Conversations

Conversations

WILLIAM JEFFERSON CLINTON

sations

conver·sa'tion *n.* Informal exchange of ideas by spoken words;
instance of this; ~ piece, thing that
serves as topic of conversation, painting of group of people conversing

FROM HOPE TO HARLEM

Janis F. Kearney

Writing Our World Press
Chicago

First Edition
Printed in the United States of America

10 09 08 07 06   6 5 4 3 2 1
Cover design and inside layout by Denise Borel Billups, Borel Graphics
Edited by Amy Mantrone and Mellonee Carrigan Mayfield
Back cover photo of William Jefferson Clinton in the oval office, 2001

Library of Congress Control Number: 2006904041
ISBN: 0-9762058-1-5

www.writingourworldpress.com

Rodney [Slater] was up here introducing me and said some reporter asked him whether I really felt all of this or if this was just some elaborate political strategy that I've carried out for 50 years now. Mostly only white people ask that. And they don't get it, people who ask that. Sometimes they ask that because they're afraid their editors won't like it if they don't run a partially negative piece, but mostly it's just a continuing manifestation of the absence of necessary human contact.

They haven't done enough laughing and crying and fighting and burying and marrying and eating and praying across racial lines. They never went to John Gammon's wild game dinner in Crittenden County and heard a woman sing "If I Can Help Somebody" a cappella with a hailstorm coming down on a tin roof for accompaniment. They never sat in a little wooden church house in the summertime and watched the preacher inducted when there were 300 people in a church built for 150 causing even more than the normal number to be afflicted by the Spirit; or brought a community center to Wrightsville or a sewer system to a poor Delta town.

—William J. Clinton, accepting the Black Hall of Fame Award

Contents

PART I—HOPE AND HAPPENSTANCE

PART II—CONVERSATIONS: HOPE, ARKANSAS

PART III—HOT SPRINGS: ARKANSAS' LITTLE PIECE OF HEAVEN AND HELL

Contents

Contents

PART VII—A DAY IN THE DELTA

PART VIII—CONVERSATIONS WITH BLACK AMERICA

Contents

PART IX—THE CLINTON PRESIDENCY: BLACK AMERICA'S REPORT CARD

Acknowledgements

Thank you to the following individuals and institutions who helped make this book a possibility: Henry Louis Gates and Harvard University's W.E.B. DuBois Center for African and African American Studies; Jacqueline Taylor, Jonathan Gross and Anna Vaughn Clissold of DePaul University's Humanities Center; David Alsobrook, director, and Racheal Carter, audio/visual specialist at the William J. Clinton Presidential Library; the North Little Rock Laman Library staff; Cheryl Batts, and the P.H.O.E.B.E./Uzuri Project, in Hot Springs, Arkansas; the Hot Springs Historical Society; *The Sentinel-Record* and *The Hope Star* newspapers. Also thanks to the interviewees from throughout the country, and most especially those from Hope, Hot Springs and central Arkansas, for sharing their precious time and memories; and to a dedicated, hard-working editorial and production team for their long days and sometimes sleepless nights: Amy Mantrone, Mellonee Carrigan Mayfield, and Denise Borel Billups.

Finally, thank you to William Jefferson Clinton, for being a leader worth writing about; and to Bob and D.K., for continuing to believe in my dream of helping to change the world through stories.

Prologue

William Jefferson Clinton, the 42nd president of the United States, enjoyed astounding popularity throughout America and most foreign countries during his eight years in office. Beyond that, he enjoyed unparalleled popularity in America's black communities.

Throughout his 12 years as governor of Arkansas and his eight years as U.S. president, the attribute that stood out most in this Southern politician was his ostensibly genuine ease in interfacing with black Americans and addressing the race issue—not only before black audiences, but also before the masses.

In a 1998 issue of *The New Yorker*, Toni Morrison wrote that William Jefferson Clinton was America's "first black president," noting his uphill battle with white America and Capitol Hill's palpable discomfort with his way of doing business. Though Morrison's descriptor was tongue-in-cheek, hers was a serious theme—that it was Bill Clinton's humanity, his inherent empathy with those different from him that sometimes put him on the outs with mainstream politicians, particularly conservative Republicans.

In truth, throughout Bill Clinton's 30-plus years in public service, political pundits have continued to question the validity of his humanity, suggesting often that Clinton's feel-your-pain style might serve the brilliant strategist well as he plays to his adoring public. In essence, they believed that empathy bought him votes.

After Clinton found himself president of the United States, the questions didn't end, but became private fare for politicians, journalists, and other media types. At the national level, where the stakes were higher and the issues were supposed to follow suit, few white journalists or commentators addressed the question head-on. There seemed no politically correct way to say that Clinton's empathetic way with black America discomforted white America.

When the subject was broached, it was in the context of whites' perception of black Americans' sophomoric allegiance to Bill Clinton. This was viewed as an example of his Southern charisma and his ability to imitate black folks' emotionalism. Few in the mainstream media dared admit that much of white America's unease with Bill Clinton was because this different kind of thinking might somehow upset the nation's hierarchical apple cart.

In spite of a voluminous number of books written about this popular president, none except DeWayne Wickham's *Bill Clinton and Black America* has devoted much space beyond footnotes to the 500-pound elephant that stood in the middle of America's living rooms for eight years: Bill Clinton's inexplicable relationship with black America.

The ignoring of this profound, intrusive issue suggests that it was never a real concern for America. Yet, according to most black Americans interviewed here, particularly those who knew William Jefferson Clinton when he was simply "Bill," his strengths and weaknesses are cast from the same die: his in-your-face position on race and civil rights.

"He was a different kind of white politician who never minded speaking out about America's failure to confront race," one longtime Clinton admirer said.

Conversations: William Jefferson Clinton, From Hope to Harlem does not claim to offer universal answers to the questions that bubbled beneath the surface throughout the Southern politician's career; nor does it attempt to justify why America's 42nd president is the leader he came to be. Conversations is a collection of oral histories, personal opinions, personal experiences and shared memories; all centered around William Jefferson Clinton's leadership, his presidency, his race legacy, and his humanity. The conversations make real the man so many see as a phenomenon of America's South.

Most Americans were introduced to Bill Clinton in 1992 through television and newspapers. What they don't know is that the man's facility, comfort, and inquisitiveness about black culture did not begin on January 20, 1993, when he took up residence at 1600 Pennsylvania Avenue. If anything, the glare of the mainstream press muted what those who know Clinton best view as his compassion, an almost quixotic obsession with righting the historical wrongs created by America's race conflicts.

This empathetic attitude toward those different from him began long before Clinton left Arkansas for Georgetown University and later Yale Law School. His relationships with African Americans began in his birthplace, Hope, Arkansas. His keen observations of his environment began as a teen in his second home, Hot Springs, Arkansas.

While the title "Friend of Bill Clinton" took on new meaning after 1993, many African Americans held that title well before Bill Clinton was *the* Bill Clinton. In fact, the state of Arkansas is populated with African Americans, men and women, who consider themselves "friends" of Bill Clinton. Hundreds are sprinkled across the country.

Interview subjects from across America contributed hours recounting their experiences, disagreements, and astonishments with William Jefferson Clinton. None of these men or women believed the man's affinity for black America was anything but genuine.

Conversations: William Jefferson Clinton, From Hope to Harlem examines an enigma: a white man from Arkansas—a president of the United States—who removed the curtain from the discussion on race and never stopped digging at what he describes as America's most languishing, nettlesome sore. This book promises entertainment, education, and a background palette for the world, the culture, the times, and the environment that helped shape the William Jefferson Clinton we know today.

Introduction

I thought seriously about another title for this book, *The Ten Most Frequently Asked Questions About William Jefferson Clinton*, but that would have muddied the waters. Instead, I have sought to focus on the single most frequently asked, and unasked, question about William Jefferson Clinton: "What kind of environment produced such an atypical Southerner, politician, and American?" And I ask this question of a primarily African American interview pool.

This is not a tell-all book, and it does not offer a deep analysis of the Clinton administration. What it does offer are panoramic views of the history, the environment, and the places in Bill Clinton's past. While there were certainly intrinsic forces that helped shape Bill Clinton's childhood, no amount of discussions, interviews, or research is likely to illuminate which forces carried the most weight.

William Jefferson "Billy" Blythe III was born at Julia Chester Hospital on August 19, 1946, to 23-year-old Virginia Dell Cassidy Blythe, who had lost her husband just months before her son came into the world. The young widow memorialized her husband by giving his name to her only child and spent the next three years being a part-time parent while she trained as a nurse anesthetist in New Orleans and Shreveport, Louisiana. Billy Blythe would later become William Jefferson Clinton, taking his first stepfather's name as his own when he was in high school.

The child spent his first six years in the town of Hope, from 1946 to 1953. Many of today's child psychologists believe the early years are the most important and impressionable years of anyone's life. Some suggest that beyond the first five or six years, there are few changes in the pattern that helps determine who and what one eventually becomes.

Billy Blythe is remembered as a child with a voracious appetite for life and knowledge, a "walking sponge" who internalized whatever he came in contact with. And in a place like Hope, in the pre-civil rights era of the 1940s and 1950s, that could make for some interesting internalization.

Hope, Arkansas, had its high points during its 100-plus-year existence, including a few memorable characters that would show up in American and Arkansas history books. But in spite of its claims to the contrary, for most of its years, Hope was a town typical of most small, Southern towns—nothing much to write home about. Most of the residents moved there from other small towns, bringing with them typically small-town attitudes. There were variables, however, that might explain a phenomenon such as Bill Clinton: Eldridge James and Edith Cassidy and their daughter, Virginia Dell Cassidy.

There were endless reporters' questions throughout Bill Clinton's political career as to how he turned out to be so different from most people born in Hope, or even in Arkansas. James Eldridge Cassidy was Clinton's consistent response. Cassidy, he pointed out, helped shape him into something more than his surroundings. This grandfather, who seemed more like a father, Clinton says, planted the seed of color-blindness in his conscience very early on.

Virginia Cassidy, the young mother who left her son with her parents as she traveled to Shreveport to complete her education, would later complete the job her parents had started, making up the missed time by blowing up his ego to almost bursting capacity and buffering him from their sometimes harsh reality by assuring him of a destiny for greatness. She was, in the end, the cheerleader who made William Jefferson Clinton believe he could hang the moon if he so chose.

"Paw Paw," as young Billy endearingly called his grandfather, was the source of Bill Clinton's love for people in general and his interest in people different from him, which in Hope meant black people. Paw Paw's carefully planted seeds blossomed over the years into a heavy-laden conscience and an obsession with fixing the country's thorniest problems, beginning with the thorniest of all: the Southern Arkansas Delta's racial conflict.

Eldridge Cassidy also, reportedly, spoiled his grandson rotten, painting the world for him in beautiful blues and yellows instead of grays or even black and white. This included stirring the child's imagination with tall tales and stories of his past.

This child had an unquenchable thirst for knowing all there was to know about the world around him and would inherit his grandfather's renown for talking the best of conversationalists under the proverbial table—and continuing the conversation as they rested up underneath.

But then, there was also Edith. While Eldridge Cassidy gave young Billy his over-sized heart, Eldridge's wife, Edith, a practical nurse described by many as a straightforward, tenacious woman with a heart evenly mixed with gold and steel, passed on to her grandchild a keen intellect and an almost maniacal drive to succeed.

Edith Cassidy's work ethic was legendary, and it was this example that Bill Clinton would later emulate. The young grandmother (she was 45 when Billy was born) was known for helping women in need, no matter who they were. It is said that she often sojourned into the black community to nurse ailing mothers when no one else would do so.

While she heaped tons of love on what some believed was the son she never had, Edith Cassidy also took on the role of strict disciplinarian, demanding his best at all times. Beginning as early as 2 years old, young Billy began to recognize words and, not much later, to read. Edith Cassidy, in her effort to make him the best, was said to have driven the young boy unrelentingly, drilling into him that "second best" was never good enough.

In essence, her love and her own personal ambition created this driven scaler of heights who never acknowledged the word "can't."

Neighbors might have been a bit surprised to learn that Edith Cassidy went to bed at night dreaming of raising the smartest child in Hempstead County, not realizing that he would one day be viewed by many as the most brilliant U.S. president of all times.

From all accounts, Billy, with his interminable smile, was always eager to make as many friends as possible. To his own surprise, he somehow made just as many enemies. Billy simply refused to let friendship get in the way of always being the best. Likely, his grandparents' contrasting personalities and universal love and adulation for the child created the dual personalities. These very traits would later make William Jefferson Clinton a lightning rod for either resentment or blind loyalty.

Much to Edith Cassidy's dismay, her husband's compassionate heart seemed to win out with young Billy over her more practical lessons in life. It was Paw Paw who the child strove to emulate in those early years, as he charmed and smiled his way through Miss Mary Perkins's kindergarten class and through first grade at Brookwood Elementary School.

Yet, Edith should not have worried. Though his grandfather's persona is the first impression one gets upon meeting Bill Clinton, there is another level to his personality; one that would surely make Edith Cassidy proud. It is the Bill Clinton with a harder edge, a mind still at work when others switch theirs to "off," and a no-holds-barred competitive side—all inherited from Maw Maw.

Bill Clinton's surrogate parents should also be credited for what many described as his being a fish out of water. While he worked hard at fitting in with the other children of Hope, there was most certainly something different about him. In their actions, if not in words, the Cassidys taught Billy about living a life of purpose, one above the small concerns of every-day folk like the townspeople of Hope and the children he played with at school each day.

In embracing both surrogate parents' philosophies of life, Billy was armed for whatever obstacles that awaited him. His charm and love for people would disarm his staunchest critics, while his intellect and his strong work ethic would blow any competitor out of the water. These variant strengths, thanks to Eldridge and Edith, would protect him most of his life.

The Cassidy home was different in another way from most other white homes in Hope, Arkansas. There, young Billy grew up amidst one unashamedly kind man and two unusually strong women. He would become an early "sensitive" man before it became popular and embrace the idea of women's rights as just plain sensible.

It is also true that the Cassidys' take on race was different from that of others in the southwest Arkansas town. This was driven home, Bill Clinton has said, by his interactions with black men and women who worked for his grandfather, the black children who visited his grandfather's store, and the black families his grandmother sometimes nursed when others wouldn't. Bill Clinton grew up missing that gene that told him that people who happened to have darker skin were necessarily lesser beings.

Young Bill Clinton must have wrestled, though, even as a child, with his heart, with what he felt, in contrast to what was. Knowing, somehow, that his view of life was inherently different from others—a young white child of the pre-civil rights South questioning the morality of separation of the races? Viewing as just plain silly that he had to walk past a black school to get to Brookwood Elementary; and spending hours puzzled by the early rule that black and white children don't play together or visit each others' homes.

The Cassidy home, at 117 South Hervey Street in Hope, had been the only home Billy Blythe had known during his first five years. From all accounts, it was a happy home, with an overabundance of love and adulation. And when Virginia Cassidy Blythe completed nursing school in

1950, she returned to Hope and her son. For a short time, while she took on nursing and private duty jobs at various hospitals, Billy remained at the Cassidys' Hervey address. But his life would change in two ways that year: his mother would marry the handsome car salesman of whom, it is believed, neither Edith nor Eldridge approved; and with that marriage would come Billy's move from Hervey Street to 312 East Thirteenth Street—geographically, just a few miles away from his Paw Paw's home.

Two years later, a bigger change in Billy's life came about when his stepfather decided to move his family to Hot Springs, where he would take over sales at his brother's Buick shop and Virginia was promised a better nursing job. While 7-year-old Billy Blythe was likely excited about a new move and the possibility of new friends—and though Hope, Arkansas, still wasn't much to write home about—young Billy Blythe must have known the value of what he'd be leaving behind.

Hope was never a center of either anti-black sentiments or patriotism, but it certainly did not entertain racially progressive views. Even during the war years, when the country and even some Southern towns began testing the waters of racial harmony, there was never enough concerted effort to make it stick. When black veterans returned from the war angry, hopeless, and in need of jobs, the community leaders offered them share-cropping opportunities, jobs as field hands in their cotton fields, or other manual labor.

No welcome mat was set out to greet integration when it did finally find its way to Hope, Arkansas. Federal laws forced some changes but did little to change townspeople's hearts or minds about the mixing of the races. If anything, the integration heyday rankled the God-fearing men and women, who believed they would do the right thing in their own time, or when God came down and told them it was time. They viewed the federal government and the Supreme Court as enemies of the states. This time and place would play a large role in the making of young Billy Blythe.

Conver

PART I
HOPE AND HAPPENSTANCE

And I think that if you look all over the world, all the trouble spots of the world, most countries and most people get in trouble when they try to organize folks around hatred or disdain or disregard for people or groups who are different from them. They either look different than they do, they worship God in a different way, or they're just different. And it's hard to get to the point in life where you can have an honest disagreement with somebody and still acknowledge that their humanity is just as valid as yours, and that life's a lot more interesting, because they're not just like you are.

—President Clinton, One America Event

CHAPTER 1
— HOPE'S —
History

The state of Arkansas started out as part of Missouri Territory—a small corner of Arkansas County, Missouri. It was eventually split off from Missouri Territory by Congress and officially made Arkansas Territory. A new county in this Arkansas Territory, Hempstead, was named in honor of one Congressman Edward Hempstead, an attorney who was born in Connecticut and lived for some time in Indiana. He then walked cross-country to St. Louis to practice law and was one of the early petitioners for incorporation of that city.

Southwest Arkansas was a trackless wilderness at this point in its existence; white men had hardly set foot on its land. The *Old Town Speaks*, a compilation of documents from Hempstead County's old courthouse, offers: "The only avenues of travel were the rivers—going north and south. The only trail across the country was Military Road, which was first a buffalo trail, then an Indian trail over which 'tis said (Spanish explorer Hernando) DeSoto traveled in 1541. This trail became known as the Old Military Road, from its having been cut out, or widened by the United States troops in President Jackson's day, when that president was driving Indians out of the South and needed a wider trail or road."

The U.S. government encouraged settlement in this new Arkansas Territory, going as far as asking Spain to allow settlers from the Texas side of the Red River. Cotton farmers, they hoped, would flock there, given the rich bottomlands. Spanish settlement, in fact, was essential to building a large economic base in the area.

Early settlers cut out roads, established ferries on the rivers, and cleared up the farmlands. There were no domestic animals early on. The settlers lived on wild fruits, berries, fish, and the flesh of wild animals until their farms began to yield food. Bear meat took the place of bacon and pork; the opossum and raccoon were also plentiful. It was not unusual for the heads of families to get up before daybreak and go a few hundred yards from their homes to kill a deer or wild turkey or even a bear, or to fish at the river bottom. Buffalo roamed the Plains just across the Red River, and once or twice a year the settlers banded together, traveling by boat up a stream to what would later become Clarksville, Texas. They returned with boatloads of buffalo and divided it among the families.

Trading posts were established on the banks of the Red and Little rivers as well as the Cossatot and the Little Missouri rivers, at which points the settlers made contact and traded with the Indians. Washington's Travelers' Inn became something of legend in the area. Located on Franklin Street, in the heart of the town, it was one of the earliest structures built there. The two-story building had a wraparound veranda and a dozen or more spacious rooms separated by a long, wide hallway. A large auditorium on the second floor was used for balls and public meetings. The Inn was also a stagecoach station; men would come to smoke their pipes; women to socialize, gossip, and receive or post letters to relatives.

By all accounts, this inn served as temporary housing for some of the more interesting names in the southwest, including Davy Crockett; Colonel James "Jim" Bowie of Bowie knife fame; James Black, the silversmith who actually made the Bowie knife for the colonel; Stephen Fuller Austin, known as "the father of Texas"; and his brother-in-law, James Bryan. It was at Washington's Travelers' Inn, reportedly, that Davy Crockett spent his last days before sojourning to the Alamo, traveling from Shreveport to San Antonio, where he would meet his death.

After some years, the old landmark was purchased by local newspaper publisher William Etter and used as his residence until after the War Between the States. Etter published the first issue of the *Washington Telegraph* in the old tavern. Ironically, the building was eventually sold to blacks for a time before finally being torn down by the city.

While the residents of Hope and Hempstead County toed the same line as those of other small, Southern towns when it came to race, local historians swear there was something a little different about how they handled relationships between blacks and whites. Theirs, they contend, was a sense of community spirit that often included slaves; a sense of fairness that went beyond the color line.

Even so, slavery was a reality in Hope and Washington and Fulton and the rest of Hempstead County. Most Hempstead County farmers were not wealthy enough to own more than a few slaves, and the smallest farmers had to work side by side with their slaves in the fields. One farmer in Ashley County, according to author Al Paulson, was brought to court because he was too kind to his slaves. This was considered obnoxious behavior, even in Hempstead County with its sense of community, in those days when slavery was a serious matter.

Paulson offered his own rendition of slavery in Hempstead County:

> Nearly every white adult in the Washington (Hempstead County) area owned slaves. They worked the fields, ran the households and raised the children. Trusted young female slaves went to New Orleans by steamboat to learn haute cuisine from the finest rich chefs. Others might learn dressmaking, hairdressing. Slaves attended one of the four local churches with their masters, sitting in the balcony with all the black and white children. Every service—whether Baptist, Methodist, Presbyterian, or Episcopal— included a special time when a spiritual was sung from the balcony. But slaves they remained. They were bought and sold. They were commonly given as wedding presents by doting parents. Slavery was woven deeply into the fabric of life in antebellum Washington.

Paulson's compilation of interviews with over 800 slaves depicts a horrid commercial trade that included brutality little spoken of by genteel Southerners. The whip and the auction block belied the myth of the happy, contented slave, in spite of the fact that some slaves had fond memories of their masters.

But Paulson did believe that the relationship between slaves and their owners in Hempstead County, and in Washington in particular, was somehow different from the rest of the state. He points to a "sense of community among blacks and whites" that was most evident when the Civil War began; and soldiers wearing both blue and gray were seen streaming into the towns after the Battle of Prairie D'Ane. He admits that that sense of community became strained after the war.

CHAPTER 2
WASHINGTON COUNTY
JOINS THE *Confederacy*

Washington County rewrote its history when the town chose to follow the Gray rather than the Blue. It would seem that no matter the level of affection the good people of Hempstead County held for their slaves, the question of whether or not they would remain slaves was never entertained. As part of the Confederacy, Hempstead County would make its position clear. Volunteer soldiers proudly formed themselves into the Hempstead Rifles for the Fourth Arkansas Regiment of the Confederate Army. One of its officers was Daniel Webster Jones, who would later become governor of Arkansas.

One impassioned proponent of Hempstead County's move into the Confederacy was John Eakin, once a staunch Unionist. Eakin was hired by the local newspaper publisher, William Etter, just around the beginning of the Civil War. This new editor was not only a strong proponent of the Confederacy in his writings, but also a vocal politician who took every opportunity to espouse his separatist ideals. Obviously an effective politician, he was in short order elected mayor of the town of Washington. Eakin's philosophy of separate and unequal can, as much as anything, be credited with ushering in a real change in the social climate of Hempstead County.

The war, though, took its toll on Washington and Hempstead County, and things changed for the worse when the Union army set up a blockade of New Orleans. This suspended the county from exporting cotton, its economic bread and butter, and dried up the money. Inflation became uncontrollable; and staples such as salt, needles and thread, and the most critical of all, medicine, went lacking. People in the area died by the hundreds, as measles and other diseases infected the very young and the old.

Even the vocal Eakin was forced to admit that the area was defeated when General Frederick Steele captured Little Rock on September 10, 1863. Governor Harris Flanigan moved the government records from Little Rock to the Hempstead County Courthouse, and Washington became the Confederate capital of Arkansas for a brief time.

Refugees of this war began to filter into Hempstead County, and the people of the town and nearby areas sheltered and fed them. Refugees, in fact, would fill every resident's spare rooms, attics, barns, and empty slave quarters. Tents were soon erected on residents' lawns.

Ironically, both Union and Confederate soldiers were housed in Hempstead County. The town doctor, Nathan Smith, who had vocally opposed secession, came out of retirement to treat the wounded at the Baptist church. He ended up treating his own wounded son, a Confederate soldier who had joined the war against his father's wishes.

The area suffered throughout the Civil War. Bitter cold settled into the atmosphere; rain soaked wood that might have been used as firewood. The beautiful pine pillars of churches were eventually chopped up and used as firewood to warm the Union and Confederate soldiers. Soldiers from both sides were buried in the Presbyterian cemetery.

Washington didn't suffer alone. Times were hard throughout Arkansas during the Civil War. According to one writer, "Anarchy, desolation . . . ruled most of Arkansas. Disease was lord over it." Newspaper publisher Etter twice led wagon trains of cotton to Mexico, where they were traded for trainloads of desperately needed medicines and supplies, as the people of Washington continued to die.

With the influx of war refugees, Washington's population swelled to as many as 30,000 people toward the end of the war. Most of these were not permanent residents of the town, but included soldiers and war refugees. Many of the men, once they recovered from their wounds and illnesses, helped with the work needing to be done, since most slaves had been pressed to join the war. Local blacks held a charity ball and raised $1,147 to help the sick and wounded of all races sheltering in Washington.

John Etter, on June 7, 1865, wrote this epitaph for the Confederacy: "With it dies all obligations of allegiance. Each man is free in conscience, without loss of dignity or self-respect, to take the oath of allegiance to the United States. We are satisfied that our single devotion to the Confederacy, during its existence, has fulfilled all the obligations of patriotism. With a conscience clear of offense, we are willing to transfer that allegiance, so left in abeyance, to the government of the United States, and hope to observe it quite as faithfully."

But other residents were still in denial that the Confederacy had lost the war. As Union soldiers came in to overtake the town and county, there was bitterness in the air and fear of what this meant for their farms and their livelihoods.

All of Hempstead County—black and white—would feel the burden of the Confederate army's defeat. Blacks who had suffered as slaves were now free, but they now stood to suffer a different kind of hardship with this new federalism. Freedom, from where they stood, seemed to be something quite different from what they'd dreamed. Not unlike many in the white community, they were in dire need of the basics—food, clothing, and shelter. Planters needed laborers but had no way of compensating them.

One aspect of the South's Reconstruction era that historians continue to study and document is the fact that a number of former slaves were so quickly elevated to political office. Hempstead County boasted at least two former slaves who became lawmakers during that time: Archie Shepperson was elected sheriff for a time, and Richard Samuels represented Hempstead County in the new state assembly.

It was soon acknowledged that there was an obvious need to find ways to educate the former slaves. One school for blacks opened in the

Baptist church, while a separate school for whites was operated in the home of one Alchyny Delony. The county's two academies didn't reopen because the county could no longer afford them. Everyone was bankrupt; fields were barren, storerooms were empty.

Shepperson and Samuels would both serve in the Reconstructionists' State Legislature, and Samuels would eventually found the Colored Methodist Episcopal Church. Shepperson would later become a county judge. Another black resident of the county, James Tyrus, was appointed county tax assessor. A black man by the name of John Williamson founded the Episcopal Academy, which drew students from five surrounding states.

Robert McWhorter, who was sent by the carpetbaggers to govern Washington, quickly gained the respect of the community after marrying a local woman. He can also be credited with the placement of the small number of blacks in the county and state's new political structure.

Nothing in this southwest region of the state was as it had been. Lawyers who had fought in the Confederacy were disbarred. Hempstead County had been known for its ample supply of attorneys, but they were all now mostly unemployed. Augustus Garland represented the lawyers before the Supreme Court, citing the disbarment as unconstitutional, and won. He was rewarded by being elected to the U.S. Senate in 1867, but was refused a seat because delegates from the Southern states weren't recognized. Instead, the people of Arkansas made him governor. He would later be admitted to the U.S. House of Representatives, then to the U.S. Senate.

In fact, a number of Hempstead County residents became nationally renowned after the Civil War, including Daniel Webster Jones, who eventually became state attorney general and served two terms as governor of Arkansas. Grandiose Royston would eventually lead the state constitutional convention.

CHAPTER 3
—HOPE AND THE—
Race War

By the time Hope became an established town, African Americans had fully realized the irony of their freedom. Abraham Lincoln's Civil War, and later the Emancipation Proclamation, had inadvertently given hate groups such as the Ku Klux Klan more reason to resent blacks and justification for acting out their hate.

Unlike some later years, when Southern blacks would catch the train to the North and Midwest seeking their piece of the American dream, most freed slaves settled in the South, and many settled in small, rural towns such as Hope. They brought to their new address an almost visceral fear and hopelessness that overshadowed the momentary exhilaration of freedom. Ironically, their fear and hopelessness would serve the majority community quite well. The community quickly drove home these two points: freed slaves were not recognized as full citizens, and the only interaction most whites wanted with blacks was as manual laborers or house servants.

Thus, one dismal way of looking at it is that while Mr. Lincoln had provided the key to unlock blacks' shackles, white America had no idea how they were supposed to deal with unshackled slaves. This mostly uneducated population had been given leave of the degrading and physically dangerous environments they'd known, only to be thrust into a new environment that was just as dangerous and even more hostile.

Moreover, while the more progressive Southerners might no longer openly condone slavery, they certainly weren't progressive enough to

9

accept the free blacks as anything near equals. The Jim Crow laws that followed Reconstruction may, in fact, have done more to harm the status of the freed slaves than slavery did, damning them as dangerous, untrustworthy, sexually deviant, immoral, and not worthy of inclusion in American society.

One vivid indication of the post-Reconstruction Hope, Arkansas, was the announcement of the incorporation of the Daughters of the Confederacy in Hope on January 21, 1952, after being chartered on March 7, 1896:

> The Pat Cleburne Chapter No. 31 in Hope, Arkansas, was chartered on March 7, 1896. This was the first chapter to be chartered in the state of Arkansas and second west of the Mississippi, with Mrs. C. A. Forney elected chapter president . . . . The first annual convention in Arkansas was a call to Hope, Arkansas, on October 14, 1896, for the purpose of organizing an Arkansas division. By this time there were four chapters with three required to organize.

CHAPTER 4

HOPE RISES FROM
—— THE ASHES OF THE ——
Civil War

The Civil War had an odd way of elevating small towns while taking others down a notch or two. The town of Washington had long been the central site of activity in Hempstead County and continued to grow for a time shortly after the war. Residents were finally accepting the fate of the war and beginning to rearrange themselves around that fate. A new, larger Hempstead County courthouse was erected on the town square and a new jail was built smack dab behind the Methodist church.

The vaults of the Hempstead County courthouse yet contain quaint and curious documents such as one legal document from a William Cravens of the county of Rockingham, Virginia, who did "emancipate, set free and forever discharge from slavery, my Negro woman, Nance, who I purchased from Esther Cravens, widow, in the year 1795, then aged about 23 years old."

But Washington's growth would end with the advent of the new railroad that ran through Hempstead County but bypassed the town of Washington altogether. According to some historians, Washington refused to have the railroad come through the quaint town, fearing what it would bring with it—unwanted strangers, noise, and smoke. The loss of the railroad was only one of the town's mishaps. During this same time, two large fires would devastate the town; and the former toast of southwest Arkansas, which had peaked at a population of 780 before the Civil War, began to lose its momentum.

Just a few miles up the road, Hope's economy boomed while the economic fortunes of Washington stagnated, then declined. Along with Hope's growth came the desire to become the county seat, and so began the 60-year struggle between the two towns for that honor. Hope, of course, cited its population increase and, most importantly, its new railroad station. Hope was, in fact, the impetus for the railroad route through the area, thanks to its location 112 miles southwest of Little Rock and 34 miles northwest of Texas. Given these two variables, Hope was now the new center of commerce and economy for Hempstead County. But Hempstead County pointed to their beautiful new county courthouse and their longer history of holding the title.

As fate is so often the great equalizer, the city of Hope encountered a huge setback in 1884, when a fire came very near to destroying the city's business district. Though every able-bodied man and woman participated in efforts to save their city, many buildings were lost in the fire. Ironically, the fire was the precipitator for more building and rebuilding in the city. By 1888, Hope had an opera house, six churches, two banks, lumber mills, a wagon factory, a cotton compress, an abundance of stores and smithies, and a population of about 2,000 people. The beautiful little prairie had become a prosperous town.

Hope residents were so confident that they would win the county seat that they built a new courthouse in the late 1880s, hoping to affect the election. The ploy failed, and they eventually used the courthouse as their city hall.

CHAPTER 5
HOPE
—— AND ——
Happenstance

The American railroad has long been a symbol of America's successes and challenges, its civil liberties and its racial conflicts. For decades its progress served as a gauge of America's greatness and its failures. The town of Hope's significance was greatly increased by two variables: it was the birthplace of former President William Jefferson Clinton; and the small southwest Arkansas town was established solely in relation to America's industrial transformation, namely the railroad.

It was during the days just prior to the turn of the century, a most turbulent political and social juncture in Southern history, that James Loughbougher, railroad commissioner and attorney for the Cairo & Fulton Railroad Company, traveled Arkansas' back roads, scouting routes and stop stations to expand his railroad company. The railroad lawyer became intimate with rural Arkansas' unexplored, unexploited, wooded acres of land and, in doing so, happened upon a ragged patch of land in Hempstead County. Loughbougher would unknowingly impact Arkansas and American history on August 20, 1872, when he sanctioned the backwoods tract of land as a bona fide train station and, in a sentimental gesture, named the station after his 4-year-old daughter, Hope.

What Loughbougher and his railroad crew witnessed in their early stops in Hope Station were endless patches of trees, weeds that reached many of the railroad crew's shoulders, and populations of small, indigenous animals—rabbits, raccoons, squirrels, opossums, deer, fox, wild dogs, and, every once in a while, a 500-pound black bear hidden up in the hills. If he strained his eyes, Loughbougher might have spotted the sparsely populated communities beyond the train stop and the one or two well-populated small cities such as Washington, the county seat, and Fulton.

Further down the road was Texarkana, which wore its mixture of Southern and Western origins boldly and proudly; often sharing the hair-raising stories of how the two collided. Texarkana—a good-sized town sprawled across the southern edge of Arkansas and within spitting distance of both Louisiana and Texas—boasted its own pioneer history.

Yet, most south Arkansas towns in the adjoining counties of Hempstead, Columbia, and Union claimed only a handful of families— most dirt poor, simple folk living off the land and hacking out a life in agriculture or lumber in these post-slavery days. They all had one thing in common: their perennial bitterness toward Reconstruction.

Because this was the dawning of the train era for Arkansas, Hope Station would attract crowds of spectators from the surrounding towns: wide-eyed, mostly barefoot children, some sporting their one pair of everyday shoes; mothers wearing home-sewn dresses; and fathers dressed in Sunday suits or work overalls. A few lucky families waited placidly in their horse- or ox-drawn wagons to witness south Arkansas' transformation.

While trains were fast becoming a common sight across America's Plains, and Hope Station was not unique to the South, it was an anomaly for Arkansas. The trains and their stopping points were part and parcel of a new post-war America, and to some extent a target of the perennial resentment that small-town Southerners felt toward the progress they saw forcing a compromise of what they knew.

Thus, Southern Arkansans vacillated between overwhelming pride in "their" moving locomotive and a feeling that the North had infiltrated every crevice of their lives—a love-hate fascination with the new world so boisterously forcing its way into their insular one.

But the train oglers came in dribbles, then droves, from the small towns of Washington, Fulton, Nashville, and Springhill. Polite, gentle, shoving sometimes—stirring up little dust bowls right there beside the train tracks—as the good, simple country people sought the front of the crowd, not wanting to miss out on that indescribable feel and sound of the hot or cold air escaping the large, iron machine as it rolled slowly, heavily to a stop.

More titillating than the sight and feel of the big train, though, were the sights inside those trains as spied through the wide picture windows. The sights would stay in the minds of the people of Hempstead County for days and nights. That awe that just hundreds of miles away lived Americans much like them, but alien in so many ways. Women and men dressed to the nines on a weekday and riding the trains as if they were born to do just that. Women who wore manly skirt suits or billowing dresses and hats; and men dressed in dark, rich, wool suits and top hats or Derbies. Just as riveting were the train porters, colored men in spit-pressed blue suits and caps, smiling, some of them, none looking like the coloreds that lived in south Arkansas, or as if they'd ever picked a sack of cotton in their lives.

Though the people of Hempstead seldom witnessed colored men or women passengers riding these trains, some were politically astute enough to know that there was a law in place allowing such a thing. The Civil Rights Act passed in 1873 by the last Reconstruction Legislature barred racial segregation in common carriers, hotels, saloons, restaurants and places of public amusement—a temporary legislation offering temporary freedom of racial intermingling. That law was upstaged by the Separate Coach Act of 1891, which required "equal but separate and sufficient" railroad passenger coaches and waiting rooms. The test for determining who was to be segregated, the law pointed out, was "a visible and distinct admixture of African blood."

So as the locals stared into the train's picture windows, they often found slightly amused eyes staring back. These travelers in fine clothing and fancy hats, sometimes smoking long cigarettes, found the country folk of southwest Arkansas rather quaint.

Further down the road of Southern progress, politicians and lawmakers representing both sides of the political aisle would seek ways to utilize this political steam engine to further their or their constituencies' own agendas. According to Harry S. Ashmore's *Arkansas: A History*, the Democratic leadership quickly took up railways as an effective tool to make their position of "keeping things as they were" clear on race relations.

By 1893, clearly anti-Negro legislation had been authored by the Democrats that called for Jim Crow segregation of the races on the railroads, one way white Southerners expressed their anger and resentment toward Northerners and free blacks arriving in the region to take free rein with their Reconstructionist views. Their anger was directed specifically against Northern blacks and carpetbaggers' efforts to change the Southern way and the "natural hierarchy of whites and blacks."

It was in the midst of this environment, tainted by deep-seated anger and conflicts between the states about slavery and race, that Loughbougher moved his family from Carondelet, Missouri, to Little Rock, Arkansas. It was no longer the wild, southwest Arkansas Territory through which he'd laid those tracks. The man and his family would soon be designated a place among the much-esteemed pioneer families of Little Rock.

While Loughbougher named the train station for his young daughter, there is nothing to substantiate that Hope ever set foot in the small, rural town that carried her name. There is inference, however, that Hope Loughbougher shared her father's love for travel and exploration. She was said to have embarked on travel throughout her adult life.

Long after her father's contributions to the development of Hempstead County and Little Rock, Hope Loughbougher settled into a dual life of her own. A spinster, she insulated herself from the world with books and a far more exciting life of travel to worlds that represented cultures far different from what she knew.

Her ultimate dream was to travel to France to live and work for the Red Cross. She had, in fact, begun plans to do just that in 1917, but that chance at a new life was lost when Hope died at her brother's home in Little Rock, just months before her planned trip to France. Her obituary, published in both statewide newspapers, described Hope Loughbougher as a well-traveled scholar and linguist who had lived almost half a century in Little Rock, traveling and dreaming of another world. She was buried between her parents in Little Rock's Mt. Holly Cemetery. Her funeral was officiated by an Episcopalian minister.

CHAPTER 6
──HOPE'S──
Reconstruction

The first settlers in Hope, Arkansas, arrived in 1873, shortly after the train tracks were laid and the train began its regular route. It was a time of upheaval for the country and for the South, as Arkansas grappled with dramatic economic, social, and political changes in the state's landscape.

Arkansas' Legislature held a special session in April 1865, ratifying the 13th Amendment and abolishing slavery. The next decade, and certainly the two years of presidential Reconstruction, would force Arkansans' hands. Would they stand up for their Confederate history or do what was morally right? Arkansas, for all practical purposes, was still Southern in every way in spite of the fact that the new Republican Party was formally organized under one General Edward Ord; and for the first time in history, almost 22,000 black voters were registered! The gates of the South were torn down by Northern carpetbaggers who alighted on the South like locusts to take the political and economic reins from the state's leaders.

Ashmore writes: "There were only nine native Arkansans among those convened to determine the state's future, and three of these were ex-slaves. There were 23 carpetbaggers, newly arrived to exploit the possibilities of Reconstruction; 30 scalawags, as Unionist locals were called; and a dozen of the old conservatives."

Major William E. Woodruff, new publisher of *The Arkansas Gazette* and grandson to its founder, wrote: "The bastard collocation, whose putridity

18

stinks in the nostrils of all decency, now in session at the Capitol, has very conceited ideas of its importance and pretentious opinions of the scope of its powers. As a matter of some trifling interest to those who have not witnessed the exhibition of the menagerie, we would state that the Negro members, eight in number, occupy seats on the western side of the hall."

Arkansas, after much wrangling about freed blacks having the right to vote, was finally readmitted to the Union on June 22, 1868. The larger problem for Arkansas and other Southern states, however, was how to stabilize the South's unsteady economy. Realists knew that the only salvation for the state's economy was to join the bankrupt whites and the newly freed slaves at the hip "under a system that would restore the agricultural productivity upon which the state depended."

Such newspaper ads as this one from *The Arkansas Gazette* became common: "One hundred laborers wanted to work on a plantation on the Arkansas River. Proprietors to bear all expenses and will pay one year with provisions, food, comfortable houses, and firewood."

Sharecropping fast became the South's new economic collaboration between white farmers, former slaves, and later the heirs of both groups. Sharecropping also brought out the worst in human nature. Black freedmen had few options in the South, and for many, this collaboration was little more than a step up from slavery. The system thrived, however, because the post-slavery days were desperate times for both blacks and whites, and, with all its boils, it was something of a balm for the economically challenged families of the South, both black and white.

Unwittingly, the town of Hope and the ever-increasing railroad tracks played a role in these changes, as more and more non-Southerners were transported and deposited into the area. The times and the environment of this new territory gave rise to risk-takers, men with innate traits for recognizing and seizing opportunities without question or hesitation.

George McLanahan was one such man. A contractor, McLanahan was responsible for building the railroad right-of-way through Hope. After learning that some of the land along the route was owned by the government, McLanahan made an overnight trip to the county's homestead office in Camden, Arkansas. He returned home the next day with a claim to 80 acres of land, including the site that later became Hope's business center.

The Arkansas Gazette mentioned Hope, Arkansas, for the first time on August 22, 1873, when the newspaper "commissioned" a reporter to board the train and record eyewitness observations during the train ride from the southwestern corner of Arkansas:

> The track-laying gang on the southern division of the Cairo & Fulton Railroad has passed Hope Station, on Prairie d'Roane. This is the point where passengers leave the road for Washington, Hempstead County, which is nine miles distant. As soon as regular trains run to Hope, stages will connect and run through to Washington the same day. Travelers can now make the trip from Little Rock to Washington by daylight.

One week after that article was released, another reporter penned an article:

> The first passenger train to Hope . . . on Wednesday morning last, the first passenger train for Hope station left this city (Little Rock) in charge of conductor Brown and John Kline on the engine. Several prominent citizens were on board, bound for Hot Springs and other points south. All along the road at various stations, many improvements are being made.
>
> No incidents worthy of note transpiring until we arrived at Hope. This embryo city is situated in Prairie d'Roane and already has a saloon in full blast. The depot building is going up, besides several other structures.
>
> A side track is laid and stocked with cars . . . the road is a very good one. On the road, we found wagon after wagon laden with merchandise. The citizens of Washington talk of little else than the railroad, although it is nine miles away. They regard it almost in the light of a miracle. Thursday a number of them visited Hope in a body, accompanied by the Silver Cornet band, to welcome the train and the officers of the road. The road has opened up a wonderful country and advanced all the material interests of the state.

On September 6 of that same year, another reporter visited Hope and wrote:

> A sign of the progress of civilization and refinement in south-western Arkansas was exhibited in the large, fine piano on the freight platform at Hope Station. A large crowd of people welcomed the arrival of the train and was greatly surprised when it did not tarry longer. The train left Hope on its way to Fulton, and after running about a quarter of a mile through the tall grass, entered the woods.

Hope received its charter in 1875. By that time, its population had grown to 1,500 people. The town, however, didn't get a sewer system or natural gas pipe installed until around 1910. Cotton was indeed king throughout the Arkansas Delta as well as in Hempstead County, where the town boasted a number of cottonseed mills. During its first three years of settlement, locals migrated from already settled communities like Rocky Mound, Spring Hill, and Washington, bringing their household goods and all they owned in ox carts. Acres of handmade tents decorated the small town's landscape until homes were built to replace them.

One early settler and local historian, Tom McMath, noted that the town attracted a small influx of foreigners that he was sure enhanced the town's allure. In addition to a group of German immigrants, McMath wrote: "There was Bill Friganza, the Spaniard with a very romantic background who was so determined to make a place for himself as a solid citizen that very few of those that thought they knew him well, realized that he was an accomplished guitarist and singer. He achieved his high purpose. He was highly respected and his family ranked among the highest."

Hope's leadership established an Immigration Association during the town's first year and advertised the new town in a 32-page publication, targeting pioneers seeking homes in the southwest. The pamphlet described the current town as well as its history:

Where the town of Hope now stands, there was nothing to be seen except a partially finished depot building, a few temporary buildings for workmen, and a home or two.

What was at that time a beautiful little prairie, which had perhaps from the advent of the red man furnished a field for the sportsman, was then to offer grounds for the erection of a little city, of which the people of south Arkansas are justly proud, and is a place of as much, if not, more commercial importance than any place between St. Louis and Texas.

Today there are in the city as many as 50 well-finished brick storehouses [one, the Racket Store—today's version of the dime store—was located at 111 West Second Street] with several others to be completed by the opening of the coming cotton season. No other place south of Little Rock can say as much.

Lands may now be had cheap, say from $2 to $5 for wild, and from $10 to $30 per acre for improved farms. There are some 60,000 acres of railway lands yet to be had in the county . . . . This county seat of Hempstead County thrived through droughts and plenty."

CHAPTER 7
HOPE'S
Post-Reconstruction
──── Era ────

Hope's black community understood and acted according to their white counterparts' preconceived notions of who they were. They lived throughout Bill Clinton's childhood, and after, in this kind of between-a-rock-and-a-hard-place environment. Most black women worked in the homes of whites, taking care of their children, while the men were relegated to jobs no whites would do.

Many of the former slaves, in fact, accepted a different kind of slavery, using their years of taking care of white men's farms to hire on with wealthy landowners as sharecroppers, renting and working the land for measly compensation at the end of the year. There are countless horror stories documenting how unfair this often one-sided work relationship has been over the years.

Like those in the rest of the South, whites in southwest Arkansas blamed Lincoln and the Reconstructionists for the onset of race problems in the country. In their minds, slavery had been a respectable part of the state's growth and economy for the 30 years before Emancipation. Thus, it was the freeing of the slaves that precipitated most of their problems.

Most whites in the town of Hope were genteel Southerners who declared a desire for racial harmony after the war between the conservatives and Reconstructionists finally died down. But real racial harmony, below the surface, mostly eluded the community. One reason for the ongoing bad feelings between the races was that poor white Southerners were in as desperate need as freed blacks.

It was with the ex-slaves' final realization that their freedom was little more than a word that some courageous men and women began efforts to gain broader civil rights, demanding equal political and legal status. Congress felt compelled to award the Civil Rights Acts of 1866, 1870, 1871, and 1875, with the intent to penalize innkeepers, proprietors of public establishments, and owners of public conveyances for discriminating based on race. These acts, however, were basically invalidated in 1883 when the Supreme Court ruled that the matters they addressed were not properly civil rights and thus not a field for federal legislation.

After the Civil Rights Act of 1875, no more federal legislation regarding civil rights was passed until the Civil Rights Acts of 1957 and 1960, although some states passed their own civil rights laws. But states such as Arkansas and towns such as Hope felt comfortable continuing "business as usual" when it came to their "coloreds."

When a young future governor and president declared to his future wife, first lady, and senator that he hailed from the Watermelon Capital of the World, he wasn't just whistling Dixie. Hope and Hempstead County's biggest claims to fame were their gargantuan watermelons.

Even with its impressive growth, most people outside the state knew only one thing about Hope, Arkansas: the city's annual Watermelon Festival, featuring an infamous seed-spitting contest. The Watermelon Festival began after a new hybrid of watermelon seeds were introduced to the city, and cultivation of the fruit quickly became a source of city pride. Until the early 1920s, Gibson's Drug Store, the local distributor of the new watermelon seeds, offered an annual prize for the largest watermelon grown.

Farmers' interest in the crop skyrocketed when Hope sent a 136-pound watermelon to President Calvin Coolidge in 1925. Shortly thereafter, the town became known as the Watermelon Capital of Arkansas and, later, of the world. The festival began in 1926 and lasted through the early 1930s. Beginning in the mid-1920s, the town's chamber of commerce staged a one-day festival each year at which citizens served huge slices of ice-cold watermelon to passengers as trains stopped at the station.

The highlight of this yearly celebration was the parade and the "Watermelon Queen" Pageant. The world-renowned Watermelon Festivals attracted more than 20,000 people in a day until the early 1930s, and the onset of the Great Depression. The Hope Watermelon Festival's crowds first dwindled, then came to an abrupt end.

Even with the Depression, however, competition continued among Hope farmers seeking the title of owner of the world's largest watermelon. O.D. Middle reported a record 195-pound watermelon in the 1930s; the prize-winning watermelon was sent as a gift to movie star Dick Powell, a native Arkansan. That record wasn't broken until 44 years later, when Lloyd Bright reported his watermelon weighed in at 200 pounds. The Bright family beat their own record in 1986, when they reported a 260-pound watermelon.

CHAPTER 8
—HOPE'S—
Depression

Hope, Arkansas, had just been declared the county seat for Hempstead County, and town leaders had just announced plans for a shiny new courthouse, when the country's economic walls came tumbling down. It was 1929, and President Herbert Hoover was at the helm. It was also the year that James Cassidy moved his family to the fast-growing town of Hope, Arkansas.

The Stock Market Crash of 1929 changed the landscape of towns like Hope which were just coming into their own. It dissipated the optimism that filled the air in Hempstead County, putting an end to the festivities that represented the town, like the popular Watermelon Festival and Pageant. Rural and farm families throughout Arkansas suffered the loss of their farms; sharecroppers were evicted from their leased homes: and many went homeless. Cities lost businesses. The people of Little Rock, in a panic, withdrew over $5 million from the banks, almost bankrupting the state capital.

The roles of men and women would change forever. Many women in Hope would roll up their sleeves and do whatever was necessary to help keep bread on their family's table. Many men, for the first time, stayed home jobless while their women worked. Women, in fact, made up about a quarter of the workforce in the Southern Delta during this time, but their new roles garnered resentment from men who claimed they were taking the good jobs from men.

Fewer couples married. Men simply couldn't support a family. Many men, in fact, walked away from the families they had, leaving the women to provide for the children or move into the emergency shelters that housed indigent families. When emergency shelters were filled to capacity, indigent families were forced to move to the cardboard homes, temporary homes made from paper and other scrap material. These pitiful excuses for housing were called "Hoovervilles," because of President Hoover's inadequacy in stemming the economic disaster or helping those in need.

Franklin Roosevelt's New Deal government program, including his Works Progress Administration (WPA) program, was a saving grace for many, especially blacks and women. Arkansas was the first state to fill all of its WPA slots for women, who served hot lunches to school children, made clothes in sewing rooms, tended the sick in household aid programs, and taught adult education classes as part of this program.

The Depression era, for all its negatives, afforded the people of Hope and other parts of the country an opportunity to learn new ways of persevering. Women raised gardens and canned fruit and vegetables for the winters. Many sewed theirs and their family's clothes, sometimes from flour sacks or other scrap material. Quilting with throwaway scraps became a popular pastime in both the black and white communities.

Cotton was hardly king during these years, when the price per pound went down more than 60 percent from its normal price. Countless farmers walked away from their cotton crops and other crops they couldn't afford to keep. For the first time since Hope's settlement, people were moving away from town as fast as they were moving into it. Men and women sought something more, traveling either together or separately to find a better life. Teen-agers were often left to fend for themselves. At the worst point of the Great Depression, 250,000 teen-age hoboes were said to roam the country, searching for food, homes and jobs. Many teen-agers left their homes to lift the burden off their families.

As if loss of jobs and homes was not enough, a large part of Arkansas, including Hempstead County, was affected by the Dust Bowl of the 1930s. Though the natural catastrophe was mainly restricted to the Texas panhandle, southwest Arkansas was also greatly affected. And while the Dust Bowl of the early 1930s was not the cause of the Great Depression, the loss of land contributed greatly to the South's ongoing economic problems. Farmers went bankrupt; their land turned over to the banks or the government.

This ecological and human disaster, also dubbed the "Black Blizzard," lasted 10 years. The reason for the Black Blizzard, scientists and ecologists believe, was a combination of the drought of 1930 and farmers and ranchers' relentless abuse of land and soil, including the overgrazing of livestock.

Over 50 million acres of land were destroyed by the Dust Bowl and another 50 million endangered. Those caught in the middle of dust storms were left with damaged lungs or died due to inhalation of dust in the air. Even cows developed health problems and often died from eating dust-coated grass.

The largest migration in American history, famously fictionalized in John Steinbeck's *"The Grapes of Wrath,"* included over 2.5 million people who left Oklahoma, Kansas, Texas, New Mexico, Nevada and Arkansas— the Dust Bowl areas—and headed for California's promised land.

Yet in the midst of these ominous times, Americans found ways to forget their lots in life for moments, even hours, at a time. Some of the era's most memorable movies were produced during the Great Depression—fantasies, comedies, and science fiction, produced to take Americans' minds off their hopeless situations. Movies such as *"The Wizard of Oz,"* the Andy Hardy movies, *"Snow White and the Seven Dwarfs,"* *"Frankenstein,"* *"Dracula,"* and *"The Invisible Man"* drew record crowds. Actors such as Shirley Temple, Mickey Rooney, and the Three Stooges became symbols of make-believe lives during that period.

For a mere 10 cents, Americans could put their troubles on hold or pretend they didn't exist for one or two hours at a time. The films drew audiences from every spectrum of society, from the poorest to the richest, taking in from 60 million to 75 million movie tickets each week.

Even criminals had their 15 minutes of fame during the Great Depression.

Americans romanticized the lives of America's Most Wanted, following their Hollywood-like stories with almost as much interest and fascination as they did the radio soap operas. Al Capone, Bugsy Segal, Bonnie and Clyde, and Lucky Luciano all became household names.

By the 1940s, many blacks had joined the area's white soldiers marching into war, fighting and dying for America and democracy. But war veterans—black and white—returned home from that war angry and hopeless and in need of jobs. Though blacks had proven their patriotism, their mental, social, and economic oppression would continue to be a way of life.

Hope was a town of good Christians who fervently believed in God and morality, but there were no bleeding heart liberals there, no avowed abolitionists. The people of Hope, like those across the country, were victims of their times and their environments. This was part and parcel of being white and free and holding onto their God-given rights. Patriotism, however, didn't give rise to a bothered conscience when it came to the morality of enslavement or "separate but equal."

Historians will discover that, except for a few brief instances, blacks are not included in Hope's historical archives. Hazel Simpson, a president of the city's NAACP, has lived in Hope most of her life and recalls that "separate but equal" was the official law during this time, although not the reality. For every institution, there was a dual existence.

Hope's all-white town leaders must have made mention, during their city council meetings or chamber of commerce gatherings, of what was going on in the rest of the country. There may have been a tinge of fear that one day they, too, would have to give a second thought as to how they did business and how they dealt with blacks in their town. But like most Southern townspeople, they pushed the thought of change as far back in their consciousness as possible and went on pretending that change would never come.

A good indication of America's racial attitudes during Bill Clinton's childhood was the fact that something as groundbreaking as Jackie Robinson's breaking the color line in professional baseball, on April 15, 1947, garnered not one front-page banner headline from mainstream media.

But someone must have kept an ear to the ground, assessing the tenor of the growing rumbles of discontent throughout the country, rumbles that came from discontented blacks and indignant liberal whites, embarrassed by their country's racist environment. Surely the rumors that some Southern states were giving in to the integration nonsense gave them pause.

This was the Hope, Arkansas, with all its good and bad and shades of gray, that spawned a boy like William Jefferson Blythe III. The Hope, Arkansas, that Bill Clinton was born into on August 19, 1946, was in most ways typical of most Southern Delta towns of the pre-civil rights era. These towns were rife with racial inequalities, with unwritten rules of conduct for blacks, and even with well-articulated restrictions as to the places blacks could or could not go.

Given the times, the place, and the entrenched attitudes of those around him, it is indeed miraculous that Eldridge Cassidy would teach his grandson the worth of all human beings and the common sense of treating all men as equals.

Yet Hope's early settlers saw themselves and their town as slightly different from the rest of southwest Arkansas. One prominent Hope resident who moved there in the early years was Tom McMath, who wrote in 1960:

> Hope was an extraordinary town then, as it is now. Unique in its history, unique in its character and personality, Hope never really belonged to any particular category. It was essentially Western, since everybody who lived there was from somewhere else . . . yet, it had a Southern setting.
>
> It had no antebellum traditions; and there was a sizeable mixture of Northern and foreign folks, all there for one purpose, to work and build, and hopefully, to make money in the pioneer community. So there was little or no laziness or leisure.
>
> It was a rough, busy, dirty, smelly town—in the damp, still air of evening every privy contributed its quota of perfume—but you couldn't help but love it. Some of the finest people to be found anywhere lived there, and there was a wealth of color and drama in their daily lives.

Most conversations with members of Hope's white community reveal a town without a racial history that stands out in any way. But in many respects, Hope's way of dealing with race mirrored every other small town across the state. The town, in fact, toed the Confederacy line with its philosophy of oppression and dual systems for blacks and whites that most in the South embraced.

James Eldridge Cassidy was born in Parker, Arkansas, on August 19, 1898—the same month and day on which his grandson would come into the world nearly 50 years later. Cassidy moved to Nevada County, five miles from Hope, in January 1922, to a little town called Bodcaw. Seven years later, he and his wife, Edith Grisham Cassidy, along with their 6-year-old daughter, Virginia, would move again, this time to the fast-populating town of Hope.

Cassidy's grandson, who would one day become the 42nd president of the United States, was born just miles from two historic sites. One was the former Confederate capital of Arkansas: Washington, Arkansas. The small town lost that distinction to Little Rock after its capture by the Union Army in 1863. Somewhere near the center of town was the town's sole blacksmith shop, the site where the first Jim Bowie knife was forged. Just a few more miles south, a visitor would happen upon historic Spring Hill, a small town that once boasted an exclusive female academy, the only one in the Southwest. Rich planters and farmers throughout the region sent their daughters there to learn the three R's and ladylike deportment.

Farmers within the southwest region made weekly trips to the town of Fulton to unload their bales of cotton and other crops onto the banks of the Red River. They stood around, visiting with each other and gossiping gaily, as they waited to see the steamboats pull up, gather their goods, and leave again to transport their load to ports down the Mississippi River and to market.

CHAPTER 9
—HOPE'S—
Miracles

The Great Depression hit this small town hard. The city lost one of its three banks, a number of businesses, and many jobs for its residents. But, in 1941, Hope was selected by the Roosevelt War Department as the site for a $15 million proving ground that would serve as a test site for war ammunition. A surprise to the surrounding counties, the fact was that Hope was already cutting its teeth on good, old-fashioned political wheeling and dealing.

Arkansas Governor Homer Adkins and Hope's own U.S. Senator Lloyd Spencer had hatched this deal that would put Hope and Hempstead County on the regional map. Hope finally got the notice it had strived for for so long. It was now the envy of the rest of the state and the region, and its fate, many thought, was sealed as a "special" kind of town. The truth is, no one except the politicians who helped make it happen imagined that such a windfall could actually happen to the small town.

The Southwestern Proving Ground, built on the outskirts of Hope over a one-year period, was a testing site for small bombs, rifle shells, and flares that would be used in the upcoming war. Five thousand workers were brought in to work on the site, and 1,000 permanent employees took over the operation of the 37,000-acre complex. Amazingly, the army took over and cleared what many believed was the county's best farming and grazing land, an area about five miles wide and 15 miles long.

Tenants, sharecroppers, wage hands, and 424 "regular" families living in the "approved site" were asked to move. Of that number, 117 were landowners. A large number of blacks lived there and were said to have left behind not only their homes but also their livelihood, in the form of gardens. The government issued National Guard tents as temporary homes for the families who had no place to go and were unable to relocate.

Officers and technical experts in charge of the Proving Ground lived in Hope until officers' quarters, a colony of new homes nestled in a pleasant grove of trees, were built on the Proving Ground site. There might have been some that saw this move as something less than laudatory, but they were in the minority. And almost overnight, the small town became a bustling city. Highways leading there were widened and paved, and utilities extended to the south, where headquarters were located.

How could the residents grumble about Hope's new Municipal Airport with three 5,500-foot lighted runways, each 150 feet wide, built as part of the Proving Ground complex. The airport would maintain the status of being the largest airport in the state for many years afterward. More importantly, Hope residents believed the Proving Ground added to the rest. They saw the reality of jobs for their families and themselves. But amidst the excitement and grand expectations of the Proving Ground was another reality—ongoing, hushed grumbling from the black community.

Blacks who lived on the original site of the Proving Ground recall that it was then called Oak Haven. Rumors persisted long after the site was closed that many of the residents were forced to move without prior notification and without places to go.

Stories spread of displaced families forced to leave their homes, gardens, and belongings to move to other towns.

Children who played in the area told of finding and accidentally playing with ammunition left behind on the grounds and in the lakes. The family of one longtime resident of the area, Cora Bell Young, worked as sharecroppers on land owned by a local farmer, Gus Savage. Young says

34

her family, like many other sharecroppers nearby, was forced to pull up stakes when the Proving Ground came to Hope. Many black families relocated to McCaskell, a few miles down the road from Hope.

Young recalls: "We could hear the bombs day and night; and it sounded like they were right over our houses. We actually saw the planes go up and drop the bombs down, then heard the blasts. The blasts shattered windows for miles around. Even when we moved to Nashville, about 20 miles away, we could still hear the bombs. No matter how much it bothered us, nobody could afford to move away. All that ammunition hitting the ground, it was sometimes impossible for anyone to sleep."

Churches including Goff Chapel Church, which had been donated to the community by a black family, were moved from the Proving Ground area, Young says. At least two cemeteries, one white-owned and one black-owned, were moved by the War Department. One black cemetery, located on a plot of land donated by white landowner Bryce Bean, remained in the area: "It was saved because it sat on Highway 24, right outside the big fence surrounding the Proving Ground," according to Young.

But the Proving Ground, for most of the people of Hope, was the beginning of a new, prosperous time that never quite left, even when it closed down four years later. This hopeful new city seduced pioneers throughout the States; and many an immigrant family put down roots there.

On April 5, 1942, one year after the War Department had set up shop, Hope residents witnessed firsthand the changes the department had made. Within a two-hour period, 1,250 automobiles carrying 6,250 people passed through the gates of the Southwest Proving Ground. Unfortunately, residents were only allowed to view the complex from their cars; no one could leave their cars to walk around the site.

In 1946, due to economic constraints, the War Department phased out the Proving Ground. The workers dismantled, packed up, or destroyed as much of the operation as possible. They left a few memorials that would assure the people of Hope wouldn't forget them—the Municipal Airport;

the Industrial Area; a Game and Fish Commission Preserve; and Oak Haven, the suburban community in the pleasant grove of trees. Former owners were given an opportunity to repurchase their land. As much as possible, they cleared off the dangerous ammunition and put the land back into cultivation. Highways were widened, and utilities were extended to the south.

By the time young William Jefferson Blythe was born on August 19, 1946, Hope had metamorphosed into a prosperous incorporated town that boasted: "Episcopal, Baptist, Christian and two colored churches; a white school, and a black school; a good hotel, the 'Barlow;' and a courthouse capable of seating 350. There were two banks, both a lumber and planning mills, a wagon factory, a cotton press, and a number of special and general businesses, blacksmith shops, etc. There were also an artesian well 300 feet deep, which supplied the town's water . . . and telephone connection with Texarkana and Washington."

Like most of the rest of Arkansas, Hope's economy was based mostly on agriculture. And thanks to Hempstead County's rich soils and favorable climate, Hope had never suffered a complete crop failure. The town's farm products gained recognition from as far away as England. The Liverpool Board, for a number of years, gave special quotations for Hempstead cotton. And in 1904, the Louisiana Purchase Exposition in St. Louis awarded the state's alfalfa a blue ribbon.

Hope attracted business pioneers like Paul W. Klipsch, a lieutenant colonel who came to the town at the Southwest Proving Ground. When Klipsch left the armed services, he told his superiors he planned to "build a better loudspeaker for radio and entertainment use." He and his wife started a shoestring company and attempted to do just that. The first thing he had to do, however, was learn how to make the speaker and how to educate the masses that there was such an improved device. Then he had to convince people they needed it. Much later, Klipsch and Hope were able to boast that the business was world-renowned for building some of the best audio speakers in the world.

CHAPTER 10
HOPE'S
Dual School System

Hope, like the rest of the Southern Delta and the rest of the South, operated a dual educational system for black and white students. Mary "Nell" Turner, Hope's historian, says Hope School District was formed in the 1880s, a few years after the town was officially established. The journalism and English teacher spent most of her 30-year career in Hempstead County at Hope High School where, she points out, Captain C.A. Bridewell was the first teacher employed there.

D.L. Paisley, who had taught in the schools under Bridewell, became superintendent of Hope School District after Bridewell was elected mayor. Paisley would later write: "When I came to Hope in 1904 (as a teacher) there were two school buildings, one for whites and one for Negroes. The course of study in the high school was limited to four subjects taught by me except some help in English. There were 809 students, six graduating seniors . . . and a 5-mill tax."

The first major undertaking of Superintendent Paisley and Hope's school board was the construction of a medium-size frame building at East Avenue and North Main Street. It was a red framed, two-story structure and was used from 1888 until 1922—first for the entire school, then for the high school only. The graduating class of 1888—all eight of them—held their commencement ceremony at the Murray Opera House.

In 1905, Hope's school board purchased a large piece of property in College Addition, and in 1908 foundations were laid for the "splendid building which is the pride of our city," as one local pamphlet described it. Garland School was completed that summer at a cost of $40,000, and elementary classes were transferred to the new building that fall. The high school's population was 66 students in 1906. By 1911, that number had reached 130. There were now 15 teachers, a superintendent, a high school principal, a grammar school principal, and a music supervisor, as well as an athletic team and a high school magazine.

Billy Blythe's first year of public school was spent at what once was a Catholic academy. Superintendent Paisley had purchased that building in 1918 and made it into Brookwood Elementary School. Before Mr. Paisley's departure as superintendent, he would OK the construction of a $150,000 high school, built "way out on Main Street in an old cornfield . . . that isn't even in the city limits." The city limits, of course, were extended; and people were told that a good gravel road led to the school.

The completed school, which drew national media attention, was described as "outstanding." It boasted the first intercom system in any Arkansas high school, and its vocational building was the first in the nation to be constructed by National Youth Administration labor.

CHAPTER 11
— HOPE'S —
Colored School

I n 1886, as Superintendent Paisley was working hard to make Hope's
white schools the envy of the rest of the state, a young black man by
the name of Henry C. Yerger came to town. As was true all across the
South, a dual education system was still in operation in Hope and
Hempstead County. Henry Yerger, however, would work to prove that
separate didn't always have to mean less excellent when it came to
Hope's black student population.

Henry Clay Yerger, born in 1860 in Spring Hill, Arkansas, was the son
of Anthony and Sally Yerger. Anthony Yerger, a doctor, had opened the
first black hospital in the southwest. His young, handsome son was
considered a pioneer in "Negro education" when he came to take over
Hope Colored School. The young professor had graduated from Little
Rock's Philander Smith College and had studied at Hampton University
in Virginia. His home was in the neighboring town of Spring Hill, and he
must have felt he was moving up a step when he came to Hope. Yerger's
first school was a one-room building located on South Hazel Street. And
it was a few years later that they moved to Shover Street and renamed it
Shover Street School.

Professor Yerger was liked by both black and white Hope residents,
and there was probably no other institution in the town that engendered
more pride from both races than Hope Colored School. Shover Street
School, in 1886, boasted two rooms and two teachers. In a short time,
there were four rooms and four teachers. In 1895, Yerger established the
first training school west of the Mississippi for Negro teachers, and
subjects were being taught through the 11th grade.

By 1915, he had built a second story onto the building, and three teachers were added to the faculty. Yerger, a sophisticated lobbyist for his school, gained the support of the Rosenwald Fund, the Jeanes and Slater Fund, and the General Education Board. They all were instrumental in helping to make possible a school for Hope's black students. For a long time, Shover Street School was the only black high school in this section of the state. Students from all over the state and from surrounding states went there for their education.

In 1918, Shover Street School was upgraded to serve as a headquarters for teachers and shortly thereafter became one of only three summer school sites in the state, joining schools in Little Rock and Pine Bluff. The State Department of Education endorsed Hope's State Summer School for Negroes, and a dormitory was built to accommodate out-of-state teachers and students who had come for training. Again, Yerger received funding from the General Education Fund and the Smith Hughes and Slater Funds to establish courses in home economics and agriculture.

By the summer school's 23rd session in 1929, teacher enrollment for the six-week program had grown to more than 336 teachers from Arkansas, Louisiana, Texas, and Oklahoma. In the midst of such interest in the program, a year-round, teacher-training department was established.

In 1931, the school was renamed Henry Clay Yerger School in honor of the educator who had nurtured it to this point. The school, by this time, boasted a faculty made up of the best crop of teachers in the state as well as some from adjoining states who had been recruited to the school. Professor Yerger was recognized by the Hope community as an outstanding leader. He was the first black to receive the Citizens Award for community education and religious services. He was touted as a statewide educational leader, serving as president and treasurer of the Arkansas Teachers Association, the black teachers' association.

Thanks to the Rosenwald Foundation and the General Education Board, in 1931 the school board purchased five adjoining acres for the building of H.C. Yerger High School and a park. The all-black high school became one of only 13 schools in the state with an "A" rating from the State Department of Education.

The Rosenwald Foundation's involvement in the history of Hope's education system was part of the Foundation's efforts to make a difference in black communities throughout the South. In 1917, Julius Rosenwald, president of Sears, Roebuck and Co., initiated a school-building program that was to have a dramatic impact on the face of the rural South and in the lives of its African American residents.

Through the Julius Rosenwald Foundation, more than 5,300 schools, shop buildings, and teachers' houses were built by and for African Americans across the South and Southwest until the program was discontinued in 1932. The Rosenwald School program has been called the "most influential philanthropic force that came to the aid of Negroes at that time." In all, the Rosenwald Foundation contributed more than $4.3 million to construct schools across the regions, and more than $4.7 million were raised by African Americans to build the schools.

Today many of these Rosenwald Schools are gone, victims of changing times and communities. However, interest in the history of the schools and the preservation of the surviving structures has been growing. In 2001, the state of Mississippi included Rosenwald Schools on its 10 Most Endangered Historic Places list, and Alabama initiated a survey of remaining schools. In North Carolina, where more than 800 Rosenwald Schools were built, a preservation effort is well under way. And in both North Carolina and Arkansas, the state historic preservation offices have put out calls for assistance in documenting and preserving the history of the Rosenwald Schools.

Had William Jefferson Clinton, public servant and political leader, and Julius Rosenwald, founder of the Rosenwald Foundation, lived during the same era, they surely would have had much to discuss about Arkansas and the South's educational systems and, more importantly, the failure of the region to adequately serve all of its youth.

Conver

WILLIAM JEFFERSON CLINTON
FROM HOPE TO HARLEM

PART II

CONVERSATIONS:
HOPE, ARKANSAS

Dr. King once said, "We refuse to believe there are insufficient funds in the great vaults of opportunity of this nation." Today, there is a new understanding that actually building one America replenishes the funds in the vaults of opportunity, that this is not an act of charity or kindness, or even constitutional obligation, but enlightened self-interest.

—President Clinton, One America Speech

Autrilla Watkins Scott is a tall, thin woman. Though she is well into her 70s, she remains spry and active. Her Long Beach, California, home is decorated with photos of the family she left in Hope. On the mantle sits black-and-white pictures of a good-looking young couple, Autrilla and her young husband, Olen, and one of Olen's parents. Also there is a more recent photo of Autrilla with President Bill Clinton, and a framed local article describing Autrilla as the president's babysitter.

I might have spent more time with Billy Blythe than any other black person in Hope. I wasn't more than 16 when I started babysitting little Billy Blythe, and the job really happened by accident.

My family moved from Ogden to Radical Hill and finally to Hope in 1929, before I was born and right before the Depression hit. I was delivered by the town's black midwife in 1930. Mama couldn't go in the white hospital, and we couldn't afford the one black doctor in town. My daddy was a drayman in Hope, but we still were really poor, especially after the Depression set in. People were moving every time you looked around . . . sometimes clear out of the area to try to find work or a cheaper place to live.

I went to school at the all-black Yerger Elementary School on South Hazel Street. I started school in 1936. From that first day, I loved learning, but school had to take a back seat when Daddy died. We had to live, and I was the only one around to help Mama for the longest. My daddy died in 1939, when I was just 9 years old. That year, I started working outside the house to help Mama out with the household. It was hard times back then.

One of the jobs I took on when I was in high school was as part-time housekeeper for Roger Clinton, from Hot Springs. He had a car dealership in Hope and wasn't here all the time, but he had an apartment that he shared with another man. My brother, Hosea, was the one who referred me to Roger when Roger told him he needed somebody to clean his duplex on weekends. I was just cleaning his apartment for a while, but later, after he started dating Virginia, I started babysitting, too.

At the same time, I was also helping Mama wash and iron rich white folks' clothes. Some of the white women in Hope worked in the post office, so they'd hire black girls or women to do their housework while they went to work. Sometimes we'd take their washing up to the house in a paper box. Some of the white women would say, "Autrilla, why don't you ask your mama if you can come

45

over here and play with my girl when you get outta' school?" Some of these same people would expect us to step off the sidewalk when we passed them during the day.

I always dreamed of getting out of school, going to business school, and then finding a good job that would let me continue to help Mother. I had started babysitting for white folks when I was about 12, because my four brothers and a sister went off to the war—three brothers went to the Navy, and one brother and one sister went to the Army. That meant it was just me left at home to help out.

My brother, Hosea, owned a hamburger place called The Blue Room, not far from Roger Clinton's Buick car lot. It got real busy a lot of times on the weekend, and I'd work there when I wasn't in school. Roger Clinton came there just about every day to eat lunch. He'd order chili and hamburgers just about everyday. I remember how much he loved chili and hamburgers!

He came in one day I wasn't there and told my brother he and his roommate was looking for somebody to clean their duplex during the weekends. Hosea asked if I wanted to do it, and I right away told him I did. I started that next week. I'd go over to the Buick place to pick up Roger's key after I got off from school, then go to the duplex and clean up. It wasn't a lot of work. All they had was a living room, one bedroom, a den, and a kitchen.

One weekend I was there and had finished cleaning, but decided to take a break before I left. I drank a coke and started listening to the radio and forgot all about the time. Before I knew it, I heard a key in the door, and a few seconds later, in walks Mr. Clinton with this young woman and little boy. I tell you, they almost scared me to death . . . I guess I scared them, too. I knew, then, I'd stayed much longer than I should have.

I think Roger was a little upset that I was still there. I could see it in his face, but all he said was, "I thought you would'a already been gone by now." I told him I was getting ready to go and started gathering my stuff, but then he changed his mind, saying as long as I was there, would I mind looking after little Billy for a while. I don't remember Virginia and Billy saying anything during this whole time.

That was how I first met Billy. After that day, it pretty much came to be routine. When I would come to clean the apartment, Roger and Virginia would drop by and drop off little Billy for me to watch. That child would be so excited to see somebody new. It was like he had been saving up things to ask me . . . and he couldn't get them out fast enough. He was a really good little boy, kind of serious, but full of energy and full of questions.

There was a few times when I was trying to finish my work, and he was talking and asking questions, nonstop. I finally said, "Billy, you can go on outside and play for a while." As much as that child liked to run his mouth, he was always real glad to go outside and play. I never had to worry about him getting dirty or anything; he was real good about minding. But I just needed to catch my breath, 'cause he could sure run you ragged with a million questions a minute.

When Bill Clinton became president, the first thing I thought to myself was: Lord, I use to send that boy outside because he didn't let me do my work, for trying to answer his questions!

I kept babysitting Billy, off and on, for about two years. When I graduated from high school, Virginia surprised me with a pretty blue, ruffled blouse. I'll never forget that.

Olen and I left Hope in 1955, a few years after Billy and his mother moved to Hot Springs. Hosea would visit Roger in Hot Springs and always told me how little Billy would ask about me and wanted to know why I wasn't visiting him. I look back, now that he grew up to be president of the United States, and think about the kind of child he was. I'm not surprised at all that he did so well. He was a serious child and always wanted to know so much about everything!

☉

David Johnson, married and a grandfather, is a former University of Arkansas Razorback football star and was drafted in the mid-1970s to play for the Dallas Cowboys. A knee injury ended his football career while he was with the Houston Oilers. Johnson returned to Hope in the late 1980s and became a community leader and public servant.

I was born before the Civil Rights laws were passed, but my father was bent on my brother and me learning to mix with others. Most people outside Arkansas don't believe it, but we actually attended a white school, Guernsey Elementary, years before integration came to Hope.

I was in seventh grade when Dr. Martin Luther King was shot, and as the only black child in my classroom at Guernsey

Elementary, I sat there as my white classmates celebrated the death of someone who meant so much to me and my family. That was the loneliest I've ever been. Since then, I've visited the Lorraine Hotel in Memphis where Reverend King was killed and invited some of those same white classmates to make that journey with me.

My interest in sports began with the bad feeling around integration in Hope. It seemed my brother and I weren't completely accepted by either the whites or the blacks after integration took place. I found out I was good at football and became an All-American fullback for Hope High School's team and was offered scholarships by four major colleges. My first choice was the University of Texas, where I was scheduled to room with Earl Campbell. But just one night before signing with Texas, my mother convinced me to stay in Arkansas.

Coach Frank Broyles and John Richardson, the first black football player on the Razorbacks' team, recruited me one month before finishing high school. Coach Broyles and I are still good friends. When a friend of mine was injured in a Razorback game, I was the only player Coach Broyles trusted to drive his 1965 T-Bird to the Springdale Hospital 10 miles away.

My father shopped at the Cassidys' grocery store when I was a child. Bill's Uncle Buddy was the first person I ever knew to buy steaks for his dog. I met Bill Clinton at a nightclub in Ozan, Arkansas. James Taylor was a longtime friend and supporter of Bill Clinton, and he sponsored a barbecue and rally that night. The second time I met him was in the mid-1980s after a horrible flood of southwest Arkansas' Red River. I picked the governor and his aides up in a van and got a chance to talk to him during that time.

Floyd Young, former educator, administrator, and the first black mayor of Hope, Arkansas:

I was born in McCaskell, right outside Hope, and attended elementary school in Nashville, another small town in the area. I finished high school at Blevins Training School and went on to college at the former AM&N College in Pine Bluff, Arkansas.

I began teaching right after college. I taught mathematics at Marked Tree and Cloud High School. I also taught in Hope public schools for 10 years. When I started teaching in Hope, I started out at Yerger High School. I was a counselor there, just a year, when the school board sent me over to Hope High School. Integration was finally here, and they thought they needed a black person to deal with the students. I worked closely with Nell Turner, the white counselor.

We went through a tense period as the school administration tried to decide where to send teachers. I always thought the administration saw Yerger as the place to put marginal teachers, and I was very upset that they would do that. There were some excellent teachers there and such community and school pride there. The administration was smart to decide that during this transition, they would have a black counselor and a white counselor at Hope school. I made trips over to the school before the year began to try to figure out what problems we might have.

Interestingly, if you ask anyone who didn't have the day-to-day experience of working there or going to school there, they'd say Hope schools' integration process was a smooth transition. Compared to other places, that's probably true . . . but there were some bumpy times, some misunderstandings on the part of both blacks and whites.

I questioned why so much of what meant a lot to the black community were discounted. The Yerger students lost their alma mater, their mascot, their school colors. All of this was replaced with Hope High School's symbolism. I couldn't understand why there couldn't have been a more equitable compromise.

Though I went to high school in Blevins during the 1950s, a lot of our activities were here in Hope. There were separate colored and white waiting areas in the train station, but it was still the central gathering place for blacks who worked during the week. Some, who had cars and trucks, would drive to Hope to spend their day. Others would "bump" rides back and forth or ride the bus.

There were two movie theaters back then—the Saenger and the Rialto theaters. Normally, the young people would go to the movies and stay most of the day. When it was time to return home, youngsters would catch a bus that ran from Nashville through McCaskell to Hope. Though we were all from different towns and went to different schools, it didn't matter, because we saw each other every weekend. The grownups sometimes gathered at a black café on Cotton Street. That street was renamed Walnut Street.

After integration became law, the people of Hope began efforts to peacefully integrate the whites-only establishments—the hotels, the restaurants. That was around the same time I began working at Yerger as a math and science teacher. I worked with the Neighborhood Youth Corps, after I saw how black students were unable to get jobs at the businesses where we traded so heavily—the restaurants, banks, and clothing stores.

A breakthrough in race relations happened in 1966, when Will Rutherford, the black principal of Yerger, became a Hope chamber member. He was the first. After that, I started counseling young people on applying for jobs in town, advising them not to go to interviews with a chip on their shoulders, not to appear too aggressive, to make sure the owners knew how bad you wanted to work. The students would tell me how the interviews went. I collected that information for two years before finally going before the chamber and sharing it with them. After that, a number of our students were hired by local businesses.

I knew Bill Clinton's Uncle Buddy and worked closely with Vincent Foster, Sr. I didn't know Bill Clinton but knew Mack McLarty and George Wright, Jr., who grew up in Hope and were Bill Clinton's friends. There were some good people in Hope, but they were all the products of the times and the environment. Most white people with money didn't want to see real growth because that would mean too much change in the way things had always been. The townspeople weren't quick to accept newcomers, even their own kind. People always had to prove themselves. I've always thought they saw the Cassidy family as outsiders, and that probably had a lot to do with who Bill Clinton turned out to be.

Hazel Simpson, one of Hope's first black female entrepreneurs and former vice president of Hope's NAACP:

I graduated from Yerger High School in 1959, Hope's all-black school founded by Henry Yerger, one of this town's great black leaders. Ours was the only school south of the Mississippi River to attract black teachers from surrounding states. Teachers came to Yerger to finish up college degrees. Most black residents of Hope feel deep pride in the Yerger legacy—the school and the outstanding family who remained involved in the school's administration up until 1949. That year, Will B. Rutherford took over as principal. Yerger's alumni are scattered throughout the country, but most of them come home each year to participate in our school reunions, and we contribute to this city's economy to the tune of $125,000 to $150,000 during that weekend.

In Hope, as in most places, blacks have always had to make demands to achieve anything. In 1988, our local NAACP sued the city to get more blacks on the school board, and we ended up getting four members. Our public schools integrated in 1969 but today they are predominantly black. We made more progress in the black community and in bringing the races together from 1969 to 1989 than we've made during the last 10 years.

I remember Bill Clinton's grandfather and how he treated blacks fairly, here. But we have to realize also that his store was located in our part of town, and it simply made good common sense and good business sense to have a good relationship with black folk.

W. LaDell Douglas, a Bowden, Arkansas, native, pediatrician, and former chairman of the board of Hope Medical Center:

I was born in the small town of Bowden in 1943. Like many Southerners, my family took part in the Great Migration: blacks leaving the South in search of better economic and racial environments in the North. The Douglas family left Hope in 1953 and ended up in Chicago, where they would remain for over 20 years.

I was born at home in Bowden but moved to Hope before I turned 1 year old. I went to Hopewell Elementary School up until my parents moved to Chicago. We moved just one day before my 10th birthday. What I remember most about those early years in Hope is how hard my father worked to make sure we had the necessary things to do well. He was a schoolteacher, a politician, a carpenter, and an insurance salesman. Most people tell me he was a hell of a good teacher.

My father campaigned for Governor Francis Cherry in the early '50s and would take me with him when he drove around the state speaking, or whatever. I also traveled with him as he sold burial insurance throughout the area.

I went to a segregated school in Hope, and the one time I went to the movies, I was directed to the balcony. That was where black folk sat if they wanted to watch a movie. It was common knowledge that if we went downtown, we had to drink from the colored-only fountain and go to the colored-only bathroom.

51

By the time I was third or fourth grade, we would always take Fridays off to pick cotton. I always competed with a boy named Jimmy McFadden, but he always beat me. The most I ever picked was 150 or 160 pounds. On weekends, my mother, sister, and I picked up pecans, our weekly family activity. We were paid 50 cents a bushel.

My mother had a beauty shop that she closed when we left in 1953. When she and my father moved back in 1974, she started it up again. My father owned a service station with his two brothers for a year after moving to Chicago. Within a year, though, he started his own and operated it until they moved back to Arkansas.

I finished medical school in 1974 and did my residency at Duke University. I started practicing in Durham, South Carolina, in 1978, but moved to Jacksonville, North Carolina, a city on the North Carolina coast. My sister returned to Hope in 1984. Not long after she moved back, she started calling to tell me that Hope Medical Center was looking for a pediatrician. The head of the medical center started calling and continued to call me for some time, in hopes I would return home to practice medicine. Finally, I said yes to their invitation to visit the center.

I came down that Christmas and brought my family. I spent time with the medical center staff and director but told them I wasn't interested at the time. They called me back almost as soon as I got home and asked what would it take to get me down there. I sat down and wrote out a long list of requirements, expecting not to hear back from them. But they responded right away, agreeing to my entire list.

So I returned to Hope in January 1994. My mother lived for one year after I got back. I was glad I was able to spend that time with her. I understand during much of the time I was away, there was a bustling black business community in Hope. That doesn't surprise me. There always was that tenacity by blacks to really try to advance. Even through segregation, they seemed able to find a way to advance.

Mary "Nell" Turner is an octogenarian and descendant of one of the earliest families settling in Hope. She is a slight, well-preserved woman with a kindly smile and a sharp memory. For many years she has served as something of a historian for the city (of Hope):

I was born in Hope in 1920. My family lived on Elm Street, in downtown Hope. I was a teen-ager during the years that Bill's granddaddy, Mr. Cassidy, delivered our ice. We had iceboxes back then, and men would haul big blocks of ice to our homes to keep our meat and milk and butter from spoiling.

My family and neighbors considered the Cassidys as country people, who moved into town. They moved here around 1929 in a horse and wagon. The family didn't own a car for the longest. Mr. Cassidy brought us groceries, milk, and huge blocks of ice in his wagon. I never drank homogenized milk until I went away to college.

Not many families had cars back then, but I was good friends with Frank McLarty—Mack McLarty's daddy—who came from a pretty wealthy family. Frank owned a car, and so did another friend, John Wilson. Back then, teen-agers always traveled in groups, mostly so that all of us could ride in the few cars available. When we went parking, there was a whole group of us; and we would sometimes exchange dates.

In 1936, a bunch of us went exploring out in this park area outside town. I vaguely remember we carried a watermelon with us to snack on . . . we usually did. We all ended up going through this abandoned house. Somehow I ended up spending the night there with one of my girlfriends.

In the middle of the night, my friend had a nightmare. I think it was because of the sheer curtains that kept blowing over the bed we were sleeping in. Later on, I learned that Virginia Cassidy and her first husband, William Blythe, had moved into that house when they first married. After Bill Clinton became governor, then president, I always joked that that I'd spent the night in the house that Bill Clinton was born in . . . in the very room Virginia and her husband slept in.

That house was first built by a wealthy man by the name of H.J.F. Jarret. He'd built the house as a wedding gift for his son, who fought in World War I. But his son and his new wife only lived in the house for a short time before they divorced. They both ended up moving away from Hope. By the time Virginia and William Blythe moved into it, it was a rent house. One of my friends lived on the street directly across from the old Jarret house and recalls her mother inviting Virginia and William Blythe over for homemade ice cream.

Hope had just one high school when I was growing up. It went from seventh through 12th grade. In fact, I was in seventh grade before the school was built, I think. Nobody had a lot during that time, but none of us knew it. I graduated from high school in 1937, went to college at Henderson for the first two years, then dropped out, because it was my sister's turn to go to school.

Even without a college degree, I got a job teaching down near Smackover at Lou Ann School, right in the middle of oil country. The Lou Ann School had an outdoor bathroom, but also an oil pump sitting out back. I was paid $75 a month—a lot of money then—and saved enough to go to summer school after that first year. I loved teaching down there, but I also enjoyed teaching in Hope for 27 years, even without the oil fields.

I remember Virginia being real popular. After she came back here to practice nursing, she got to be known as the best registered nurse in the area. Her mother, Mrs. Edith Cassidy, was well thought of, too. People always called on her for their nursing care, or even when they needed someone to just be there with them. People stayed in the hospital for a long time then. When I had my child, I was in the hospital for 10 days. She was said to be so good with people. She was something of a legend around here.

Virginia did anesthesiology, not nursing like Mrs. Edith. She had a cousin, Dale Drake, who she was real close to. I think after Virginia moved to Hot Springs, they talked almost every day on the phone. Bill was going into the second grade when he left Hot Springs.

Hope schools integrated around the late 1960s. I remember it being an extremely smooth integration. Will Rutherford was the principal of the black high school then and I think what made the difference was the counseling sessions with the teachers and that they brought in psychologists to talk to us. We all worked on different committees to get ourselves prepared for the changes.

I remember having a young black student, a young girl who I just didn't seem to get along with. She and I just didn't understand each other. I called Mr. Rutherford one day crying after we'd had an altercation. He came and met with me for about an hour, and I think I got a better understanding of our problems.

I allowed the students to have panel discussions on integration, and I really think that helped them. It was good to have blacks and whites talking together. I just did everything I could to see if it worked . . . you just do what you have a gut feeling about.

I lived in Hope my whole life and never had thought there was class disparity here. But there was a young, black girl who came on Saturdays to help me in the house, and one Saturday, she told me she couldn't go to the library. I just was so surprised, because it had never occurred to me before that everyone didn't have access to the library. I didn't grow up with prejudice, but it was there, I guess.

The truth is, there were class differences made even within the white race. When families moved from the country into town, they met with prejudices. My mother and her family came here in a buggy, and they were ostracized. I heard that when Virginia came to town, some of the kids would treat her badly. She was very, very bright and had that spirit, just like Bill's. No matter what people said about her, she would do well. They didn't have money, but it didn't seem to stop them.

Hosea Watkins is a still-handsome, 90-year-old Hope native and former deputy sheriff of Hope. He remembers with nostalgia the early days of living in the small town, and his years working for Eldridge Cassidy in his grocery store:

My family moved to Hope in 1920 from a much smaller town called Radical Hill, where the first retirement home was built in southwest Arkansas. Before moving to Radical Hill, we lived in Ogden, a few miles south of Hope.

My father was a drayman. There were four licensed black draymen in Hope. They were movers and sometimes taxis. They also hauled trash, house furniture, and lots of wood for people's heaters and wood stoves. Draymen had to pay a $25 fee every year for their licenses.

That was the '30s and '40s, and most of the whites and blacks from that time are dead and gone. I met Virginia through Roger Clinton. She was pretty young when she married Roger. And it wasn't long after they married, he took her and Billy off to Hot Springs. Before that, Roger stayed in Hope to run the car dealership a lot of the time. We got to be good friends. He would come to my restaurant and eat chili and hamburgers all the time. His car dealership was right next to Wilson's Grocery Store.

I grew up during the Depression, when times were pretty hard. I went to work for the city in 1939. I thought blacks and whites got along, but mostly because black folk knew our places. We knew what we could and couldn't do. There were a lot of places we couldn't go. But there were some good white people, like Luther Hardin's family, John Wilson's family, and the McLartys. John Wilson's daddy would buy him things like baseballs and mitts and ask if we wanted to play with them. He knew our folks couldn't afford to buy things like that.

Still, the fact is, any time black folk forgot their place, whites would remind us. Back in those days, it didn't matter what it was, the white person was always right. We didn't have no say-so. Something I almost never talked about over the years was the first time my daddy took me downtown. He wanted me to see a black man hanging on a post. That was back in 1925. I wasn't more than 6 years old at the time. But my daddy brought me up there that morning and showed me what had happened to Brownie Tugger. He wanted to show me what white folks did to black folks they thought had stepped out of line.

They claimed Tugger Brown drove a white girl to Washington, the next town over, and raped her. We lived not far from Brownie's wife, Alice, for a long time. I always felt so bad about that, and it took me the longest to stop dreaming about it. The thing was, back then, black folks was only supposed to haul black folks in their taxis. Brownie was the black folks' taxi driver, and Tom McLarty was the white folks' taxi driver. I don't think anybody ever found out for sure how that white girl ended up in Brownie's taxi.

But that was what it was like in Hope, back in those days. I later on started working for Mr. Cassidy, Bill's grandfather. He hauled ice to homes throughout the city in a horse and wagon. I helped him haul ice for a long time, making 73 cents a day. He owned a general store, and I helped out around there. That was the first time I ever saw a man pick up almost 300 pounds of ice and carry it on his back.

Tillman Ross is a proud veteran of two wars: World War II and the Vietnam War. Well into his 70s, Ross is a tall, striking man with sharp memories of growing up in southwest Arkansas:

More than anything else, I'm most proud of the 20 years I served this country in World War II and Vietnam. I've been a war veteran for more than 50 years, and if the opportunity arose, I would do it all over again. My life and my wife Maxine's life still center around Bethel African Methodist Episcopal Church. I started attending Bethel when I was just 12 years old, and to this day, I serve as a church steward, trustee, usher, and president of the lay organization.

The first time I voted was in 1942. I voted Democrat in a foxhole in France. I've been a Democrat ever since. And when I left the military, I joined the party and try my best to stay involved.

I was in World War II 58 years ago, in Southampton, England, getting ready to land in Normandy Beach. In 1950, I was in Japan. When the war broke out in Korea, I was part of the first group sent there. I have no regrets. The military allowed me to learn things I have carried with me. I am, right now, the post commander for the American Legion here in Hope. All the members here are Vietnam veterans, except two are World War II veterans.

I had been in the military so long that when I first came back, I didn't know a lot of people. But I still wanted to do something for my country, so I joined some of the local organizations.

Mr. Eldridge Cassidy owned a store on the north side of town here. Though I didn't know Bill Clinton then, my family regularly visited the store and got to know Mr. Cassidy real well. His daughter, Virginia, was born out in the country, about five miles from where I was born.

Back in those days, hardly anybody had cars. Everybody used horse and wagons. We'd drive the wagons from Sutton, where I was born, to Bodcaw, where Mr. Cassidy lived at that time. It was nothing unusual for people to stop at neighbors' or even strangers' houses to ask for a drink of water. That was how I got to know Bill's uncle, Buddy Grisham. I was 12 or 13 years old, and my daddy and me stopped by his house to ask for a drink of water. Mr. Grisham asked my father if he would cut him some stove wood and take roosters as payment because he didn't have enough money to pay him.

Of course, my father was proud to hear him say that. We had a big family and could certainly use those roosters. We walked back to the chicken coop with him, and, sure enough, there was these big old roosters strutting around the pen.

Daddy wasn't about to look a gift horse in the mouth in those hard times. We brought the load of wood and stacked it in the back yard where he told us. After that, Mr. Buddy came out and helped us catch four or five roosters. I swear, we ate roosters seem like forever, but I'll never forget daddy saying we came out ahead, 'cause of that rooster laying with the hens and giving us more chickens that spring.

Mr. Cassidy was very friendly, willing to help you in a time of need. Back in the '30s and '40s, times were hard and people were suffering. He had this little store, but he would hardly ever turn anyone down if they didn't have money. In 1946, when Bill was born, I was just getting out of the service.

Race relations here were pretty bad when I was younger. There were limits to where blacks could go. The places you wanted to go, you were barred from going. I would walk by and look into the pool hall, but we couldn't go in. We weren't allowed to go into clothing stores or restaurants. In restaurants, we had to go from the front to the back to be served. We walked past the white people sitting at the counter eating or drinking. The only place to get ice cream was the double-dip stand. Black customers would be lined up half a mile to get the double-dip ice cream on the week-ends. There were hamburger stands—a front part for the whites and the back part for the blacks.

Blacks gathered at the Hope train station, in a small area designated for us to sit. I remember that our water came straight from the water line. The whites had cool water from the fountain, but we knew never to go to the fountain. There was a huge grocery store that sold all kinds of food in large quantity. Country folk would come there on weekends to shop. In the middle of the downtown square were two large water barrels—one for white people and the other for blacks. If we wanted a drink of water, we had to share one dipper. The white people's water barrel had disposable cups. We were glad to get it, though, because it was cold. They kept it full of ice all day, and it was free.

School integration took place in the late '60s. I lived right across the street from Yerger Junior High School. Though I worked at Lone Star Ammunition Plant in Texarkana, that first day of integration, I stayed home, sat on my porch, and watched that transition. I was shocked to see how smoothly it went. There were no problems, no troubles. Everybody who could get off work was there watching, too. Police were patrolling the schools.

I remember how, in 1957, I got leave from the army and traveled from Germany to be with my wife during the birth of one of my children. When I arrived in Little Rock, I couldn't believe what was going on. There were all kinds of upheaval about the integration of Central High School. Being over in Germany, I didn't know anything about all these problems in the schools. When I returned to Germany, everyone over there had already got the news. They knew all about Governor (Orval) Faubus and Central High School.

Conver

WILLIAM JEFFERSON CLINTON
FROM HOPE TO HARLEM

PART III

HOT SPRINGS: ARKANSAS' LITTLE PIECE OF HEAVEN AND HELL

We are white and black, Asian and Hispanic, Christian and Jew and Muslim, Italian and Vietnamese and Polish Americans and goodness knows how many more today. But above all, we are still Americans. Martin Luther King said, "We are woven into a seamless garment of destiny." We must be one America.

—William J. Clinton, on race, the Shorestein Center

CHAPTER 12
——A SECOND HOME FOR——
William Jefferson Clinton

William Jefferson Clinton spent most of his youth in the city of Hot Springs, Arkansas, located almost halfway between the state capital where he would spend the balance of his adult life, and his birthplace, Hope, Arkansas.

It was 1952 when 7-year-old Billy Blythe moved with his mother and her new husband, Roger Clinton, to Hot Springs, where Roger would continue work with the Clinton Buick company. Mrs. Virginia Cassidy Blythe Clinton would become a popular nurse anesthetist with the Hot Springs Ouachita Hospital, where she would come to be known at the best in the area.

By the time the Clinton family moved to Hot Springs, it was a city reborn, having bounced back from the trouncing it took from the Civil War and become an internationally renowned tourist town. This quaint yet progressive community boasted a population that included many non-Southerners and some foreigners. Despite Arkansas' reputation as backward and insular, Hot Springs attracted nationally recognized entertainers and well-known celebrities who enjoyed the "freedom" of the town, including it medicinal spas and open gambling.

Was the political timbre of Hot Springs as left-leaning as was its social environment? *The Sentinel-Record,* on June 26, 1959, wrote that Representative Ray S. Smith, Jr., of Hot Springs, was recognized for his courageous civil rights move in casting the lone vote against Governor Orval Faubus' school closing bill in 1959. Smith received the Edmond G.

Ross Award, named for the Kansas senator who had sacrificed his political career by casting a deciding vote against the impeachment of Andrew Johnson.

Bill Clinton was 11 years old in 1957, when Arkansas became infamous around the world for the integration crisis at Little Rock's Central High School. That one incident, Clinton would later say, symbolized much of what he would spend his life fighting against.

In an interview that took place during his presidency, he reflected on those tumultuous early years of integration in Arkansas: "I was only 11 years old when the nation's attention was riveted by the scene of nine black children being escorted by armed troops on their first day of school in Little Rock's Central High School . . . it had a profound impact on me.

"I was concerned about the racial separation between blacks and whites that was taken for granted by so many of my neighbors and friends. When I was a very young boy in Hope, I spent time in my grandfather's grocery store. Many of his customers were poor and black, but he treated everyone, black or white, with the utmost dignity and respect. I often played with black children. My grandfather tried to explain why a little black boy I played with couldn't go to school with me, or why the streets in the black neighborhood were not paved like the streets in the white part of town.

"My grandparents were not well educated or well off; and I don't know how they came to break from the conventional white opposition to racial equality, but I'm so grateful to them for what they taught me."

During the 10 years Bill Clinton spent in Hot Springs before going off to college, he would shed much of his rural, small town persona and begin to assimilate comfortably into the more cosmopolitan Hot Springs environment. He would also shed the name that had been his biological father's and take on his stepfather's surname. No longer Billy Blythe, he became William "Bill" Clinton. His peers saw in him a bright, popular young man with an infectious personality and a natural talent for music, especially the saxophone. In March 1964, he was selected as co-first chair for the tenor saxophone; it was the first time Hot Springs High School had ever awarded two first chair winners.

He was never very involved in school sports but had a great interest in cars and could often be found hanging out at the Clinton Buick dealership. He graduated with honors from Hot Springs High School in 1964, and his peers predicted that in 20 years he would become "a social worker in a prairie dog colony."

Hot Springs, though, with all its exotic airs, was still the South. Bill Clinton attended a segregated elementary school and high school. The Clinton family lived in the white part of town and had the privilege of eating in the segregated restaurants and watching movies in segregated theaters. Although the Cassidys instilled in Clinton the importance of looking beyond race, his new home, Hot Springs, might well have taught him a practical lesson about the importance of presenting a racially harmonious face to the visitors to the city, many who came from a more liberal North.

While both Hot Springs and Hope had been proud participants in the Confederacy during the Civil War, the two cities' similarities went little further than that. Hot Springs' outside-the-box persona likely had much to do with Bill Clinton's joie de vivre and maybe his open acceptance of people and situations that others find harder to accept.

It was during the 1950s and 1960s that the unarticulated questions that pestered young Billy Blythe in Hope began to reintroduce themselves in the form of what was happening within and outside the state. During the height of the civil rights struggle, the teen's deep-felt sensitivities on race began to bud, and it was in Hot Springs that he forged his own philosophies and ideals about America's race conflicts. Those theories and ideals, for the most part, would remain with him.

CHAPTER 13

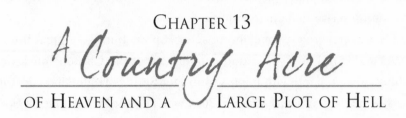

A Country Acre

OF HEAVEN AND A LARGE PLOT OF HELL

According to legend, in 1541, Spanish explorer Hernando de Soto and his troops were the first Europeans to see the mysterious hot springs that flowed down from a mountain slope. French trappers, hunters, and traders became familiar with the area in the 17th century, and it was from the French that Americans acquired the area as part of the Louisiana Purchase in 1803. The following year, Thomas Jefferson dispatched an expedition led by William Dunbar and George Hunter to explore the newly acquired springs. Their report to the president was widely publicized and stirred up interest in the "Hot Springs of the Washita Mountains."

In the years that followed, more and more people came to Hot Springs to soak in the waters, which were believed to have medicinal qualities. The idea of "reserving" the springs for the nation took root, and a proposal to that effect was submitted to Congress by the territorial representative, Ambrose H. Sevier. In 1832, the federal government took the unprecedented step of setting aside four sections of land there, the first U.S. reservation made simply to protect a natural resource. Little effort was made to mark the boundaries adequately, and by the mid-19th century claims and counterclaims were filed on the springs and the land surrounding them.

In the 1870s, the government continued to control the springs and to reserve certain areas as federal property. Hot Springs came to be called "The National Spa," and such slogans as "Uncle Sam Bathes the World" and "The Nation's Health Sanitarium" were used to promote the city. Private bathhouses were built under the supervision of the federal government. These establishments ranged from the simple to the luxurious. The government even operated the U.S. Government Free Bathhouse and a public health facility.

By 1921, the Hot Springs Reservation was such a popular destination for vacationers and those seeking health remedies that the new National Park Service's first director, Stephen Mather, convinced Congress to declare the reservation the 18th national park. Monumental bathhouses built along Bathhouse Row about that time catered to crowds of health seekers. These establishments, complete with the latest hydrotherapy equipment, also pampered the bather in artful surroundings, featuring marble- and tile-decorated walls, floors, and partitions. Some rooms sported polished brass, murals, fountains, statues, and even stained glass. Gymnasiums and beauty shops also helped visitors in their efforts to feel and look better.

Just after World War II, as medical technology and Americans' use of leisure time changed, there was a rapid decline in use of the bathhouses, and one by one they began to close down. Today, only the Buckstaff Bathhouse operates as a traditional bathhouse.

Charles Moss Williams, a historian of small Arkansas towns, wrote during the turn of the century about a quaint village—a stopping point for Civil War veterans—that would soon become world renowned not for its gigantic watermelons but for its hot natural springs, and later for its access to man's darker proclivities.

But growth for this unique Arkansas town would be slow in coming, mainly because of two roadblocks: first, outsiders' access to the area was extremely difficult given its mountainous landscape. More importantly, politics and decades-long disputes between local land developers and the federal government prevented the area from ever reaching its full commercial potential. While several different residents held claim to the area,

Congress passed a bill in 1832 reserving four sections of the land, with the springs in the middle, for future use by the U.S. government. Although citizens held prior claims, this reservation supposedly wiped out the possibility of private ownership of land within a mile of the springs.

The land dispute was a drawback for the area even though it would be decades before the government ever enforced its claim. With the true ownership up in the air, development and improvements of facilities were slow to take place. N.P. Woods, the town's assistant marshal in 1850, offered this: "The hot springs . . . are celebrated from Vermont to Texas for the cure of all kinds of rheumatism and syphilitic complaints; and if the title was settled there would be great improvements made so that more people could be accommodated, which would be a great benefit."

One visitor from Mississippi described the town as something of a camp meeting. "The houses are situated about the same and are all little frame or log cabins, situated in a valley between two mountains." Even geologist David Dale Owen, who came to the town in 1858 to analyze the waters, pointed out that "everything about the baths, hotels and boarding houses is of the most temporary character." But the problem of how to get to this town enshrouded with warm, medicinal water prevailed. According to one writer:

> From Little Rock to Hot Springs, the distance is about 60 miles and has to be traveled in the old-fashioned stage coach over a broken mountainous country . . . you may form an opinion of the comfort we enjoyed on the way when I tell you that twice we came near upsetting, broke down once absolutely, and had sundry other mishaps . . . a ride of 15 hours brought us to the springs.

Thus, the primitive and temporary nature of Hot Springs gave it the likeness of the wild frontier of the Old West. It was duly noted in letters and correspondence that the people visiting Hot Springs during the pre-Civil War days were to a great extent those seeking fame and fortune through gambling and other unsavory sources. According to one writing:

And here are to be found people from all parts of the country, and all sorts of ills to which flesh is heir to are well represented. There are also hundreds of persons here afflicted in no way except in lack of a proper sort of brains, but who come to gamble, to drink brandy and to murder. The day we got here a man was shot, though not dangerously. Nothing was done with either of the parties.

Hot Springs, in spite of its harsh traveling conditions, seemed to have found its mismatched claims to fame during the years leading up to the Civil War: healing waters and a Wild West environment. One *Arkansas Gazette* article described the city's success thusly: "The crowd is greater than ever before; the hotels and boarding houses here and in the surrounding country are full."

On November 2, 1829, the Territorial Legislature ordained this new area Hot Springs County, taking it from an edge of Clark County. The first county seat, however, would be a much less noticeable town further southwest called Malvern. In contrast to the mostly flat terrain of Hempstead County, Hot Springs' landscape included forested ridges and river bottomland. The Ouachita Mountains in the north and west gave the city an otherworldly feel, and the rolling hills suggested a place of peace and contentment. Of course, that would only describe part of Hot Springs, and only during some hours of the day.

CHAPTER 14
HOT SPRINGS
—— AND THE ——
Civil War

According to one writer, Wendy Richter, in an essay entitled "The Impact of the Civil War on Hot Springs, Arkansas," the small town was almost totally destroyed during the course of the Civil War. Most of its small population was lost as residents fled what became a dangerous and desolate location.

When the war broke out, the men of Hot Springs and surrounding areas flocked to Hot Springs and Rockport, organized companies, and moved to Little Rock to sign up in the Confederate forces. On their way to Little Rock, the men gathered on the banks of Ten Mile Creek and trained for two weeks. Most became part of the 3rd Arkansas Calvary. Some northern Hot Springs County residents enrolled at Mount Ida in Montgomery County in July 1861. This group of volunteer soldiers was mustered into Confederate service in Missouri. Of the hundred or so men who left with this company—mostly farmers, but also mechanics, builders, tradesmen, blacksmiths, and one stagecoach owner—less than 15 would return.

The makeup of the company was consistent with most in the area. None of the local men had military experience, but they were described as "hardy, stout, determined men . . . and used to a Frontier rifle, though not a man in the company knew anything about military tactics."

Like Hope would in 1863, Hot Springs found itself thrust into Civil War history when, in 1862, the small village became the temporary capital of the state of Arkansas. This happened when Union General

Samuel Curtis invaded and occupied Batesville, less than 100 miles from Little Rock. Governor Henry Rector feared the troops might seize the state capital and, in a rush decision, loaded the most important state records onto a steamboat on the Arkansas River and transported them to Hot Springs. *The Arkansas Gazette* wrote this about the dramatic action:

> At Dardanelle the records and archives of various offices were taken off land. After much difficulty, a train of wagons was procured, in which the boxes, weighing in all some fifteen or eithteen [sic] thousand pounds, were sent over the mountains. Hastily packed, in rough boxes, and carried in wagons without covers.

The temporary capital was set up on property owned by Governor Rector in a two-story home in the park. Some of the records were stored in a log kitchen, which was separate from the house itself. Movement of the capital drew criticism, particularly from Little Rock's true Democrats:

> We would be glad if some patriotic gentleman would relieve us the anxiety of the public by informing it of the locality of the state government. The last that was heard of it here was aboard a steamer "Little Rock" about two weeks ago, stemming the current of the Arkansas River.

In spite of the loss of Confederate soldiers in Arkansas, Hot Springs would enjoy a miraculous rebirth during the post-Civil War era. Shortly after the war ended, the town began to swell in population and change demographically. Past residents returned to their homes, and people from adjoining towns and even out-of-state visitors settled in the city. A great number of the new settlers were, in fact, former Union soldiers who'd first learned about the area during their military forages across south and southwest Arkansas.

The town began its claim to fame as a health resort, and word of the medicinal value of the hot springs in the city spread throughout and even outside the country. Many Americans had moved west of the Mississippi River after the Louisiana Purchase, but few had made their way to Hot

Springs until after the Civil War, even though there had been national publicity about the town's claim to fame, medicinal waters for those suffering from rheumatism and paralytic afflictions. The 1830 census showed a population of only 84 residents in the township of Hot Springs; 30 years later, the town's population had grown to only 201.

In 1860, Hot Springs boasted two main hotels, the Hale House and the Rector House, and a number of smaller boarding houses. There were several doctors practicing in the town, including a Dr. J.C. Grafton and Dr. George Washington Lawrence, both arriving in 1859. There were smaller pavilions on the east side of Hot Springs Creek, each having a narrow bridge extending across the stream. The few professional buildings and homes were scattered along Hot Springs Creek and the hillsides surrounding it.

Hot Springs County became Garland County on April 5, 1873, formed from territory cut off of Saline, Hot Springs, and Montgomery counties. Malvern, however, lost its role as county seat, and that distinction was awarded to the new and exciting Hot Springs.

Garland County was named in honor of Augustus Hill Garland, a private citizen who was practicing law in Little Rock when the county was formed. Garland was born in Tipton, Tennessee, in 1832, but his parents moved to Miller County, Arkansas, shortly after his first birthday. After his father's death, the child moved with his mother to Washington, in Hempstead County. His mother would marry Thomas Francis Hubbard, who would eventually become a notable judge in that area.

At the age of 21, Augustus Garland followed in his stepfather's footsteps by becoming an attorney; he practiced in Washington for several years and then moved on to Little Rock, where he partnered with prominent attorney Ebenezer Cummins. Fortuitously for young Garland, Mr. Cummins died the next year, leaving all his cases and clients to the young man. Garland's newfound role at the firm required that he visit state and federal courts throughout the state as well as the U.S. Supreme Court, where he was later admitted for practice in December 1860.

Garland was a Pulaski County delegate to the state convention that considered the state's secession from the Union. Like the majority of the delegates, he voted against the secession. After the infamous clash in Fort Sumter, however, a second meeting of the convention was called, and this time Garland voted along with the majority for Arkansas' secession from the Union. In 1861, he was elected a member of the Confederate Congress, where he served until 1864, and to the Confederate Senate, where he served until March 1865. In 1867, Garland was elected to the U.S. Senate, but was refused a seat because of his position on secession.

When Arkansas adopted its post-war constitution in 1874, Augustus H. Garland was elected its first governor. He was inaugurated in November 1874. In 1877, the Legislature elected him U.S. senator to succeed Powell Clayton and re-elected him in 1883. President Grover Cleveland appointed Senator Garland U.S. attorney general in 1885. He served for the first four years of the Cleveland administration—the first and only Arkansan, for many years, to serve as a member of a president's cabinet.

Garland died in January 1899 while arguing a case before the Supreme Court. He was buried alongside other prominent Arkansans, including the Loughboughers, in Mount Holly Cemetery in Little Rock.

Hot Springs' economic base was beef and dairy cattle, hay, soybeans, and rice. Industrial development included lumber mills, brick plants, metals, and small industry. Many residents commuted out of the county for work.

Hope had its watermelons, while Hot Springs' early county seat, Malvern, had its bricks. It was, in fact, dubbed the "Brick Capital of the World" and celebrated this dubious distinction with a Brick Fest each year. In 1936, the WPA built the county courthouse using Malvern's own locally manufactured bricks. The county was also said to be the site of some 65 varieties of valuable minerals, including the nation's greatest concentrations of novaculite, vanadium, and magnet ore, which was found in the roadbed of U.S. Highway 270, which ran between Hot Springs and Hope.

The Sentinel-Record, Hot Springs' main newspaper, announced the opening of the city's new main hospital, the Army and Navy General Hospital, on October 19, 1933. This hospital replaced a wood-structured, 150-bed army hospital that had been built in 1887. Between its opening in 1933 and its closing in 1960, the hospital provided medical care to thousands of military servicemen and women, veterans, military retirees, and their families, as well as congressional members and other dignitaries including General John J. Pershing, President Harry Truman, and President Lyndon Baines Johnson. In fact, it was estimated that at least one third of the citizens of Garland County had received care from the hospital, especially during World War II.

In 1874, the idea of providing medical treatment with the aid of the thermal waters in Hot Springs was born when a prominent and noted physician, Dr. A.S. Garnett, and another Hot Springs pioneer, Charles Cutter, became convinced that the U.S. government should provide facilities for its veterans who were crippled as a result of war injuries. Among Dr. Garnett's patients in the spring of 1882 was General John Logan, a former army officer and then an Illinois senator.

With Senator Logan's help and the help of local businesses and professional pioneers of the new city, the plans for the hospital unfolded. By June 1882, a bill appropriating $100,000 for the establishment of the Hot Springs hospital was passed. By July, the War Department had authorized its construction. The Department of the Interior donated 24 acres of park area to the War Department for the hospital site; the cornerstone was laid that year, and the hospital was completed in 1886, officially opening in January 1887.

While politics had made the Army and Navy hospital a reality for Hot Springs, it was politics, again, that brought its demise. From all accounts, infighting within the Army Department closed the doors of the much-heralded hospital. All hope was not lost, however. In 1960, the Hot Springs Rehabilitation Center became a reality, bringing new industry and economy to the area. The center was one of the first in the nation and became a national leader in rehabilitation services.

Visitors from outside the state were attracted not only by its outstanding service but also by aesthetics such as marble designs inlaid in the floor, marble wainscoting, and a pink marble entrance. Within three years, it was rated one of the top four rehabilitation centers in the nation. Due of the acclaim of the rehabilitating springs, the center attracted national and international conferences, workshops, and entertainment. Visitors from around the world came to Hot Springs to learn about the center and to sample the hot springs.

CHAPTER 15
HOT SPRINGS . . .
—— A PARODY OF ——
Liberalism

A ccording to the 1950 U.S. census, Hot Springs' total population was 36,687, almost one-fourth of which was Africa American. In 1959, six years after young Billy Clinton moved from the ultra-rural town of Hope to the unusually cosmopolitan Arkansas resort area, an interesting article entitled "A City of Racial Harmony" appeared in a local Hot Springs newspaper. The article, written by one Edna Lee Howe, describes the southwestern resort town known for its medicinal spring water, its gambling proclivities, and its Broadway-like entertainment district as nothing less than the "real" land of opportunity for black Americans:

> Since Hot Springs' earliest days, the Negro has been an integral part of this community, working side by side with the white man and endeavoring to play his rightful role as a citizen in all walks of life.
> Today there are between seven and eight thousand Negroes residing in this resort, representing close to one-fourth of the total population of the city proper, based on the 1950 census. With all the integration strife rampant over the country, leaders of the Negro community are convinced that nowhere in this country does a better relationship exist between the two races than in Hot Springs.

T.J. Collier—one of the city's leading black physicians, a member of Hot Springs Mayor Dan Wolf's advisory committee, and the first black to serve as vice president of the Hot Springs Garland County Medical Society—called race relations "super excellent . . . it is something that has developed through the years. It has been a natural thing. There is a feeling of kindness and understanding between the races. No special effort has been made to establish such a relationship. It is something that has existed through the years."

Collier believed the harmony between the races was due in large part to the city's cosmopolitan atmosphere. But Collier went on to say: "Things are not perfect, but yet we have tried to be conservative in our requests; and we are looking forward to things being even better. We shall not attempt to accomplish them militantly, however. There is a movement in Hot Springs to keep agitators out . . . we do not want that. We have labored hard to keep them out."

A newcomer to the city, Reverend Brown, lauded the white community for sitting down with black leaders to discuss problems and planning for the future on a peaceful basis. "I think this will be the solution, not only in Hot Springs but everywhere."

Edna Howe points out in her article that the "fine churches and schools; beautiful homes, many of which are surrounded by landscaped lawns and flower gardens; a flourishing business district; a community center where a well-planned youth program is carried out;" were all indications of the exemplary racial harmony of Hot Springs.

Education was important to blacks in Hot Springs. There were approximately 900 students attending Langston High School. Douglas Elementary School, which sat on the same street where Billy Clinton and his family lived, was the oldest black school in the city, dating back to the Reconstruction era. It began as a brush arbor, built by freedmen after the Civil War. Goldstein Elementary School was named for Percy Goldstein, onetime principal of Langston High.

The three schools employed a total of 37 faculty members. Langston was named by a distinguished legislator from Virginia elected during the Reconstruction. A 14-room brick building located on Silver Street, it was the largest of the three black high schools in the city. The school had been razed by fire twice, in 1903 and in 1913, but was rebuilt both times.

According to Howe's 1959 article, "Hot Springs has many fine Negro churches, religion being an important force in the life of the race. There are a large number of Protestant churches, and members of the Catholic faith also have their church, St. Gabriel's."

St. Gabriel's Negro Catholic Mission was founded in the 1940s by the Reverend Father Haines. By 1959, the mission had added a school for Negro children, administrated by the Sisters of the Sacred Heart of Mary. The first Negro church organized in Hot Springs was Roanoke Baptist Church on Whittington Avenue in 1863. It was also the site of the first public school for Negroes.

Many young blacks who left Hot Springs attended well-known colleges and universities, including the University of Illinois, Howard University, Meharry Medical College, and the University of Arkansas' medical school, whose first African American graduate, Edith Irby Jones, was a native of Hot Springs. Many returned to Hot Springs and became leaders in the community as teachers and business owners

There were already two Negro patrolmen on Hot Springs' police squad, Howe pointed out. A third patrolman, who was "affectionately known by blacks and whites as 'Papa Meathouse' " and was also a local disc jockey, had died the year before. Negroes also played a vital role in Hot Springs politics, Howe says. In the city's infancy, one J.A. Carr served one term as police judge, and D.H. Harris was city clerk at one time.

The article points out that more than 200 Negroes were employed in the "thermal health-giving waters" known as hot springs, the town's chief industry. Blacks were employed in the various bathhouses and hotels. Many had followed in their parents' footsteps in attaining these jobs, and many had worked for half a century in these roles.

According to this and other documents, Hot Springs' black business district was centered on Malvern Avenue. Howe described the 1959 environment this way:

The general business life of the Negro here centers on Malvern Avenue with its clean, up-to-date cafes, barbershops, shops, taverns, and clubs. Also on the avenue are located two bathhouses—the Phythian, owned by the National Order of the Knights of the Pythias, and the National Baptist Hotel and Bathhouse, first owned by the Woodmen of Union Fraternal Organization, which erected it in the early 1920s. Both of these establishments are owned and operated by Negroes. The National Baptist Hotel and Bathhouse was later purchased and renovated by the National Baptist of America Convention, Inc., and is now operated by that organization.

Hot Springs boasted two Negro funeral homes; and a 23-bed county home for the elderly and disabled was replete with a dietician and practical and registered nurses.

John Webb is a familiar name in the city of Hot Springs. Webb came to Hot Springs in the early 1920s and became one of the greatest benefactors of the Negro race there. He was an organizer and builder and was largely responsible for erection of the National Baptist Building. The building's main auditorium had a seating capacity of 2,000 with a lower auditorium that seated another 500 people.

The city prospered from the large number of visitors and conventions that flocked there, and some of the largest conventions held in Hot Springs during that time were made up of Negroes. The National Baptists Convention attracted more than 2,000 delegates there each year. The Apostolic Convention attracted more than 2,500 delegates. The Arkansas State Teachers Association's annual convention attendance was also estimated at 2,500 per year, and in 1962 it attracted 3,000. State Baptist meetings convened more than 1,000 members and small meetings accounted for another 1,000. The Bishops Council was another of the larger gatherings there. The city also attracted visitors from as far away as Africa, the Bahamas, and Canada.

Hot Springs had a disproportionately large number of Negro physicians for a town of its size. More than 10 black doctors resided and worked in the area during the late 1950s and early 1960s. Dr. John Eve, a renowned surgeon in the city for many years, operated the first Negro hospital, Woodman of Union, a class "A" institution recognized by both the American Medical and American Hospital Associations. He later established the Alice Eve Hospital, located in the Phythian Hotel, which he operated until his death.

The Emma Elease Webb Community Center at Pleasant Street, and Gulpha, a United Fund agency, was the only center in the city where Negro youth can go for supervised recreational activity. Built in 1918, the center also served as a school and dormitory building for nurses and bathhouse attendants at the Woodmen of Union Building. Prior to becoming a dormitory, the building had been a neighborhood grocery store, a restaurant, a drug store, and offices.

In 1888, Francis J. Scully wrote a book called *Notes From Cutter's Guide*, which focused on early Hot Springs. According to Scully, the black community of Hot Springs sprang up around Visitors Chapel AME Church, which was located near the town's train stop and became the stopping place for blacks traveling the route. The book included photos of Negro shanties in 1888 and mentioned that local Negro women's work was mostly washing the clothes of Hot Springs' visitors, while men had jobs bathing clients.

John Webb, an African American contractor, is believed to have built both churches and homes on Hot Springs' Pleasant Street. There were a number of black bathhouses in Hot Springs during the 1890s. The Independent was a bathhouse used by black clientele only and was managed by a local black businessman, A.C. Page. Eventually, however, a white business owner purchased the Independent and changed the name to the Maurice Bathhouse. He also re-segregated it to whites-only.

In 1890, the Phythian Sanitarium Bathhouse, later renamed Phythian Hotel and Bathhouse, was built on the location which currently houses the historic Austin Hotel. The Phythian was built by the Colored Knights of Phythian. In 1904, this group had opened and operated the Crystal Bathhouse on Malvern Avenue, but that bathhouse had been destroyed in the fire of 1913.

In 1948, arrangements were made by the National Baptist Church Convention, a very large church denomination, to replace the old bathhouse formerly operated by the Woodmen (the church likely created another business entity to operate the bathhouse).

According to John Webb's documents, baths continued at the old site from 1926 until the new building was completed in 1950, with full facilities for the baths for the convenience of colored persons. The new bathhouse was replete with nickel-plated brass fixtures and an abundance of marble. The end of legal segregation and the waning use of public bathhouses contributed to the decline of the National Baptist Hotel. It closed in 1981, still under the management of Mrs. Ardelia Davis.

According to the *Social Register*, a locally distributed pamphlet published by Herbert Bonner, a local black businessman, there were at least 22 black-owned businesses along Malvern Avenue, Cottage Street, Garden Street, Church Street, and Pleasant Street, which all made up the Negro business district. The businesses surrounded the Phythian, Visitors Chapel Church, and the Woodmen of Union Building, and included hotels, furnished rooms, restaurants, barber shops, dry cleaners, mortuaries, an ambulance service, a chiropodiatrist, a pawn shop, a construction company, dentist office, beauty salons and eight doctor's offices. The businesses also included a law office, a billiard parlor, drug stores, cab companies, grocery stores, photographer studios, and eventually a radio station and the Gem Theatre.

The Gem Theatre was established in 1932 and was owned by a prosperous black family, the Trumans. Mrs. Claire Truman played the piano and organ for the movie house on 425 Malvern Avenue. According to Scully's Guide, the theater was sold in 1940 to Reverend and Mrs. A.E. Humbard of Gospel Temple, a non-denominational congregation.

81

The development of Hot Springs' first African American residential and commercial district, known locally as the John L. Webb neighborhood, began with the construction of Visitors Chapel AME Church in 1870. The opening of Hot Springs' Army and Navy Hospital in 1887 fueled residential and commercial development of the neighborhood to support African American workers at the hospital. At the turn of the 20th century, several spas were built near Church Street to serve African American patrons.

The neighborhood prospered in the 1940s, particularly through the end of World War II. Following the war, medical advancements in the treatment of arthritis and other diseases weakened the popularity of Hot Springs as a destination for those seeking the "cure." The mostly African American hotel and bathhouse labor force began to seek employment elsewhere as the popularity in spas took a turn.

John Webb's Woodmen of Union Building served as a center for African Americans' social, cultural, commercial, educational, and health care activity for many decades. As such, it was a significant monument to African American history during the time of the Jim Crow laws. During that era, many African Americans struggled to improve their conditions and accommodate themselves to harsh segregation.

The Great Depression and legalized segregation brought about a dramatic decrease in business for commercial enterprises like the Woodmen of Union Building, the National Baptist Hotel, and the Gem Theatre. The end of segregation meant that African Americans were free to choose among the other hotels and businesses in Hot Springs. Other factors, such as the introduction of chain stores and the out-migration of many African Americans from Hot Springs and the rest of the South, resulted in the closing and demolition of most commercial buildings in the John Webb neighborhood.

Conver

WILLIAM JEFFERSON CLINTON
FROM HOPE TO HARLEM

Part IV

Conversations:
Hot Springs, Arkansas

Part of Martin Luther King's dream was that somehow we would learn to "work together, pray together, struggle together, go to jail together, stand up for freedom together." If I could leave America with one wish as I depart office, it would be that we become more the one America that we know we ought to be.

—President William Jefferson Clinton, at the Martin Luther King Commemoration

Jan Paschal was a young home economics teacher, new to Hot Springs, when she met Bill Clinton.

I met Bill Clinton during my first year in Hot Springs. I taught home economics at Central Junior High School during the first year of integration there. There was lots of anger that the school board had closed Langston Hughes High School, which the black community had great pride for and their children had attended for many years. These children were now forced to attend the formerly all-white Central High School.

I was teaching 47 students in one class. The summer I arrived in Hot Springs, Bill Clinton was preparing to leave the States for his year at Oxford University in England, but his mother's best friend, Marge Mitchell, introduced us before he left. John Paschal, my future husband was pretty legendary for his civil rights activism in Hot Springs.

The first thing I noticed about Bill Clinton was how much ahead of everybody else his age he was. He was, even then, so concerned about the state of the world . . . wanting to make changes. But more than anybody else his age, he was a true patriot. He could see that we had a long way to go, and he felt responsible for helping make things better.

He had a sense of the people as a whole, regardless of hue . . . I just can't stress enough how far ahead of his time he was— that, and the fact that Arkansas and Hot Springs were so far behind the times. At that time, while there were lots of people coming into the city from different parts of the country, it was not a cosmopolitan city. Blacks certainly held jobs, but most were menial jobs such as doormen, hotel clerks . . . jobs in which they took care of the wealthy clientele that visited the state.

Of course, there were racial problems then. That's why there were demonstrations and marches. There wouldn't have been a need, had there been no concerns. I recall when Spiro Agnew visited Hot Springs as vice president. That was when Winthrop Rockefeller was governor. The governor called John and told him he didn't want to embarrass the state with a march or demonstration while the vice president was there. John told him, "Governor, you got your job to do . . . and I got mine." But it was very uneasy times during the mid- and late '60s.

I remember Bill driving around town in his black convertible with his curly hair . . . everybody knew him. Back then Hot Springs had lots of block parties, and Bill made them all. He was very popular. It was Bill who introduced me to my late husband, John Paschal. John was a civil rights leader in Hot Springs, and he lost his teaching job because he spoke out, marched, and demonstrated for change. While John was much older than Bill, I think Bill admired him a great deal . . . for his position on civil rights and the fact that he would risk his life for what he believed in.

There is no question that Bill is completely comfortable around blacks, maybe he is at his most comfortable. So many blacks knew and loved him in Hot Springs.

I think Bill Clinton knew he couldn't do what he wanted to do in the Delta, because the decisions were being made in the back rooms, by powerful white men. The most telling thing about Bill Clinton was that as a very young man—21 years old—he didn't have a real need to help or work with black children, but he always did. I believe he knew even back then that it was the children who were our future.

I was working in New Hampshire when Bill Clinton started his run for president, and when he came to New Hampshire he hardly had anybody with him . . . unlike the other candidates who brought big entourages. Most of the candidates didn't realize when they came to the school how sophisticated the children were about politics, and I have to say they ate most of them for lunch . . . except Bill Clinton.

It was a little boy by the name of Michael Morrison, who had cerebral palsy, who coined the phrase "Bill Clinton is our REAL education president" after the governor spoke to the kids and had them eating out of his hand. After that speech, the students and I went out and got sweatshirts made with that phrase, "Bill Clinton is the REAL education candidate," printed on them. We used Bill Clinton's credit card to pay for them. Everywhere he went in New Hampshire there were huge crowds of kids with their sweatshirts and their signs. It was as if we had been there a year laying the groundwork for his campaign.

Glenn Mahone, an authentic "Friend of Bill," grew up in Hot Springs. The two young men shared a love of music and a desire to change Hot Springs and America's status quo.

I first met Bill Clinton in Hot Springs. We both grew up there. I cut yards in Hot Springs for extra money and happened to stop at his house one day. Of course, Hot Springs was segregated at the time. In the mornings, I would go to the black neighborhoods and cut grass; and in the afternoons, I would go to the white neighborhoods.

On this particular afternoon, I went to the door and Bill's mother, Mrs. Virginia, came to the door and told me she didn't need my help because her son always cut her yard. She thanked me, and so forth. I was leaving, and Bill rode up on his bike. He asked me what I was doing, and I told him. He kind of shrugged and said, "Oh, yeah, I do cut the yard . . . I'm sorry." We chatted for a while. His mother was married to Mr. Clinton, and his family was in the automobile business. I left, but I remembered how inquisitive he was.

Several years later, Hot Springs started changing some. Bill was already away at school by then. I was a senior about to graduate from high school, but I had a band, a rock band called the New Banana. We were playing all over, at high schools and various places throughout the state. I had about a 12-piece band. I was a singer, and Bill was a saxophone player.

I was kind'a surprised when he asked if he could play with the band. We were playing for money by then, and I wasn't sure whether I wanted to cut our share with another person. I was pretty hesitant about it. But we got to talking and remembered that we had met during that time in front of his house. So I went on and said he could join the band.

So he started playing with us. He was away at school most of the time we played, but he was there most of the summers. We were pretty good, played all over, played in the "Battle of the Bands" and actually won a couple of times.

In the summer of 1968, the first year of integration at Hot Springs schools, the Jaycees wanted to do a block party to bring black and white kids together. Our band played and some of the black guys asked some of the white girls to dance, and that literally almost started a riot. Bill and I were right in the middle of it—me on the black side and him on the white side. After the fight subsided, we tried to keep playing for a while but ended up stopping before it was over because there was still a fair amount of tension from both sides.

Now, we both always tell the story that single-handedly, he and I almost started a race riot in Hot Springs; then together, we stopped a race riot from happening. But that was a time! Bill never tried to sing, but he was a heck of a saxophone player, and at that time we were playing some of everything, Sam and Dave . . . . He use to love to play "Hey Jude" and "Soul Man," and I use to love to sing it. It was a lot of fun.

During that same summer, as integration was starting, we decided that there were enough of us in the Jaycees to integrate the all-white swimming pool. There was me, Bill, and a guy named John Paschal, who ran an organization called the Council for the Liberation of Blacks. I wouldn't say Bill was actually a member of COLB, but he was pretty active in it. Most times, I'd describe Bill as the calming force. He was young and spirited and had this ability to see beyond what most of us could. He always said that the world was changing and Hot Springs had to change along with it . . . but he wanted to be there to play the role of keeping tempers down.

We did some other rather radical things around Hot Springs, and Bill was always one of the first people to say, "Let's do it, because . . . it's just not right." I remember we would sit and talk late at night . . . Bill; Jeff Rosensweig, a Little Rock attorney; Jay Dierks, whose family owned a big farm and the Weyerhauser Company; Elizabeth Reader, whose father owned a drugstore in Hot Springs. We would get together and talk about what was wrong in Hot Springs and in Arkansas. I was usually the only black in that group. Bill had a special sensitivity when it came to the race issue . . . I think it was just there. He was one of them, but he was also one of us. He crossed over very easily.

He was reaching out when, in Hot Springs, people didn't reach out. I think it goes way back; even when I first met him there was this inherent warmth he displayed. I sometimes thought that something had to have happened early in his life, because you could tell black folks weren't new to him. I never got the impression that he did any of that to get noticed, because it certainly wasn't popular then. I'm sure he got telephone calls or his mother got telephone calls because of it. I think he just saw that something wasn't right, that there were injustices and he wanted to make them right. It was just real genuine, it really was.

Bill continued to play in the band that summer, and he knew my mom real well, so he would come by my house, and I'd go by his house. His little brother, Roger, started playing with us because he knew some of the younger guys in the band. It was a totally integrated band, and Bill was the oldest of us. He certainly gave us direction and literally was the force that kept us together.

Within our group, he always led the conversation, always wondering, always asking how I felt about certain things—about Martin Luther King, Jr., or about segregation. He was always inquisitive about the whole race thing. I think that helped mold who he later became. Sometimes he would pick me up because I wasn't driving at the time, and we'd just drive around and talk. In fact, the night after the almost-riot, he drove me home because some of my friends shunned me.

Hot Springs was a very segregated city. Things really got bad in the '60s. Bill was there then, and it almost seemed he was always on our side, but in truth, he tried hard not to take sides but to be a calming force. I think Bill realized there needed to be someone young, with long hair, who we could relate to, not the city fathers. He definitely made a difference. You could probably go back and ask anyone there and they'd tell you he did.

John Paschal and Bill became good friends. When my dad passed, Bill sent flowers and came by. He was in school at the time, so he wasn't able to come to the funeral. But he really enjoyed hanging out with my father, talking to him, asking him all kinds of questions. I always thought he must have been mentored by older blacks, probably in Hope.

It's so amazing to think that Bill never attended an integrated school before leaving Arkansas. Hot Springs High School was all-white. He was already in college when it integrated. It integrated the year I became a senior.

After the first term of losing, Bill Clinton settled in as governor; and he really wanted to move the state forward. He did welfare reform, even back then. I think he could have appointed more blacks . . . maybe he made up for that when he came to D.C. I was a big fan of Governor Winthrop Rockefeller. Dale Bumpers was a moderate governor who did a pretty good job for the state. But Orval Faubus left the state in such a terrible position that anything after him was perceived in a better light.

Junius M. Stevenson, Hot Springs native; former educator; Democratic Party leader

I was born in Red Bluff, near Texarkana. My family moved to Hot Springs in 1921. I was 5 years old at the time. I finished high school in 1934 and left Hot Springs for Chicago in 1936. I returned to Arkansas to go to college at AM&N College in Pine Bluff. I didn't finish there because the school at the time was too focused on agriculture. I transferred to Tennessee A&T.

In 1945, I moved to Chicago and lived there until 1982. I worked two jobs most of my life. I worked at the post office at night, and taught seventh and eighth grade science for 22 years.

Hot Springs is different from most places in the state. I was a musician, and this was a city full of musicians. There was a vibrant business community when I was growing up—doctors, lawyers, dentists.

By far, for the black community, the most important person to set foot in Hot Springs was John Webb. Before he came, blacks had to call on white doctors to come to them because they couldn't go into the white hospitals. John Webb built a black hospital; recruited doctors and nurses; and put training in place for them. John Webb helped turn Hot Springs' bank around but was never able to open a black bank.

I always thought Lyndon Johnson contributed most to black America. He was capable of getting through the Civil Rights Act. By coming forth with the Voting Rights Act, he freed a great deal of blacks; and they, in turn, went into the Democratic Party. Blacks always voted here. Black organizations would pay poll taxes (a discriminatory tax that many Southern states imposed as a way of keeping blacks from voting) and control a lot of the voting. One thing they always did was give the Negro Civic League the last ballot box. That meant about 300 to 400 votes that could push the vote either way.

This was a resort town; and that worked to the blacks' advantage to some extent, because any kind of public racial strife would have destroyed tourism. That kept the lid on any possible problems with race relations.

I went to Langston High School when it was a segregated school. We had good teachers. We were taught manual training and home economics, but no arts and no music. We had science on alternating years. My mother and father were attendants at the U.S. Government Free Bathhouse. It was the health spa for declared paupers. My mother was paid on commission, while my father worked on straight salary. When I graduated from high school, the superintendent sent for me to come down to get a job there. I left that day to seek my fortune.

When I was growing up, if I was walking down the sidewalk the same time as three or four white boys, I knew to step off the sidewalk and let them pass.

☺

The late Larry Bonner inherited his career and his barber shop business from his father. Larry Bonner recalled, with fondness, the Hope of yesteryear when entertainers and celebrities often made Hot Springs a regular stop:

I was born in Woodruff County, and when I was just 17 months, my family moved to Hot Springs. We were a typical, poor black family. But we were also hard workers and very proud. My father worked in Johnny Woodson's barbershop when he first moved to Hot Springs. Then, a few years later, he opened his own shop at 339 Malvern Avenue.

Thanks to that barbershop, we were able to survive the Depression. Over the years, my father expanded his barbershop to include tailoring and a beauty shop. There was competition right across from us, but we had good business. I started working with my father when I was in ninth grade and never stopped.

Langston High School was the black high school here, and all six of my kids graduated from the school. I was taught by my father, and I still believe, that you can do what you want to if you are willing to work hard enough.

I remember the Clinton family here in Hot Springs. Roger had a car dealership; and I remember seeing Bill working on cars at the shop.

Hot Springs, back when I was growing up, was something else! During my 70 years here, I've seen people like Lucky Luciano, Roy Campanella, Joe Black, Luke Easter, Bill "Bojangles" Robinson, Joe Louis, John Henry Louis, and so many others—all right down on Malvern Avenue.

They used to call Malvern Avenue "Black Broadway"—it was a hot spot of entertainment. There was always something exciting

93

going on. There were all-black entertainment clubs, featuring people like Sarah Vaughn, Aretha Franklin, Ray Charles, Lionel Hampton, Phineas Newborn, Little Milton, Kool & the Gang. Sometimes, when entertainers were in town, they'd come over to Langston High and sing or play for us students. Henry Glover grew up here. He was a black man who wrote country-western songs. He managed Langston's football team in 1939.

Ⓠ

The late Early Marbley, native of Goodwater, Alabama, spent most of his life in Hot Springs. During his lifetime, he held many and varied jobs. But one he remembered fondly was his work for Raymond Clinton's Buick dealership. That was how he became acquainted with young Roger and Bill Clinton.

I was born in Goodwater, Alabama. My mama died when I was 8 years old, and at that time I lived with my grandfather for a while until he died. I began working when I was 8 at a sawmill in Goodwater. That same year, the old man who worked at the mill hauling timber would take me with him. Later I found out he needed somebody to drive when he slept. He taught me how to drive the timber truck. I worked at that timber mill until I was 10 years old.

I left home at 11 years old and went to Georgia, then Florida, where I met and started working for a couple from Hot Springs. Mrs. Francis Brown and her husband were vacationing in Gainesville, Florida, at the time. I started chauffeuring for Ms. Brown in 1931, when I was 20 years old and moved back to Hot Springs to continue working for them. Once I moved to Hot Springs, I went to work for Mr. Martin Eisner, Mrs. Brown's father.

In 1942, I went to the Army and was stationed in New Guinea for three years. I came back to Hot Springs in 1945 and started working again at Mr. Eisner's drugstore. Though he had passed while I was in the Army, he had written me and said when I returned from the Army I could have my job back,

I worked for Raymond Clinton for 17 years. After that, I worked for the Vapors Club. While I was working there, some white man walked up to me and asked if I knew any colored people wanting to work at the post office. He said he was going to the racetrack and when he came back he'd check back with me. This man had a contract at the Hot Springs post office. When he came back I told him I was interested in working there. I ended up getting the job; it was a contract, and I worked there for 15 years, until 1963.

When little Billy came from Hope, he was 6 years old. They bought a home and moved it up on Park Avenue. I was working for Ray, his uncle at that time. Billy just about grew up in that parts room in the Buick place. He was always there, always asking questions. He worked there a lot of summers until he left and went to college.

I use to take his younger brother Roger to school a lot. When Bill became governor, I sometimes drove Roger to Little Rock. Even after he became governor, Billy loved my pound cakes, so I would send them up to Little Rock for him. The last time I sent him one, he was in the White House.

❧

Ruth Atkinson lived most of her life in Hot Springs, worked in several of the local bathhouses and has fond memories of Bill and Virginia Clinton.

I was born in Muskogee, Oklahoma, but got married early and moved to Conway, Arkansas, then from there to Hot Springs. This was a nice place to live; and I found a job when I got here. I've worked for a number of different white families, including the Swifts, the Stewarts, and the Sumners.

I worked at Club Belvedere and got to see people like Ella Fitzgerald and Pearl Bailey come through there. Dave Harrison managed the club then. I sometimes made $200 or $300 a night working there. Some big spenders would come in there with $6,000 or $7,000 and not leave with a dime . . . just burned money like it was nothing.

I worked at the Tower Club and Vapors Club and would see people like Elvis Presley and Al Capone, who both really loved the spas. Somehow or another I got along with all kinds of people like that. I would work in the women's lounge some, in the checkroom. Sometimes I served trays of food and drink.

I kept Bill Clinton for Mrs. Virginia when he was a young boy. He grew up with my son on 372 Cedar Street. and was always real smart, with a mind all his own. He was kind'a hard-headed and loved to talk politics even then. By the time he was 10 or 11, he was already telling people he was going to be a big political man. I told him he could be just about anything he wanted to be.

He called me "Mama Ruth" and would spend the night with me and Carl lots of times. I think Carl and Bill stayed friends a long time . . . they may still be friends. Virginia and I got along because I think we were a lot alike. She was high-tempered, and so was I. We went to the races together a lot and really enjoyed that. I'd bet $25, then quit and go home. I'd cook dinner, and Virginia would come over and eat with me. Whatever I cooked, she'd eat. Bill always liked my cooking, too. He especially liked turnip greens and corn bread.

When I went to the hospital and had to be put to sleep, I told the doctors I didn't want anyone else giving me anesthesia except Virginia . . . because when she popped her fingers, you were out; and before you knew it, you were awake, with no problems. She was the best at what she did, better than anybody in this state.

Petrilla Bonner Pollefeyt grew up singing the gospel in her local church. But she also spent a lot of her time listening to country and western music on her radio. The Hot Springs native was perhaps the first and probably remains the only black female country and western singer.

I grew up in Hot Springs during the '50s and left Hot Springs to attend Lincoln University in Jefferson City, Missouri, in 1964. After two years, I returned to Arkansas and finished up at Philander Smith College in Little Rock.

If schools had been integrated when Bill and I were in high school, we would have been classmates. My family knew the Clinton family well. And my father, a barber in downtown Hot Springs since he was a teen-ager, always bought his cars from Clinton Buick.

Ironically, if Hot Springs had been a different place . . . maybe at a different time, Bill Clinton and I would have been friends. Music is so important to both of us. I grew up singing in the AME

Church, and he was a member of one of the local bands in Hot Springs, the only integrated band during that time. My mother always entered me into the local talent shows there in Hot Springs. But when people ask me how I ended up singing country-western, I tell them it wasn't a choice . . . the music chose me. Probably Bill Clinton would tell you the same thing about politics. Sometimes our paths are laid for us, and we just follow that path.

Hot Springs was always a unique town because of its natural resources and, for a while, its gambling casinos. This gave both blacks and whites a more diverse upbringing. Blacks were always very involved in Hot Springs' famous bath spas, its entertainment businesses, and the gambling industry there. Most times, however, they held the menial jobs, doing the cleaning, bathing, and taking care of the visitors and clients.

At the same time, Hot Springs had an unusual number of professional blacks in comparison to the rest of the state. There was definitely a middle class, and even lower middle class people were always working to rise above where they were. My dad was a barber and worked at the casinos at night. My mom worked as a domestic in white people's houses and as a nurse's aide at the hospital. She eventually moved up to the physical therapy department at the Arkansas Rehabilitation Center before she passed in 1990.

Blacks in Hot Springs lived modestly; and yes, the city had its share of poverty and projects. The people of Hot Springs didn't fight against integration as much as some other parts of the state did. Downtown stores integrated pretty smoothly after removal of the Jim Crow laws.

Even though we had our own black section of town, there were always whites living in those areas as well. It was never completely segregated on our side of town. With this in mind, I believe Bill Clinton, who spent his childhood there, would feel pretty comfortable around both races because of Hot Springs' unique dealing with the race issue.

While he didn't live in the black section of town, Bill's parents, who lived on Park Avenue, definitely wasn't considered part of the upper echelon of Hot Springs. Those were the people that my grandmother, mother, and even I worked for. His uncle owned a Buick dealership on Hobson Street and had a reputation of always financing blacks for car loans.

As early as 1963, my parents built a new home in a mixed neighborhood. So you see, Hot Springs always was considered more accepting of blacks than most places in the state. The town was always pretty diverse, with the exception of the schools. While our football teams played at the white Rix Stadium, all the concession stands were owned and operated by whites.

I am very proud to have grown up in Hot Springs and that the city produced someone like Bill Clinton. I truly believe he is who he is because of the racial environment he grew up in, in Hot Springs. I think his love and compassion for all people is genuine and, to some extent, comes from that early environment. That's how I feel, being a country-western singer. I grew up listening to all kinds of music, including country and western. I think it expresses my heritage as well as others'.

I found it pretty ironic when President Clinton was being ridiculed for his affair . . . because this has always been a Southern gentleman's prerogative. Many Southern women pretty much knew their husbands or fathers had mistresses. I don't think Southerners were as appalled as others who pretended it was outside the norm. Not that it should be condoned, but it's reality, and I don't think it ever stopped any of those men from doing their jobs to the best of their ability.

Bill Clinton has a sixth sense when it comes to the black community and gaining the black vote. Somehow he knows how we think and even what's in our hearts. I've always known him to encourage us, as minorities, to always seek to improve our place in society. He did a lot for this country and, before that, for the state of Arkansas. He was the first governor to devote so much money and time to improve the education system in Arkansas. He challenged teachers to challenge themselves.

Tommy Sproles, a Hot Springs native and former army medic, was tapped by Governor Clinton to become the first black Arkansas Game and Fishing commissioner.

I met Bill Clinton in the '70s in the Union Bank Building in downtown Little Rock. I was working there at the time. He was leaning against the wall with his arms folded, and when I came into the elevator, he straightened up and I shook his hand. He introduced himself as Bill Clinton. I didn't see him again until he was running for governor. He was a thin, tall, dark-haired guy at that time.

A great leader is able to be a boundary spanner. There is a difference in being an administrator or a high-technical person and being a great leader. Great leaders have to be able to expand the boundaries, to look for outside opportunities in addition to working inside the circle. A person that can look for outside opportunities, yet manage what they have inside the circle is a great leader. I view people like Jocelyn Elders as a great leader of the most recent times. The things she talked about 15 years ago, when they were taboo, are being talked about publicly now. She was ahead of her time.

Bill Clinton was a great leader. Napoleon was a great leader. He was able to make people follow him and wasn't afraid to go out and venture into uncharted territory, wasn't afraid to lose the fight on the shore in order to discover new oceans.

I lived in Memphis most of my early childhood and was introduced to racism there. I had to get up early to catch the bus to go to the field. If I made $3, we were able to keep a quarter. The farmers who owned the cotton fields had no respect for women or men working in the field. I was so little, I was the mule boy. I was the one responsible for taking the cotton up to the bailer.

When I was 11 years old, I left Memphis and moved to Hot Springs. I was already supporting myself and knew I had to get a job. I shined shoes at the Arlington barbershop, waited tables, cooked, and supported myself all through high school. I also played football and participated in the band. I'd leave practice and go to work.

I encountered racism in Hot Springs the same as in Memphis. When I worked in the Arlington barbershop, the customers would make racist remarks like, "I want my shoes to be as black as you." Once when I was working at Kempners' clothing store, my job was to wipe the windows and get the boxes together. They would say, "Don't touch the clothes, because we don't want grease or blackness to rub off." As far as physical violence, I didn't encounter that until I went into the Navy.

Integration in Hot Springs was a smooth transition. A group of friends and I integrated the bowling alley. We expected a fight, but they invited us in, no problem.

I had a band called the Five Teens, made up of Gerald Frazier, Bill Butler, I played piano, Charles Knox played drums. John Puckett was my music teacher. He headed up the choir and gave private piano lessons. Carl Pleasant was the band director. He taught me trumpet and baritone horn. There was a lot of music in

Hot Springs, good music teachers. I remember Bill Clinton played saxophone. I grew up in a Pentecostal church environment, played piano there. But between church, music, fishing, and hunting, I didn't have time to get into trouble. I still love Hot Springs.

Bill Clinton gave African Americans more opportunity than any other governor. Dale Bumpers and David Pryor were good governors; and they had a few African American staff members. But Bill was like a risk taker. He didn't act based on what people thought about him.

I remember when he appointed me to the Game and Fish Commission. He took a lot of blows with that. There had never been a black person in the country to head up wildlife management. He took a chance on me. I don't think any other governor would have taken that chance at that time. I remember getting threatening phone calls from sportsmen, saying, "Don't come up here." Everybody carried guns in Arkansas. I was told to resign, don't accept the appointment.

The day he made the appointment, there were people parked out in front of our house. The state wasn't ready for that, but Bill Clinton was. I was, and the Masons were ready—they wrote some strong letters. We had a team in place that went out and got support of this appointment.

Most people never knew, but that was a very serious appointment for Arkansas. There were a lot of rich people who wanted that appointment, who had been big supporters. In the back of his mind, I'm sure he was wondering whether he should go through with it, but he had some good advice from people like Bill Norman of Greenwood. Some good people like Dr. George Cole— they all talked to him and vouched for me—assured him he could take a chance on me.

With the pressure he was getting from the black community and the support from the white community, he did what was in his heart and stood by me those seven years I was there. He only questioned one decision I made but told me it was my final decision. I was chairman my last year.

Bill Clinton's contribution to the state of Arkansas was giving minorities opportunities to go out and make it for themselves. In his administration, we weren't held back the way we were before. It wasn't like he ever said he was going to give our community a bunch of money. His philosophy was not to give you a fish to feed you for a day, but to give you the opportunity to learn to fish . . . where it would benefit you for a lifetime.

I remember traveling to a picnic in Jasper, Arkansas, with Governor Clinton. I was the only black person there, but we walked around that crowd, and he introduced me to all those white folks. We used to ride over the state together, and one time we were talking about wildflowers. I was telling him about this one flower called a Tickseed Coreopsis. He was really interested and a little surprised. He asked me where I learned all about that plant, and I told him that it was one of the things I learned at the Game and Fish Commission—the job he'd gone out on a limb to appoint me to.

Conver

WILLIAM JEFFERSON CLINTON
FROM HOPE TO HARLEM

PART V

ARKANSAS MOVES FROM
A WORLD WAR TO
CIVIL CONFLICTS AT HOME

My fellow Americans, we must be concerned not so much with the sins of our parents as with the success of our children, how they will live and live together in years to come. If those nine children could walk up those steps 40 years ago, all alone, if their parents could send them into the storm armed only with school books and the righteousness of their cause, then surely together we can build one America—an America that makes sure no future generation of our children will have to pay for our mistakes with the loss of their innocence.

—President William J. Clinton
40th Anniversary of the
Central High School Integration Crisis

CHAPTER 16
── ARKANSAS AND ──
the Great War

Just as Arkansas began its slow recovery from the Great Depression of the late 1930s, rumors of another war slowly traveled throughout the state. This poor, mostly rural state had languished consistently at the bottom of the heap of poor states since its establishment in 1836, and the Great Depression had just about stretched its resources and the morale of the people to their limits, or so they thought. President Franklin D. Roosevelt's New Deal, though, had been the lifesaver for both black and white Arkansas.

Rumors of another war—the second one of the 20th century—were hardly what the people of Arkansas wanted to hear. Although the Great Depression had impacted the world, America, and certainly Arkansas, the people of the state yet maintained their isolationist attitudes, worrying about their small corner of the world and leaving the rest to fend for themselves.

The reality of World War II, though, would change that sentiment forever, in particular, the news of Adolph Hitler's plans for the ethnic cleansing and eventual decimation of the Jewish race. Even with America's own race and civil rights problems, Arkansans viewed such blatant hate and misguided power as a danger that threatened every corner of the world.

Historians cite 1939 as the official beginning of World War II, although little real war conflict occurred until 1940, with the onslaught of the Blitzkrieg—lightning warfare—of the new German army. It was then that President Roosevelt was convinced, and convinced Congress, that not just the United States but the world was in danger.

America's involvement in this war, he said, was about the protection of the four freedoms: freedom of speech, freedom of worship, freedom from want, and freedom from fear. Shortly thereafter, Congress voted to pass legislation and allocate funding toward the strengthening of America's military might.

Whether it was Roosevelt's patriotic speeches that helped change Arkansans' minds or something else entirely, the state leaders now accepted that what was happening in Europe would impact them. Arkansas' governor, Carl Bailey, went so far as to order the state police to explore any signs of Nazi plots within the state and called upon everyday Arkansans to report any pro-German actions.

When the Japanese bombed the American fleet in Pearl Harbor on December 7, 1941, it sent a deafening message around the world. No corner of the world was safe from this war against evil. Nearly one-third of the Pacific fleet was destroyed or badly damaged. President Roosevelt wasted little time announcing, during one of his "Fireside Chats," his declaration of war against Japan. Once again, the U.S. military was fully engaged in another world war.

Before its end, more than 200,000 Arkansans—more than 10 percent of the state's population—would serve in the armed forces. Patriotic blacks enlisted in large numbers, even though they were still relegated to all-black units with white officers. Over 4,000 of these soldiers, both black and white, died protecting their country's freedom.

A large number of women contributed to the war effort as well. Women joined and served in all branches of the military. Those who stayed home found creative ways to help the cause—buying bonds and collecting scrap metal and rubber to be made into war weapons. Members of the all-black MacArthur Knitting Club of Pulaski County knitted sweaters for soldiers after working a full day outside their homes. Families planted "victory gardens" to raise enough food to help see the country through the war. Coffee, tea, sugar, meat, gas, and tires were in short supply and rationed.

Undeniably, the war proved an economic boom for the country and certainly for Arkansas. Bauxite, a lightweight metal used for the outer lining of most airplanes, had long been a staple of Arkansas industry. During the war, however, its production increased 12-fold. New bauxite plants were built in other Arkansas towns, including Jones Mills and Hurricane Creek. Land was also leased to the Aluminum Company of America for its operations.

Major defense plants, all making some form of arms, bombs, or chemicals for the war effort, were built in Camden, Jacksonville, Maumelle, and Pine Bluff. Much of the farmland in Hope was transformed into a large testing range with its own airport. Camp Robinson in North Little Rock became a training site for soldiers, as it had been in World War I. The U.S. government began building Camp Chaffee in Fort Smith just before Pearl Harbor, but expanded the site after the war began to train thousands of soldiers. Other army bases were scattered throughout the state, including in Blytheville, Newport, Stuttgart, and Walnut Ridge.

The government also helped build dams to produce more power at Blue Mountain, Lake Catherine, and Lake Norfolk because Arkansas' power supply was far less than needed. Still, 70 percent of the power was brought in from other states.

During World War II, more than 28,000 people were hired at the defense plants, and it is estimated that the state's economy grew by $400 million.

Arkansas cities grew and prospered. Those near defense plants and bases reaped the benefits of the jobs and income they provided. Little Rock grew by 25,000 people in six months during 1940. Hope grew from 7,475 people in 1940 to 15,475 by the end of 1941. There were not enough houses to go around, and people sometimes had to live in tents, garages, or warehouses.

The war dramatically changed Arkansas' domestic scene. Women were taking men's places in the workplace as men went off to war. Nationally, the number of women working outside the home increased from 13.9 percent in 1940 to 31 percent after the war began. In Arkansas, where there were fewer defense plants, the incidence of women working outside the home was only 20 percent of all workers—smaller than the national growth, but a significant increase from Arkansas' past.

Women worked in machine shops, operated radios and river aircraft, and did sheet metal work, woodwork, and drafting. They also managed farms. Because of the labor shortage in private businesses, women for the first time became bank tellers, newspaper reporters, cab and bus drivers, and mechanics in auto repair shops. Some left Arkansas to work in plants in other states.

Arkansas schools, already at the bottom of the scale when it came to offering quality education to its students, suffered even more during World War II. By 1945, more than half of the pre-war educators—teachers and principals—had left either to join the armed forces or to take higher paying "war jobs." At one time during the war, more than 60 percent of Arkansas' teens had dropped out of school simply because there were no teachers to teach them. A large number of students from small, rural areas migrated with their families to urban districts. While Congress proposed special help for the schools, most Southern lawmakers refused federal aid, fearing it would mean enforced desegregation. The effort by the state's General Assembly to raise the sales tax to allocate more money to schools also failed.

As is often the case in wars, Americans' deepest fears and prejudices came bubbling to the surface. Japanese Americans would bear the brunt of these fears, and the ongoing violence and retributions against Japanese Americans became a national concern. President Roosevelt responded to the problem with what was described as a military measure: 117,000 legal Japanese Americans citizens were rounded up and distributed throughout the country in interment or relocation camps. Two Japanese-American centers were set up in southeast Arkansas, one in Rowher and another in Jerome.

By the summer of 1942, roughly 8,000 Japanese Americans resided in each of these centers. The government supplied housing, food, schools, and medical care for the families. Forty years later, an apology would be offered and retribution payment would be made to Japanese Americans.

Ironically, Arkansas also became something of an international holding cell for foreign prisoners of war. Twenty-five thousand German prisoners of war and a smaller number of Italians were held in Arkansas until the war ended. To make room for the new residents, the Japanese Americans were moved from the Jerome Camp to Rowher or to camps outside the state. German and Italian prisoners were also housed in Camp Robinson, Camp Chaffee, and in Dermott. Small branch camps were situated in Arkansas' eastern Delta and in the Grand Prairie areas of the state. Many of these prisoners of war were used as extra labor by Arkansas farmers. After the war, the Germans and Italians were sent back to their home countries and the Japanese Americans were freed. A few Japanese families chose to remain in the state.

Though Arkansas sits squarely in the middle of the Bible Belt, the war perpetuated serious strain between patriotic Americans and members of the Jehovah's Witnesses religious denomination. Jehovah's Witnesses drafted into the military appealed the decision based on their sacred vows, namely "Thou shalt not kill" and "Thou shalt not make unto thee any graven image."

These vows, they argued, prohibited them from participating in war combat or from saluting the American flag. In 1942, violence erupted in Arkansas as members of the religion made their way to a meeting with military personnel. Seven members of the group were shot. In a ruling by two U.S. Supreme Courts, the Jehovah's Witnesses were assured exclusion from war based on their religious convictions.

To a great extent, it was during this era that black soldiers began to take note of the irony of their roles as protectors of America and the world's freedoms, considering that they were not allowed to enjoy full freedom or equality in their own country. The black soldiers' disillusionment with the military and anger at what they knew awaited them at home after risking their lives for the four freedoms served to escalate unrest back on American soil.

Blacks had actively and voluntarily participated in three wars, yet they were little closer to full citizenship than they had been in the Civil War. No matter what their rank or their contributions to the war, it was legal to relegate black soldiers to the most menial of jobs and to pay them significantly less than white soldiers doing the same jobs.

Ironically, the war was an effective backdrop for early civil rights efforts. Black leaders were well-positioned to speak out and demand full rights for black soldiers and for the rest of the black citizenship. New York's A. Philip Randolph, the president of the Brotherhood of Sleeping Car Porters, a black labor union of Pullman Porters, was one of the first black leaders to speak out on this issue.

In a meeting at the White House, Randolph insisted that President Roosevelt order tax-financed defense plants to hire and pay blacks on an equal basis with whites. When Roosevelt balked at Randolph's impudence, Randolph threatened a huge march on Washington, promising that more than 100,000 black demonstrators would be there.

Using Eleanor Roosevelt as a go-between, President Roosevelt negotiated a truce with Randolph. The march was canceled in exchange for Executive Order 8802, which outlawed racially biased hiring in public job training programs and private industries that received U.S. contracts. The president also formed a Fair Employment Practices Commission to make sure business firms followed the new rules.

Although Executive Order 8802 was effective in improving job options for blacks, much of its success was tied directly to the reality of wartime labor shortage. The real impact on future civil rights laws could be credited to the Fair Employment Practices Commission. Randolph's planned march on Washington was revived in 1963 when a brilliant young minister, the Reverend Martin Luther King, Jr., made his memorable appeal for the rights of all men.

In spite of Roosevelt's executive order, the armed forces were not prepared to change at this time. Arkansas, along with other Southern states, still maintained separate units for black and white soldiers. Black soldiers from outside the South who had been assigned to Arkansas for training got their first taste of legal separation of the races.

The culmination of the effect of the armed forces' race culture on everyday life in Arkansas occurred in March 1942, when Thomas B. Foster, a black sergeant stationed at Camp Robinson, was shot and killed by a white policeman on Little Rock's 9th Street, then a bustling black business corridor. The shooting was decried by black leaders. Daisy and L.C. Bates, publishers of the state's only black newspaper at the time, launched a vocal campaign for the hiring of black police officers.

Pressured by the The *Arkansas State Press* newspaper, the black community, and the Negro Citizens Council, the Little Rock City Council agreed to hire eight black patrolmen. This was a major step for Little Rock's city government, but it came with stringent restrictions. The black patrolmen could work only in the black communities, could not arrest white citizens without the help of a white officer, and would not receive the pensions that white officers received.

It would be decades after the war before Arkansans could point to their education system with any semblance of pride. Throughout the war years, the system was dismal for most of Arkansas' students, both black and white. This was especially true in the state's rural districts, especially in the black-only school districts, where practically every item was secondhand, used, or less than usable.

Many black students' educational inadequacies were beyond shameful. The end of the war would exacerbate these problems, as soldiers returned home and families grew. The baby boomers would stretch the size of classrooms even more than before. As a whole, the state contributed embarrassingly small sums of tax money toward educating their young. Many schools were dangerous and unhealthy. Resources were at a bare minimum, and classes were overcrowded as a general rule.

While nothing was being done about moving Arkansas from the bottom of the heap when it came to teachers' pay and spending per pupil, legislators locked onto school consolidation as a way to resolve their problems. In 1921, the small state had 5,112 school districts. That number was reduced to 1,598 in 1948, and after new laws were enacted the number of school districts in Arkansas dropped to 424.

After the war ended, many veterans returned to the state seeking training for jobs. Thanks to the GI Bill, which provided educational benefits or training to veterans, there was a large influx of black and white war veterans entering colleges. Blacks would begin to make small gains at the college level during these post-war years.

The state had long recognized the need to maintain a healthy supply of black teachers, doctors, and lawyers to serve the black communities and had helped fund many bright young students' out-of-state educations. But by the late 1940s, both the need to cut spending and the threat of Supreme Court interventions brought this to a halt.

Thus, shortly after the war, Silas Hunt and Jackie Shropshire would become a part of Arkansas' civil rights history as they became the first blacks to enter the University of Arkansas' Law School.

Edith Irby Jones, a bright young pre-med student from Hot Springs, would make her own imprint on history when she became the first black to enter the University of Arkansas' School of Medicine in Little Rock. While these young students would make history by being the "firsts," they would also suffer gravely from white students and instructors for the sake of their education.

A young black Arkansas teacher by the name of Susan Morris also helped change Arkansas history when she sued the Little Rock School District for pay inequity. In 1941, white teachers in Arkansas earned $625 a year, compared to blacks' salaries of $367.

After the U.S. Supreme Court ruled in favor of a black teacher in Virginia, Arkansas lawyer Scipio A. Jones filed a suit on behalf of Morris, a teacher at Little Rock's Dunbar High School. The attorney asked for equal pay for his client, based on her qualifications and her experience. Future U.S. Supreme Court Justice Thurgood Marshall—then a lawyer with the National Association for the Advancement of Colored People, the black organization that monitored and advocated for civil rights—assisted in this case.

In 1941, 22 percent of white teachers in Arkansas had less than one year of college training. Susan Morris, who had been teaching for seven years, had a bachelor's degree from Talladega College in Alabama and had completed masters-level English courses at the University of Chicago, for which she'd received only A's. The school board's defense was that "regardless of college degrees and teaching experience, no white teacher in Little Rock is inferior to the best Negro teacher."

Judge T.C. Trimble found in favor of the school board, but his finding was struck down by the U.S. Court of Appeals in 1945. Susie Morris had won a major victory for herself and other black teachers. In retribution, however, the school district promptly fired her. It was six years before she worked in the school district again.

One freedom that President Roosevelt failed to include in his patriotic speech leading up to World War II was the freedom to vote. In fact, this freedom would be one of the hardest fought for by Southern blacks. In Arkansas as in most other Southern states, voting would not be a right easily won by black Americans. The resistance was most blatant in the Democratic Party, the stronger party in the South at the time.

A 1944 voting rights case in Texas—the Smith v. Allwright case— challenged the legality of blacks being prohibited from voting in state primary elections. The Supreme Court ruled that such voting restrictions were indeed illegal. That same year, Arkansas' black voters would vote for the first time in the state's primary elections, runoffs, and general elections.

In response, the all-white Democratic Party of Arkansas strategized to impose new rules for joining the party. The new rules called for holding two sets of elections, one national and one state. That meant taxpayers had to cover the cost of four elections—two primaries and two general elections. Most blacks would not be able to afford the cost of four elections. For most Southerners, poll taxes are therefore synonymous with the voter rights discrimination that was legal throughout and after the war.

The war officially ended in May 1945, and many white war veterans returning to the state were just as resolved to gain full practice of Roosevelt's four freedoms as blacks were. In what would become known as the GI Revolt, former soldiers—mostly whites—took on the seats of political power both locally and nationally. Sidney McMath was one of these young war veterans who aspired to political office. He ran for prosecuting attorney on the platform that he would challenge Hot Springs Mayor Leo McLaughlin to clean up the city's gambling machinery.

Though he did not actually end gambling in Hot Springs, McMath became a popular politician, and in 1948 he ran for state governor and won.

McMath bucked the system by placing black Arkansans on state boards for the first time since Reconstruction. Blacks also made gains during this time in local races, earning seats on city councils in Malvern and Hot Springs.

McMath also sponsored laws to end lynching and bills to end the poll tax, though the members of the General Assembly refused to pass many of his reforms. The least controversial program passed by the General Assembly during McMath's tenure was a highway program. Arkansas had been known as the state with the worst highways and roads for years.

One carmaker advertised the durability and strength of his cars by saying they had passed the "Arkansas mud test." In 1949, the state borrowed money through a bond issue to pay for repairs and new highways. Nearly $80 million, both state and federal, were spent to improve roads.

After retiring from politics, McMath become an ambassador for the state and a friend of President Harry Truman's. In one public speech documented in Jim Lester's *A Man for Arkansas: Sid McMath and the Southern Reform Tradition*, Arkansas' 35th governor said: "We are not spending all our time on white-columned verandas sipping mint juleps and plotting to keep our people in economic slavery. In fact, there is abroad in all the southland a vigorous progressive movement—a growing demand for the development of the human and economic resources of our region."

By 1950, during President Truman's leadership, the United States would participate in yet another war—the Korean War, which the president would refer to as a "police action." This so-called police action included sending thousands of American soldiers to South Korea to assist that country in its fight against communism as embodied in its enemy, North Korea.

This war, according to most military historians, was founded almost entirely on America's fear of communism. Many Arkansas veterans of World War II who had joined the Army Reserve or the National Guard were called up to fight again, and younger men were drafted into the war. The undeclared war ended in 1953 after taking the lives of 461 Arkansas soldiers.

CHAPTER 17

THE NEW DEAL,
ARKANSAS FARMING, AND THE
Great Migration

Arkansas was in for more change as the great agricultural transformation got under way in the 1940s and 1950s. Thanks to new, bigger and better farming machines and farming techniques, the culture of farming went through a major metamorphosis throughout the state. As a result, the number of farmers and farm families in the state dropped, with the number of people living on farms falling from more than 1.1 million in 1940 to 595,000 in 1954.

Ironically, it was Roosevelt's New Deal that initiated this dramatic change in Arkansas' farming landscape, in essence killing off Arkansas' small farmer. The program favored larger landholders, allocating them money to purchase new farming machines such as cotton pickers, thus doing away with the need for manual labor in many instances.

The types of farming changed as well. In the hills, small farms switched to cattle or poultry. In the Delta, cotton lost its kingdom to soybeans and rice. Food processing became a large industry in the state. Small family farms were gobbled up by large farming businesses.

The migration of blacks from Arkansas to the North was precipitated by this transformation of farming in their home state. Most of the departing blacks had been sharecroppers, tenant farmers, and small farmers who simply couldn't afford to farm anymore. Arkansas lost about 10 percent of its population during this era, which resulted in the loss of one of its six seats in Congress after the 1950 census. But blacks were not the only people leaving the state. Arkansas lost 6.5 percent of its overall population between 1950 and 1960.

Chapter 18

Orval Faubus
Puts Arkansas on the Map

Orval Eugene Faubus became Arkansas' 36th governor, tying with Bill Clinton and Mike Huckabee as the longest-tenured governor of the state. Each of the three men led the state for four terms. Faubus could easily be listed as both one of Arkansas' most popular governors and certainly one of its most controversial.

Orval Faubus was born in Huntsville, Arkansas, into a poor populist and socialist family. After graduating from high school, he attended Commonwealth College, also called "The Little Red School House," in Mena, Arkansas. The school was closed shortly after he attended after rumors spread that it was staffed by communists. Faubus taught for a while in public schools but joined the Army shortly after Pearl Harbor. He rose to the rank of major during the war and was appointed postmaster shortly after returning home. He would also purchase the local newspaper and publish it for a time.

Governor Sid McMath appointed Faubus to the state's highway department in the mid-1940s. This was where Faubus' political education took root. McMath lost his bid for a third term amid a cloud of scandals, including reports that there were improprieties in the way his friends had received highway contracts. Francis Cherry, a relative unknown in Arkansas politics, defeated McMath by blowing the highway department scandal out of proportion. Cherry would serve as governor for one term before losing to McMath's appointee, Orval Faubus, whose country-boy wit and humor appealed to the common man.

Throughout most of his four terms as governor, Faubus would be viewed as a moderate politician with a speck of liberal leanings. Even after 1957, most Arkansans would continue to paint him as a political pragmatist rather than a segregationist. He came into the position of governor at a time when Arkansas, like the rest of the country, was on the cusp of change. The war had brought about many of these changes. A large number of people were moving away from the rural areas of the state and settling in the larger towns and cities.

Women now worked outside their homes, gaining decent jobs and pay. Many displaced farmers were leaving the state, and blacks were either moving up north or settling in the state's urban areas, where better jobs could be found. The average per-person income in the state in 1955 was $1,142—60 percent of the United States average.

In 1955, Governor Faubus established a state commission, the Arkansas Industrial Development Commission (AIDC), with the sole responsibility of attracting jobs into the state. His prize appointment to this commission was a newcomer to the state—a Yankee, no less— Winthrop Rockefeller, a World War II veteran who had risen to the rank of lieutenant colonel. More importantly, this Rockefeller was grandson to the wealthy John D. Rockefeller of New York.

Winthrop Rockefeller had arrived in Arkansas for a visit on the invitation of an Army buddy by the name of Richard Newell. He wasn't there long before he decided he'd stay. Rockefeller bought a large plot of land at the top of Petit Jean Mountain in Conway County.

He built an enormous home and ranch and spread cattle across the hundreds of acres. The Rockefellers immediately became active in Little Rock's civic and cultural affairs, and this proved helpful in his new role as a business magnet for the state.

Beyond the Rockefeller name, his biggest drawing point for businesses was that Arkansans were desperate for work and were willing to work for 30 percent less than the nation's average wage. The state saw a miraculous economic transformation during Rockefeller's nine years at the AIDC. More than 600 new plants and factories and 90,000 new jobs are said to have come to the state during this time, a 57 percent increase in jobs and 65 percent increase in income.

Orval Faubus would have had to be blind not to see the volatility of change that threatened Arkansas in his early years as governor. In 1954, the U.S. Supreme Court had directed schools throughout the country to move "with all deliberate speed" toward desegregation.

The NAACP was growing in numbers and strength. Young, educated blacks who returned to Arkansas after time spent up North brought with them little patience for the slow wheels of justice found in the South. They carried back stories of equal opportunity in other parts of the country and questioned why it wasn't a reality in Arkansas.

Slowly, there appeared some signs that Arkansas intended to uphold the law, and some stores and restaurants removed their "Coloreds" and "Whites Only" signs from their doors. Yet, while there were interracial committees such as the Little Rock Council on Education who spoke out on the need for equal education, there were also a growing number of voices speaking out against the mixing of the races, even in the classrooms.

Groups such as the White Citizens' Council and men like "Justice Jim" Johnson of Hoxie, who proposed an amendment of the state constitution that would defy the court ruling. Johnson, an avowed separatist, would run against Faubus in the next election. Though he lost his bid against Faubus, Johnson's proposed amendment won by 185,374 to 146,064—a searing indictment of where white Arkansans stood on civil rights. The more race relations seemed to progress in the North, the more vocal integration opponents became.

In 1956, when it was evident that Arkansas schools were not moving "with all deliberate speed" to integrate the schools, Daisy Bates, the president of the state's chapter of the NAACP, along with 30 black parents, filed suit against Little Rock School District Superintendent

Virgil Blossom and the school board, citing that black children had been denied entry into the school. The Supreme Court upheld their earlier ruling that the schools were to be integrated "at all deliberate speed."

Faubus had not made his positions on school desegregation public. When asked point blank, he said his position was neutral on the Brown v. Board of Education ruling and that it should be up to local school districts to decide how they wanted to handle the issue. During his 1956 campaign for re-election, however, he learned that most white Arkansans had no such laissez faire attitude toward the court's ruling.

A wily politician, Faubus proposed a tax increase to the 1957 General Assembly, much of which would go to schools and provide equal pay for black teachers. In exchange for this tax increase, he agreed to support east Arkansas segregationists in the passage of their laws, one of which would end compulsory school attendance and gave state aid to districts threatened with court suits.

The segregationists wanted the NAACP to publish its list of members. They wanted a state sovereignty commission to protect Arkansas from the U.S. courts. It was possibly his socialist father's teachings that prohibited the governor from agreeing to the segregationists' demands after passage of the tax increase. But he would find that to be a political misstep.

Faubus' sense of political survival eventually won out against the values instilled in him by his father. The governor would paint himself into a box in 1957, as he took a starring role in the Central High School Integration Crisis in Little Rock. His overzealous action against the integration of Central High School—ordering armed troops to the school to bar nine black children from entering—is what the rest of the world remembered about the state of Arkansas and Arkansas' governor, Orval Faubus.

Harry Ashmore, then editor of *The Arkansas Gazette*, which would win a Pulitzer Prize for its coverage of the harrowing incident, analyzed Faubus' position on the school's integration. "Many of Faubus' supporters accepted him as a racist ideologue, and he was usually so portrayed in the national media, but few of his antagonists in Arkansas ever did. The *Gazette* contended from the outset that he had no real concern with racial matters one way or the other, but was exploiting the highly charged school desegregation issue to maintain himself in power."

Orval Faubus' father, Sam Faubus, was convinced that his son was untouched by simple race prejudice. Though Sam Faubus admitted he had never seen a black person until he was a grown man, he had nevertheless taught his son that racial equality was essential to progress and justice.

Sam Faubus was convinced that his son's vocal and well-documented stance against integrating the school was a ploy to garner favor with Little Rock's leading citizens, who wouldn't stand for the Feds forcing their integration policies down the throats of God-fearing people. They were incensed that the poor whites in the urban areas would be forced to send their children to school with blacks while those living in the upper-income areas wouldn't.

It would take the president of the United States to ensure that Central High School was integrated in September 1957. The stain on Arkansas' history could not be erased, but the president's decision to uphold the authority of the federal court was a step toward setting things right.

The president removed the Arkansas National Guard from Governor Faubus' command and placed them under the command of the U.S. Army, then ordered units from the U.S. Army's 101st Airborne Division into Little Rock, where they set up guard posts around Central High School and a command post on the field behind it.

The nine black children were swooped up by the guardsmen in an Army station wagon and deposited in front of Central High School amidst the white mobs' protests. The nine children were then escorted by a rifle-toting guards up the steps and into Central High School.

This was far from the end of the story. Governor Faubus closed the school for the entire next year. White students went to private schools or didn't go to school at all. When the schools reopened in 1959, some blacks attended Central High and others went to Hall High School. Complete integration of the schools wouldn't trickle down to the lower grades until the early 1970s.

In spite of how the rest of the world viewed Arkansas' governor, Arkansans decided they had a keeper. Faubus' political instincts had been right on the money, at least for his state and his constituency. He won great support from the people of Arkansas for his "handling" of the Integration Crisis. He had stood up to the Feds, and, in a way, Arkansas had won the tug of war, at least for a time.

During his 12 years in office, the power of the governor's office continued to grow. Faubus wielded power over agencies, commissions, and the General Assembly. He turned out to be good for the state. State programs expanded, schools and colleges received more money, highway budgets increased. Alas, he was not able to avoid the taint of scandal.

CHAPTER 19
A Yankee Republican
—Takes Arkansas—

The rich Yankee war veteran Faubus handpicked to bring business into the state turned against him during the Central High crisis. Winthrop Rockefeller, the moderate-to-liberal Republican from the North, took issue with Faubus' position on the school's desegregation. Even setting aside his personal position on the Little Rock Integration Crisis, as head of the Industrial Development Commission, Rockefeller saw the incident as very bad for business. While eight plants had opened in Arkansas the year before the crisis, none moved to Arkansas in the next two years.

In 1964, Rockefeller challenged Faubus but lost by a small margin. But in 1966, Faubus' former AIDC commissioner threw his extra-large cowboy hat into the ring again. Had it been another time and another Republican candidate, he would never have had a chance in the Democratic state of Arkansas. But even though Arkansas' Republican Party was weak, Rockefeller had a few aces in the hole—his name, his money, Arkansas Democrats who were still angry with Faubus, and the state's black voters, who now viewed Faubus as an impediment to their own progress.

Rockefeller's opponent in the Republican primary was none other than "Justice Jim" Johnson, the segregationist from Hoxie, who lodged personal attacks on Rockefeller's wealth, pedigree, the fact that he was a Yankee who divorced his first wife, and even that he had a drinking problem.

In contrast, Rockefeller ran his campaign as if the race were being held in New York City. He used big money, computers, polls, and more radio and television advertisements than the state was used to. He traveled all over the state and met with Democrats and Republicans, blacks and whites.

Rockefeller's win was historical—the first Republican governor in Arkansas since 1872—though he'd only won 54 percent of the vote. The 90 percent of blacks who voted for him, most of whom had never voted Republican before, gave him the edge he needed to win. While Jim Johnson refused to shake hands with blacks, Rockefeller welcomed them.

Rockefeller promised an "Era of Excellence" but would not be able to pull it off. He would never win over the Democratic General Assembly. There were only three Republican legislators at the time. Though he offered considerable reform legislation, he was crippled by the assembly's lack of support for his programs.

He was able to pass some laws through the 1967 Legislature, adopting the state's first minimum wage, tightening tax insurance regulation, adopting a law guaranteeing freedom of information, and finally closing down the gambling houses in Hot Springs.

He might best be remembered, however, for his role in reforming Arkansas' prison system. After a report from the state police that the state's prisons were hotbeds of crime, Rockefeller brought in a professional criminologist named Thomas Murton to fix the problem. Whether or not Rockefeller intended him to do so, Murton attracted a great deal of national media attention.

Over time, that attention would increase when Murton ordered that graves at Cummins Prison Farm be dug up. He had been told, and believed, that there were murdered inmates buried on the prison grounds. This turned out to not be true, and Murton was eventually fired when his ambition became a liability to the governor.

In 1970, a movie, "*Brubaker,*" was released depicting prison scenes that were said to be loosely based on a book written by Murton called

Accomplices to a Crime: The Arkansas Prison Scandal. That same year, a U.S. court declared the entire Arkansas prison system unconstitutional, describing it as "a dark and evil world." Rockefeller, a vocal advocate for changing the capital punishment laws, would authorize clemency to 15 death row inmates, reducing their sentences to life in prison.

Rockefeller's moderate politics paved the way for the next three governors—Dale Bumpers, David Pryor, and Bill Clinton—all of whom were either moderate or moderately liberal. Rockefeller's liberal views on the race issue were not welcomed with open arms by Arkansas' more conservative citizens. But he nevertheless changed the culture of state government by placing blacks in agencies for the first time in Arkansas history.

In a dramatically courageous move for an Arkansas politician, Rockefeller held a public ceremony of mourning for the death of Martin Luther King, Jr., on April 4, 1968. He was the only Southern governor to do so, perhaps saving the state from the race riots visited on other states after the civil rights leader's assassination.

Governor Rockefeller won re-election in 1968 with a strong black support base and lukewarm support from white voters. That same year an ultraconservative Independent, George Wallace, carried Arkansas for the presidency.

Rockefeller's second term was filled with turmoil and conflict with the Democrat-led Legislature, especially on the issues of tax reform and raising tax rates. Rockefeller had mounted a tax increase campaign under the name "Arkansas is Worth Paying For," but obviously not many Arkansans agreed with him. Moreover, the governor's personal problems began to add to his political struggles.

Though he had promised not to serve more than two terms, Rockefeller ran for a third time in 1970. There was little Republican opposition, but there was a large number of Democrats vying for the job, including a little-known lawyer from Franklin County by the name of

Dale Bumpers. This young, attractive, untainted politician beat Rockefeller by a large margin: 375,648 to 197,418.

Much of Rockefeller's agenda would be adopted by Governor Bumpers, including reorganizing state government from hundreds of agencies into a small group of departments.

Conver

WILLIAM JEFFERSON CLINTON
FROM HOPE TO HARLEM

PART VI

CONVERSATIONS
IN ARKANSAS

You know, I never thought about this in the way my appointment of people of color, and lots of women, to important positions—in the way most people think about it. I always figured we'd do a better job if our government was more representative of the rest of the people in the country. I always thought we would make better decisions. I always thought empowering people and communities was a positive good. I never thought it was something I was doing for somebody else—I just thought I was trying to make Democracy work.

—President Bill Clinton

The late Ernest Joshua was recognized by President Reagan as an outstanding small business owner, and since then his company has expanded to Africa and the United Kingdom.

I met Bill Clinton around 1980, shortly after he lost his second campaign for governor. It was at a barbecue. After that, we went duck hunting together, and that was the beginning of our friendship. Bill Clinton was not only the most brilliant politician I've ever met, but he was a politician who had a heart and vision. Like all politicians, he rewarded those who helped him achieve his goal. But, unlike many others, once he's done that, he went about the business of serving the masses—not just those who helped him, but all Americans.

When Bill Clinton took office, the country was on a downward spiral. Eight months after he was sworn in, the nation was moving upward. No wars, changes in the Old Guard, minorities were being appointed to important roles in government. His finest hour was when he decided to take a trip to Africa. He chose to spend enough time there to talk to the leaders, learn their concerns and their resources. He was the first president who can say they learned a great deal about Africa firsthand.

William Jefferson Clinton's leadership style is a combination of some other great leaders—Truman, Roosevelt, John F. Kennedy, and Johnson. I'm not ashamed to say that Ronald Reagan was a friend of mine, but he was light years away from the vision Bill Clinton had for the country and the world.

Clinton's greatest accomplishments were putting policies in place to help women, children and families and moving our economy forward for eight years. There are no more important issues. He moved black Americans from the outside or sideline of government into the inner circle within eight years' time, something no other president did.

His missed opportunities were basically the time he spent dealing with the scandals. That time should have been spent running the country. Although his faults were personal and moral, his opponents used that to hurt him and ended up harming the country.

His Race Initiative was good in principal, but getting Americans to go along with it was a big challenge. Even with missed opportunities, he did a better job as president than most people, even his followers, thought he would do. He was young, was governor of a small state and hadn't really spent a lot of time in the D.C. culture. I think that showed just how much of a quick study and what a brilliant politician he was.

The media's portrayal of Bill Clinton didn't change my opinion of him one bit. I think I knew him a lot better than anyone writing about him did. He has always been a thoughtful man who cared about people at every level. Bill Clinton will one day be viewed as one of our greatest presidents nationally and internationally. He was brilliant, had vision, and used both to make a better world.

Minnie Jean Brown Tricky, one of the Little Rock Nine members, made her home in Canada for more than 30 years. But she returned during the Clinton administration and served as an Assistant Secretary in the U.S. Department of Interior:

> I met Bill Clinton in 1987 during the 30th anniversary of the Little Rock Central High Integration Crisis. As governor, he was very instrumental in that event taking place. I was living in Canada at the time, though I'd heard about him.
>
> But during the anniversary ceremony in 1987, Governor Clinton spoke at Central High School and talked about this amazing young black man, a rising star, who had been killed in an accident. To see this politician bare his emotions brought back memories of the only other Arkansas governor I knew of— Governor Orval Faubus. The difference between the two men was so substantial.
>
> The Little Rock Nine and our families were invited to the governor's mansion that evening, where we ate, talked, reminisced, and even sang old songs. Clinton's daughter, Chelsea, and my two young girls even joined us. I have always wanted to thank Bill Clinton for that day, because it was truly the beginning of my recovery from the 1957 Integration Crisis. When I left Arkansas as a teen-ager, there had been no public or private acknowledgement of that awful wrong. We really needed to hear someone of his stature apologize. That meant so much.
>
> Bill Clinton's greatest contributions to our country and to black America are the very things some people see as failures—his effort to make universal health care a reality in this country. The fight he

had with Congress over universal health care said a lot about his courage. His dialogue on race was very important. And he gets really high marks for bringing in outstanding people to run the government, to make sure diverse experiences were brought into the mix.

Toward the end of his administration, I had an even greater appreciation for what he'd done: bringing in people he believed would do the right thing for America; and the realization that so much of his efforts to change the country for the better were stonewalled.

I returned to the U.S. during his second term and went to work in the Department of the Interior. I was proud to call him my president. I think he made most Americans proud. Not a single president was perfect, but Franklin Roosevelt and Bill Clinton will be viewed as great leaders because they used the federal government to take care of the country. They didn't just help one part of America, but all Americans.

<hr>

Carol Willis, a McGhee, Arkansas, native; attorney; former Clinton aide; and Democratic National Committee consultant:

I met Bill Clinton at the University of Arkansas law school and knew him as the young, white professor who always had a few black students in his classroom. I volunteered to work on his campaign against Paul Hammerschmidt, even though there were few African Americans in the 3rd District at that time. Another black lawyer, George Van Hook, and I volunteered up in Fort Smith and in the black community in Fayetteville.

We quickly became frustrated, though, after the campaign office managers directed us to water the rocks down on the parking lot. As law students, we didn't think that was too cool, but we watered the rocks. Later, we met Bill and Hillary in the headquarters office and told them how our day went.

My first impression of Bill Clinton was that he was a laid-back, easygoing but eager person. He was a "golly gee, wow!" white guy. We were going into the end of the black revolution at the time, and my friends and I considered ourselves revolutionists. We viewed Clinton as a bleeding-heart liberal, a hippy at heart, and Fayetteville probably was the most liberal place in Arkansas at the time. He wanted to reach out to us but didn't really know how to do it. It was like he was trying to keep from stepping on egg shells to keep from insulting us. That changed over time, though, after he got to know us. But, back then, we would push his button just to see what his reaction would be.

The thing that always reverberated about Clinton was that he always came across as a sincere guy. Sometimes we thought he was conning us, but most times we knew he wasn't. Usually, he always made the right decisions. We had to push him on some things, though. And over time, it got be a lot of pushing back and forth.

He was the kind of guy that could accept being pushed. You could push him, raise hell with him, then all of a sudden he'd get mad and start pushing back. I think that made him tougher. Because he was the golly-gee white boy who went to Yale, he was also sensitive and genuinely wanted to help. When you compared Bill Clinton to the rest of the law professors on campus, there was no comparison, when you're talking about interaction with the black students.

• • •

A great leader understands the people he's leading, their plight. He or she has to be willing to take on the big, tough issues and make some hard decisions. I think you have to be egotistical to a degree, because you have to believe you can do what you say you can do. You have to be comfortable with yourself, because most time you will be alone in your decisions.

• • •

What Bill Clinton provided for Arkansas was an atmosphere of change. Blacks and whites learned to work together. After losing his second term as governor, he regrouped and brought in a different team. I was part of that group, so was Rodney Slater and Bob Nash. We worked as close with him as most people in the governor's office, but each one of us brought something different to the table. The amazing thing is that he knew to bring in three blacks with diverse backgrounds and strengths.

One of his greatest attributes is his ability to provide an atmosphere of interaction and exchange. He threw together a black revolutionist like me with an Orval Faubus appointee, Maurice Smith—a classic white politician, by the way. Clinton just expected us to work out our differences. In my very first conversation with Maurice Smith, he told me, "Look, if you want power, you got to understand that we got to elect this guy governor . . . it ain't about whether I worked for Orval Faubus or whether you're for black power . . . it's about us working together. The end result is the only way we can get the power and influence we want. We got to get this guy elected."

He guaranteed me that if I sat outside his door and watched the way he worked Arkansas politics, I'd learn a hell of a lot from him. "Watch my hat . . . if my hat is in, I got a deal going, so just sit there and listen." And I did, and I learned a hell of a lot about the intricacies of politics from Maurice Smith. Maurice and I ended up becoming good friends.

The governor brought in people like Betsy Wright, Gloria Cabe, Mary Ann Salmon, Kay Goss, Joan Roberts, Judy Gaddy, Nancy Hernreich . . . all of these people brought different experiences and strengths. They all came from totally different worlds. Clinton was a master at pulling together those kinds of coalitions, and he was even better at getting these people to work together.

He applied this to the whole state, and it worked. I could run off a long list of guys from all parts of this state who had nothing in common—farmers, hunters, the good old boys, the rednecks, the Baptists, the Jehovah's Witnesses, the Churches of God in Christ, the segregationists—this hodge-podge of followers that Bill Clinton pulled together to make it work.

The black community started progressing during the Rockefeller years, but Clinton built on some of the initiatives Rockefeller started or tried to put in place. He was a lot better at getting black folk involved in the process. Sid McMath, Bumpers, and Pryor were moderates and did their parts to move Arkansas forward.

Unfortunately, we didn't get the education system Clinton always wanted and promised Arkansas. But a lot of that had to do with the attitude of the Legislature at that time. The state's economic development structure wasn't developed the way it could have been. And as brilliant a politician as he is, Clinton has always taken on too many issues, tried to get too many things done at one time. If he had concentrated on four or five good issues, rather than 10 or 12, he probably could have done much more.

While he did well in appointments of blacks to boards and commissions, we failed to institutionalize diversity in state government. He made a lot of good appointments and some bad appointments, too, black and white. One of the few real heated exchanges the governor and I had was when he decided to appoint one of my good friends.

He looked at the guy's resume, saw he had a PhD from Harvard, that his wife had a degree from MIT, and said, "This guy will work." I reminded him that he'd quickly run out of people in Arkansas with those kinds of credentials. Then what would he do? I thought he was trying to clone himself and Hillary in his appointments. I think I called him an "intellectual bigot."

Boy, did that set him off! He went on for at least a minute, then reeled it back in. Finally, he asked me, "Well, do you want me to appoint your friend or not?" I told him there were a lot of people out there just as qualified that didn't have that kind of pedigree, that most of the people he had advising him and agreed with most of the time were not graduates of those kinds of schools. He laughed it off, but knowing Bill Clinton, he definitely gave it a lot of thought.

But our failure to leave some concrete model for black and moderate white communities to continue to work toward change allows conservatives to turn back the clock, because there's nothing concrete there to assure they don't.

The very strengths he exhibited in Arkansas, he continued to exhibit on the national stage. He gave minorities, the disenfranchised, opportunities they hadn't been afforded before. Bill Clinton has a good heart, but he is also a smart politician . . . he understood political payback. I give him credit for taking on some tough issues as president, as during his campaigns. He even took on the black leaders who disagreed with him.

His greatest contribution as president, again, was providing an atmosphere of change and opportunity. He made some good international decisions, although he received some bad counsel from his advisors. He tried to keep his loyal group around him to some degree, but I think he made a mistake of trying not to make the Carter mistake.

Whatever opportunities were lost can be attributed to the hits he took—all the scandals and constant battles with the Republicans and (Kenneth) Starr. That took at least four years off his presidency. I believe he would have made some stronger and bolder choices had he not had the fights and ongoing battles. He screwed up on Lani Guinier (who Clinton nominated as the first black woman to head the Justice Department's Civil Rights Division) by bailing out on her because of the conservative, white community. The stupid mistake with Monica Lewinsky will be a part of his history, unfortunately.

In the end, Bill Clinton was a man at the right place at the right time. He came from the right background at the right time. He was smart and courageous enough to include disenfranchised people and women who had never been included at the table before. The Mideast photo with his arms stretched around (Palestinian leader Yasser) Arafat and (Israeli Prime Minister Shimon) Peres says a lot about what was important to him. That will always be his strength, bringing people, and even worlds, together . . . to cut through the minutiae and get to the real deal.

Clinton grew into the job. I remember during those campaign days, I'd look at him and think, "Damn, Beaver Cleaver is gone be the president of the United States." The world stage still needs him. He is the same idealistic Bill, if you don't look too closely at the scars—some self-inflicted. He's still sincere in what he tries to do. If he's not, he is one hell of a con man and has convinced someone not easily convinced. You still can't stay mad at him because, in a lot of ways, he's still Beaver Cleaver.

☙

*Jack R. Kearney, Gould native; former director, Arkansas Ethics Commission; Little Rock attorney:

I was in undergraduate school in Fayetteville when I heard about Bill Clinton from black students who were excited about this new, young professor from Yale. I recall him looking even younger than he was and seeming progressive in his thinking. I know some students saw Hillary as very bright, but they found it hard to get used to her Midwestern ways.

Bill Clinton, on the other hand, was pretty down to earth. He sometimes hung out with black law students and enjoyed a lot of the popular music. I went to law school at Syracuse the year he arrived in Fayetteville, so I never got to know him that well, except I took one of his summer courses. My brother, Jesse, had told me a lot about him. He thought he was great. I was taking his class to pass the summer, but I think he was pretty disappointed that I wasn't more like Jesse . . . or, at least, that I didn't stay awake in his class.

A great leader is someone with a clear vision beyond what the ordinary person has. A president needs to have a clear vision of where they're taking the country and why . . . so that ordinary noise

*Note: Five members of the author's family—the Kearney family of Arkansas—are interviewed here. Each member was either law students during Bill Clinton's tenure at the university; served as a governor's appointee, or as presidential appointees.

and distractions don't change your focus. I do consider people like Abraham Lincoln, Muhammad Ali, Billy Graham, and Bill Clinton as great leaders.

Bill Clinton was a completely new kind of person in the way he dealt with Arkansas state government and with minorities. He followed three governors who also contributed to the state's movement forward. Winthrop Rockefeller was really catapulted into great leadership by default, I think, because of the times and because he followed an awful governor, Orval Faubus.

Dale Bumpers was brilliant and had lots of integrity, and David Pryor kept moving the state forward. He was, like Bumpers, a very personable governor. But Bill Clinton is the best politician we'll ever see, a brilliant man and a brilliant politician. I do think he might have been too ambitious a politician to focus the way he should have on things that should have been done in Arkansas.

President Clinton's greatest contribution to the country was what he did for the economy and his stewardship for the government during his tenure. Because we felt secure economically and safety-wise, we were able to focus on a lot of other issues. He also opened up the government to include blacks and minorities like no other president before. I'm sure he did it for political purposes, but I also believe he genuinely believed it was the right thing to do.

The biggest loss was that the Republicans never viewed him as a legitimate president because of his progressivism and his position on race. I'm convinced many of them viciously hated him and ended up attacking him on every turn. All of this resulted in big distractions for him, kept him from focusing on some of the issues that were important to him. I think his position on and signing of the welfare reform bill issue was an example of his giving in, when he must have understood they were out to "kill" welfare.

He is an absolute political genius. People can't appreciate it now, but there will never be anyone to compare him to. He survived what I don't believe any other leader could have. He connected to people and engendered loyalty that is rare. Unfortunately, he also gave his enemies ammunition, and that disallowed him from reaching his potential. The Republicans' endless and shameless attacks on him robbed the American people of an opportunity to have a spectacular presidency. Their attacks, I'm certain, would have distracted even Jesus Christ himself.

Bill Clinton matured during his presidency, and that's to be admired. For the most part, he stood behind political negatives such as the Race Initiative, health care reform, affirmative action, bringing blacks and minorities into high level roles in government . . . things he did because they were simply the right things to do.

Because he is such a charismatic, bright man, he will always attract those who love him and detest him. His focus on world issues, on AIDS, is good. He will have an impact on politics, on the country and the world, for a long time to come.

❧

Jesse L. Kearney, native of Gould, Arkansas, served as an assistant attorney general for the state of Arkansas and was later appointed as a juvenile judge for Lincoln County:

I met Bill Clinton during my second or third year in law school, around 1975. I was impressed that he was significantly younger than all the other professors and that he had experiences outside Arkansas. Many of his theories and approaches to law certainly didn't originate in Arkansas.

During one of his classes, he gave us an assignment based on a case he was working on and invited his students to do research on the case. I volunteered for the research and obviously did a pretty good job. He later told me that my research had allowed him to win his case. Later, we would talk quite often about Arkansas estate law; and that eventually evolved into a friendship. I never liked estate law before, but through my research I gained an appreciation for it, and that is a big part of my law practice now.

• • •

A great leader must have passion to lead and an innate ability to relate to people. A great leader is also someone who is willing to think and act outside the box: people like Alexander the Great, Napoleon, Bill Clinton, Martin Luther King, Jr., and Abraham Lincoln.

• • •

Arkansas remained on the lower rung of Southern states and the country for years, before Bill Clinton brought a different way of thinking to state politics—challenged Arkansans to think about what the state should be doing to bring itself out of poverty, to resolve some of our social and racial conflicts, and to break down the "good old boy" system.

As governor, one of his first rude awakenings was how he would have to work within those layers that represented the status quo before he could move people to the next step of thinking about changes. Clinton actually came nearer getting around that than any leader before or after him.

One of Clinton's legacies will be his involvement of people of color in state government, in both the attorney general's office and the governor's office. That simply hadn't been done to that extent under the old system. Blacks had been involved to a limited degree during the Rockefeller administration, but generally they were involved in decision-making only to the extent that it affected the black community. In the Clinton administrations, blacks were placed in significant positions of responsibility that affected the entire population.

Winthrop Rockefeller, a Republican, laid a lot of the groundwork for the accomplishments we saw in the Clinton administration. He did it with old money and an international name and an attitude that he was there to do what he felt was right. But for the first time, a governor involved blacks in state government.

There was no reason Bill Clinton should have lost to Frank White in 1981, but unfortunately, there was still a large holdover of Arkansans wanting to cling to the good old boy system. As one of his aides, I encountered countless white Arkansans who saw it as just plain offensive to have to deal with a black person representing the governor.

Bill Clinton's ambition was actually one reason for his loss and one reason he didn't get even more done. I don't think he knew just how strong the motivation to uphold the status quo really was. Possibly, if he had curbed his drive to make immediate changes, the good ole boy network would have been more willing to accept them. In that way, he still would have done what he set out to do in the end.

His greatest contribution as president was his economic policy. He has always had a real understanding of economics, but he was also smart enough to rely on some very brilliant, visionary economists. The fact that, so early in his administration he was able to pull together an economic package that actually became reality in front of America's eyes was something that made everyone—his followers and detractors—pay attention. And whatever happened after that, good or bad, it couldn't touch the significance of that. It impacted every level of the American community.

It was refreshing to have a president talk about reconciling differences between the races in the country. But I would have liked to see him fill a couple of positions on the Supreme Court with African Americans.

The health care reform package should have passed. The administration's position on Rwanda was a big disappointment. It angered me when our position was that we didn't want to risk our soldiers' lives by getting involved, while we watched American soldiers being sent away to lose their lives in other parts of the world. A different position on Rwanda would have put him in good stead with Third World countries. He did make an attempt to get the U.S. involved in the continent of Africa, which had been ignored by American presidents up until his administration.

His legacy is that he lived the American dream and made it possible for a lot of us to come closer to it than we'd ever imagined. He is a leader who didn't come from wealth or a perfect environment; but through an outstanding education, a desire to lead, and an ability to view people based on their individual value, he was able to move to the highest position in the world. I hope he considers serving as Secretary General of the U.N. He could carry his one-world philosophy to a universal stage.

He is still basically the same Bill Clinton. He's obviously grown considerably. He has the same basic tenets and values. He still has a healthy sense of humor. He's obviously seen the world from the mountaintop and has the vantage point that the average person doesn't have.

❦

John L. Kearney, Gould. Arkansas, native; law professor; Arkansas attorney:

I met Bill Clinton in 1973 when I was a law student at the university. He was intelligent, gregarious, and mature beyond his actual age—probably around 25 at the time. I noticed that he had a knack for identifying students having academic difficulties, and I watched him go about trying to help many of them. He attended a number of study sessions with students and made himself available to answer questions and give pointers on studying certain subjects. He also attended social functions where he was very often the only non-black person present, or one of a very few. I vaguely recall his run for Congress and that he didn't do well.

A great leader is someone who has not only a clear vision of where he wants to go, but his vision matches the majority of the people he's leading. Just as important as that is getting his constituency, followers to understand where he wants to go and where he wants to take them, and to get them to understand that that vision is in everybody's best interest.

This describes leaders like Harry Truman; Abraham Lincoln; Booker T. Washington; Mr. and Mrs. Johnson, the principal and teacher at my segregated high school; and Bill Clinton, as far as recent leaders.

● ● ●

Governor Clinton broke from traditional thinking in a very radical way and was particularly good at doing and saying things that other politicians were afraid to say. And he did it in a way that made it difficult for the masses to disagree with him. While some white Americans might have disagreed with his inclusiveness of blacks and minorities, I think most Americans understood and appreciated what he was trying to do.

His primary contribution was in education. He started to preach educational excellence at a time when we were losing interest in it. And I think a lot of that loss of interest came about because we were coming out of a number of years of forced busing and forced integration, and white people were trying to get around doing the court-ordered integration.

Clinton started us thinking, again, of education as an investment in the future and in individuals. The school consolidation effort, putting more money into schools, raising standards as teachers—not only to assure quality education, but for teachers to become true professionals—all of this was good for the state and good for setting examples for the country.

His inclusiveness of people, in addition to education, brought in folk who had a different way of looking at things, people who weren't politicians. He involved people who had different and fresh ideas. At the same time, there were limitations to what he could do for the state. So there were a lot of good starts with no completions. Education reform is a good example.

President Clinton, jokingly, mentioned that some people called him the first black president. What other president would joke about that? There was, in fact, a time when it was a crime for a person to accuse a white person of having black blood or to be related to black folk. And for a Southern white man to feel comfortable enough about himself to even joke about it, says a lot about him.

He appointed a number of people who weren't longstanding politicians or big money contributors to his administration. Most times, that's how blacks and other minorities are left out. His greatest contribution as president was to help America economically. We had unprecedented economic growth, stability, and progress, and everybody shared in that, from the lowest to the highest. That will be his lasting legacy. We weren't just better off, economically, but Americans felt better off. We felt secure as a nation.

It was to a great extent thanks to his leadership that there was some semblance of peace and stability in the Mideast, an area of wars and conflicts since 1947. He built relationships with our former enemies—Vietnam, Korea, and the communist countries.

I wish he had done more, or something different, with the criminal justice system in terms of our sentencing guidelines. And I know this is not something he's particularly responsible for, but the sentencing guidelines are still unfair. And that's something that could have been done, and he maybe could have used the governorship as a bully pulpit to get some changes made.

His legacy will portray Bill Clinton as dynamic, futuristic, all-inclusive, giving to us a sense of responsibility to one another, a sense of getting involved in trying to improve ourselves individually and, in so doing, improving the nation as a whole. I'd like to see him continue to speak out to both black and white communities about race. He still has a lot to teach America about race relations. I'm frankly impressed by how little he's changed.

Judge Andree Roaf, Arkansas Supreme Court:

My husband, Cliff, and I moved to Arkansas in 1969. The first year and a half, I didn't work, because we decided to have that second child. We became very involved in voter registration here in Arkansas and especially down in Pine Bluff, my husband's hometown. I grew up in a family that had always been involved in politics. The year we moved here, Dale Bumpers ran against Winthrop Rockefeller and beat him. I was working the polls that year and trying to learn about the city at the same time. I knew just from conversations that that was an important political transition for Arkansas.

In the mid-'70s, Bill Clinton called and said he wanted me to serve as co-chairman of the local Democratic Committee. When I told him I had four small children, I thought that would make him change his mind, but it didn't seem to faze him. Of course, Bill Clinton saw that as an unacceptable excuse. I know he thought it was an honor, but I was thinking how it all sounded like a lot of hard work and travel.

We invited Governor Clinton to Cliff's 40th birthday party. He came and of course was the life of the party. Cliff and he were quite close and would often spend time together at political meetings in Little Rock. I took a back seat in politics, while Cliff got very involved.

• • •

Intelligence is a prerequisite for great leadership; someone who has spent their lives preparing themselves, inspiring a certain amount of confidence, not just with intimates but the larger arena. Adlai Stevenson was a great leader but not a great communicator. Franklin Roosevelt . . . I remember the day he died, my mother was crying. He had such an impact on the country and all of us. Like a Martin Luther King, Jr., sometimes it's just being the right person at the right time and stepping up to fill that role.

• • •

As governor, Bill Clinton certainly brought more blacks into state government at higher levels. That was unprecedented at a time when Arkansas was still transitioning past the Central High Crisis, though in a sense, I don't think we'll ever get past it.

Until Rockefeller was elected, there were no blacks in state government. So someone like Bill Clinton coming along after that kind of pattern was a ray of hope that the state really will get past all that. After that we got Dale Bumpers, David Pryor, then, Bill Clinton—all were outstanding leaders. It was a heady time to be in Arkansas, to watch this unfold. For a small poor state, we've had a great caliber of leaders.

As president, he was consistent in his effort to bring blacks into government at the highest level. You hear about the glass ceiling in corporate America; with Clinton in the White House, there was no glass ceiling in federal government. For eight years, I think, we were all proud to say that we had a brilliant, thoughtful, compassionate president in office . . . a president deserving of being there.

What Clinton wanted to do and tried to do with the Race Initiative was great, but America just wasn't ready. So in a way, that whole effort was a lost opportunity, because we weren't ready to talk about race. His decision to travel to Africa was good, but I'm just not sure what kind of lasting effect it will have. The positive side of that was that he showed respect for a continent that had been ignored for so long. I truly wish he had been more aggressive with appointing federal judges.

Bill Clinton moved us years ahead, more than his eight-year term would represent, in terms of full participation. America and black America needed his leadership so desperately. I don't think he has changed as a human being . . . you can tell when people are genuine. You can't fake that for that long, for that many years.

Judge Henry Jones, Little Rock, Arkansas, native; U.S. magistrate, Eastern District:

Bill Clinton was attorney general the first time I met him. It was simply a chance meeting, but I was quite impressed. He was an energetic, idealistic young lawyer who wanted to do great things for the state of Arkansas.

• • •

A great leader is someone who is able to make tough decision for the benefit of principle and for those that he is entrusted with affecting . . . be it a baseball team or a country. Great leadership presupposes integrity. Without integrity, you can't make those kinds of principled decisions that are necessary.

• • •

Governor Clinton's greatest contribution was that he was able to convince people of color, women, and the state's non-privileged that they had opportunities. One way he did this was the appointments he made, the people he surrounded himself with . . . the personal interactions he had within our community. All those things demonstrated a view that women and blacks are competent and can govern at the highest levels.

The kind of legacy he left was the principal of inclusion. He stood for inclusion. Even if you disagreed with him, you knew he believed in what he stood for. It was a matter of diversity vs. representation, bringing all that you have . . . he understood that.

His legacy will be as a governor, a leader who saw the potential in all people and included those whose capabilities matched a need, regardless of their color or race or gender. My view is that the people who normally talk about this have not come to grips with the importance of this issue. Their view of merit has no basis. They criticized his position on affirmative action, when what they are doing is attempting to redefine merit. This is a crazy notion, when in fact there has never been the "best qualified." There's always been selection based on comfort level of those making the final decisions.

As governor, he missed some opportunities with education. He did some things but, for some reason, didn't go far enough. One of the things he made miscalculations in, as governor and president, was in regards to health care, and it was really unfortunate when he and Hillary abandoned that fight. As president, he missed the opportunity to stand up for his nomination to the Civil Rights Commission when he refused to stand behind Lani Guinier.

Yet with his feel for domestic issues, Bill can be an outstanding statesman, touch all kinds of people, bring folk together to discuss and resolve issues. I'd love to see him use that incredible mind to help resolve some of our domestic issues.

My one stay at the White House was at the same time as Bill's friend, Calvin Hill, who I went to college with, was there. As Calvin and I were leaving the next day, Bill ran out to stop us and convinced us to stay and chat with him. He wanted to talk about this book he had just finished reading, which dealt with the theory of the underprivileged and the permanently underclassed. I'll always remember the kind of passion he exhibited around those issues. That is who Bill Clinton really is.

Judge Joyce Warren, Little Rock, Arkansas, native; former assistant attorney general; Arkansas Supreme Court judge:

I actually met Bill Clinton at a party out on Kavanaugh Road, here in Little Rock. Vashti Varnado, a brilliant young woman who had been his student and later worked for him, introduced us at a social event. He was very personable, very down to earth, and very unpretentious. He had a knack of really engaging people in conversations, and I think he announced that night that he was running for attorney general. I was clerking for Judge Darrell Hickman at the time, so I didn't volunteer in his campaign, but my husband, James, did.

• • •

A great leader is someone who is cognizant of their strengths and weaknesses, someone who surrounds themselves with people who give them information they need, then sifts through that information and takes what they think is important. The great leader will make his or her decision and stick to it. Even though it's human nature to make mistakes, a great leader will admit their shortcomings and not pretend to be omniscient.

* * *

Working as an assistant attorney general for Bill Clinton was only the second job I'd held since law school. I oversaw the criminal justice division. While it was a great experience, I didn't have a whole lot of contact with him on a day-to-day basis, but he was always accessible to his staff. He was very concerned about us serving the citizenship to the best of our capabilities.

There were an unprecedented number of minorities working as assistant attorneys general in Clinton's office. About half of us had graduated from the University of Arkansas: James Smedley, Vashti Varnado, B.J. McCoy, Jesse Kearney, and myself.

Bill Clinton has always been a workaholic. He came to work before most of his staff did and was usually the last one to leave. He'd work all day, in and out of the office, and attend all these functions in the evening. Some critics claim Bill Clinton is indecisive. I never saw that. I saw him as a leader who weighed all the pertinent information before making a decision . . . and, usually, he ended up with the best decision.

He was great at delegating duties, because he hired staff for whom he had great confidence in their abilities. He left the day-to-day operations of the office to his lead attorneys. I recall one national meeting that the attorney general allowed every black staff person to attend. I think he decided that since he always talked about inclusion, he wanted the larger community to see that he was in fact practicing what he preached. I never once thought he viewed any of us as tokens. It was a great working atmosphere. He always encouraged honest debate between the staff and himself.

Though his tenure of attorney general was for just one term, Bill Clinton was a great attorney general. The state couldn't have done any better. I never thought anything he did was just for show. He was genuinely interested in knowing what his office workers believed could be improved in the state of Arkansas.

As governor, he was committed to hiring more African Americans as part of his administration, not just as tokens, but to be part of the decision-making process. Black Arkansans have been great contributors to this state government, and not just in traditional roles.

Clinton spent a lot of time working with department heads to create policies and laws that dealt with the state's social ills. He absolutely put children and families first: education, health care, social issues, and welfare issues. Much like Governor Winthrop Rockefeller, who I worked for as the liaison to the health department; Governor Clinton stressed that our roles were as public servants, and we were responsible to the people of Arkansas.

❦

Judge Olly Neal, eastern Arkansas Delta native; Arkansas appeals court judge:

My most profound meeting with Bill Clinton was in 1981, shortly after he lost to Frank White. He agreed to have dinner with a group of us from east Arkansas. We met at Fu Lin's restaurant near the state capitol . . . Jimmy Wilson, the attorney who sued the state for Lakeview Schools; Leon Phillips, Lakeview's superintendent; Wilma Bond, a Lakeview school staff member; and my daughter, Karonna, who was 6 or 7 years old.

We wanted to encourage Bill Clinton to run again for governor. We advised him, too, that he should spend more time up in northwest Arkansas next time around, where his heaviest loss was. We promised him during that dinner that if he ran, we'd deliver the Delta for him. And for umpteen years, we did. He carried Lee, Phillips, and St. Francis counties with a 90 to 95 percentage victory every time he ran.

I was a rabble-rouser in the east Arkansas Delta. All of my efforts, since 1969, had been toward trying to change the quality of life for the poor people of the Delta. I missed a lot of good opportunities to try and get that done, but I was always realistic about politics and politicians. I never thought anyone was going to deliver any miracles to us in the Delta. But probably the thing that was most impressive about Bill Clinton was that he created an atmosphere where we felt we had access, possibilities. As some black leaders have said, "As long as there is hope, there is some possibility of improving the quality of lives." Bill Clinton kept that hope absolutely alive, there's no question about it.

Clinton had a style about him, and I can't exactly describe it . . . and I'm not sure anyone else has ever described it, from all the

The Arkansas Years

1) Governor Clinton voting at the polls in Little Rock with daughter Chelsea

2) Governor Clinton at 1992 Presidential Campaign fund-raiser

3) Governor Clinton with Wendell Griffin, appointed as PSC Commissioner

4) Governor and Mrs. Clinton at Black History Exhibit in Arkansas

5) Governor Clinton with top black aides: (from left) Mahlon Martin, Bob Nash, Rodney Slater and Carol Willis

The Arkansas Years

1) Rodney Slater, Mr. and Mrs. Wiley Branton Sr. and Governor Clinton

2) Governor Clinton talks to children in Little Rock

3) Governor Clinton presents 4-H Award to LaVerne Feaster

4) Presidential candidate William J. Clinton and the late NAACP leader Benjamin Hooks

5) Governor Clinton and the Lower Mississippi Delta Commission

6) Governor Clinton with former ARKLA executive Sherman Tate

1

The White House Years

1) President Clinton with AR Bank Executive Charles Stewart

2) President Clinton and civil rights leader Daisy Bates (seated)

2

3

3) Mrs. Lillian Ross, longtime Clinton Campaign volunteer

4) President and Mrs. Clinton with the late Ernest Joshua and Mrs. Joshua

5) President Clinton with Arkansas minister Reverend William Robinson

6) President Clinton with childhood babysitter Autrilla Watkins

4

5

6

© William J. Clinton Library

1) President Clinton with African American White House Staff

2) President Clinton honors 100-year-old Charlotte Filmore, former Eisenhower seamstress at Radio Address

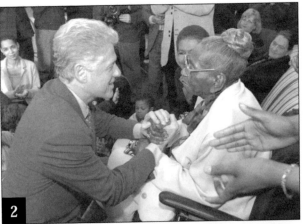

© William J. Clinton Library

1) President Clinton meets with Vice President Al Gore, Rodney Slater, Ernie Green, Lottie Shackelford, Bob Nash and others before his One America announcement.

2) President Clinton with White House Personnel Director Bob Nash (left) and HUD Secretary Henry Cisneros

3) President Clinton with The Little Rock Nine/ Congressional Medal of Honor recipients

4) President Clinton joins (from left) Reverend Jesse Jackson, Mrs. Coretta Scott King, Congressman John Lewis and other black leaders in symbolic march across the historic Pettus Bridge in Selma, Alabama.

5) President Clinton meets with (right) Dorothy Height, Jesse Jackson and other national black leaders

6) President and Mrs. Clinton bestow Presidential Award upon Congressman John Lewis

The White House Years

1) President Clinton with former black mayors (left) Wellington Webb of Denver and (right) Marc Morial of New Orleans

2) President Clinton signing Transportation Bill as Transportation Secretary Rodney Slater looks on

3) President Clinton with South African President Nelson Mandela

4) President Clinton with civil rights icon Dorothy Height and Sen. Edward Kennedy (back row)

5) Senior White House officials: (l to r) Ben Johnson, director, One America; Charles Duncan, deputy director, White House Personnel; Al Maldon, deputy director, Legislative Affairs; Bob J. Nash, director, White House Personnel and Thurgood Marshall, III, director, Cabinet Affairs;

6) President Clinton presents Presidential Award to baseball great Hank Aaron.

readings I've done. But he could walk into any room, among any group of people—any group of people, whether it was a bunch of very radical blacks or a group of redneck whites—and in short order, he was one of them. It always impressed me to watch him go from a black church where he could lean on a podium and preach like one of them black boys, then hang out with a group of whites who were absolutely against making things better for black folk. He could establish a rapport immediately with either one of those groups. He had this gift, absolutely.

Of course, Bill Clinton is quite a brilliant guy. He may not have acted so brilliant in some of his personal life, but he was clearly able to grasp a large set of facts and distill them into something that made some sense, and go forward with a plan based on that. That's, I think, what helped carry him along. Just amazing . . . how he could establish this rapport with all these different groups, something I can't explain.

I remember when he came back to Arkansas a few years back to speak to the black preachers. It was my intention not to be that enthusiastic about seeing Bill Clinton, because I was still miffed that he didn't deliver a research lab to the Delta that he'd promised, years ago. We really thought we'd get that lab in Helena, and my thing was, if we could deliver that lab to Helena, it would bring 15 or 20 PhDs to the Delta area.

That lab was so critical to the Delta for lots of reasons, and I was not happy that Bill Clinton didn't deliver it. When he visited the Delta during his presidency, I quickly reminded him that (Senator) Trent Lott was delivering more to Mississippi than he was delivering to Arkansas. So I had no intention of being glad to see Bill Clinton when he came home to visit the black preachers. Yet . . . when we saw each other, it was just like the old days. That boy just has a real skill at that. In fact, if you want to stay mad at him, stay away from him—analyze what he produces for you from afar.

●   ●   ●

I think that leadership has to do with politics, and politics is the art of the possible. It's not a matter of saying all the right things but a matter of getting some things done, and making some things different and better. I don't think we all have to be on the same wavelength all the time, because we're different human beings, but leadership is like politics: it's the art of the possible. It means . . . can you bring folk together to accomplish some mission, or some goal, or some objective?

147

I think a lot of folk who raise the issues are important. But great leaders, I think, are those people who make things happen, not those who bring the issues. I pride myself on being able to take ideas and turn them into something that will make something happen. My own claim to fame was the Lee County Cooperative Clinic. But I've always said I didn't come up with the idea to create that clinic; there were some little VISTA volunteers—white kids down in the Delta—who did that. Of course, my involvement was critical to making it come into reality. Greatness is delivering on something rather than just reciting the theory.

● ● ●

As governor, my grading of Bill Clinton is, selfishly, based on the Delta more than anything. I thought, in his leadership role, he might have been even more aggressive in doing something with the education system. The Delta, consistently, has the highest percentage of schools failing to prepare students for entry into the world—any world, whether it's the work-a-day world or the academic world.

I can't point to one specific thing he failed to do in that area, but it seems that it became a larger issue. It seems to me that Bill Clinton, more than any other leader we've had, understood what was going on in the Delta. Because of that, and because he was such a popular governor, he could have put a little bit more of his political capital in instituting long-term changes.

But even with my disappointments, Bill Clinton yet stands taller than any other Arkansas governor in what he tried to do and the accomplishments he made. Rockefeller made a difference, but not in quantity. He came close to equal Clinton's in quality. He began the process of opening up state government. Dale Bumpers built on it and had the right title behind his name. You will probably find the largest turnout of black votes ever in 1970. Rockefeller was the kind of leader who took on things that other people wouldn't. Of course, his money had a lot to do with that: he was permanently retired all his life.

Dale Bumpers was a good governor. He told me he was born and raised in Charleston, Arkansas, and never understood anything about the relationship between blacks and whites. When we were trying to get some construction facility over there and the whites were doing everything they could to block it, he made the mistake of giving me his home number and his mansion office number.

● ● ●

As for Bill Clinton's presidency, what he did with the economy is his greatest accomplishment. Of course, there were some things he did I didn't agree with, like NAFTA. But there's no way I can believe that that didn't have substantial impact on our economic prosperity. If you look at the economy when he got there, and where it was when he left, you can't help but give him credit. Even among the black community, there was a substantial improvement, although there still is that hard-core bottom that ain't been touched in a real way.

And then we still have our kids going to prison in droves. That demographic hadn't been touched, because they're still in the penitentiaries around the country. Blacks make up 16 percent of the population and 60 percent of the prison population. That just doesn't compute at all for me.

I was really disappointed he missed in the Mideast peace effort, but it sure in hell wasn't because he didn't try. He got way out there. And I thought that required some real nerve, because in this county, if you're going to be a political factor, you almost got to be pro-Israel to the extent that you're anti-Palestine. I think that's unfortunate, but I think it is reality.

Then, his seamless effort to put blacks at every level of government operations will make it extremely difficult to have an absence of black faces in federal government or the White House in the future.

When I went to school back in 1958, I decided I wouldn't be a doctor because I didn't know anybody who looked like me that was a doctor. The two doctors I saw there weren't anything like me. While I don't like Clarence Thomas, it's better to have a Clarence Thomas than a white man who thinks just like him. It's best for our kids to see a Clarence Thomas on the Supreme Court than 12 white men. Bill Clinton put black folks, other minorities, and women in leadership roles, and he didn't put them there just to sit there; he put them there to help run the government, to call the shots. That's important, very important for our kids.

Of course, the Lewinsky scandal cost him, in terms of his ability to make things happen in that second term. As much as I am in awe of his mental capacity, that was inexcusably stupid. Like a lot of Southern men, I was raised to believe I can be with every woman I can be with, but I have had to turn opportunities down . . . and I'm not even a brilliant man.

I don't blame him for the Whitewater stuff—I think that was just the conservatives coming after him—but I do blame him for the Monica stuff. At the time it came, it must have been just a desire to take a risk . . . like playing Russian roulette. He lost a lot of political capital with that.

I compare him to Lyndon Johnson, who we know had his personal issues, but he definitely used his political capital to make things happen. Kennedy had the ideas and presentation, but I don't think he made things happen the way Johnson did. But Bill Clinton's contributions are considerably broader. Johnson was in a different era, for sure, but Johnson's role was critical. He made crudeness all right.

The Bill Clinton legacy is that he was willing to take real risks to make some positive things happen. He had the natural charisma and the brainpower to do that. He was willing to get out there, to hold on to his concepts and delegate them out for other people to implement. He had the uncanny ability to keep it in his grasp and farm it out, increasing the number of Bill Clintons running the country.

He hasn't changed substantially in terms of his character. I remember the picture we took at dinner that time, because President Reagan had just nominated Sandra Day O'Connor for the Supreme Court . . . and Governor Clinton said, "Well, now we've got a woman on the Supreme Court." And my 7-year-old daughter chimed in and said, "No, she's been nominated, she hasn't been confirmed by the Senate yet." He was amazed, and just laughed. He's reached the epitome of politics. He's able to make money. He could easily sit back, but I think he's still engaged and that's good.

☉

Judge Wendell Griffin, Altheimer, Arkansas, native; Arkansas Appeals Court judge:

I met Bill Clinton in the fall of 1976. I was a first-year law student at the University of Arkansas, and he was an assistant professor and one of the point people for the Carter presidential campaign, I think. He was also running for attorney general. I met him at a coffee machine in the Law School, and we talked a lot about the Carter campaign. Since then, I've learned his eagerness to share was genuine.

By the time we met, he'd lost his run for the 3rd Congressional District seat and had won the Democratic primary for attorney

150

general. It was clear he would be our next attorney general. This was his last semester at the university, and though everyone seemed to agree he was a great instructor, the joke on campus was that Bill Clinton was a full-time politician and a part-time law school professor. Those of us who were in his criminal law class weren't complaining, because that meant he wasn't there very often.

● ● ●

What is great leadership? It's multidimensional. If you look at it in political terms, Bill Clinton is probably the greatest electoral politician in my lifetime . . . maybe the greatest electoral politician in the 20th century. Franklin Roosevelt may have come to rival him. After Roosevelt, Johnson would be the third greatest politician. But Bill Clinton, in terms of being able to translate his personal charisma, his vision for government, and his sense of political relationships into votes and political offices, makes him the greatest politician, electorally.

Greatness has to be looked at in another sense: how well does one govern. As for Arkansas' governors, Bill Clinton's stature ranks second to Rockefeller . . . one would think he would rank first because of the length of time, but the governor's office in our state is weak, and the power of government really reposes in the state legislature.

A lot of Clinton's tenure . . . the first part of his tenure, the first several years, he had to deal with powerful career politicians in the Legislative Council who contradicted everything he stood for. And in Arkansas, they really controlled the state's bureaucracy. So I don't think his tenure allowed him the experience of exercising power, except in appointments.

Clinton's political vision puts him in the category as a great leader. Again, the other leaders that come to mind are Roosevelt, Kennedy, Johnson, and Truman, because they were able to communicate a vision for the nation that took hold. As much as I personally found (President Ronald) Reagan's policies offensive, he has to also be viewed in that group.

What made Governor Bill Clinton stand out was his hiring practices. I was impressed that he hired black lawyers that I knew in the attorney general's office, the first time more than one black lawyer had been hired in that office. That impressed me, that anyone, especially someone so new to politics, could leverage that.

For example, the Arkansas Court of Appeals was created in 1978 or 1979 and began working in 1980. Governor Clinton named an African American, Judge George Howard, Jr., who had been appointed to the state supreme court by Governor Pryor, to the initial court of appeals. So the court of appeals, from its inception, had a person of color on it.

He made a significant appointment of a woman to the initial court of appeals, and when Judge Howard was elevated to the federal bench, he named W. Harold Flowers, another black attorney, to the court of appeals. Later, he appointed Richard Mays to the state supreme court. Again, this was the first time in the history of the state that you had a new court established that had people of color and women.

He was doing the same thing with other boards and commissions. So what we saw in the first gubernatorial term was a much more diverse approach to government, much more receptive, much more sensitive to people of color and women—people who had not been viewed, historically, as politically connected. I think that became the signal feature of his political base in Arkansas, and, to some extent, was a source of vulnerability for him in Arkansas as well-a double-edged sword.

Bill Clinton got on the national map in 1978 because he was the youngest governor. Later, he got on the national map because of his policy on education reform. But my opinion is that the education reform he initiated was not as effective in communicating the kind of fair message that someone would have expected from Bill Clinton. What the message of teacher testing conveyed was that somehow there was an educational validity in a test result that was not equal to other indicators.

So you had all these educators, black and white, who produced folk like you and me with little or nothing, bright people for whom test results were meaningless. Someone as brilliant as Bill Clinton failed to challenge the myth of objective testing. He bought into the myth that if we can test it, or validate it statistically, public policy ought to flow from it. Black folks' history refutes that.

The tragedies of the 20th century will be that the vision of Johnson's Great Society was stolen by the Vietnam War, that Jimmy Carter's vision of a new political culture was rejected by the Reagan era, and that Bill Clinton's vision of an engaged American community was squandered by internal and external forces.

Bill Clinton's greatest positive contribution was the Clinton approach to inclusiveness in government. During his terms, we saw the largest number of people of color nominated for the federal judiciary and the largest number of people of color within political position in regulatory agencies. Inclusion was the signal, just as it was in Arkansas . . . his calling card, politically, nationwide. It was also, ironically, just as in Arkansas, a point of vulnerability for him.

I was very disappointed when Bill Clinton failed to uphold his appointment of Lani Guinier. When he abandoned her nomination, it signaled to Congress that he would not expend political capital to get his civil rights agenda enforced. It also signaled that he would take a less-than-aggressive approach to pushing judicial nominations. Keep in mind that the same committee that would have had to confirm Guinier, would have had to confirm federal judgeships.

I think that decision might have hurt him, politically, as much as the Lewinsky scandal. The Lewinsky scandal will be what the historians write about, because it had major consequences. After Lani Guinier's nomination was pulled, though, we saw a lot of energy from the black and women community, as well as other minority communities, taken out of the political calculus.

Another disappointment is that, at the end of the Clinton era, the federal judiciary was not populated with folks who have an approach to justice consistent with Clinton's moderate political philosophy. The courts are still made up of many people who have more of the Reagan philosophy.

Other missed opportunities were criminal justice, welfare reform, and health care reform. During Clinton's tenure, the criminal justice system became more Draconian and less trustworthy because of the so-called War on Drugs.

Bill Clinton, of all people, could have projected a different and more humane approach to welfare reform, so that poor people and people with addictions aren't barred, for life, from getting welfare benefits. We know of the relationship between addiction and poverty. However, that message didn't come through, so now we don't have that dealt with. And because health care reform was not passed, the people who were underinsured in 1992 are the same ones uninsured now.

Bill Clinton is yet young, creative, energetic, and incredibly intelligent. I hope he will keep focused on the problems that still plague our communities and tunnel his energies, through his presidential library, in the areas of interracial, cross-cultural, global understanding. Bill Clinton is the best communicator of any national or international leader.

He is not the unabashed visionary that he was in 1992. He's still thinking about the future, but he has a much clearer sense of how personally expensive the vision is, and how vicious some people can be who are threatened by that vision.

Judge Wiley Branton, native of Pine Bluff, Arkansas; Arkansas juvenile court judge:

I knew of Bill Clinton before I actually met him. My dad, Wiley Branton, Sr., actually was the one with the Arkansas connections. He and Hillary served on the Rockefeller Foundation board together, and I'd often heard him make reference to both Hillary and Bill over the years. Rodney Slater made a point of introducing me to Governor Clinton when I moved back to Arkansas from Washington.

● ● ●

Great leaders . . . some people might look at Hitler as a great leader in that he could mold people and get them to follow his agenda. But for me, a great leader would be somebody who can basically get people to follow an agenda that would be good for humanity as a whole. Most folks . . . even great leaders we know of, don't have that global reach. I believe great leaders can have flaws. I'm thinking of people like Gandhi; Martin Luther King, Jr.; Franklin Roosevelt; and Winston Churchill.

Most great leaders find themselves in power during a time when a great crisis is at hand. Their greatness is based on the fact that led the people in the right direction. To be a great leader, you almost have to have a crisis at hand to exhibit that kind of leadership, or lack thereof.

● ● ●

Governor Clinton, I am convinced, was sincere in his efforts to bridge the racial divide. Other politicians have paid lip service to that when it was convenient, but with Clinton I don't think it was just for political convenience. He also made an effort to involve a significant number of blacks in his administration, more than all the other Arkansas governors combined. Rockefeller was the governor who probably came closest to Clinton's ideals about diversity.

I would rate him as a great president. He was courageous to risk the Democratic backlash when he cast himself as a New Democrat. He tried to balance the need for economic growth with having ordinary people have a better quality of life. Here, again, Bill Clinton was one of those great leaders with flaws . . . but if you look beyond that, I think he will go down in history as a great president.

As for expectations, I don't set my expectations too high when it comes to politics. In one sense, he did what I expected he would do. Still, there were some things that weren't done that I would have liked to see happen. The health care effort is one. In a country as rich as this one, we shouldn't be in a position where folk don't have at least minimal access to medical services. I don't necessarily blame him for that. The fact that he went out on the limb about being an ethical administration ended up hurting him and his administration. I would have liked to have seen more done with education. Our public education system is still a mess, especially pre-K through 12. It needs a major overhaul.

The Clinton legacy will be a complex one, because you have to separate his accomplishments from the scandal . . . and that picture gets a little muddied. Historians will, of course, look at that scandal, but they should write about how the persecution of Bill Clinton was far worse than any indiscretion on his part. That's the greatest tragedy of his presidency: that this country spent tons of dollars on a witch hunt. While the indiscretion was wrong, that's all it was. And the media played into it while there were so many more important issues to deal with. And it wasn't just Bill Clinton being treated unfairly, but the country got cheated. He could have done so much more if he hadn't been pinned down by this constant barrage and constant attack on issues like these politically motivated attacks.

Of course, I was angry at Bill Clinton. He had to know the conservatives and Republicans had it out for him. But still, the American people should never have allowed that to go on—we should never have allowed him to come under that kind of scrutiny. Now we know that one of his greatest attributes, obviously, is his ability to compartmentalize. Most of us would have been paralyzed with all that swirling around us every day. But he still functioned each and every day. What an interesting character trait, that in the midst of all his troubles, he could still function as president. That's amazing.

Julius D. Kearney, former Public Service commissioner; former director, Arkansas Disability Services:

I met Bill Clinton in the spring of 1974, when he was a professor at the University of Arkansas' Law School. A couple of my brothers had taken law classes under him, and I remember going to a political rally where one of my brothers introduced me to him. I recall we talked about Yale and Arkansas, about public service and his running for office. In some ways, he was like other quasi-liberal whites I had known in Arkansas, but in other ways, he was more open, more intelligent, and much more in tune with everyday issues. He was, in fact, quite interesting.

We discovered that we had a mutual associate, Professor Robert Leflar, dean of the University of Arkansas' Law School, who I often talked to about race and politics. Dr. Leflar grew up in Siloam Springs, a small town up in northwest Arkansas where, incidentally, one of my sisters-in-law grew up. Dr. Leflar, I remembered, told me the only time he ever saw blacks in Siloam Springs was when two black men were running down the street toward the railroad, because whites didn't want them in town. It was interesting for Clinton to be running for office in that part of the world, especially after I got to know his politics better.

● ● ●

A great leader has to have a vision of where they're going, which means they have to understand something of history. Their vision has to include some things that can't be done right now. The greatest leaders are always moving in the direction of what must be done. Many visionaries, however, aren't good leaders. Leaders have to be able to move people, and many people with good ideas just can't communicate them. Examples of great leaders in our lifetimes would be Theodore Roosevelt, Franklin Roosevelt, Richard Nixon—who I didn't agree with, but he did have the ability to move the country—and Bill Clinton.

If you look at what Bill Clinton was able to do, with all the baggage, he was able to move the nation forward in many ways. Even during the worst of his personal trials, he was able to forge a community with conservatives, liberals, and radicals to get some things done. He was able to do what no other president I know could have done.

Though he had a vision of where he wanted to take the state, I personally feel his first term as governor was too ambitious for Arkansas. He went out of his way to get what he considered the best and brightest, which meant he was getting people from outside the state, many of whom were very bright . . . but they weren't Arkansans.

Arkansans, both blacks and whites, are very much into having people pay their dues before we give them our vote of confidence. Most folk want you, in addition to paying your dues, to be a part of the struggle all your life.

Many of the blacks Clinton initially brought in were not necessarily a part of the old cadre of black leaders. So he took some time just gelling into both the black and white communities. He did a good job of opening everybody's eyes to what our opportunities were. Much of the Old Guard in Arkansas, especially, wasn't prepared or willing to concede the status quo for change. When he returned in 1982, he knew Arkansas politics better and was able to implement some of those changes.

I disagreed fundamentally with some of the education initiatives during his administration as governor. I think there was an opportunity to do something major in the area of education in Arkansas, and he would have been the one to do it. Many years ago, we discussed school consolidation and making some changes in school funding. That would have been a steep battle for him, politically, and I don't think he wanted to expend his political capital on it.

But Arkansas has long needed to do a major revamping of our education system. When he and Hillary were working in 1983 and 1984 on education standards, I was really happy about that, but I never believed that was the major problem in Arkansas. The problem is there are still far too many school districts, they have no accountability to anyone, and they are broke for the most part. I think there should have been a bigger effort to make more fundamental changes in the standards.

Another education-related issue was the proliferation of colleges. Arkansas is still one of the poorest states in the nation, and we seem to want as many colleges as Texas or California. We used to call them technical schools; now everyone has a college, and they're growing and expanding. It makes no sense. If you're going to have any of them become excellent, then you're going to have to cut down on the number and feed them good curricula.

As president, Bill Clinton set a tone where the American people could get some sense out of the budget, could plan their lives around their income. That was even more important for most minorities than the general population. He brought saneness to the budgeting and spending process which allowed us to know that we didn't have to have a wild deficit. That was very, very important.

Along with that was his ideal of an inclusive nation that does not stifle business, but instead partners people with businesses to help move the country forward. I think it really helped the African American community, but it also showed Hispanics and other minorities that there were opportunities as well for them. And it helped businesses.

Bill Clinton did something that we've not seen another president do in my lifetime: he made most of his appointments on merit. Maybe not on the same characteristics of merit that other folks did, but he did not go down party lines. He made a lot of Democrats and Republicans mad, because he selected people who would do a good job. He was criticized for his appointments of judges, and some of them went against him, but he appointed people who did a good job.

I remember Governor Clinton and I were on a plane together some years ago, and he was telling me his uncle was mad at him because he had appointed a man who was running against his uncle. He said, "You know, Julius, I couldn't have done it any other way, because the man I appointed is a good man . . . in fact, I didn't know he was running. But if I had to do it again, I couldn't do it any differently, because he was the best man for the job." That's very telling about his sense of fairness.

The Clinton administration lost a great deal of momentum because of the Lewinsky scandal. He wasn't able to put the emphasis on the Middle East, and at the point when he could have really pushed diversity, he was tied up with that foolishness. He couldn't make the bold statements we all expect from him.

He could have done a whole lot more, if his last three years hadn't been tied up in foolishness. It would have been so important to America's future if he had gone the full measure on working with the Arab and African worlds. Those are the things that will come back to haunt America. He visited Africa, but he didn't put the substantive type of emphasis there that should have been placed there.

● ● ●

His legacy will portray Bill Clinton as a man who sought to do good for the country. He came into leadership having given more thought to it than anyone in the history of the world. I'm convinced the presidency was something on his mind as a child. He did think about it and sought solutions to various problems. His legacy will say that he succeeded in most things he set out to do. His governorship was constrained by a Democratic legislature, a one-party system that was made up of folks who were, in many ways, self-serving. It wasn't Republicans who defeated him in 1980, it was Democrats.

Even though he had been trained and had thought about it, he had to go from being governor of Arkansas to being president of the United States. I think he learned quickly. He did hit the ground running, made some errors but learned from his mistakes.

By the end of 1993, which was early for any president, he was running full steam and had put a mold on the office, did a very good job of setting his agenda to the extent he had the Congress with him. He did a good job, but the American people, partly because of the homosexual issues and the health care efforts, decided to divide Congress.

His future should include involvement with world issues, poverty, and race. I think President Carter has really set the curve for that. Clinton should continue to talk publicly about the Middle East and Africa. I think the world will listen to what he's saying. He is wiser now. While I didn't consider him a hippie, he was a young man thinking like a young man. He's still idealistic and the fastest read I have ever run across.

I remember when it was that I fully realized the kind of governor we had. It was during a 1983 trip we took together. He had appointed me to head an agency, and we were flying to D.C. to testify before a Senate panel. This, mind you, was an issue he had never heard anything about before. And we spent our whole flight between Arkansas and St. Louis talking about my hometown of Gould, and all kinds of issues other than the issue we would be testifying about. And when we stopped in St. Louis, he spent all his spare time talking to everyone he saw.

Finally, when we got back on the plane, and during the flight between St. Louis and D.C., we talked briefly about the issue we were testifying on. We got to the Senate and he absolutely blew them away. I was flabbergasted, couldn't believe it! The Senate, finally, had to remind him that I was supposed to be the expert and he was just there with me.

☉

LeRoy Brownlee, former commissioner, Arkansas State Board of Parole and Corrections:

I first met Bill Clinton at the University of Arkansas at Little Rock. He was teaching a course out there, and I met him with James Reynolds, a former classmate of mine. It was the early '70s, after he had lost that congressional race up in northwest Arkansas. We were students of Dr. Bob Riley's and were there as part of a project to interview Bill Clinton.

159

We were constantly looking for leadership for the party at that time. Bill was one of the bright stars on the horizon, we were told, and Jim and I decided that night that it was true. He was extremely bright, very articulate, and very energetic, all the qualities you sought in a future leader.

Bill Clinton's leadership was above average. If he was graded, he would definitely receive an A from me, in some instances, an A+. Of course, there were some areas where we felt more should have been done. There were some disappointments, but his accomplishments balanced it all out. There was a genuine effort to move the state forward in the areas of education and economic development. His hands were tied, to a great extent, by so many Old Guard legislators he had to deal with.

The state hadn't cared about educating our children, especially the ones in impoverished areas. The complete system was pretty much in shambles. I think Clinton was convinced that unless we get that part of it right, we could give up on moving Arkansas forward. His work through the Arkansas Industrial Development Commission—actually established by Faubus— really helped the economic environment. Many of those international companies are still in Arkansas, making a difference.

By far, our biggest disappointment in the Clinton era was over in the Delta area. We just expected so much change, more improvement than ever took place. The failure to make a real difference in the Delta was a big disappointment for Arkansans. Even as president, though, he tried to reach back and do something, through the Delta Commission. I remember seeing him at a hearing one night, it went on past 1 a.m., and he was still there, listening to Delta residents talk about their plight. Finally, the hearings ended around 2 a.m. I don't know how he did it, but I know he genuinely wanted to see some changes over there.

Bill never received the sweeping majority vote; he always had just enough. If you look at the coalition of those who helped him win—blacks, women, liberal or progressive whites—that kind of coalition tells you that everybody wasn't satisfied with him, yet everybody benefited.

During his two terms as president, Bill Clinton tried his best to level the playing field. We were so proud when he made his cabinet appointments and there was more than one appointment of color. We were familiar with the "rule of one," like Robert Weaver at HUD (the Department of Housing and Urban Development) and Patricia Harris at HEW (the Department of Health, Education and Welfare).

We couldn't believe he was doing the same thing at the federal level as he did in Arkansas. Who would have dreamed there would be our own Rodney Slater running transportation for the entire country? We would pick up the newspaper or turn on the television and see one of us, and we knew they were at the table.

Those who say he could have done more aren't thinking about what he did for poor people and black people through programs like HUD, SBA, USDA; the housing and small business initiatives; the water, sewer, and electricity projects in places that had never had those amenities. Then there was the historically black colleges and Universities who benefited from his tenure.

We benefited when he maintained peace throughout most of the world and when he passed laws like the Family and Medical Leave Act. I think what we sometimes look for are the big things that only benefit black folks. What we don't realize is that anything that benefits the masses, benefit us as much or more.

We can't compare his presidency to a Lyndon Baines Johnson's . . . different times. Johnson was the accidental civil rights president during a time when the country would have gone to hell in a hand basket if he didn't get those laws passed. Integration was going to happen with or without him. Johnson was in the right place at the right time for greatness. The difference is, if we could look into his heart, in contrast to a Bill Clinton's . . . according to Johnson's chauffer, it wasn't unusual at all for Johnson to use the N-word when he hung out with his boys.

Bill Clinton had the distinction of probably having the worst group of enemies than any president. They pounced on him from the time he announced he was running for president and didn't let up until after he left the White House, when they finally issued a report on his investigation. There were so many obstacles . . . I don't see how he could have done more than he was able to do. He wasn't going to be allowed to do more than he did.

There was an event in Memphis for the Church of God in Christ, when Bishop Louis Henry Ford died. Clinton was there paying his respects. I've not seen much of that since he left. I have a memorable picture of Bill after winning one of his campaigns. He was sitting up on my shoulder, holding court with somebody behind us. I'm satisfied and proud that he did the best he could, more than anyone ever expected an elected politician to do—certainly as much as his enemies would allow him to do—as governor and president.

Les Hollingsworth, former Arkansas Supreme Court judge; Little Rock attorney:

Bill and Hillary both worked in the presidential campaign of George McGovern and came to the University of Arkansas after he lost. When he ran for Congress in northwest Arkansas, not many of us expected Bill to beat Paul Hammerschmidt. He was new to Arkansas politics, and he wasn't one of the "good old boys."

Ironically, one of my early law cases was with Marianna High School where Rodney Slater was a junior. It was a major school case involving a student boycott. All the black students at the school were boycotting because the school wouldn't recognize Black History Month (or maybe it was Reverend King's birthday). Rodney Slater was leading the boycott.

We met with Rodney and the other student leaders and school officials for a couple of hours, but no compromise came out of it. That was around 1971. Little did I know that this young, quiet revolutionary would become a state leader and close aide to a U.S. president.

I was invited up to the University of Arkansas by George Knox, the only black law professor at the university in the early '70s. He asked if I would come up to speak to the black law students. The university had committed to bringing more diversity to the law school, so George was trying everything he could to recruit more black students there. More importantly, though, he wanted to help them assimilate as smoothly as possible into the law school environment and maintain a healthy black student attrition rate.

So he'd invite black attorneys to present at symposiums, to talk about our experiences and allow students to ask questions. I was in that first group of blacks to graduate from the university and had some experiences a little different from some of the later graduates. It happened that Bill and Hillary attended my symposium and got very involved in the discussion. After the symposium they invited the black lawyers over to their home, and we spent the rest of that evening talking about politics, the state, and how to get more black students into the law school.

By the next year, Bill and Hillary were on the student entrance committee, and for the first time, the university had about 30 black students enrolled in the law school. The law school enrollment that year surpassed black enrollees for any other college in the university. In 1969, there had been no more than 10 black lawyers in the state. Four or five years later, there were 35 black students in one class. More blacks started passing the bar exams, and by the end of the '70s, we had more than 100 black lawyers in the state.

Can you imagine what a revolution that was in the legal system of Arkansas? I'd give 99 percent of that credit to Bill and Hillary Clinton. They made it happen. While we'd been agitating for it for years, people like Richard Mays and me, but Bill and Hillary actually made it happen.

It was apparent to just about everyone who met him that Bill Clinton was politically ambitious. And Richard Mays, who was always very astute at reading people and their strengths, told me one day as we were driving back from Fayetteville, "Les, this guy is going to be president of the United States one day." I didn't believe it, but Richard was convinced. I paid particular attention to Bill Clinton after that.

Though he lost his first political race, he got right back out there and ran for attorney general and won. After that, things began to fall into place for him. He knew all the black lawyers . . . had taught two-thirds of them. No other attorney general in Arkansas history had more than one black assistant attorney general working in that office. He had five. No one since him has come close to that.

Bill Clinton did an outstanding job as attorney general. More than anybody who had held the job before him, he made that office relevant. It was almost as if fate had smiled down on him in 1978, when Governor David Pryor ran for the U.S. Senate seat and won. All the formidable opponents—(Jim Guy) Tucker, Thornton, and Pryor—were running for Senate. In my mind, Bill Clinton had already done his homework and figured it out: the way to be president was to first be governor.

His getting beat in 1980 by Frank White was a fluke. It was Arkansas slapping his hand. Frank White had no capabilities to lead a state. He switched from Democrat to Republican to take advantage of the white voters' anger at Bill. That was the only time I was ever grateful for a two-year term limit. I wasn't surprised at all at Bill's re-election . . . or his concerted effort then to make a four-year term limit the law. He began to deal with substantive issues like education and teachers testing and was able to bring about a dramatic reform.

So all during this time, he had done nothing but distinguish himself. At the same time, the Democratic Party was going to hell in a hand basket, and they really needed new leadership. Well, everyone had started looking at him as the chosen one, and he was selected to make the speech at the Democratic Convention in Atlanta. You know the rest of that story . . . he made that long speech and was lambasted nationwide. I don't know whether the response from the speech had anything to do with it, but somehow he figured out that it was probably George Bush's time.

I got a real introduction to the depth of Bill Clinton's intellect during my work on the state's federally mandated redistricting effort. I worked closely with him for months as lead attorney for that redistricting piece. The attorneys in the case would meet and strategize in the evenings and come up with what we thought was a pretty good plan. The next day, we'd proudly show our plan to the governor for review. Within minutes of looking through it, he would come up with a better plan . . . on issues that were clearly against the state's traditional positions.

There were times that we differed with his opinions, like on the Senate and Pulaski Country redistricting effort. The bottom line was politics reared its head in those cases, and he had some people he had to protect. The biggest problem was the districts in the Arkansas Delta. That area had always had the largest number of African Americans but was now steadily losing numbers. We lost a congressional seat because of that. But he was very helpful in the federal judiciary redistricting effort. At that time, we only had one black federal judge in the state, Joyce Warren.

By 1990, he had already pulled together an exploratory committee—at the height of Bush's popularity. He was spending a lot of time out of the state but made a point of communicating directly with us, and we would meet with him in the mansion when he returned to the state.

In 1986, Lani Guinier and DeVal Patrick, both of whom were with the NAACP Legal Defense Fund, joined us in Crittenden County. We had filed to desegregate county clerks' offices in all 75 counties, knowing that we'd likely fall short of all 75 counties. It was amazing to watch. Clinton and DeVal Patrick actually worked that case without any help from the rest of us. Lani and I decided they definitely didn't need us. All the clerks were women, and all of them were mesmerized by these two young, good looking men. Not only did that affect voter registration across the board, but it definitely increased the number of blacks we were able to register. If he'd been running that year, I know Bill would have been re-elected that time.

Lani Guinier got married that year, and we all went to her wedding, including Bill and Hillary. They had all become friends in law school, and she joked that most of the black folk knew him because he hung out with them a lot, talking with them about black issues.

I worked for one governor, and that was a Republican governor, Winthrop Rockefeller. Rockefeller's revolutionary administration actually set the stage for moderate Democratic governors like Dale Bumpers and David Pryor. He definitely made it possible for Bill Clinton to implement some of the things he wanted.

I have to give Rockefeller credit for his creativity, and Bill Clinton the credit for creating the ideal in state government. Both Dale Bumpers and David Pryor were moderate governors who didn't turn the clock back for the state, but they weren't a Bill Clinton. Bill Clinton brought Arkansas into the 20th century.

As president, most people thought Bill Clinton would bomb during his first term. Most people don't know him. He is a person who doesn't take anything lightly. He studied, did his homework, and learned the players. He set a high standard for himself and for the people running the federal government.

Most important for our community, he made it possible for a phenomenal number of African Americans to participate in presidential politics and in the operation of the White House and the cabinet-level federal government. As far as comparing him to other presidents, I think it's fair to say that Lyndon Baines Johnson did pass the most substantive, aggressive civil rights legislation in history. Eventually, Johnson might have even come to believe in it himself.

Unfortunately, I can't be objective when it comes to Lani Guinier. That was a huge mistake on his part. It wasn't as if she was just someone off the street. Lani was a straightforward, no-bullshit kind of person. She was more than deserving to get that appointment.

Bill Clinton was a substantive leader, though. I can still hear his talks about our responsibility to make America better, and how America couldn't afford to leave one human being behind . . . and how fired up he'd get. There are some people who say his presidency was not beneficial to the state of Arkansas, but history will accord him with doing a great job for all the country. It will mean more because of what he had to overcome, how bent his opposition was on destroying him. Amazingly, he was able to separate his personal travails from his presidency and continue to lead the country.

Loretta Lever, native of Fordyce, Arkansas; former director, NAACP's Regional Fair Share Commission; originator of the Arkansas Minority Set-Aside Program:

I met Governor Clinton in the early '80s, when he was young, aggressive, and very ambitious. He didn't seem to carry the baggage of other governors, and no allegiances to the party. He was like fresh air for Arkansas politics. He had all these new ideas and just needed the opportunity to implement them. He was anxious to see changes in the state, especially the state's civil rights history.

One of the early and memorable events during Clinton's tenure was a celebration of Martin Luther King, Jr.'s birthday, held at the state Capitol. The NAACP memorialized Reverend King by planting a tree in his honor at the state Capitol. Governor Clinton spoke at the event. We were all really on a high after such a significant day, and we joked that Orval Faubus would never have let this happen under his watch.

● ● ●

A great leader is a visionary, able to communicate his or her vision with the masses and to strategize on how to implement that vision. It's a person whose vision encompasses the full community, not just a segment of the community.

● ● ●

As director of the NAACP's Regional Fair Share Program Commission, I attended meetings where the governor was in attendance. Discussions were often about the impact of our community's financial problems, how local banks were not cooperative. My concerns, as I told him, were that blacks contributed millions of dollars toward purchasing goods in the state, but we received less than one percent of the state agency's contracts.

During one of those meetings, I suggested the 10 percent minority set-aside program for state contracts, which would not only help blacks wanting to start businesses, but would help the state with jobs, taxes, and removing people from welfare. The governor thought such an initiative might work and encouraged me to do some research on it. I started pulling people together to create a bill for the 10 percent minority business set-aside.

From the beginning, I was told, "Loretta, you'll never be able to do that." But I was extremely determined, so I started meeting with national NAACP attorneys to discuss different attorneys general's opinions. I wanted to make sure the bill would pass the test, so we lobbied the Legislature, and thanks to help from the late Senator Jerry Jewell, we met with the Senate committee and successfully moved it through committee.

The state purchasing board spoke against it and made it very difficult. We ended up rewriting the policy to include women in our definition of minority. When we went before the House committee, the state purchasing board chair was absent, and virtually every white legislator walked out. The bill passed by three votes. It was a front-page story the next day. Fortunately, the white legislators were so embarrassed, they were anxious to work something out with us.

There was another civil rights issue on the table at the time, so we were given three days to bring our bill back before the committee. We met with Governor Clinton to ask for his support. He was concerned, but we convinced him that the bill could pass if he supported it. Like I've seen him do so many times, the governor worked his magic with the Legislature, and the bill was brought back up and passed.

There were two major contributions Bill Clinton made to our state. He made certain that African Americans were a part of Arkansas' government on all boards and commissions, in decision-making roles at departments and agencies. His was the most comprehensive effort of inclusion any governor of any state had made.

The other significant thing he accomplished was working with African American leaders to make the 10 percent set-aside a reality. That was a historic step for this small Southern state. No other Arkansas governor would have dared gone before their constituents with such an initiative.

As president, Bill Clinton continued much of the work he began in Arkansas, breaking barriers by appointing minorities to positions they'd never had the opportunity to hold before. Whether they were boards, commissions, or departments, the good ole boy system was broken, and that troubled a lot of people. I'm convinced that his appointments, his inclusiveness, his speaking out on civil rights and the race issue, all contributed to the problems he had in the White House. When a president of the United States sends that kind of message, there is no way things can't change.

Though we do not excuse his bad judgment or the scandal that resulted from it, as a race, we refused to turn our backs on him. He was so much more than those moments of weakness. He had reached out to us when no other leader would have. We had been through years of uphill battles together. We chose, as a race, to forgive him and, in fact, to rally behind him.

Bill Clinton is still the same inside, but he is a refined, more worldly and sophisticated Bill Clinton. I think the same issues and concerns are there, but more in global context now. He still enjoys an amazing level of respect from most Americans.

♁

Martha Dixon, small business owner:

I met Bill Clinton through Hillary in 1985. She had bought one of my designs from a boutique in Little Rock and called to tell me how much she liked it. Governor Clinton had just won an election, and she asked if I though I could make her inaugural gown. I remember making a matching cummerbund and handkerchief for the governor.

That opportunity introduced me to Arkansas politics. I had never worked in politics, really, but after meeting them, I became involved in his campaigns and got to know them personally. I have been in and out of the governor's mansion a lot over the years, and I always had to pinch myself, because I'd never dreamed I'd be invited to the governor's mansion. Everyone knows how much energy he has. I had to catch him on the run and throw a measuring tape around his waist.

Bill Clinton was more than smart. He was a very caring man. Once the gowns were done, I continued to assist Hillary with other tasks she'd ask me to do. He would sometimes invite blacks to the governor's mansion, and I was included sometimes. On one of those visits, I told him I was interested in starting my own small clothing manufacturing business. He asked me a lot of questions, then told me he thought mine was a great idea. Then he proceeded to tell me who I needed to talk to.

I cried tears of joy all the way from Little Rock to Arkadelphia. Having the governor take a personal interest in my little dream was so much more than I could have expected. Shortly after I got home, I started my business plan but ran into some stumbling blocks. I called on him again, and he steered me in the right direction.

Bill Clinton is the same Bill Clinton I met back in 1985. I remember telling him when they were getting ready to leave for Washington, D.C., how proud I was that he was going, and by the time he returns, his hair would be as white as snow. I was right.

I've always been comfortable talking to him There are some powerful people I don't feel comfortable with, but he's not one of them. He's an amazing person, and I don't think there ever will be another Bill Clinton. I hope I live to see another leader do half the things he's done. I honestly doubt I will. Whether his gift is something he was born with or something he practiced until it became a part of him . . . I wish he could clone it and share it with others.

℗

Cleon Dozzell, former appointee to the State Advisory Committee for Juvenile Services:

I was first appointed to the State Board for Juvenile Services in the '70s by Governor Dale Bumpers, then Governor Pryor reappointed me, and when Governor Clinton came in 1978, he decided to keep me. I was the only black on the board at that time, and when I retired from the board in 1989, Governor Clinton dedicated the new juvenile services building in my name. He always made jokes about me serving on the board that long and told me he didn't see a need to change things when they were working so well. I told him I was happy to serve under three of Arkansas' best governors, and longer than anyone else in the state.

When he became governor, there were only nine blacks on boards or commissions. It didn't take him long to change that. It was one of his first promises when he became governor.

I worked the voting polls at Dunbar Center, at Dunbar Middle School, during Governor Clinton's election campaigns. I remember he would bring little Chelsea to the polls with him. One time I was voting at the same time, and I told him, "Now, Governor, you know ladies are first." He and Chelsea laughed so hard at that. Later I found out that the newspaper had taken a picture of me and said I had made the governor wait in line to vote.

Bill Clinton was, by far, Arkansas' greatest governor. He was good for all of Arkansas, not just the black community. Nobody had anything good to say about our state for the longest. He moved us forward, especially in education. He did things most of us never thought were possible or thought we'd see in our lifetimes. There were blacks heading up many of the state's largest departments and agencies.

Governor Rockefeller, whose leadership was closest to Bill Clinton's, served as a board member of the National Urban League for some time and attended every event the Urban League held. One of the funny things about him was his souvenirs. During his campaign, he gave away these little packets of sewing needles with his name on it. I was always fascinated at how large his hands were . . . never met anyone with hands that size. But Rockefeller was genuinely concerned about the black community. He supported different black groups and was responsible for the musician Henry Shedd getting his start in Las Vegas.

When Bill Clinton became president, it was the most wonderful thing for blacks in this country. We had never really had anyone in the White House who viewed us as equals or recognized us as part of this country, really. Johnson was great because he passed the Civil Rights bills, but his heart wasn't in the same place as Bill Clinton's. He was there at the right time. It was such a blessing to attend President Clinton's first inauguration . . . that was something I would have never imagined I'd do before leaving this earth.

Othello Cross, Mississippi native; former Arkansas school educator; attorney:

I first met Bill Clinton in the fall of '76 at the University of Arkansas. I remember him as an outstanding teacher who encouraged students to express themselves freely, without any constraints, on anything we wanted to say, and he was always actively engaged in our discussions.

● ● ●

A great leader is a person that can gather information, decipher that information, and make the best decision based on the information he or she has gathered. Great leaders move forward to make sure decisions are implemented to solve problems that exist.

● ● ●

Although I almost went to work for Governor Clinton in 1979 as a liaison to the Arkansas Department of Correction, I ended up being appointed to the Claims Commission by Republican Governor Frank White in 1981. After Bill Clinton beat Frank White, I remained on the commission and got a chance to work in his administration and to see him in action and to learn why it was that this governor was able to get things done that other leaders couldn't.

Bill Clinton's key was never putting a motion on the floor unless he had the support to pass it. He lobbied Democrats and Republicans and was able to get a number of things done, because he saw things from both sides and was able to compromise. The end result wasn't always exactly what he wanted, but he almost always got some movement toward the direction he wanted it to move.

It was during my years at the law school when I took several classes from Hillary Clinton that I learned how committed she was to improving education in the state of Arkansas. Because I was a former schoolteacher and coach, we would often discuss some of the state's education problems. While the governor, naturally, gets the credit for education reform, Mrs. Clinton played a significant role in that whole effort to move Arkansas' education system into the 20th century. That whole minimum standard testing was her initial idea.

Governor Clinton's greatest contributions to the state were his appointments of African Americans to state government positions and his effort to move the educational system forward throughout the state, but certainly in the Delta area. I know for a fact that he used a lot of his emergency fund to underwrite a number of projects in the predominantly African American school districts.

President Clinton's economic achievements for the country were good for black America, but it was also good for the whole country. His diverse appointments proved a point to the rest of American society and to our own youth: if they are qualified, they could aspire to be a cabinet member one day. In all the years I've known him, I never detected one iota of racial prejudice in Bill Clinton. I found out when he was governor and at the university, he never saw color. He was the first and only person I can say that about, black or white.

God, how I wish the Lewinsky incident had never happened. That was the one thing that may leave a mar on his years of contributions to this country. You can't erase history, so I just hope people will put it in the right perspective. This should not be the only thing he's judged on. You also can't erase the fact that he achieved more, economically, than any president in the history of this country.

While I think he was a great leader for the country, Bill Clinton's departure from Arkansas created problems in this state because the federal government began investigations which proved hurtful to all of us. They embarrassed him and his family, but also the people of this state. None of the investigations disclosed any wrongdoings on their parts.

I am confident Bill Clinton will be seen, years from now, as one of America's greatest presidents. My prayer is that he continues to share his compassion and brilliance with us, especially our leaders. There is no greater contribution he could make.

***

Ozell Sutton, native of Gould, Arkansas; former regional director, Office on Civil Rights, Department of Justice:

I moved from Arkansas to Atlanta in the early '70s and have worked in the Office of Civil Rights in the Department of Justice since 1972. I had served in basically the same capacity for the state of Arkansas and as the state's first black governor's aide under Winthrop Rockefeller. But even before he became governor, I worked for Rockefeller on his farm, Petit Jean Mountain. Everything the Rockefellers had, my wife, Joanna, and I had. The Rockefellers, Winthrop and Jeannette, saw to that. We lived like rich people up there.

Winthrop and I didn't always agree, though. I told him one day, "Mr. Rockefeller, as a white man, even though you're a good one, we're not on the same level on these issues . . . you weren't born in Gould, come up on Mr. Charley's plantation." I told him the story of the pig and the hen.

The pig and hen went to breakfast one day, and they pulled up on the counter and looked up on the walls and saw this beautiful ham and eggs. The pig jumped down and grabbed the hen's hand and literally dragged her out. The hen said, "Why are we running?" It occurred to the hen that it was then they were finally safe. The hen said, "We can now stop." The pig said, "No, we can't stop, because to you it is mere contribution, for me it's a total sacrifice."

Even to this day, he is probably the closest thing to Bill Clinton than any governor in Arkansas, and that's why he lost the election. But I decided a little later to leave Petit Jean. With all the benefits of working and living there, I couldn't let the civil rights movement pass me by.

So to Joanna's dismay, I left there and moved back to Little Rock to satisfy a burning desire since I was a child to help right some of the wrongs in this country. I immediately missed living in Pinnacle Mountain, where there were all the finest accoutrements. Joanna cursed mightily that we didn't have air-conditioning any more.

Winthrop came into governorship at a critical time in the history of the state. Faubus had done the state in, with his rabid positions on segregation. There was no industry coming into Arkansas because people—blacks and whites—saw it as a place to stay away from. Industry didn't want to move their workers into Arkansas. It was dead in terms of economic development.

Two things Winthrop brought with him to Arkansas: a name . . . Rockefeller, which meant contact with great, industrial giants. The name was magic at that time . . . considered the richest folk in the country. So the governor brought an attitude that was so distant from Faubus', of inclusion and participation.

When he brought me on board, black leadership came together after Reverend King was assassinated and made some demands on the governor. There's a picture somewhere with Rockefeller singing "We Shall Overcome" on the steps of the Capitol with black leaders. At that time there was not a single black head of an agency, not a single black on a board or commission. He agreed to move in that direction.

Winthrop Rockefeller won with 96 percent of the black vote, three bodies of people: 96 percent black vote; a disillusioned, progressive white voter; and a handful of Republicans. Those whites were so disillusioned, and it was hitting them in the pocketbook. It was the right time for someone like him. Insurance executives, bankers, businessmen—all of them with money were all losing money. He offered a solution to Arkansas, which up to that point had been a disaster.

After he brought some sense of pride to the state, a moderate Democrat was able to come along and win back the governor's office. When they could afford to go back to the Democratic Party, they did. Other than Faubus, it was not traditional for a governor to win three terms. Faubus won four times, because of his segregationist stance. Arkansans found who they were looking for in Dale Bumpers.

But we did have differences. Once, he was invited to speak to the Economic Opportunity Agency, and, of course, I was there with him. Governor Rockefeller got up at this agency's convention luncheon and criticized the audience about the "Say it Loud, I'm Black and Proud" statement. He saw that as anti-white, anti-establishment, and he said that.

That night, when I went down to the banquet, the members jumped all over me . . . saying they thought Rockefeller was "beyond that." The next day, I went straight to his office and questioned him about it. He stood his ground, said he didn't like the "Black and I'm Proud" statement and that he thought it was anti-white. I explained to him that it didn't have anything to do with white folks, but simply meant that we were finally at the point of being proud of who we are. I told him we were talking to and convincing ourselves. He still didn't see it. About a week later, he came to my office and said he had been thinking about what I said, and he finally understood.

I was already in Atlanta when Bill Clinton came on the scene in Arkansas, but I kept up with him and saw that he was responsible for a lot of positive changes there. The first time I met Rodney Slater was when I'd come down to speak at Philander Smith College. After my speech, Rodney came over and said he wanted my advice about his role as special assistant to the governor. He knew that I held a similar role with Governor Rockefeller and wanted to know how I operated and survived as a black assistant. We talked and compared notes between the two men and the two administrations. The last time I saw Bill Clinton, I told him how slighted I felt not to be invited to his White House more.

Bill Clinton's greatest contribution was inclusion, to bring blacks into the intimacies, high levels of government. I was so proud of all the White House appointees and the cabinet-level appointees and others in his administration. Most importantly was his willingness and dogmatism in doing that . . . to make this country more "for all the people."

As for the nation, it was his ability to include all peoples into this government, regardless of their color or race. I always say, other country's effort to dominate us isn't the problem. Our biggest problem is the lack of a truly functioning democracy within our own country as a shining example to the world. Clinton went a long way to make that happen; and I will forever be indebted to him for that.

Lyndon Johnson, like Clinton, had the guts to do what no other president could do. There is no way we could've got the Civil Rights bill under Kennedy . . . good man, but not willing to or courageous enough to confront this country and do the things that had to be done. LBJ did only what LBJ could do. He was the master politician. He came from an element who were bitterly opposed civil rights and was just mean enough to whip them into line. He pushed that Civil Rights Act . . . drove it home with opposition of people among whom he grew up and among whom he came into prominence. He stayed on the case. The 1964 Civil Rights Act, the 1965 Voting Rights Act, can be attributed to his tenacity.

There were a number of times I disagreed with Bill Clinton. There were times I didn't think he moved as forcefully in dealing with South Africa as I thought he could or should . . .when I didn't think he dealt with Africa equitably or adequately.

There were times when he didn't show as much courage when it related to blacks. Sometimes he showed a great personal commitment but didn't use the presidency as well he could have. On his personal commitment, that was unquestioned. But there were times he didn't use the presidency to advance the causes as much as he used his personal interest and commitment. But I know how that goes in politics. Sometimes, what he believed personally and what he was willing to use were two different things.

☉

Patsy Gatlin, former governor's aide, Office of Boards and Commissions; current assistant to the Arkansas attorney general:

I met Bill Clinton in 1986 through Dr. Paul Root, who was a friend of his and worked at the Department of Education. He stopped by to speak to Dr. Root one day while I was visiting. I had been volunteering for his campaign and told him that. About three weeks later, I got a phone call from his office. One of his aides asked if I was interested in a position as an assistant in the Boards and Commissions appointments office. I went to work there that next month.

Bill Clinton's leadership style was different from any I'd known. I had worked in pretty bureaucratic offices, but in his office everyone seemed to be on the same level. All his aides and assistants seemed to feel so comfortable with him. The governor's office at that time had a laid-back atmosphere, even though you knew they all worked very hard and they definitely got things done.

Governor Clinton's greatest contribution to the state was changing the complexion of state government, setting a tone for how race relations should be. Unfortunately, after he left for Washington, the atmosphere changed too. No other governor has lived up to what he accomplished.

As president, he carried over so much of what he did as a governor to the White House, particularly in the areas of education, children, and the family. The same as in Arkansas, my only regret is that he didn't have another term to finish some of the things he started.

A lot of us in Arkansas were hoping he would return to Arkansas after the White House. We really missed his leadership. But he is now a global leader, and while the current administration doesn't seem to use him the way they could, he could really help this administration in foreign affairs. If I were writing the Clinton legacy, I would describe him as one of the few leaders who actually kept his word. He didn't make promises he couldn't fulfill.

My first year on the staff, I was invited to the mansion for the governor's annual Christmas party. I was so nervous. Everyone was singing Christmas carols, and I was too scared to even sing. The governor looked over at me, smiling, and said, "Come on, Patsy, let's hear you sing." I was embarrassed, but I was also very pleasantly surprised that he even knew who I was. That was the kind of man he is.

***

The Reverend R.J. Hampton, a Newport, Arkansas, native who's known mostly for running on the Republican ticket for governor against "Justice Jim" Johnson in 1968:

I became involved in Arkansas politics while I was in college in 1957, during the Central High School Integration Crisis. In 1964, I managed the local Lyndon Johnson presidential campaign. Some of the people I worked with in that campaign were Jack Fowles, who was president of the Young Democrats then; John Boyce of Newport; and the late Jim McDougal. It was an unusual campaign year: Goldwater was this ultraconservative Republican running for president, and Faubus was this quasi-conservative Democratic governor. What most people didn't know was that, though Faubus pretended he was supporting Goldwater, at times he was supporting Johnson. Faubus, in fact, financed much of Johnson's campaign.

I jumped from the Democratic Party to Republican in 1968, when there were very, very few black Republicans in the state. It was the year "Justice Jim" Johnson ran for governor against Rockefeller. The newspapers called me, and I told them, "If Jim Johnson is running, I might run, too." The Arkansas Democrat newspaper later called me "the resident black Republican" when Richard Nixon became president and asked me how I viewed his administration. I told them it would go down in history as one of the worst in history . . . and I was right.

I was working at Shorter College in Little Rock back in 1971, when a young man by the name of Glenn Mahone introduced me to Bill Clinton. His exact words were, "You have to meet this man, R.J.; he's going to be governor one day." I learned then that he was from Hot Springs, the same place Glen was from, and that they'd been friends early on. My impression of him never changed—he was a very brilliant man with a sense of purpose, extremely focused, very normal in a lot of respects, but he's not so brilliant or focused that he's lacking in everyday common sense.

• • •

Great leadership is a combination of circumstances. If there is no need for great leadership, no matter how hard you try, you can't develop it. It is the situation they find themselves in that brings out the latent capacity for leadership in most great leaders.

Even in Bill Clinton's presidency, if there had been more dire circumstances in the country, you would have seen an unquestionable greatness in his presidency. Bill Clinton, unlike most politicians, went to great lengths to prepare himself.

In 1990, during the Iraq War, Clinton told me he wouldn't have done it that way. He was already preparing himself by watching the way George Bush, Sr., was handling the situation. He more or less lived out the presidency long before he became president. Normally, Arkansas governors would not be thinking like that.

• • •

To a large extent, Governor Clinton's administration followed the blueprint of the old Rockefeller administration. Rockefeller was the first governor to include African Americans in his administration. Clinton's, however, was a more natural relationship. He lived the life of an All-American. What set him apart more than anything else wasn't his brilliance but his focus, and he knew very early what he wanted to do, whereas many people get into politics to figure it out.

Orval Faubus was actually a pretty good governor until he became drunk with power and led by politics. He was obsessed with power and smart enough to make lots of people wealthy. I think he hired one black person during his whole four terms as governor. What most of us remember about Faubus is what he showed us during the 1957 Integration Crisis.

Winthrop Rockefeller was the governor who started the movement forward for blacks. This was a volatile time in Arkansas. I recall AM&N President Lawrence Davis inviting Reverend Martin Luther King, Jr., to be commencement speaker at the college one year, and the higher education board tried to oust him for that.

But Rockefeller put a black young man by the name of Sonny Walker over the Office of Economic Opportunity, and Sam Sparks, whose father had worked for Rockefeller, was one of his key advisors to the cabinet. What many people remember is that he granted clemency for everyone on death row before leaving office.

Dale Bumpers was a statesman even as governor. He was always seen as a very honorable leader and kept his administration clean from scandal. I think the same is pretty much true for David Pryor. Neither of them is remembered for outstanding actions, but they both moved Arkansas forward and also continued to bring blacks into state government.

Bill Clinton's administration, of course, set a new bar for inclusion of minorities in government. One of the reasons he was so successful was that he kept a pulse on all of his constituencies, not just blacks. But he had high-level aides who maintained close ties with the African American community.

There wasn't much that went on in our community that his office didn't respond to. It's difficult to point to just one particular policy or issue to prove he impacted the state and the African American community . . . he made most of us feel good about his being there and was a good ambassador for the state.

Bill Clinton never stopped being a politician, but he also believed in giving all people a fair shake. At the same time, not even Bill Clinton seemed able to get their hands around the problems in the Arkansas Delta. I'm not sure what it is that our leaders keep missing, but that's where we missed so many opportunities.

He will have a phenomenal legacy. I see him moving in other directions. He'll have tremendous impact around the world in the years to come. He's not tired, still filled with ambition. Clinton is even more powerful . . . he's one of those people who can articulate the world's problems and define some resolutions. History will burn away some of his human frailties, and he will be remembered more for what he did, despite all the years of distractions.

Q

Regina Favors, Jonesboro native; vice president, Blue Cross Blue Shield:

I met Bill Clinton at the Safeway grocery store on Main Street in Little Rock. He asked to borrow my pen to write himself a note. While he was writing, I excitedly told him I would be working in his upcoming campaign. He was really grateful and asked my name, and after that, never forgot it.

His greatest contribution to our state was the education initiatives he put in place to improve our quality of life. He also worked hard to improve race relations throughout the state. More than any other governor, he saw black input as valuable to the progress of this state.

His presidency was something we were all especially proud of. He gave the common person the opportunity to live a decent life. There has not been a president for whom people have felt so good about. We were able, as a community, to get decent jobs, invest our money, and achieve for our families.

There was a time when we imagined what it might be like if our struggles would completely disappear. People that I know, my colleagues and friends, felt nearer than ever before to living that American dream. I'm excited about the Clinton presidential library and what it can do to continue to heal racial scars.

His legacy as governor and president are much the same: he provided strong leadership, reaching out to all people. During his presidency, he brought a respect for public service that hadn't been there and reached more youth than any president before him. More people voted and registered to vote. He gave young people hope that things could be better, so they were inspired to become involved in politics and government. For a long time, young people didn't feel a part of our government.

Q

179

The Reverend Hezekiah Stewart, native of Liberty Hill, North Carolina; director, Watershed Community Development Center, Little Rock:

I came to Arkansas in October 1976, when Bill Clinton was attorney general. I met him in 1977, and we've considered each other friends since then. I met him in College Station—East Little Rock, considered the black part of town—when he and his young daughter attended a community event there. Believe it or not, Chelsea spent a lot of time in East Little Rock when she was a child, playing with some of the kids who went to school with her. Bill Clinton never seemed to have reservations about bringing his daughter around blacks.

● ● ●

A great leader is a man or woman who is compassionate, visionary, clear about where they're headed.

● ● ●

As for Bill Clinton, it never was a matter of his intelligence or knowledge of government: he literally cared about the people he was put there to serve. The rest of his abilities and his intelligence was just a tool he used to run this country. In 1978, after he'd been elected governor, I worked with the state's Youth Employment Support Program. People referred to him as the "whiz kid" who never forgot a name or a face. I guess part of that is having a photographic memory. The other part is caring about the people he met. Everyone knows that one of the most beautiful things is having someone remember who we are . . . and when that someone is a governor, that's magical. He remembered your name and the circumstances around your meeting.

When we were looking for funds to put the first health clinic out in poor little College Station, he stepped in and helped us with that. In fact, he made a lot of things possible for us to help the poor people of College Station. When one of our local activists, Annie Mae Bankhead, died, I developed a whole new appreciation for Bill Clinton. I saw clearly that he was the kind of governor who would be with us, not only during our celebrations but through our sorrows, too.

After a few years of his being governor, none of us were ever surprised to see him at a funeral, eulogizing someone we all knew in the community. For all practical purposes, people started to receive him almost as a family member. He often came to the

Watershed office during holidays with his checkbook and a basket of fruit to distribute to the needy. He was always concerned about the poor people in this state.

One night the governor drove by my office here and brought me this book by Taylor Branch, *Parting the Waters,* the first one he wrote on Martin Luther King. That convinced me that Bill Clinton understood the issues we were working on, that he knew the importance of helping to create a better life for the poor people of the state, to help them find jobs and get their GEDs.

When Channel 4 named me "Man of the Year," I looked out in the audience and there was the governor with tears in his eyes. Those are the kinds of things about Bill Clinton that were not revealed during his political years. Here was a governor coming out to East Little Rock with me, fixing baskets, passing out food. The people who didn't know Arkansas or the people of Arkansas—who didn't see the part of him that we did; those who were at odds with him politically—would never ever see that, and that was unfortunate.

James Lee Witt, his FEMA director, who had run the disaster office in Arkansas, said basically the same thing: the people of this country never, ever saw his heart, and that was a tragedy within itself. First of all, there were so many who were dumbfounded that he made it, they could never see his heart.

He stopped me one day while we were at a conference at Hilton Inn and asked what would I do to change the welfare system in this country. I told him I didn't think it was beneficial to allow welfare recipients to continue to receive resources without asking something of them in return. I suggested funding be used toward scholarship stipends so that welfare recipients were able to go into some kind of training, so the money could help them to grow and not stay stagnated in the way they were living.

I have to believe he used some of what I said in crafting the welfare to work program. The thing with the welfare to work program is, you have to instill love and motivation and inspiration in people before they will believe in the process. And that's what Bill Clinton envisioned for the program.

Back in 1991, I introduced him at a program held at Bethel AME Church in Little Rock, and I told the audience that they were looking at the future president of United States. He just looked at me, shook his head, and smiled. But I had been watching him and knew he was going to be president.

When he awarded the Little Rock Nine the Congressional Medal of Honor, it was a moment in time that vindicated all that had happened back in 1957, including Orval Faubus' role as governor. It was one more way he tried as president to correct some things in America's history, sins against humanity and against the minorities in this country. His acknowledgement of the sins of slavery and apologizing for slavery meant a lot.

In 1997, when the tornado ripped through College Station, he came here and prayed with me, and we walked together through the damaged area. The people in College Station were so grateful to have him here, dispensing his special brand of charm, his genuine compassion, and touching the people. When he went back to Washington, he sent his cabinet members and aides to ask us what we needed. The Mennonites came in here and built 22 new homes and helped repair about 85 homes. Transportation Secretary Slater, HUD Secretary Andrew Cuomo, FEMA Director James Lee Witt, Senator Dale Bumpers, and so many more.

After all these years of needing one, College Station now has a sewer system. If Bill Clinton hadn't been president, that likely would not have happened. We would not have gotten the kind of rapid response this area received. A lot of good things came to Arkansas thanks to Bill Clinton, whether people will acknowledge it or not.

When he was going through that deal with Monica Lewinsky, it was like a whole lot of us felt as if we were going through it with him. I wrote him a letter and told him in the letter, if you're innocent, stand your ground, but if you're guilty, tell the truth, because those of us who love you on this side will love you on the other side. He sent a note back thanking me.

His contributions as president are many. His unwavering policy on inclusion, from the attorney general's office to the White House. He allowed this nation to see that African Americans were just as capable of handling this country's most important offices as any other human being. Bill Clinton was the motivating factor for many young African Americans going into politics and law. America will one day see the impact he has been on our community, above and beyond any other president's impact.

His legacy will be that he had an uphill climb in everything he did, yet he came out the victor. America was the beneficiary. He was the president anointed by God to lead the nation into a new era of economic development and racial harmony: a caring president and an extraordinary politician.

CONVERSATIONS IN ARKANSAS

The Reverend Larry Ross, North Little Rock native, former vice president, Southwestern Bell:

I met Bill Clinton in 1978, when he was attorney general, and I was a member of the Art Porter Trio. Though his future definitely lay in politics, he loved music, and I think he actually considered playing saxophone with the Art Porter Trio at one time. The trio was performing at one of the Little Rock clubs when I met him. He walked up and introduced himself, and we started shooting the bull. We were just fellow musicians that night, talking about music and a host of other things. I learned that night that he could talk nonstop about any subject.

* * *

A great leader must first be a good follower and a good listener. One must have integrity, vision, and a willingness to take a stand. Like one old Negro spiritual goes, "Even if I go by myself, I'm going."

* * *

As governor, Bill Clinton stood out for his philosophy of inclusiveness. He went well beyond what he had to do to place blacks in decision-making positions. I don't know whether that was something he consciously set out to do, but for the first time, blacks were appointed to every state commission and board. We became players in state government. I thought that was refreshing—a statesman who was also proactive.

But also, Bill Clinton wasn't fulfilling quotas. When he made me the first black member of the Arkansas State University board, he'd done his homework and learned that I'd done some work in that area with early education programs. That's the way he operated in making appointments.

He reminded me to a great degree of Governor Winthrop Rockefeller. I actually got my start in politics as a Republican . . . which was very unusual in Arkansas, until Winthrop Rockefeller came here. My mother worked for Governor Rockefeller, and in 1966, she became one of the first African American Republican committeewomen.

Thanks to Mrs. Rockefeller, the Henry Shedd Trio—the band I played in during my college years—was invited to play at the National Republican Party's Convention in New York and other Republican Party events. Much like Mrs. Clinton, Mrs. Rockefeller had a lot to do with the governor's progressive points of view. So a lot of things Bill Clinton did to move the state forward, racially,

183

Governor Rockefeller tried to do during his two terms. There will never be another Bill Clinton.

Of course, even as loyal as black Arkansans are to Bill Clinton, we also know that there were things that didn't get done under his leadership. He had a lot of battles to fight and a great deal of opposition to some of the changes he tried to make in the state. While there was much effort to move the state forward in the area of education, we should have actually moved a lot further along. Education was never funded at the level it should have been. Even through his tenure we maintained regressive taxes, high sales taxes, and exemptions for forestry.

There is no question that moving from a small, rural state like Arkansas to the center of power and the White House must be quite a journey. Imagine the change from working with legislators who you know by first name, probably visited in their homes and know all their kids, to a legislative body made up of people from different cultures, different regions of the country, and many different views on how to run a country and structure legislation. Unfortunately, a lot of people in Arkansas expected him to be able to have free reign over laws and policies in D.C. just as he did in Arkansas.

His greatest contribution was economic stability for the country. Many business people were able to increase their bottom line, and more people were able to access capital. The John Johnsons of the world and the Bob Johnsons of the world definitely benefited. My hope is that we will see, years later, how the economic trend trickled down to the masses and to our community.

My disappointment in his presidency, however, was that he didn't put at least one person of color on the Supreme Court. That would have made a significant, long term impact.

The Clinton legacy? At a very critical time in Arkansas' history, a young visionary happened into the political arena and made a difference in everyday Americans' lives. He took that responsibility serious, even as a young man with a vision, a high energy level, and a drive to actually make a difference in the lives of people.

Bill Clinton never saw a problem that he didn't think he should solve. I sincerely hope his future will include continued work on the big three: education, economics, and opportunity, especially in the Delta areas in this country. His foundation and his will to do good are both still intact.

The Reverend William H. Robinson, Jr., pastor, Hoover United Methodist Church; founder and CEO, Community Developers Corporation:

I met Governor Clinton in his office at the state Capitol. He was meeting with the Christian Ministerial Alliance, which was up in arms about the governor's position on capital punishment. I was a part of that group of ministers that included Bishop Walker, Reverend Young, Reverend Willingham, and others. We had concerns about the disproportionate number of African Americans executed in the state. This particular meeting, though, was centered around one particular stay of execution. As I recall, our request for a stay was granted.

My first impression of Bill Clinton was that he was very politically astute. He knew the issue, had studied it. Apparently, pressure was coming from his conservative constituency, who wanted to continue capital punishment without any real study as to why so many African Americans were being executed. Later, he spoke to the Ministerial Alliance about his platform and why he should be elected. I think we all thought he would make a good governor.

● ● ●

A great leader is a person who is politically astute, able to get a task done without total alienation of a body, but is also able to look at himself and make changes. Politics is the art of compromise.

● ● ●

In terms of bringing equity and justice across racial lines, he did a superb job. Rockefeller was the other governor who stepped out when it came to inclusion, but Rockefeller had the where withal to underwrite the positions he placed blacks in, since the state wasn't willing to add them to their budget.

The fact that Rockefeller followed Faubus and had deep pockets to hire people was a great incentive for Democrats and Republicans to vote him in. Without the rich white folks' support during the 1957 Integration Crisis, I'm convinced that Faubus would have taken a different approach to that whole thing. There's no doubt there were other powers calling the shots.

But Clinton went several steps beyond Rockefeller, of course, in appointing blacks to positions with authority. He did a yeoman's job with diversity in the state government. He also surrounded himself with people who represented both sides of the spectrum.

He was, without question, the most progressive governor we've had in Arkansas and the first governor to have such vision to make things happen.

As president, Bill Clinton made history with appointments such as Ron Brown, Rodney Slater, Bob Nash, Alexis Herman, Togo West, and all the rest. In making those appointments, he said to America, these people have the ability to be in high profile roles and do a good job. It's helped young blacks feel that they can achieve not just the glass ceiling but beyond that.

He was politically astute enough to put a new wrinkle in politics. He was strong enough to cope, even against the odds. I was in Washington two years before the election for a workshop and told a group about Bill Clinton dedicating our first HUD house, how he went back and started calculating how many HUD houses were in the state. I half-jokingly announced to them that President Clinton came by, and they thought I was crazy. Even then, a lot of us believed he was destined for the presidency.

I think how he played out his last term was politically smart, in that he was able to play out his last term. I wish he had been just a little bit more supportive of Jocelyn Elders. I think her statement was a substantive one based on reality. There were some things he couldn't say, but he could've used others to fight that battle. At the same time, I understand politics and the fights he was up against.

Even during the scandal debacle, most people accusing him fell even before he did. The Democrats didn't really challenge Republicans, who I thought were far more unethical. He couldn't do it himself, but I wish there had been a closer look, early on, at people like Newt Gingrich. The Democrats just didn't play dirty ball, and this time they should have.

I wish there had been more interest in supporting Somalia and some of the other countries where killing and genocide have been happening for years. I'm a pacifist, but when we're the only ones who feel we can manage the weapons of mass destructions . . . that's a form of terrorism in itself. Bill Clinton started off with a boom when he moved his office to Harlem. I think that pretty much demonstrated that he walked the walk. He could've settled for just being another Jimmy Carter.

Richard Mays, Little Rock attorney; international business consultant:

I met Bill Clinton in 1973 when I served in the state Legislature. He just lost a race for Congress against Paul Hammerschmidt, so I thought it was strange for the losing candidate to be addressing the joint session of the House and the Senate. After his speech, though, I fully understood why he'd been invited down to speak.

Though he was very young, he was already poised and full of charisma. I remember thinking that Bill was like a younger John F. Kennedy. There was certainly that Kennedy image, that Kennedy charisma and intellect, but I think Clinton had a lot more going for him.

Once he became governor, it was clear there was a lot more to him than just his charisma. I was pleasantly surprised when Governor Clinton called me up on the phone one day and asked me if I wanted to serve on the Supreme Court. My first question was, "What Supreme Court?" And he laughed and said, "The only one I have any power to appoint you to." I recall saying to myself, if a lawyer doesn't have the time to serve on the Arkansas Supreme Court . . . he should probably be a doctor. So I was his first African American appointee to the state Supreme Court. Even then, I didn't know him that well, though I knew and served in the Legislature with his good friends Rudy Moore and Steve Smith, and I knew Hillary.

●   ●   ●

A great leader has to have a true vision of where he or she wants to take his constituency and have exceptional communication skills to influence that constituency. He or she has to have courage to swim upstream at times and has to have the energy and imagination to excite the constituency and bring the best out of that constituency.

●   ●   ●

Clinton was the greatest governor Arkansas ever had. He really created a partnership in government by giving African Americans opportunities beyond anyone's expectations from a Southern governor.

●   ●   ●

When I campaigned for him, I'd remind voters there had been only one black ever appointed to the attorney general's office before Clinton. He appointed five black assistant attorneys general. His level of commitment to involving African Americans and creating diversity was just unheard of.

When I graduated from law school, Les Hollingsworth and I were invited to a meeting with L.C. Bates, Governor Rockefeller, and a black Republican by the name of Ronald Coleman. I don't remember the issue, but it was my first opportunity to meet L.C. Bates, who was very forceful and deliberate with Governor Rockefeller.

Governor Rockefeller recruited people like Sonny Walker, Les Hollingsworth, Sam Sparks, and Ozell Sutton, and placed them in positions we'd never held before. He appointed Judge George Howard, who was a Little Rock lawyer then, to the State Claims Commission.

The fact that Rockefeller came after Orval Faubus highlighted the change that took place in state government at that time. Before then, most blacks with promise left the state. Rockefeller made some of us realize that we could make a difference inside the state.

Bill Clinton's greatest contribution to the state was to serve as a symbol of what a true democracy can be. The dream is what Bill Clinton personified. He prepared himself to run the state, and though he was very brilliant, he maintained the common touch, using all his experiences to change the infrastructure.

Arkansas didn't really know him at that time, didn't have a reason to trust him, and, to a great extent, waged a political battle against him. It was very much similar to the theme of David and Goliath, and I would say he won a number of those intermittent battles.

What he proved is that Arkansas' leaders don't have to be rich or famous or liked by all the powers to be. What was very important, as he tried to change Arkansas for the better, was that he was able to be independent without being controlled by the power base or money interest in Arkansas.

He was able to communicate with the conservative white Southerner, yet maintain his principle and commitment to the African Americans. He was able to bring people together and get the best out of them with the force of his personality, charm, and energy.

I do think Bill Clinton should have been more political when it came to bringing resources, especially economic resources to his own state. I can certainly appreciate his not wanting to play politics that way, but there is a certain level of acceptance in politicians showing favoritism. Arkansas had a huge role in helping create Bill Clinton, the great politician. Many Arkansans believe they didn't get the kind of returns they expected.

As much as some people want to ignore it, Bill Clinton's involvement of blacks at the social and political level was unprecedented. And I never once thought he was less than genuine and real. But he didn't just serve us . . . he created a climate of stability for the entire country.

He made Americans feel proud to be Americans and able to enjoy that time and place. And though few political writers will admit it, he created a comfort level between blacks and whites that just could not exist before Clinton. Not even Johnson's civil rights bill did that.

His legacy will be that ability to bring people together of all different nationalities and interests. There is no comparison to him, anywhere, when it comes to a human being being able to open lines of communication among people.

He should continue working with Third World countries, become an intricate part of this evolution. I would like to see him focus more on a stronger link between an economic and political vision. He should keep working on corporate America, making them understand the common sense and urgency of reaching out to minorities and women, making them a part of the infrastructure.

Bill Clinton has changed very little, and I imagine that's been hard, given all the changes in his life. I watched him during his campaigns as he began to travel at warp speed and was amazed at how he handled that speed as effectively as anyone possibly could.

The real contributions of Bill Clinton to America and the world will be seen more clearly in the future. Clinton's weaknesses were primarily that he was a man. He held so much promise for some, but that very promise frightened others. He was scrutinized like no other president before him, because he was both a promise and a threat.

I'm convinced one of the reasons he wasn't able to make some of the systemic changes we wanted was that he never fully understood and never waged an offense against the powerful group of politicians who both feared and hated him. My concern is that the opportunity will never avail itself to us again. Who, in the next century, will have that kind of vision, that kind of compassion? His lost opportunities seem greater, because he was our only hope for change and because God bestowed such gifts on him.

There are two instances that defined the complexity of Bill Clinton. The first time I saw Bill Clinton most stressed was before he made the decision to pull his support from Lani Guinier.

I happened to be in the White House meeting with Mack McLarty that day, and Bill Clinton came in and said he wanted to talk to me. He and Vice President Al Gore were having lunch, and after lunch, he asked me to stay for a meeting he was having with advisors on the Guinier decision.

There were about 15 to 20 people in the meeting, including a few African Americans—Maggie Williams, Vernon Jordan, Alexis Herman, and myself. All the usual players were there, including George Stephanopoulos, Mack, and the rest. It was a very interesting meeting, with some rare insights into his advisors' positions. I'll just say the people who advised him to continue his support were far outnumbered, and they weren't the people you'd expect.

Mack asked me after several people spoke what I thought. I simply said the meeting was too large. He took a break and pared the meeting down and moved to his study. About eight people remained. In that meeting, he asked again what I thought, and I said my heart said she should be submitted to the Senate, and my mind wanted to know from him what the price would be. Stephanopoulos said the Senate would deal with the issue in three to four days.

I empathized with the president, because I saw him trying to force an answer when I think in his heart, he knew he wasn't right. If he was taking an exam, he would have failed. Both Gore and Stephanopoulos said, "Submit her."

When the meeting broke up, the president said he needed to go and think about it. I've never seen Clinton in so much distress. He knew the right thing to do, but his political instinct wouldn't let him do it . . . he could see his opposition using it against him. He was torn emotionally, almost like trying to figure out a way to do it without confronting himself.

It was a time I'd seen him literally at a loss . . . even more than the issue with Lewinsky, in a way. Though I disagreed with his final decision, I gained a lot of respect for the anguish he was in . . . the desire to do right.

One of the other times when he gambled on doing what he felt was the right thing to do was when he sent troops to Haiti. He did not have the support for that. He played chicken but made the decision to commit before he knew the general was going to back out. That was a time he showed a willingness to take a big risk . . . but he knew that whites didn't want to see deaths there, either. Bill Clinton is a very complex man with a deep sense of right and wrong, no matter how politically brilliant he is.

❂

Arkansas State Senator Tracy Steele, North Little Rock native; former Rice University basketball star:

I met Governor Clinton at a fund-raiser for Easter Seals. I was on my way back home from Chicago. I'd recently graduated from Rice University and was working for a small marketing firm. I went to this event with a friend, and Bill Clinton was the speaker. One thing he said stuck with me, that it was important to keep Arkansas' educated youth in the state.

I was on my way to an interview for IBM in Dallas, but I decided to hang around to try and meet the governor. When I introduced myself, he already recognized me from my basketball career at Rice. We struck up a conversation, and he asked me what my plans were for the future. I told him I was particularly struck by what he said about keeping young people in the state and had a particular interest in coming home one day. I happened to have a resume in my pocket and gave it to him.

Two days later I received a call from Bob Nash, his top economic advisor. Bob asked me to come by his office to visit with him. I figured he was simply doing a courtesy call, but, in fact, a week after our meeting, I was offered the job as Coordinator of Rural Development. So Bill Clinton and Bob Nash are directly responsible for me starting my public service and political career here in Arkansas.

● ● ●

A great leader doesn't mind letting people know what they stand for and don't stand for, regardless of public opinion or outside voices. I count people like Dr. Martin Luther King, Reverend Billy Graham as great leaders.

● ● ●

Bill Clinton did in the 1990s what John F. Kennedy did in the 1960s. He brought another generation of Americans into public service, whether it was voting or getting involved in politics. Bill Clinton and John F. Kennedy did that more than any other president.

He put African Americans in positions of leadership in the state, and his cabinet was the most diverse cabinet in the country. He put good, smart people of color in positions of leadership and changed the public face of the state of Arkansas. That was especially important because of Arkansas' history. We had long been remembered for our negatives.

I have no desire to change what happened in 1992, but his rural development initiative, his Delta Initiative, and his contract with other states could have all been tremendously successful if he had remained in Arkansas. He was very committed to the Delta Initiative. And all the momentum we saw during his last term was lost. The Delta area is still in trouble. The population is steadily decreasing.

His greatest contribution as president was stabilizing and growing the economy. When he was elected, I think a lot of people who had never had confidence in our country and our economy were suddenly converted. Once mom and pop businesses started growing and everyday people began entering the financial arena, it spurred the stimulation of a successful economy. No other president has ever done that. I think that's why it remained strong so long and allowed him to fund a lot of his initiatives that no other president has had the opportunity to fund.

Arkansas could and should have done much better under his presidency. But the biggest reason was all the negative attention we received around Whitewater. The jury is still out as far as what Arkansas will eventually gain. I was involved in a couple of efforts to secure contracts for the state. There's no question we would have gotten those contracts had it not been for the conservatives' attack on Clinton. People were just a lot more wary. Even Congress had a much more careful, watchful eye about any federal assistance the state received. The entire state was hurt by it.

The Clinton Legacy? He changed politics. He won't get the credit now, but history doesn't discriminate. Everybody has a campaign bus now, everybody does town hall meetings. Bill Clinton reminded people that you can touch and feel the most powerful person in the world. He made people proud to be

Americans. His greatest legacy is what he did for race relations, the leadership he provided. He made the promise of an administration that looked like America and fulfilled it.

☉

Sherman Tate, native of Marvell, Arkansas; vice president, AllTell Corporation:

I met Bill Clinton in 1978 during one of his campaign events, just prior to his first election as governor. I remember his energy and natural excitement about the political process. He relished having an audience to talk politics, social issues, and economic development. As a pretty good judge of character, I sensed in him a genuine sincerity. I have always believed Bill Clinton honestly believed in the issues and causes that he promoted. I've always respected that.

● ● ●

A great leader is smart enough to know what they know and smart enough to know what they don't know. Great leaders, down through history, have always exemplified honesty, integrity, courage, and a humility that allows them to remain grounded.

Bill Clinton was a courageous leader who promoted and supported unpopular issues that had a direct impact on minorities and African Americans. The diversity of his cabinet and staff proves this. He was the first president who reached out to qualified people regardless of their race or ethnicity. In fact, he committed to bringing in people of color to represent the full diversity of America.

I think history will record that, eventually, hopefully, for the value and the significance it really represents to this country and to the younger generation. Especially, it says all the things that need to be said in terms of the value of people and the importance of doing what Martin Luther King called "judging people on the content of their character" and, in this instance, also their knowledge, skills, and abilities, and not the color of their skin.

In a way, Clinton was like Franklin Roosevelt, who led our country at such a critical time, through the Great War, from a wheelchair. I can recall my dad saying when Roosevelt spoke, everybody was glued to their radio, listening to the president. And as a result of that, the country came together, and there wasn't anybody—male, female, black or white—that wasn't committed to doing whatever they could do during that war.

Henry Ford was another great American. He exemplified great leadership, vision, courage, because it was a risk. We tend to forget how dramatic that change was.

As governor, Bill Clinton made a huge historical statement when he changed the complexion of state government. Blacks served in very meaningful positions. I was director of personnel management for the state; Henry McHenry was head of the State Employment Security Division; Mahlon Martin was head of the Department of Finance and Administration, which was responsible for the state's billion dollar budget. This was a significant accomplishment for a Southern governor in a very Southern state.

One missed opportunity for Governor Clinton was that at the end of his first term, he got bad advice on taxes on car licenses. This adversely impacted senior citizens. In politics, children and senior citizens are golden. You have to be very careful about policies that impact those constituencies. That's like messing with motherhood and apple pie. Had he paused long enough to think about it, he never would have had a break in his term as governor. He would have sailed right through. That was certainly how Frank White capitalized and wrested the governorship from him.

Bill Clinton used the two years that Frank White served as governor as political moratorium, to regroup. During his first term, he had surrounded himself with very bright people, mostly Eastern-schooled whites but some African Americans. Many of them, though, were novices when it came to Arkansas state government and the political process. He put a lot of trust in these young folk, who were not politically savvy to the process.

Actually, as much as he did for race relations, he missed a lot of opportunities to build coalitions between white and black communities. He would have been better served with some older, more experienced folk on his staff, at least enough to balance the youthfulness of the young people he had.

I watched from my perch as administrator in the Office of Personnel Management, where we dealt with wage and salary administration with state agencies. A lot of the folk we had to interact with on behalf of the governor didn't understand the state's budgetary process.

The Clinton legacy? Bill Clinton gave America the opportunity to say we had probably the most brilliant leader in the world, an intellectual stalwart. How many countries can boast that their leader has the capacity to grasp and retain an endless reservoir of information, technical and otherwise?

He wasn't ashamed to support social issues that were designed to improve the quality of life for the masses, not just for those who already have. What most writers and journalists overlook is that many of those social initiatives benefited more white folks than blacks.

While his legacy will reflect that moment of a lapse in moral integrity during his presidency, I don't see that overshadowing his accomplishments of trying so hard to bring peace to the Middle East, his sleepless nights as he bartered peace for the world, and his successes in many areas. This will certainly be a part of his legacy.

As a former president, he can be a major influence in current issues that our current president and key leaders continue to grapple with—civil rights, in particular. It is naïve and short-sighted to think that America can suddenly take civil rights measures off the docket.

More than ever we need leaders with the ability and the capital to express how important these things still are. He should continue to push America on issues like health care. He probably has as much or better understanding of the issues as anyone out there that will affect the American people for generations to come.

Bill Clinton has matured and is much wiser than he was in 1993. The elderly say we learn by our hard knocks, that we are baptized by fire. By normal political process as well as the self-inflicted wounds, he has grown. He will continue to generate excitement, regardless of what side of the issue you're on, a die-hard opponent or loyal supporter. Through it all, Bill Clinton is a human who has shown his humanity. He'll continue to work toward something more perfect for all of us.

Senator Irma Hunter Brown, Arkansas state senator, Little Rock:

I had just run for the state Legislator in 1976 when I met Bill Clinton. We'd cross paths on the campaign trails when he was running for attorney general. Then later, during his campaign for governor, his campaign staff was looking for African Americans to host fund-raising events. My husband, Roosevelt, and I volunteered to host a fund-raiser at our home. I remember a young African American by the name of Rob Wiley joining him that night. But what I remember most is how Bill Clinton talked that entire night. The man never meets a stranger.

To some extent, I think you could say Dale Bumpers and David Pryor paved the way for Bill Clinton's open administration. They were good governors, though more moderate Democrats than Bill Clinton. Each of them had a limited number of African Americans in their administrations, but there was not the outreach effort to make the state government diverse the way Bill Clinton did.

After he was elected in 1978, Bill Clinton made it clear that one of the things at the top of his agenda was diversifying the makeup of not only the state agencies but the state's commissions and boards, too. Meetings were held, early on in his administration, to discuss adding minorities to all the state boards and commissions.

The late Senator Jerry Jewell and I agreed that the best way to get this done was to get the governor to endorse our recommendations. Rather than make our task harder by attempting to replace existing positions filled by whites, we solicited names of qualified blacks, submitted our list to the governor, and suggested he expand the boards and commissions to accommodate a more diverse membership.

That was, by far, one of Governor Clinton's most lasting legacies. Unfortunately, no governor since him has seen fit to assure that diversity is maintained throughout the state government. Ironically, the state's Highway Commission, which Rodney Slater headed before Governor Clinton left Arkansas, currently has no black membership.

After we got the 10 percent minority set-aside law passed here, a number of legislators were working hard to actually get it implemented at the state government level. It was a very difficult law to implement. I remember meeting with the governor with another black legislator who represented East Little Rock on the issue.

We were sitting there discussing the ins and outs of it, giving him an update of where we were and just telling him what a hard time we were having trying to get some of these agencies to take the law seriously. Basically, we told him we needed him to use his bully pulpit to let the agencies know how important this was to him. I'll never forget, the governor stopped us in the middle of our complaining, and said, "Look, you all are going to have to make me do this."

That was a rude political awakening for me. In other words, it was our responsibility to come out loud and forceful and demand that the governor get something done. If he did it on his own, he would be shooting himself in the foot, politically. This would alienate him from his white constituency, even the ones who called themselves open-minded about race.

What that told me was that, while he was sincerely sensitive to the needs of our community, he also was politically savvy. The truth was, and he knew this better than most of us did, we were the swing vote, not the majority vote. He couldn't cut off his nose to spite his face.

During his four terms, there were a lot of things that might have been done had he not been concerned about re-election or moving up to president. But, to be fair, the timing just wasn't right. He made dramatic changes throughout Arkansas, and no one can take that away from him. I think virtually the exact same thing can be said about his presidency.

But if you compare states like Texas, California, and Georgia, where presidents lived, you see a great deal of funds, programs, and infrastructure designated to those places. Arkansas didn't get those kinds of perks. But if you think about it, you realize that his terms were made up of uphill battles with Congress and the conservatives. They would never have let him get away with helping our state the way most of us would have liked him to. The man was constantly under siege.

It's because we think we know Bill Clinton's heart and believe he sincerely wanted to do so much, that some of us were disappointed that more wasn't done. I think the vast majority of Arkansans are proud that he was there and took the attacks as personal affronts to our state and our communities.

His contributions to America and the black community was that, for the first time in our history, all of America was represented at the table and in federal government. He painted a picture for our young African Americans that the world can be different, that if they work hard and prepare themselves, they can move far beyond their surroundings.

As a community, we benefited from whatever laws and policies he put in place, because for the first time there were more jobs available across the board. The unemployment rate in our communities dipped lower than any other time in history. For the first time, it showed that more of us were working than ever before. It had to be based on his leadership.

Something that most whites would never consider is the fact that for the first time, blacks felt welcomed at the White House. More of us visited than in all the years leading up to his presidency. That was good for our children, to see the White House and the federal government as ours, too. My young granddaughter would see him on television and say, "That's my president." I think a lot of black and white Americans felt that way.

There were a number of things I wished had happened under his watch. I know he totally supported the colleges, the historically black colleges, but there were some things he could have done to help bring black schools up to a more level playing field, in terms of making funds a little more accessible. And a lot of small business owners still had it hard trying to access loans or grants. He could have expanded on the small business loans and increased the set-aside funding.

We made a good start in the Delta when he was governor, but once he left, practically nothing has been done. You would have hoped, with his creative ability to craft legislation, something could have been done to help move that area forward. The Delta should serve as a showplace for good, instead of for the poverty that continues to exist there.

The Clinton legacy? He was a president who believed in representation for all. He worked hard to improve the quality of life for all Americans. I think history will treat him well because of the many challenges and obstacles he faced during his presidency and his ability to overcome them. As a result of his being able to overcome those obstacles, it showed the strength of his character. I do hope he'll continue to work on the Delta, make it one of his priorities.

Thedford Collins, native Arkansan; former legislative aide to Senator Dale Bumpers:

I met Bill Clinton in Washington, D.C., in the offices of Wilbur Mills. Patsy Thomasson, a mutual friend, introduced us. He was an intern with Senator (J. William) Fulbright, and we were all at a get-together the senator was sponsoring for Arkansans. He was really young and idealistic. We were both up there in a foreign land, and he was already talking about going back to Arkansas to run for Congress. When I returned home a few years later, he was doing just that . . . and I volunteered to help out in his campaign. At that time, northwest Arkansas was a laid back, sleepy region, but they weren't ready for a Bill Clinton.

●　●　●

A great leader can visualize, put together opportunities for people to become part of that visualization. He or she explains it and makes others want to be a part of that vision. A great leader steps outside the box. They're also good followers. You have to have followed to be able to lead others. People like Franklin Delano Roosevelt, Douglas McArthur, Martin Luther King, Jr., John F. Kennedy, and Bill Clinton.

●　●　●

Bill Clinton's contributions to the state of Arkansas included his leadership in the area of education and diversity within state government. Some of the things he did, other governors could have done. It wasn't easy or noncontroversial, but it was so necessary. History will be kind to him and will take a worthy look at his advancement of Arkansas. The kind of leadership he provided was the kind that brought the disenfranchised into the process. That was unparalleled.

After Orval Faubus, blacks were just hungry for anybody to recognize us as legitimate citizens. Winthrop Rockefeller didn't just do it in state government; when he moved to Petit Jean Mountain from New York, he brought black employees with him. He had also brought a notion that blacks deserved equality. It's amazing what God and a little money can do.

As president, Bill Clinton stabilized a long-unstable economy. He started America on the road to prosperity. As part of that, African Americans were able to move up along with that rising tide. Because of his administration's diversity, it said to corporate America, "You, too, can place competent minorities and women in leadership positions . . . at the top of your companies," and we saw that happen during Clinton's eight years.

He also elevated the country's international status and changed the way the rest of the world viewed us. He made this one-world philosophy real, in a way. His effort on the Israeli-Palestinian conflict is unparalleled.

As for missed opportunities, I think Bill Clinton could have given a little more effort toward education, the kind of work he did in Arkansas. If he could have expended that across the country, we would be in better shape with our educational system, our schools. I was a little disappointed that a larger effort wasn't made to make sure our immigration laws were made equitable. Unfortunately, the darker continents continued to be the ones that were sacrificed.

The Clinton legacy? I am one of those people who believe that history will be kinder to the Clinton presidency and the man than the media is now. Probably, his most impacting legacy is that he left the country in good, solid financial shape. He involved all Americans in American government. He pushed the vision that as this country goes forward, we have to make sure no person is left behind.

Our position on the world stage was set by him, and that was one of the best positions we've held in the 20th century. This was a president, I think, who studied and understood the global consequences of any and all of our actions. Did he have personal lapses? Yes, we all do. These things, I believe, will be footnotes to the larger story.

Pretty much, he is the same Bill Clinton I met almost 40 years ago. He is more polished. He still has that uncanny knack of recalling people from long years gone by. He is using more of his God-given compassion and abilities to relate to people. He's not as visible, thank God, therefore he's not the only picture on our 6 o'clock news any longer.

His future must include him staying engaged. He can't drop out. He has too much to offer. What Bill Clinton says matters. It always will. He has a responsibility as a former president to use that power.

☺

James Thomas Kearney, Sr., Gould, Arkansas; 96-year-old retired sharecropper; farmer:

I don't know exactly when I met Bill Clinton, but it was early during his first term as governor. My son, Jesse, worked for him in his second term as governor, after he lost to Frank White, then came back. I went up to Little Rock pretty often and visited my son at the state Capitol. And one time Governor Clinton asked if I

200

had time to visit with him in his office. We sat down and talked for—it seems to me it was about 30 minutes, but it probably was half that time.

We talked about everything. He asked me a lot of questions about how I'd raised all of my 18 children and seemed real interested. He also asked me questions like what I thought he should do about different issues—welfare, education.

I sat there talking and thinking that I was just a sharecropper and had never talked to a governor before in my life. But he made me feel like he was really interested in what I had to say. He also asked me how I felt about different governors that had served. I told him about the two I thought were pretty fair—Governor McMath and Governor Rockefeller. I told him I thought McMath and Rockefeller were looking out for the whole state, not just one class of people.

I have thought about it often since then, how when I was talking to him, it was just like talking to somebody in my own family. I forgot all about he was a white man and a governor. It was just two people talking about things that were of interest to both of us.

●　●　●

A great leader . . . and a good leader is a person who does everything he promises to do and what needs to be done for the people. He keeps his word with all the people. For instance, if citizens' pipelines or streets need to be repaired, the leader should supply those needs, whatever part of the city the need is. If he is the type of leader that cares for the whites and not the blacks or vice versa . . . that's not a good leader.

●　●　●

We've had some great leaders, like Martin Luther King, Jr., and President Johnson, who I think was the best president for black folk except for Bill Clinton. He said what he'd do and stuck to it. Bill Clinton kept his word and promises to the American people. He served all the people, not just one segment of the country: white, black, poor, and rich. He was everybody's president.

When I look back at other Arkansas governors, Winthrop Rockefeller was the best governor Arkansas had for black folk, before Bill Clinton. One of the things I remember him doing was getting rid of the racist overseers at the penitentiary. I used to hear stories all the time about how they murdered prisoners, buried them on the penitentiary grounds. Governor Rockefeller heard about it and had them to dig the grounds up. I liked his platform. He treated blacks fairly. One white woman at the voting polls said she hated Rockefeller so much she'd vote for a mule before she'd vote for him.

But before Rockefeller was elected governor, black folks would go into the social service offices and would be treated terrible. He heard about it and made sure some of the people were replaced with black workers. It was something back then, to walk into some of the offices and see black folks sitting behind those desks. It took a long time for me to get used to that.

Orval Faubus was the worst governor we had in Arkansas. He was the kind of politician who started giving you things when it was time for you to vote. But he never did anything for poor black folk all the time he was there. Some people said he was a good governor . . . maybe he was, but not for black folks.

Bill Clinton was the best president we ever had, and the best we ever will have, I believe. I think most of us considered Franklin Roosevelt a good president, although he talked about fairness and equality more than he actually did. John F. Kennedy didn't actually do a whole lot, but he made people feel good about everything.

President Clinton kept his word and his promises to the American people. He treated all Americans the same and was one of the only two presidents to treat blacks as if they were truly part of this country. I don't think he made one bit of difference between the races, sexes, or classes.

When he found that there were needs in one part of the country, he had his people to investigate it and supply the needs to the best of his ability. He utilized ways to assist people any way he could. He researched things about people's conditions that they may not have even known about. He didn't just talk about changing things, he did. All the promises he made on his presidential platform, he kept them. He didn't change his words or his voice when he spoke to blacks or whites. Spoke to all of us with the same voice.

There were some things I didn't like. I never liked what happened with Lani Guinier. The Republicans worked hard to find excuses until he almost had to let her go, but I wish he hadn't. I just believe she would have done a good job.

Also, Dr. Elders had done a good job there and was a smart woman. He shouldn't have let her go just because of what she said. I think that was used as an excuse by people who didn't want her there in the first place. He must have been satisfied with her work, or he should have let her go before then.

●　●　●

Bill Clinton's legacy? Americans will remember him for how he looked out for America. He worked for and supported things that will advance America. When he came before the American people, it was a broken country left by Reagan and Bush. We were billions of dollars in debt. He paid it off. They hadn't included blacks in very much of any of the jobs before.

There are so many things he still needs to talk about. He could advise our young people about working to improve government. He could talk to both black and white. I think he could be very helpful in teaching people here and outside the country about foreign affairs. He should do a lot of speaking, especially to our communities about the race problems.

I really wish he could have run again for president. The American people wouldn't be scared the way they are now. He has gotten much wiser from his experience. But he's the same person . . . kind and easy to talk to. I think that's his nature, someone who loves his fellow man.

──────── ☺ ────────

Katherine Mitchell, Little Rock native; dean, development studies, Philander Smith College:

I met Governor Clinton during his first term, in 1978. He and Hillary were honoring women in the Grandparent Program. My mother was one of the grandmothers involved. It might have been then that I told the governor that I was born in Hope, the same little town where he was born. I moved to Little Rock really early, though. During the Central High Crisis, I was sent back to Hope and attended Washington High School until Little Rock schools reopened. I graduated from Little Rock's Horace Mann.

●　●　●

A great leader is one who knows how to follow, a person who exhibits fairness, respect for those who he leads, values everybody. People like Martin Luther King, Jr., John F. Kennedy, and Bill Clinton.

●　●　●

Bill Clinton's greatest contributions to the country were the relationships he forged throughout the country and outside the country, his domestic and foreign affairs policies. While most people didn't have high expectations for him in foreign affairs, he proved the naysayers wrong and balanced domestic and foreign affairs very effectively.

He is the great communicator, as far as I'm concerned. He's a brilliant man who knows how to engage people, whether they are friends or enemies. We couldn't have asked for a better ambassador and leader of our country. It was probably a mystery to a lot of people that he would win the presidency the first time, and to do it the second time was probably unbelievable to a lot of people.

But he has always been phenomenal. He has always been able to address diverse issues that are significant to all Americans. Not only was he an educational governor, he did a lot for education on the federal level.

☙

Dr. Theman Taylor, native of Dallas; African American studies professor, University of Central Arkansas, Conway:

I met Bill Clinton through a friend who attended Loyola University with me. B.J. McCoy returned to Arkansas for his mother's funeral in the early '70s with the intention of returning to California but ended up remaining in Arkansas. Shortly after moving there, Governor Clinton appointed him as director of a state agency called the Department of Local Services.

My first time meeting Bill Clinton was at a reception held at the home of Dr. Dan Ferritor, then the president of the University of Central Arkansas in Conway. My first impression was that here was a different kind of white politician. My experience is that most white politicians used blacks to introduce them into the black community. But, either consciously or unconsciously, Bill Clinton never really needed blacks to pave the way for him. He already knew the way.

He didn't really need blacks to go out and speak for him. He could go by himself. I don't think most black people even understood that, but he really didn't need our help in that way.

I remember, also, his remarkable memory. The man should have been a historian. If he came on this campus, he would stop by my office and say, "This is the guy who wrote that article and tried to get my wife to run against me as governor." And that was a decade ago when I had written that article.

He was not intimidated and he did his homework . . . he knew where he was going, in terms of being around people. In Arkansas, he never needed anyone to introduce him to people. If he was going to Conway, he knew what the hot issues were in Conway, whether he was going to the black community or white community. He knew what was going on there.

● ● ●

Great leadership? I studied Kwame Nkrumah, who led the revolution in Ghana in 1957. One of the things he believed was that you have to be where the people are, and you have to know where they are and deal with them from where they are. You can't go in there with the solution, because leadership comes from the people. When the Black Panthers in the '60s said, "Power to the People," I interpreted that as, leadership comes from the people.

● ● ●

As a student of history, I've concluded that Bill Clinton was as much misunderstood by blacks as whites. Many of us grew up with this Messiah complex. But Bill Clinton's greatest accomplishment as a Southern politician was giving no real credence to race, making race no big deal. To most people, race is a big deal. So you can't describe Bill Clinton as a good race relations person in the traditional sense, because it was never about race when it came to him. He was different from any other president in that.

To get the right answer from Bill Clinton, you have to ask him the right questions. You have to ask him the same questions you would ask a black person, because he would ask the same questions in Watts as he would ask in Beverly Hills and still get invited to the AME bishops' retirement parties. Putting black folk in his administration is race relations for George Bush, not for Bill Clinton.

The Clinton legacy? Clinton made a tremendous imprint on individuals, more than he did on groups. He appointed individuals to positions to make a difference, to do a job, to make lasting changes. Sometimes it was those individuals who fell short of making changes to impact the masses. The difference in politics is that most presidents or governors don't expect their minority appointees to make lasting changes. Bill Clinton did.

Gene McKissac, native of Pine Bluff, Arkansas; first black president of the University of Arkansas' Student Government Association; Arkansas attorney:

I met Bill Clinton when he came to the University of Arkansas in 1974. He was this tall, striking young man who had this following of young law students everywhere he went on campus. They hung on his every word. So, immediately, my thinking is, "Here's another young lawyer, another potential superstar with an oversized ego." I didn't know him, but I knew that was common for Eastern-educated professors who came to the law school.

He was already preparing for a run against Congressman Hammerschmidt at that time, so I met him in the context of being both a young law professor and being a potential candidate. Clinton was extremely bright and extremely charismatic. Those were the two qualities I noticed about him immediately.

I never felt he was interested in teaching law as a lifelong vocation. It wasn't that he didn't do a good job—he did—but this was just a way station to wherever he was going, as opposed to some other professors, for whom teaching was their passion.

•   •   •

Great leadership demands that the leader has a foundation whereas he knows who he is, what his value systems is, and what his values are, so he'll always have a center post he attaches himself to. Great leaders seldom stray far from their core values. A great leader also has to have a sense of service—not self-indulgence, but service.

I think every great leader has a knowledge and awareness of history. Without that, you can't fully understand how your actions, today, impact the future. Harry Truman was probably the greatest president, in my opinion. Of course, there are leaders like: Winston Churchill, Martin Luther King, Jr., civil rights leader Medgar Evers, William Lloyd Garrison.

•   •   •

What Bill Clinton did for Arkansas was create a new image that said we were finally going to break with old-line traditions as it relates to blacks. He did that in a number of his policies and initiatives, but more subtly by including blacks into his inner circle, his friendship circle. He created the image of what blacks wanted to have, even if they didn't want the substance of it, as opposed to the image of 1957. That was the image we wanted to shed.

Clinton was the boy genius, the boy wonder who, through his cabinet, his friendships, and his style, and his manner, Arkansans were willing and ready to identify with, because it was the very opposite of Faubus and the "Justice Jim" Johnson era. He was good for Arkansas, and in many ways. He changed the direction of Arkansas to think more nationally, more globally, from that reputation of being an isolated rural state. That was important for us, but it also fueled his presidential drive in many ways.

Arkansans would have revered Clinton as a great statesman if he had stuck to his guns about really making a change in the Delta and in Arkansas. But I think at some point, after seven or eight years, his national aspirations became more important than the state of Arkansas. He was moving on . . . and maybe that was his destiny.

If he had remained in Arkansas and dealt with the educational issues and the poverty issues, I think he could have made intrinsic changes. He could have made more substantive differences.

Clinton's predecessor, Winthrop Rockefeller, deserves a great deal of credit for stepping out there to change the race equation in state government, given the era in which he was governor. His attitude of inclusion actually started blacks to thinking about the possibilities of change. Clinton made many of those possibilities reality.

He was, for certain, ahead of his time. He thought outside the box, and I believe he was one man that most Arkansans would follow even outside of the box, if he had stayed around. But you have to say . . . he did it his way, whether it was as governor or president.

One of his contributions to the state, ironically, was during his presidency. Because of him, people began to take a second look at our small, rural state. To a great extent, this universal view of Arkansas as being backward, country, unenlightened, and not serious about being enlightened, changed.

As president, Bill Clinton brought to the table a sense that he was in control and that he was a great thinker. He knew where he was headed, and, consequently, the country felt safe, felt at peace, even when they didn't understand everything he was doing. The Republicans had to manufacture the feeling of not being calm, by partisanship.

For the average American, there was a saneness, a sense of equality . . . a sense that we could trust this guy not to blow the world up, not to do something catastrophic for the nation as a whole. Average Americans, whether they approved of his personal life or not, trusted that Bill Clinton understood the world he was operating in.

What he did for this country, in creating stability for growth, led to investment and a booming economy and a reduction in the national debt. This showed America that we don't have to accept a trillion dollar deficit budget forever. For African Americans, he gave us the sense that real change and progress was possible, just as he did in the state of Arkansas. Finally, a president who showed that we can be different and still be accepted. That's what really empowered a lot of black people.

Sometimes, Bill Clinton put too much on his plate . . . trying to conquer a hill that didn't need to be conquered. While health care reform is much needed, the majority of Americans didn't view it as a national crisis. He was able to bring it into the country's consciousness. Maybe if he had gone about it somehow differently .

Bill Clinton's legacy will be his visionary leadership . . . a man ahead of his time. His wisdom was a result of his life's unique experiences. That gave him a greater understanding and appreciation for all people and for all life. He tried to communicate that and translate it into policies, laws, and actions.

But maybe his missed opportunities were tied to the fact that he was so far ahead of his time. While he was an imperfect human being, he had the character to deal with his imperfections and even to lead and do a great job in spite of them.

I think the press hates the dreamer that he is, his ability to be, in terms of a leader and a visionary, what a lot of people can't be. There's almost a sort of jealousy and hatred. They talked about the character flaws as if the people speaking didn't have their own character flaws. Like King, I think a lot of people were jealous of King because of his ability to speak, and write, and to communicate and paint a picture with words, and to take moral stands, and have the courage to try.

There are many people who prefer plodding leaders, so that they can run along beside them or be ahead of them. They hate the guys who have a vision of the world and can see that it is moving beyond what they understand.

I'd like to see Bill Clinton write something beyond his memoirs. I'd like to see him write about his world visions, and how these visions can be actualized. I think that would be real important to the younger generation. Then, to write about how he's overcome the things he's overcome. I think that would be an extremely important book.

When I saw how he handled himself through the impeachment and the controversy, I knew he'd never become mean-spirited or bitter. He still has that air about him he had at the law school. He's still the self-assured young man from Hope, and I don't think that will ever change.

☉

Pulaski County Judge Marion Humphrey, Pine Bluff, Arkansas, native:

I met Bill Clinton in 1967 when we both worked as interns in U.S. Senator William Fulbright's office. I was 17 years old at the time, and Bill Clinton was a 19-year-old Yale student, working directly with Senator Fulbright's powerful Foreign Relations Committee.

Senator Fulbright would, sometimes, take us to the Senate office building for lunch, and all through the meal, he and Bill Clinton would talk nonstop about foreign relations policies. Bill had a million questions and an opinion on everything! There was another young Arkansan by the name of Griffin Smith there during that time. He's now managing editor of the *Democrat Gazette* newspaper.

I saw then that Bill was real smart, ambitious, and very friendly. There were a lot of students there who weren't as open and friendly, but none of us were nearly as interested and inquisitive about everything as Bill Clinton. When I returned to Senator Fulbright's office the next year, Bill Clinton had already left for Oxford as a Rhodes scholar.

My next contact with Bill Clinton was at the University of Arkansas' Law School. He was a professor there, and I took a criminal procedures course under him. He was a very good instructor, but I think we all knew that his real interests were in politics. A big joke around campus at the time was that he lost some of the students' test papers somewhere up in northwest Arkansas while he was out campaigning for U.S. congressman.

A lot of us law students, black and white, volunteered in Bill Clinton's campaign against Hammerschmidt. Nobody ever worked harder than Bill Clinton did, though. Northwest Arkansas wasn't as conservative as it is now, and Democrats actually had a shot back in

209

those days. But he lost the race in Sebastian County, by far the most Republican county in the state.

• • •

A great leader is a man or woman who keeps the concept of service for the people foremost in their minds and hearts, constantly working toward those policies that best enable the general population to advance.

• • •

Bill Clinton's greatest contribution to the state was the accessibility he afforded African Americans. He involved lots of African Americans in his administration, especially during his first term. During his four terms as governor, constituencies who had never had access to a governor's office or his appointed agency liaisons were able to call on people they knew to help with community projects and learn how to apply for state funds. There was an amazing amount of access to the state Capitol and the governor's mansion during that time.

As president, his greatest contribution was the number of political appointments he made to people of color at all levels of federal government. For the very first time, people of color felt they could approach agencies, departments for funding and assistance and be treated fairly—not given special treatment, but fairly.

One of the most important things President Clinton did was his signing of the executive order dealing with banks and how they dealt with minorities and making economic development opportunities available to minority communities. Many blacks see that as one of the actions that impacted our community most . . . and it was done without a lot of drama or fanfare.

There were things I was disappointed in, too. His failure to reconsider the federal sentencing guidelines and the impact they have on African Americans. Not just the cocaine/crack disparity, but federal sentencing guidelines impact the black community so negatively. It takes a judge's power away. This area was neglected by him, and I think it had a lot to do with his distractions during that time. I'm convinced that's why he didn't do more. But it would have made such a difference in the disparities in the judicial system.

Some judges feel the sentencing guidelines actually worsened during the Clinton presidency. The federal prison population continued to grow, and without a doubt, the guidelines continued to impact the minority community more negatively. The growing number of African Americans sitting in federal prisons is a national shame.

Bill Clinton was a very energetic governor and president. He was well-versed, and I think he studied for the job all his life. I think he was a president in command of the office. He was an independent thinker and never seemed to need his advisors, though he must have utilized their expertise.

But he is clearly a politician, above all things. That means there were some things that were compromised. He did a good job of maintaining his positions on policies for African Americans in the areas of domestic policy and affirmative action. He was on the right side of those types of issues. He didn't waffle too much on the basic tenets of affirmative action. A lot of times, even those who tend to believe in it often waffled on it.

Bill Clinton should continue to work on the Race Initiative, even though he doesn't have the bully pulpit any longer. More than ever, we need a voice like his to speak out for peace in the Middle East. I don't see him as someone who will just sit down and relax. He still commands an audience, though, and probably will for years to come.

☉

Annie Abrams, retired Arkansas educator; longtime DNC official:

I first met Bill Clinton when he was running for Congress, and the Democratic Party was about at the same point we are now . . . trying to wrestle northwest Arkansas away from a Republican incumbent. He and his young wife were law professors at the university in Fayetteville. Though he had left Hot Springs for an Eastern education, he had returned to northwest Arkansas, and the Democrats thought he might be one of the state's next political stars.

We certainly hoped he would overthrow Congressman Hammerschmidt, but he didn't. It was obvious that there was potential there. He had the personality, the charisma, and the drive. The party realized this first race was just an internship for his future political life.

I've been a part of politics since I was 13, when I was brought into the East End Civic League, headed by Mr. Jeffrey Hawkins. That was the most organized Democratic advocacy group I've ever known. Then, when Winthrop Rockefeller ran, I became a

Democrat for Rockefeller. When outsiders questioned that, we always said it was his philosophy on race and education that won us over.

Bill Clinton moved to Little Rock in 1975 to run for attorney general. All the black kids who had been in Bill or Hillary's classes and had relationships with him helped integrate him into the black community. When he won as attorney general, a number of those young lawyers went to work for him. Joyce Williams Warren was one of the early people he brought in and later appointed as one of the first black federal judges in the state. Clinton came in at a time when black elected officials were trickling into the state Legislature: Jerry Jewell, Irma Hunter Brown, Henry Wilkins, and William Townsend. Their relationships with Bill Clinton had a lot to do with my support of him.

Reverend W.O. Vaught at Little Rock's Emmanuel Baptist Church was Bill Clinton's pastor. Reverend Vaught was a good friend of Reverend Fred Jack, who was a friend of mine. So it was through Emmanuel Baptist that I got to know Bill Clinton personally. Of course, back then, the Southern Baptists and National Baptists didn't have any kind of race or civil rights policy, and whether he knew it or not, Bill Clinton belonged to a very conservative church.

Of course, Reverend Vaught was a man of God, and he sort of adopted Bill. Even though it was a conservative church, I sometimes visited during Christmas and Easter programs, and Bill Clinton was always singing in the choir.

I learned from the Puckett boys of Hot Springs, where Bill grew up, that the black community embraced Bill Clinton because of his love of music and, especially, the saxophone. The Pucketts were a well-to-do black family in Hot Springs who had a very popular band for a long time. I'd met them when they played for one of the Democratic conventions in Hope.

They told me, way back then, how Bill Clinton was different from most white kids in Hot Springs, and how he'd actually shared the mouthpiece of one of the Puckett boy's saxophones when he didn't have one. That was pretty much unheard of.

I did teacher training in Hope when I worked for the teacher's association in 1969. I also participated in the organization's interviewing process for political candidates. During my 27 years with the association, I met and interviewed candidates for governor, Congress and presidents. The first campaign I actually worked for was in the '60s when I walked the streets for Hubert Humphrey.

My husband was a bartender and waiter at Little Rock's Riverdale Country Club. Of course, it was segregated at the time, but Orville, my husband, worked there for a lot of years. And that gave me a bird's-eye view of what went on in a lot of those white political meetings held at the local hotels and country clubs. My husband knew Orval Faubus on a first-name basis.

When John F. Kennedy came to Arkansas to review the Murray Lock and Dam, he went to the Riverdale County Club for dinner, and my husband, Orville, came home and told me that John F. Kennedy wore tailored suits and his pants didn't have pockets. So he never carried any money and always had to ask whoever was with him for money . . . just like our own Bill Clinton.

Through my husband, I learned about some of the politicians and leaders and was able to analyze them before they came to power. I knew when Orval Faubus was coming down from the hills to be governor and that he had been "selected" by the powers that be . . . and I knew a lot of them, too.

Bill Clinton would always have some power behind him, financially. Like a lot of young politicians, the Clintons didn't have a lot of money, which means sometimes you have to carry the power people's agenda along with your own. Even Hubert Humphrey wasn't rich by a long shot.

Rodney Slater was one of the young, up-and-coming politicians I mentored. He would often ask my advice on political issues . . . like the time Bill Clinton spoke at the DNC Convention in Atlanta and embarrassed himself with that long speech, I made sure I got my message to him through Rodney.

One criticism of Governor Clinton's black appointments was that they were class-focused. Most times, he brought in people who already had class distinction, already financially secure. He was criticized for failing to reach outside a certain circle and appoint ordinary black people.

I know he felt comfortable with ordinary people, but at the same time, he was selected by privileged folk for his intellect, his charm, and charisma. The people like Fulbright and Pryor recognized that Bill Clinton was a great asset, so they adopted him like their son.

When he was first announcing in different places that he was running for president, he took a trip up to New York to meet with a group at The Waldorf-Astoria. That was in 1991, and he was there to meet the people who could secure that Eastern bloc of money that can make or break politicians.

I happened to have a friend who knew Donald Trump. I think a lot of black people in New York saw him the way we viewed Bill Clinton in Arkansas. My friend had campaigned for Adam Clayton Powell and had known his father, who was pastor of that big church in Harlem. So when Bill Clinton went to New York for the money people to look him over, here was this 60-year-old black woman sitting there to "look him over," too.

Later, she told me that someone was about to introduce Bill to her at the luncheon, and she said, "You don't have to introduce Bill Clinton to me, he's already been endorsed by Annie Abrams . . . and that's good enough for me." He just laughed and told her how he and I had been "prayer buddies" over the years.

That prayer thing started back when he was going through some difficult times, when Hillary was being criticized about not using her husband's name, and then his loss to Frank White. I would call him up and tell him I was praying for him, and we'd talk about the power of prayer. So I became his prayer buddy.

We've been through a lot with Bill Clinton. Like the night in 1988 when we were so proud he had been chosen to make the introductory speech for his friend, Governor (Michael) Dukakis. We thought if Dukakis could win, then Bill might actually have a chance.

Of course, Jesse (Jackson) was running that year, and most of us were there with Jesse. But Arkansans were so proud that Bill Clinton was making that introductory speech. When the lights started acting up, and everybody was saying he was talking too long, we did our best to keep a stiff upper lip.

The next morning, the papers came out saying he had made a fool of himself. Rodney came down to join us at breakfast, and everybody was talking about Bill Clinton's speech. We asked Rodney how he was, and he said he was really "down," that he didn't think . . . he probably wasn't coming down. Lib Carlisle, head of the Arkansas Democratic Party, and Lottie Shackelford went up to talk with him.

Finally Hillary came down, and just as she did on national television, she stood by her man. She literally whipped the group into shape and actually made us feel guilty about the way we were feeling about him. Most people don't know or don't remember that it was Hillary who came down and got the group back in fighting mode. That was an important time.

But Bill Clinton's marginal victories have always been through his black support. And I don't think he'll ever forget that, but a lot of people who worked with him did. The black Friends of Bill who traveled the country campaigning for him never got the same recognition as those few who ended up going to New Hampshire.

I recall, during his presidential campaign, Carol Willis, his political person for the black community, had rallied a group together to go to the New York convention. We had this raggedy bus and were trying to tell Carol that some of the money being spent by the campaign ought to be spent in the black community. Carol Willis worked it out for us to rent Reverend Booker's church bus. It was a raggedy old bus, but we made it to New York in it.

I told David Wilhelm, the president's political director, "We've got to do three things: win Illinois, because that's where you and Hillary are from; win New York, the little U.N.; and win our own state." And I think that's how we got to New York. By the time we got there, the president had been visiting some places in Harlem, and he saw a bunch of us had just arrived in town. Those are the times he forgets to be presidential. He hopped out of that motorcade, ran up, and hugged all of us, yelling to the media, "These are my people!" I think Bill Clinton depended on the emotional support that black folks always supplied him.

We called churches and preachers, and within 12 hours, we had to figure out who could speak where. I did a crash course on public speaking. *The New York Times* made a point that the Arkansas delegation definitely made a difference in the New York turnout and his winning there.

We traveled on that same raggedy bus to Chicago, and it was basically the same shoestring operation. When we returned to Arkansas, everyone was so proud. In Illinois, we were riding on the coattails of candidates in the Daley Machine. Besides the churches, we visited labor unions, nightclubs, and even bowling alleys.

Congressman Bobby Rush scheduled a number of places for us to visit. I remember standing up in a nightclub speaking, and the audience got so interested in the political process, they stopped the band, turned up the lights, and allowed us to take over for an hour.

When we visited black churches in Illinois, it wasn't unusual to find out you knew half the people there. A lot of the ministers were born in Arkansas, Mississippi, or Alabama. I would ask if anyone was from Arkansas, and half the church stood up. When Bill Clinton arrived in Illinois, he got a rousing welcome. He was still hopping over ropes to shake hands or hug people then.

We traveled to the very Republican state of Ohio, where the Clinton campaign was having a hard time. The lady down the street from the campaign raised $2 million in her home for the Republican Party. That didn't stop us. Everywhere we went, we told them about Bill Clinton's leadership, his caring, and how he had institutionalized inclusion in Arkansas.

As great a governor as Bill Clinton was, I am still disturbed that Marianna, in the east Arkansas Delta, is still the poorest town in the state. Our economic development is still poor. We have no black hotels, no amusement parks, no true economic anchor. We still don't have a black statewide elected official.

I know Bill Clinton's heart is in the right place, and he's probably listened to as many black sermons as I have . . . but maybe the power brokers really did have the last word when it came to intrinsic change in Arkansas.

Unfortunately, many of the people who were vital to the Democratic Party didn't come back to Arkansas. In a way, his presidency created brain drain in the African American community. We all love the man, respect him . . . but Arkansas communities are still hurting and missed out on a lot of economic benefits during his eight years in the White House.

The Clinton legacy? Bill Clinton was an ordinary person who turned out to be extraordinary. Someone from the state of Arkansas, that wasn't supposed to produce such greatness. The fact that as governor and president, he gave us opportunities, a chance to prove ourselves, the country can't deny that we are more than nannies and bubbas. The stain on his morality was unfortunate, more for us than the white community. Without that baggage, I know he would have done so much more.

Q

Arkie Byrd, an attorney with Mays, Crutcher law firm:

Bill Clinton was teaching at the University of Arkansas' Law School when I met him, in 1975. Actually, that was before I began law school. It was an informal meeting . . . just a hello as we walked through the halls. I was actually one of Hillary's students, though he still sometimes mistakes me for one of his students.

• • •

216

I don't categorize leaders in relation to their avocations because I believe it transcends one's occupation or socioeconomic level. Most important is that vision thing, which seemed to stump the first Bush White House. Also, the ability to dream a world that even you might have a hard time articulating to people. Very often great men and women visualize things before they are able to articulate them.

I think . . . in addition to vision, great leaders are people who see opportunity and take advantage of it. Part of that is knowing yourself and being honest about wanting to be a leader, not being afraid to embrace your instincts. Great leaders who have impacted our world, our communities, or their own families are usually driven by passion, but they also have an innate, intuitive sense of justice. I think of people like Alabama civil rights leader Fred Shuttlesworth, Gandhi, and Fannie Lou Hammer.

● ● ●

I was not living in Arkansas during most of Governor Clinton's tenure. I returned to the state in 1984 and hadn't particularly kept up with Arkansas politics. When I returned, I recall controversy about teacher testing. What stands out in my memory, though, is my involvement in a civil rights lawsuit that dealt with voter registration and redistricting amendments.

Several Arkansas attorneys did a voting rights case with the NAACP. Lani Guinier was one of the lawyers from the NAACP Legal Defense Fund who worked on that case. It was my first case as a cooperative attorney. She was counsel representing the NAACP, and I was the local counsel. DeVal Patrick was also on that case, and it was the first time I met him.

The case started in 1984, and we were able to settle it. Much of the credit goes to Governor Clinton, whose intervention helped immeasurably. It actually allowed us to resolve that lawsuit amicably. My hope is that it created great opportunities for access to the polls. In fact, our decree embraced motor voter. Our consent decree required the state to allow people to vote when they registered their motor vehicles, as well as at other state agencies. So Arkansas was ahead of the curve on that one, and his direct involvement was very helpful.

Since I wasn't in Arkansas most of his time as governor, I don't know which initiatives took precedence, but I recall there was a Delta Regional Initiative. But the Delta is still poor and without strong industrial economic salvation. There is still an out—migration of the population. I do think, though, that some of the responsibility of what hasn't been done in the Delta should be borne by the leadership in the Delta. The only thing they had was their vote. They certainly should have elected on that leverage they sought from any administration.

The Clinton presidency is a juxtaposition of so many things. Maybe I would think differently if I hadn't worked in Washington, D.C., and in public policy. That level of intimacy makes me know the actual realization of what actually made a difference will take time. I don't think grading his accomplishments right now is fair for his administration. I just think it will take time.

There were things I felt positive about, things I was disappointed about, and there are some things that I was just confused about. There are some things that I haven't quite reconciled. I was probably the last person in the world to read Kenneth Starr's report. I didn't read it and had no desire to. For me, I just don't want to know that stuff. It doesn't affect what has always been his positive effectiveness. I made a conscious decision during this administration not to talk to the press about the president or Mrs. Clinton. I was called often, and, basically, I still don't.

Times and tenor are so different. Certain stones were removed by the time Clinton became president. He's in a different era, with his own set of challenges. For my mother, who was born during the Depression era, a teen during World War II, there's nobody like Franklin Roosevelt.

I will forever measure every president against Lyndon Baines Johnson, a very complex man. From what I understand—and I was living during the time he served as vice president and president—he was a very passionate man and determined on the things he was determined on. I just can never forget the history of the passage of the 1964 Civil Rights Act and the 1965 Voting Rights Act; that was just so much a part of my coming of age and what I remember as being significant.

Jim Crow had not quite died out when I was born, though I don't have as strong a memory of it as my mother, who came of age during that era. But Lyndon Baines Johnson was absolutely tremendous. Yes, he was a man who was vulnerable, but so is everybody. That does not mean that this man was not significant and very powerful in his willingness to take on some of the most important legislation in the 20th century.

A very small number of presidents have used that kind of capital on issues involving race. Of course, the times may have created that, but I honestly think that man had a passion for justice at a certain level, and it informed who he was. I don't think you had to convince him it was the right thing to do . . . I think he had to convince a lot of other people, but I don't think he needed convincing. The Democratic Party has not been the same since that particular point and time.

I just think there were some people who felt there was not room in the party for a president who would help lead the charge of "doing the right thing," and those people who just came from the Old South tradition, culture, political perspective, ideology, and belief. I just think that caused a clash within that party, and I think it is still reverberating.

I've always heard money wasn't that important to President Clinton. He had excellent credentials and could have been on Wall Street. He's a smart guy, and we should give him some time to make some money. All ex-presidents, now, will be measured by Jimmy Carter. Who knew he would be a player on the world stage as an ex-president? He came into his own, and he grew.

There was a transformation that went on with Jimmy Carter. I certainly hope there will be a transformation process that takes place in Bill Clinton. I don't know if it's begun, but I think I'll know it when I see it. If he's fortunate and blessed, he'll let it happen.

Bill and Wanda Hamilton: The late Dr. Bill Hamilton served as director of Arkansas' Family Planning Agency for a number of years. His wife, Wanda Hamilton, is a former Arkansas educator in the Little Rock School District:

We met Bill Clinton when he was running against Hammerschmidt for Congress, around 1973 or '74. At that time, he was new to Little Rock politics, so he would come down from Fayetteville where he was teaching and meet with the Black Leadership Roundtable to talk about his platform. He was all over the state, talking and meeting people.

I don't think anybody really expected him to win, but the way he was carrying out his race, we thought he might win by a long shot. The Roundtable supported him in that race. After that race, he ran for attorney general, and we helped and supported him again.

I grew up in Hope, the same as Bill Clinton, but didn't realize until we got to know each other that I knew his family. His grandfather owned a grocery store that sat between the black and white communities. It was near my home, and I went there and shopped many a day.

Mr. Cassidy still used that old-fashioned accounting system—everything was recorded on note pads. He was always nice to anyone who came through his doors, and we always felt comfortable that he was an honest person.

I must have seen little Bill Clinton in that store at one time or another. That physical setting had to be good for him, helped him learn to relate to blacks and whites. He probably played with both colors and saw his grandparents provide for the needs of both black and white people. Our community was borderline poor, so that store served people from both poor and middle-class homes. I think that kind of atmosphere was valuable to Bill Clinton.

Sadly, I can count the number of memorable Arkansas governors on one hand. Before Bill Clinton, there was Winthrop Rockefeller. When Rockefeller set up the Governor's Council on Human Resources, he appointed a young black man by the name of Ozell Sutton to head it up. When Ozell left the position, he appointed me to run the council. I was so impressed when Rockefeller met with me and told me what he wanted the job to do.

Governor Rockefeller personally paid for the operation of the office. He told me he wanted me to get black people hired in state government and to work with hot spots across the state in regards to the integration of schools. He provided us with a list of the hot spots and authorized me to go out to these places and meet with groups. I spent most of my days in that job trying to increase black employment in state government.

The governor also authorized me to write letters to the agencies telling them what he wanted them to do, and to sign his name. We would give him a report of the agencies' responses. The council was a very small office. Before Wanda and I married, she worked as a receptionist in the office. Henry Jones, now a U.S. Magistrate, and Perlester Hollingsworth, who was one of our first state Supreme Court judges, worked there, too.

Winthrop Rockefeller wasn't charismatic, but he was genuine. He visited our office fairly regularly for meetings. We met in the evenings or at night. He let us know that he didn't schedule many meetings during the day. He generally wasn't around the office during the daytime. He would meet with us sometimes at 6:30 in the evening, when the rest of the workers had gone home. We had his undivided attention for about two hours.

We received reports from all the agencies, boards, and commissions telling us the number of blacks they'd hired. Governor Rockefeller would read those reports. We all knew who had no blacks and those that had no intention of hiring blacks. The state's banking commission was very segregated, and I was determined that I would personally follow up on that one.

I met with the chairman of the banking commission, and naturally he told me he'd tried but couldn't find any qualified black person. I told him I'd find him someone and get back with him. A young man by the name of Charles Bussey had just graduated from college with his master's degree. I met with him and later took him by the commission for an interview.

When we walked into the chairman's office, he quickly left and sent in the white office supervisor. The supervisor was very insulting during his interview with young Bussey. When he finished his interview, I told him it was crystal clear why he couldn't find "qualified" blacks. He was very angry.

Rockefeller consistently pushed to integrate state government, and slowly we started to see some improvements each year. We'd travel to towns where people had told us we shouldn't go, and stir things up. Texarkana was one of those places. But we saw some real changes in communities' racial interactions. Texarkana was a good example, where we did a follow-up visit and saw that integrated meetings were going on, with people from both communities fully involved.

Governor Bumpers was progressive, too, in his own way. I was with the family planning office during his term and found him to be a big supporter of family planning. He committed to increasing family planning funds while he was governor. Not only did funding increase, but he authorized expanding the program all over the state, and to assure that it was implemented in every health clinic in every county. There were a large number of those small, rural clinics—as well as the head of the state's Department of Health— who were against federal and state funds being spent on family planning. But we had the governor behind us, and it was implemented throughout the state.

I was very impressed with Governor Pryor's leadership, as well. His mother was very active in the Presbyterian Church down in Camden. I had become very involved in community service at the time, and though we were in Arkadelphia then, we had a partnership with the black church in Camden. Mrs. Pryor helped us get grants for programs for the community. We set up one of the first daycare centers for infants down in Arkadelphia. Governor Pryor and his mother were very instrumental in that.

We all saw something special in Bill Clinton when he came along. Here was this young, liberal-leaning, smart guy with all that activity he was generating around him. It meant a lot to the black community to have someone we saw would one day be significant in Arkansas politics show genuine interest in us.

When he ran for his second term, Arkansas voters—the white voters mostly—took out their anger about license taxes. The Frank White campaign was a backlash. Many people who voted for Frank White simply wanted to pass a message on to Bill Clinton. Many of my white colleagues said they didn't really mean for Frank White to win, but they wanted Clinton to get the message about the direction he was taking the state.

And then, there was Hillary. Arkansas just wasn't ready for this smart, independent governor's wife. There were even women mad at her for not taking her husband's name or staring up in his face as if he was God, the way politicians' wives are supposed to.

When he returned to the governor's office in the next term, I think he did an even better job at running the state. I was still director of the Arkansas family planning department, though Frank White had threatened that he would get rid of it and cut out our funding. We had a tremendous fight that went all the way to Washington.

Reagan was president at the time, so Governor White had all the support he needed. They put up a really good effort to close the office down. The only thing that saved us was a $10,000 Rockefeller grant that had just been approved. I think it was the largest grant they'd given us at the time. When I told the governor we'd lose the grant if he closed down the program, he decided to divert the funds over to the governor's office. He hated the family planning agency that much.

I was livid, and when I returned to my office, I called the Rockefeller Foundation. Bob Nash was vice president there and the person who had written off on our grant. He promised to take care of it and called me back later to say it was taken care of, but the money would have to go through the governor's office.

There were enough of us angry at Frank White that we formed a statewide coalition of doctors, nurses, social workers, and county health workers. We put the word out and worked day and night to make sure Frank White would lose the next election.

When Clinton resumed the governorship, we all felt Arkansas was back in good hands. Both of the Clintons are very smart people, almost geniuses, and they surround themselves with good people and use their ability to understand and empower people.

Hillary was a great leader for the Advocates for Children. Once, she was the keynote speaker for our statewide youth conference in Atlanta, and she got there about 10 minutes before time for her to speak. She asked me what we'd discussed that morning, and after I gave her a five-minute overview, she went up before that crowd and blew them away . . . without one note. She integrated everything I had told her and reinforced it with her own knowledge and experience and being the first lady of the state.

The years of the Clinton administration were good years for the most part. It was exciting to see things improve for so many people, to see hope revived, and we know from the records that things got better for a whole lot of people.

LaVerne Feaster is former president of Arkansas' Future Homemakers of America and serves on a long list of boards and commissions:

My earliest association with Governor Clinton was through my role as an educator. When I first met him, I found him to be one of the most ordinary people in high places I'd ever met. I knew both Clintons before they became famous, mostly because of their concern for ordinary people. When I was the district home economist, I did training throughout the district, and Hillary came to Hope to speak on family and child development. After that speech, all the other district leaders were so excited and impressed, they clamored to get her into their districts.

When I was appointed head of Arkansas' 4-H organization, I learned that Governor Clinton was very interested in reaching out to young people. We implemented something called the Governor's Award, which was given out at our annual state 4-H-aramas. Governor Clinton was invited each year and came just about every time to present the awards to the winners.

But he didn't just present the award and leave. He arrived before the banquet started, talked with the kids and their parents, sat and ate with the rest of us, and, after it was over, sat for a while longer to meet and greet people in the audience. He was that kind of person. I finally asked if we could have the Governor's Award winner at the mansion, and he and Hillary agreed to it. Hillary would entertain the kids during the entire evening . . . they were just like ordinary people.

I was working in Arkadelphia as a home demonstration agent for Arkansas' 4-H agency in 1965 when we finally integrated the office. The 4-H office for black people had historically been housed in the black part of town, but after integration, the office was moved to the courthouse. Winthrop Rockefeller visited the Arkadelphia courthouse during his campaign, and for the first time in my lifetime, a politician actually talked to us, not just the white agents. He promised if he was elected, he'd make some great contributions to education in the state.

It was so exciting to have Bill and Hillary Clinton leading our state. I was so honored to be a part of a small group of people the governor would call, from time to time, and ask how I thought he was doing in different areas of state government. He also asked for suggestions about what he should be doing in the black community. There was a small group of people he invited to his office to discuss the needs in the state.

Bill Clinton always looked for ways to help people with less resources—he'd never say poor people. It wasn't just when he was campaigning, but this was all the time. He valued input from ordinary people. He was genuinely interested in what we had to say.

I'd often meet with Hillary and a small group of women, too. There was Dorothy Stuck, Nan Snow, Pat Gray, and myself—we'd all meet for lunch at the office and sit there and talk. Hillary would say, "Bill has all these good old boys working for him, when what he needs to do is take names and kick butt." We would laugh, because everybody knew Bill had a big heart, and even if somebody gave him a lousy idea, he might not use it, but he'd never tell them that he wouldn't use their idea.

Bill Clinton was brilliant, but I've never heard him put anybody else down. Even if he was talking to the Pope, and he saw a sharecropper walking by, he would stop and say hello to the sharecropper. I think some people took advantage of his big heart, and that sometimes caused him problems. Even though he was smart, brilliant, he wasn't intimidated by other smart people. He realized there was plenty of room at the top.

Out of all the blacks he hired over the years, I don't think you can point to one that he hired simply because he wanted to hire a black person. They had to be capable of doing a job first. He had a gift of being able to empower people.

I was so sad that we didn't get health care reform. He can't be completely blamed for that, but it was a huge loss for the country. And then, after the scandal, he had even less leverage with the Congress. He could have done so much more. As for the state, it would have been wonderful if he had empowered some group or agency in Arkansas to sustain some of the things he put in place as governor

I'm convinced, though, that a lot of what he didn't do was because he was not one of the good ole boys. Everyone knows Bill Clinton didn't invent extramarital sex. A number of presidents before him were guilty of similar behaviors. He was an outsider, though, and the Republicans and conservatives decided to air his dirty laundry in front of the American people. Other presidents' scandals were shielded and kept from the public by the media and their aides.

His legacy is what he did for all Americans. He was progressive, and always had people around him who could carry out progressive initiatives. The status quo didn't mean much to him. He was a visionary who taught us that we should not be complacent, not be satisfied with the status quo.

☉

Bob Nash, a native of Texarkana, Arkansas, served as Senior Economic Advisor in the governor's office and was later appointed president of the Arkansas Finance Development Agency. During the Clinton presidency, he was appointed Undersecretary of the U.S. Department of Agriculture. For the last six years of the Clinton administration, he served as director of presidential personnel:

I met Bill Clinton during a political event in 1975 when he ran for attorney general. A number of friends had mentioned this young, white guy running for attorney general that I should support. They thought he seemed fair and had a history of working with African Americans. I went to the political event to see for myself.

My first impression of Bill Clinton was that he was a great speaker. He shook every hand at the event, and when he shook your hand, whether it was five seconds or 30 seconds, when he walked on to shake the next hand, you felt as if you had had his undivided attention. I was convinced that he was a different kind of politician . . . especially for the South.

● ● ●

A great leader is someone who is able to see what things that could be, the possibilities, as opposed to just focusing on how things are. It is someone who can help others see what the future could be and can rally people to work toward that. This kind of leader is able to describe that better future in a way that you can see it, feel it . . . almost touch it. Who comes closest to that definition? Three men immediately come to mind: Reverend Martin Luther King, Jr., (former South African) President Nelson Mandela, and President Bill Clinton.

There have been some presidents who I would put in that category. Certainly, I think Bill Clinton will go down in history as one of the greatest presidents. He's at the top of the list for what he contributed to black America. Kennedy and Johnson also contributed a great deal to the African American struggle, but Bill Clinton used his bully pulpit to change the culture of America, to convince us that equal opportunity for all Americans should be more than just a theory, but practiced in our everyday lives.

What most people fail to consider is that he was trying to do this in a more complex environment than the '60s. People are smarter, more sophisticated, convinced that they are already liberal, when, in fact, they are more jaundiced about morality and doing the right thing. Matters of humanity 20 years ago were seen as either right or wrong: good or evil, black or white. That, in some ways, made it simpler during the Kennedy and Johnson era.

Not taking away from what Johnson and Kennedy and even Lincoln did, I still think for Bill Clinton to make the kind of progress for African Americans as he did over his 30 years in public service was truly something not many people could pull off. We're talking about seeing what he believed take shape, not just laws or theories or promises.

As president of the most important nation in the world, he signaled to private industry, Fortune 500 companies, that it was OK to hire and promote African Americans. We had passed the litmus test when he brought us in to run federal government agencies, to serve in high-level positions in the White House, to be appointed as judges and commission heads.

Amazingly, it was a rich man—a Rockefeller, who had grown up in the East—who began to turn the tide for Arkansas' archaic racial culture. Little to nothing had been done for Arkansas' black community before Winthrop Rockefeller. He was the first governor to recognize African Americans as a viable community. I recall one instance, before Rockefeller became governor; I had a meeting in the state Capitol, and after the meeting I walked downstairs to the Capitol restaurant to eat. The workers there hurriedly told me I couldn't eat there. That was in the late '60s.

Governors Dale Bumpers and David Pryor were moderate Southern governors who successfully moved us to another level. They both acknowledged the importance of African Americans being treated fairly and equitably. They stood by the law, and more than once, Dale Bumpers went beyond just what was law to acknowledge what was "morally right."

I think most people would agree that they were good for Arkansas, men of their times, and as we all know, they both represented the state of Arkansas magnificently in the U.S. Senate for many years.

Winthrop Rockefeller probably would never be elected as a U.S. senator. He wasn't made out of that kind of material. However, as an Eastern implant into Arkansas state government, he was in a position where he didn't have to depend on funding from people who disagreed with him to pay for his campaigns. He had more freedom to be a rebel for causes he believed in, and race relations was one of the things he was sincere about, in spite of the fact he had little real experience with the struggles of black Southerners.

One of his greatest legacies as governor will be the number of businesses he brought into our rural state. That was actually done before he became governor, when he was appointed to the Arkansas Industrial Development Commission under none other than Governor Orval Faubus.

Bill Clinton, without the money of Winthrop Rockefeller, reached out to make his state Capitol and his office a diverse one. It was politically smart, and it was the right thing to do. I remember one night in 1982, after being re-elected to the governor's office, I got a call at home that night from Bill Clinton. He told me he'd been studying my work at the Winthrop Rockefeller Foundation and was very impressed.

We talked for a long time about the state's needs, about economic development in Arkansas and what he wanted the state to look like in 10 years. We talked about how other states looked at Arkansas as cheap labor, attracting low-wage industry. He said, "Arkansas is better than that."

He wanted to create new money in the state, bring in foreign industries and foreign investments, grow small and minority businesses, improve the skills level of the Arkansas work force, and promote what Arkansas had to offer all over the world. That excited me tremendously . . . things I had often thought we should be directing time and capital to.

After he had just about talked me out, he got around to asking me if I would come to the governor's office to run his economic development office. I was flattered, but I was very happy at my current job at the Rockefeller Foundation, where I was responsible for identifying quality community and state programs and funding them.

I also knew the pay at the governor's office wasn't that good and the working hours were endless. Once he talked me into coming, I told him I would not be his economic development person for the black community only. He said, "Your responsibility will be statewide." After thinking about it overnight, I called back and said I'd take the job, and even with less pay and longer hours, it was a great experience. We were able to put in place many of the very things we'd talked about that night.

What was exciting about working with Bill Clinton was seeing him walk the walk. He was committed to diversifying every board, every commission, every department and agency. He did it. He put good people in visible places, and it had an impact all over the state. Even in the private sector today, you have African Americans in all levels of private sector, because Bill Clinton sent that signal that it was "smart and the right thing to do."

When people question his compassion and passion about equity and fairness, I think a lot of that is fueled by jealousy. Some is just ignorance of what the man is about. Throughout the years I've known and worked with Bill Clinton, that question has never entered my mind, but that's because I was able to see pretty close to his heart. I've seen him vent about the futility of racism. Bill Clinton knows more African Americans, their families, their backgrounds, than any politician, black or white, in this country. What they do, what they care about—certainly more than any other president in American history.

Bill Clinton could never be accused of tokenism when it came to bringing blacks on board. As governor of Arkansas, he was known for recruiting the best and the brightest. I think he understood the argument from white America that we weren't as competent or as capable as the white person next to us. He brought in people who were viewed by both blacks and whites as competitive.

During his tenure, African Americans were appointed to run the Department of Finance Administration; the Department of Local Services, which dealt with counties and cities all over the state; the ADFA, Arkansas' bond agency; and the Department of Social Services.

Bill Clinton's vision of what could be was evident in so many instances. For many years, there was hardly any effort by the state of Arkansas to support African American businesses. People outside the state would point to us and say we were one of the Southern states without a civil rights law, and it can certainly be debated why we never passed one. But Bill Clinton was, in fact, a living, breathing advocate for civil rights for Arkansas. Throughout his four terms, he sought ways to equal the playing field for minority-owned businesses, making sure those businesses got a piece of the state mandated contracts.

Bill Clinton's White House years were, to a great extent, an extension of his years as a governor, but on a much larger platform. For the first time in the history of America, you had large numbers of African Americans at every level of government, not only as occupants but advocates for policies, laws, programs that sought to change past inequities. Most importantly, there were advocates who were able to make a difference for existing and future generations.

I didn't see him change in the middle of the stream. The same issues that concerned him as governor continued to concern him as president: health care, education, economic development, and the environment. And in just about every one of those cases, there were African Americans at the table. Not by accident, either, but because Bill Clinton said, "I want an administration that looks like America." Many of the policies passed during his eight years will affect families and people of color for decades.

It amused me when people, black and white, thought he just happened up on the black farmer's issue at USDA, that it wasn't something he really had any background with. What they didn't know was that one of the most important and effective programs he could have championed during his 12 years of Arkansas leadership was the black farmers' land reclamation program.

An important piece to black history is how black families lost millions of acres of land through unscrupulous means in the South. Dishonest whites would use methods like tax sales, adverse possessions, and partition sale to buy out a family's land ownership. Bill Clinton was the first and one of the only Southern governors to introduce and enact laws to prevent these illegalities. We worked with Southern activist programs to reclaim thousands of acres of land for blacks.

There were over 60 African Americans in the Clinton White House at various levels, and he appointed more black assistants to the president—the highest level of anyone in the White House except the president—than all the former presidents combined! There had never in the history of American government been more than one black assistant to the president at any one time, and that was Colin Powell. Louis Martin, who served in the Carter era, was a special assistant, and Bob Brown, who is recognized as helping open the doors for blacks in the White House, was as well.

There is, frankly, no comparison, when you talk about a White House with people like Alexis Herman, who served as Director of Outreach before being appointed to head the Labor Department; Minyon Moore, who ran the president's political office; Ben Johnson, who ran the One America office; Thurgood Marshall III, the Cabinet Secretary; Sharon Farmer, director of the White House photo office; Terry Edmonds, who led the speechwriting division; and Cheryl Mills, who was counsel to the president . . . and those are just the assistants to the president.

What Bill Clinton did was to find the best person for the job, regardless of race, with a mission to have an administration that looked like America. So today and tomorrow, a president can feel comfortable bringing in the best person, no matter what their color, and, at the same time, commit to diversity.

There are countless speeches in which Bill Clinton talked about all people coming together, respecting each others' differences, celebrating our differences, taking advantage of those differences—because each and every one of us can contribute something to making this a better country.

If I had to name one missed opportunity during the Clinton administration, it would have to be his failure to do more in the area of racial profiling. It continues to be a pervasive problem in this country, and we should have done more . . . using the bully pulpit and leading the way to change some old antiquated laws.

He did some speeches on it and made it known he knew it was wrong, but there should have been some muscle behind that. Even though we know it's primarily a state and local issue, the president is known to take on state and local issues when they are pervasive.

The Clinton Legacy? There were those who said the federal government was too big for one president to reduce the deficit, balance a budget, invest in underserved communities and individuals of this country. Bill Clinton proved them wrong. He did it with good leadership, vision, and good people behind him. I think he actually educated the American people on a very important fact: there is a reservoir of good, competent, capable people who are "different" but who can serve this country and serve it well.

He gave America a very basic economic lesson: the more prosperity for all America, the better off America is. Prosperity means consumerism, which means America's economy soars. He grew the number of countries wanting to become allies of the United States by reaching out to lead but not bully.

He recognized the continent of Africa in a different kind of way than any other president or world leader . . . as more than just a fuel stop or safari event. He acknowledged their struggles as well as their contributions to the world. He governed as if families and children mattered. They weren't mere numbers and facts to be relied on during the election season.

I'm convinced that, had it not been for constitutional restrictions, Bill Clinton could have served another eight years and done it well. I think, given the fact that money is not what drives him, public service will always be his driving force. He could run a Fortune 500 corporation or serve on a bunch of boards and get very wealthy, that's never been what Bill Clinton was made of.

He probably will be very rich, but he will spend the majority of the rest of his life trying to bring people throughout this country and this world together. In true Clinton fashion, his presidential library sits in an area that was predominantly black for decades. But his library will be a living, breathing, giving institution, and through that vehicle, he will continue to bring world leaders together in an effort to make the world a better place.

When historians or talking heads impress each other by comparing a leader like Bill Clinton to people like John F. Kennedy and Lyndon Baines Johnson . . . I have to think that we are either looking at our past through rose-tinted glasses or comparing apples and oranges.

Greatness comes in its own time. All three men are great for different reasons. What Bill Clinton was able to do in the here and now, neither Johnson nor Kennedy could have done in the '60s— America wouldn't have stood for it. It would have caused that second civil war we were trying to avert in the '60s. In my mind, only a Bill Clinton could have done it, and done it so magnificently.

The most definitive moment with Bill Clinton, as to who he is and why he will always be one of the greatest leaders in history, took place during the period I served as his economic advisor for the state. We were on our way to a meeting in Pine Bluff with a bunch of bankers, and, as usual, we were late. The governor had probably not slept most of the night, so he was taking his 10-minute nap that would take him through to the next day.

As we were driving down the highway, he woke up, looked over on the side of the road, and saw a bunch of farmers at a small stand. He immediately told the driver to stop. Of course, I was the handler for the day, so I suggested to the governor that maybe we shouldn't stop, since we were already behind time. He said to me, "Do you know what those bankers will say to me . . . what their complaints are?" I thought a minute and said, "Yes, we're clear on what their concerns are."

Then he looked out the window at the farmers and asked, "Do you know what those farmers out there on the side of the road are thinking . . . what their concerns might be?" Of course, I said no. We got out, spent about 10 minutes with the farmers, and miraculously got to our meeting on time with the bankers. The point is, we learned a whole lot about those farmers' concerns during that short diversion that would help us over the next months. The most miraculous part is that he knew we would.

Charles Stewart, Little Rock native; veteran banker; currently vice president, First National Bank:

I met Bill Clinton in 1979 when I served on the Arkansas State Police Commission. A fellow commissioner, Bill Wilson, and I went to the governor's office to meet with him about a man by the name of Tommy Robinson, who later became a U.S. congressman. Governor Clinton had just appointed him to head up the

Department of Public Safety. I was then chairman of the commission but still rather caught up with the fact that I was meeting with the governor. The purpose of the meeting was to let the governor know that Tommy Robinson was wreaking havoc on the state police.

It was a very candid and very interesting meeting. We laid our position out, and he listened. But the more we talked, the more agitated he got. I could tell as he began to turn redder and redder that he wasn't pleased with the way the conversation was going. Finally, he let us have it—threw in a few unprintable words, too. I think I was mostly very surprised, but I responded by laughing because I was thinking, "No one will believe this." Then Bill Wilson started laughing, and finally, the governor stopped yelling at us and started laughing.

I remember saying, "Governor, can we now get back to our conversation?" and he looked at me for a second, then just nodded and said yes. He apologized for his reaction. By the time the meeting was over, he apologized again and said, "I know you're right, and I'm going to handle it." And he kept his promise.

Great leaders are able to inspire people. They are dreamers and visionaries and are able to paint their visions so that others can see it as they do.

●　●　●

Bill and Hillary Clintons' education reform program had more impact on Arkansas and the African American community than anything else he did. While there were other governors who I thought were good for the state—Governor Dale Bumpers was very progressive, and Governor Winthrop Rockefeller broke down a lot of barriers that had never even been approached—it wasn't until Clinton's tenure that blacks were included in state government in a substantive way and actually had access to the governor's office.

What was left undone when Governor Clinton became President Clinton was the economic empowerment in black communities we had expected. I can't say it's any more his fault than the black community's itself, it's just that we had high expectations while he was at the helm.

Throughout history, there's been this debate about which is more important to our community, political power or economic power. To a large extent, we've achieved political power in the sense of having people holding political offices, but I think we're still missing systemic economic power being distributed throughout the black community.

Again, that's partially our fault. During the Clinton administration, there were opportunities where we could have made some quantum leaps. We did make some progress, but it could have, should have been more. Having served on the Arkansas Industrial Development Commission, I can honestly say he made sure there were some programs in place to increase the number of African Americans engaged in manufacturing. Unfortunately, we can see little evidence of that today.

The fact that President Clinton included blacks at the table where many major decisions and policies were being made was to his credit. The fact that he appointed more African Americans to positions of influence than had been appointed during all the other presidents combined was amazing. For the first time in my memory, when there was a period of prosperity, all people benefited from it, moved forward economically. The income disparity narrowed, and that was significant. So many times, we have these periods of prosperity, and it never trickles down to where we are.

He did something that was not only unprecedented but very courageous, when he raised the dialogue on race to the level of the presidency. That sent a signal to the rest of the country that it was okay for other people at other levels in society to engage in the debate about race and racism.

Do I think he did as much as much as he should or could have done? No, but part of that is probably owed to his political savvy, his knowing how far to push the country. I use the analogy of trying to get a snake out of a hole with a stick, with the knowledge that the more that you poke, if you're not careful, you'll send it deeper into the hole. But that is something this president made an effort to do, and he felt very comfortable doing it.

The Clinton legacy? Bill Clinton had a penchant for bringing people together across all different lines, whether those lines were race or religion or philosophy. He spent much of those eight years in office building bridges, and I think he'll be able to use those bridges around the world. Much of the strife and the conflicts today are centered around a lack of dialogue between people. Anybody that can get people to the table to talk about the problem is well on the way to resolving them.

During a recent trip to Africa, I learned just how much Bill Clinton is admired and loved by the people of Africa. That was one of the contributions he made to this country—paying attention to Africa, recognizing it as an important partner in global development.

One of the issues I've heard him articulate is his desire to help address the issue of world poverty. When we address the issue of world poverty, we'll be addressing world peace. That will be his contribution to the world, much the same way President Carter has made Habitat for Humanity his contribution.

I don't think he's changed the core of who he was. To have gone through all he has, to be, arguably, the most powerful man on the face of the earth . . . he seems to be unaffected by it all. In fact, I think in some ways he's still in awe of it.

In 1993, we went to the Rose Garden for a Little Rock city awards ceremony. After the ceremony, he gave us a 45-minute personal tour of the Oval Office, the war room, and all. He seemed as excited about this as we were. It's like doing things a hundred times but seeing it again through others' eyes. That resonated with me that he was still Bill Clinton, and he still gets excited about all of that.

His legacy will be that he worked to bring the American people together and to bridge a lot of the divides that have kept black people and white people from living together. That was the thing that sustained the unprecedented period of prosperity. He helped the masses believe in themselves.

One of the things I find interesting is people who say that crime went down because he put 100,000 policemen out on the street. I think crime went down because people had hope. People, across the board, benefited from the economic boom. That's why crime went down, and that is part of his legacy-if we educate people, give people economic alternatives, they will choose education and the legal route to economic prosperity 99.9 percent of the time.

Clevon Young, native of West Helena, Arkansas; director, Arkansas Human Development Corporation:

I met Bill Clinton in the late '80s. Even then, I remember being struck by his sincerity. He was a very generous and very open. He deals with people where they are. I've never witnessed and never had anyone say he showed any sense of discomfort around people different from him.

●   ●   ●

A great leader is a person who brings a vision of where they would like to see a country or state or organization go and are able to share that vision with others. These kinds of leaders are able to get others to buy into that vision and help them get resources to make those dreams come true. I would list Martin Luther King, Jr., Bill Clinton, John F. Kennedy, Jimmy Carter, and a local leader by the name of Mahlon Martin in that category.

● ● ●

Bill Clinton's biggest contribution to Arkansas was his efforts to bring the races together and to focus on community and economic development. I remember him saying more than once, "We are all in the same boat together, and we will all sink or all rise together."

I have no personal knowledge of many Arkansas governors before Clinton, but I understand that Rockefeller did a lot of good, as well as Governor Bumpers. But more than any other governor, Bill Clinton made a concerted effort to bring blacks into the state government, and he made a point of trying to appoint African Americans to most of the boards and commissions. There is a big difference in the way state government looks today.

Unfortunately, while he spent lots of time and attention on the plight of the Arkansas Delta, that area simply has not developed or progressed the way he or we wanted to see it develop.

The Clinton legacy is that he provided leadership during one of the longest economic recoveries the country has ever endured. All kinds of people from all levels were given the opportunity to thrive and prosper. We often talk about '92's inauguration. For the first time in history, the common people were able to be included at the seat of power.

His emphasis on racial healing was important to the country. Though the outcome was disappointing, he made a genuine effort. He raised the bar in a lot of ways, and now we see the new administration trying to at least equal his number of appointments. He put his money where his mouth was. Even after his presidency ended, he selected a site in Harlem, which was unheard of for a former president. I am sure there were endless options open to him. With Ron Brown's death, we lost a lot of momentum gained in the African continent, and, unfortunately, that momentum never recovered.

I hope he will continue to work on the issues he began working on in Arkansas. He and Bob Nash and Tom McRae and others were instrumental in putting together housing and small and minority businesses in disadvantaged communities. I hope he will continue to provide leadership and continue to help communities at local levels and continue his work in education. There is still a lot of interest in him and his presidency. He still has a huge voice in this country.

Bill Clinton could have ended up anywhere and made a success. He sacrificed a lot by staying in the state as long as he did. If income and wealth were his aspirations, he wouldn't have stayed. For many years, he was the lowest-paid governor in the country. The state benefited from his loyalty. I'll never forget how, when he appointed the Delta Commission, they had a series of meetings in Helena, Arkansas. Hearings began early one morning and didn't end until early the next morning.

Although there is still much to be done in the Delta, there is no question that he was committed to change in the Delta. He sat through the duration of those meetings all night and into the early morning. Not only was he there, but he stayed engaged in the discussions throughout.

❂

Dale Charles, president, Arkansas NAACP:

A great leader is someone with vision. Someone who knows where they'd like to lead the nation to accomplish those things which we all value dearly: home, education, and jobs. Leadership works when you are prepared to lead, and people are ready to follow you. Often, you find people with great vision, but if the masses can't see your vision and buy into your vision, then it makes it very difficult to lead.

● ● ●

Governor Clinton has, so far, been Arkansas' best governor. I'm one of those who always pushed him to do more. Certainly, there is no comparison between his tenure and that of an Orval Faubus. For one thing, he tried to reach out to the full community rather than just a favored few.

But Arkansas and the nation is still not ready for real change, so in some aspects he was before his time. What he did was, for the first time in Arkansas history, place blacks in positions we'd never held before. And he kept his promise of placing blacks on all of the state's boards and commissions.

I'm convinced that as governor he would have pushed the envelope even more if we had asked for more. It seems that sometimes we become complacent when we are given more than what we're used to getting . . . even if it isn't what we fully deserve. Imagine being the first or only black legislator, how handicapped you are in trying to affect policies. You offer a motion with no one else there to second it. It's good to place a black in an important position, but sometimes being just one doesn't help change the whole.

Real change happens when people placed in positions of power use that power to help change the status quo. One of the things this nation refuses to face, even after 9/11, is that there are still state agencies with less than a handful of black employees and none in management positions. The Arkansas Game and Fish Commission had 420 employees and only 22 blacks statewide.

Both Governors David Pryor and Dale Bumpers turned out to be good for the state. I wouldn't call them proactive, but they were effective leaders. The climate in this state was such that, if you wanted to be bold and do what you think is right, then you become a one-term governor. So, most politicians choose not to be as aggressive because they know they won't be re-elected.

Unfortunately, after Bill Clinton left Arkansas, a lot of things reverted back to the way they were before he served. Since 1992, many of the boards and commissions have been re-segregated. Perhaps this is because most blacks vote straight Democratic; and Republicans don't see any benefit in supporting our needs, since we won't support them at election time.

I was very disappointed when President Clinton fired Dr. Jocelyn Elders. I thought she was one of his most courageous appointments. She was determined to be a trailblazer for the state of Arkansas and did a good job, so good a job that she was sent to Washington, but then she was caught up in Washington politics.

Even when he was president, I was constantly urging him to do more. I personally felt if he was to be a good president, he had to do more. In numerous articles, I was interviewed about his work in the black community.

In all honesty, I've always admired Bill Clinton, but I also knew his ability to make changes; and when he didn't, I became one of his biggest critics. I was there during the first Martin Luther King parade after he was nominated for president. I thought it took a lot of integrity for him to stand in the state Capitol rotunda and say he owed a great deal of gratitude to the black community, to our support of him through the governorship and the election to the presidency.

During the 1996 election year, when Newt Gingrich was Speaker of the House, black people came out overwhelmingly and voted for Clinton. During that same time, blacks were instrumental in him not being removed from office. No doubt in my mind, he would have been removed without that support. Frank Raines was one of the most powerful appointments he made. He tried to put Bill Lann Lee in the civil rights office, but America wasn't ready for that, just as they weren't ready for Lani Guinier.

Bill Clinton deserves most of the credit for George Bush's decision to put people of color into high-level roles in his administration. It would have been hard for George Bush to put Condoleezza Rice or Colin Powell or Rod Paige into those positions, had Bill Clinton not already raised the bar.

Across this country, he nominated several individuals as district judges, Court of Appeals judges that will make significant differences given the climate of the U.S. Supreme Court. Many of those appointments are significant . . . especially the Court of Appeals.

In the state of Arkansas, some federal money was turned back to Arkansas for roads, highways under his administration. I don't think the Little Rock Nine or Mrs. Daisy Bates would have gotten their honor had it not been for him. I would have liked to see more funds come back to Arkansas, especially in the Delta. Had Mike Espy not been caught up in his situation, the state as a whole would have been better off, especially the black farmers.

I give Bill Clinton credit for not ditching affirmative action. All black folks ask for is an opportunity. Many whites and some blacks are brainwashed into believing that affirmative action is about taking jobs from qualified white people and giving them to unqualified black people. Affirmative action has never been about that.

I don't think he'll be able to be very proactive while this current administration is in power. Also, a lot of whites still blame him for bringing disgrace to the White House and placing too many minorities in important jobs. And America still doesn't want to talk about race.

Being president gave Bill Clinton an opportunity to really broaden his horizon from what he experienced in Hope and Arkansas. I think he became a better human being after realizing what he'd always preached about people being the same. He saw it on a larger scale. There's nothing wrong with being compassionate, doing what you feel is right.

☙

Dr. Beverly Divers-White, Little Rock native; former Little Rock School District associate superintendent; superintendent, Lee County School District; program director, Foundation for the Midsouth; Jackson, Tenn:

I met Governor and Mrs. Clinton in the mid-'70s, when she was serving as honorary chair of the Arkansas Advocates for Families and Children. During this event, the Clintons were announcing the formation of the Arkansas Advocates for Children. It was both a social and a media event, and they were a perfect media couple, exuding warmth and charisma.

Over the years, I often met with the governor, given my involvement in community organizations that dealt with education initiatives. I learned, then, that he was a good listener and was very responsive. I saw that African Americans not only had access to him as governor, but he also invited us to many, many sessions at the governor's mansion. Some were more social than business; others were dialogue sessions where we discussed specific issues about the state. These sessions included some community leaders and faith-based leaders.

There were often a number of outside consultants visiting, who were always taken aback at how normal it was for us to be visiting the governor in the mansion or the governor's office. Sometimes he just wanted to check in with us, to talk about how we could do things better. The Clintons were always very, very gracious hosts. I'm sure we wore our welcome out with the mansion staff. I'm sure before the Clintons, they'd never had that kind of traffic in and out of the mansion.

My more personal contact with the governor began in 1986, after the Clintons returned from a Florida trip raving about an early childhood education program they heard about on a television show. Right away, they pulled together a conference inviting people who were already implementing early childhood education programs in their home states. Mrs. Clinton was extremely interested in doing whatever was necessary to assure that the children of Arkansas received a quality early childhood education.

240

She was completely sold on the HIPPY—(Home Instruction for Parents of Preschool Youngsters) program. This was a home-based program, whereas mothers were trained to be their child's first teachers. The program was touted as building the efficacy of the parent as the teacher of the child, as well as preparing the child for matriculation into public education. The program was, and continues to be, focused on low-income children.

Both of the Clintons took a leadership role in working with the state's community leaders to help implement the program here in Arkansas. I was one of four team representatives who visited Hebrew University in Jerusalem, Israel, to review and study the HIPPY program just as it was getting off the ground. The rest of the team was Rachel Myers, a supervisor in Little Rock School District; Ruth Simmons Hertz, who worked in Pulaski County's school district; and a lady from Russellville named Joann.

We participated in the summer training institute with 17 other people from across the world. Rachel Myers and I were responsible for developing the concepts of the model for Little Rock and implementing it in Little Rock. For many years, Little Rock's HIPPY program was the largest in the state, enrolling 450 students.

In the early 1990s, $10 million was allocated to a program called the Arkansas Better Chance Program, all of which was to be used for childhood development. The Clintons wanted to use HIPPY as the primary model for that program. We all lobbied to make sure HIPPY was a key component of that program and implemented through Arkansas Better Chance.

In 1989, I left the Little Rock School District as associate superintendent to become superintendent of the Lee County School District in Marianna. That district's history, in spite of outstanding graduates like former U.S. Transportation Secretary Rodney Slater and Arkansas State Appeals Judge Ollie Neal, was a dismal one. The income level of families there was terribly low, the schools were in dangerous disrepair, and there was unbridled racism in the area.

We're talking the 1980s, but one school building flooded each time it rained outside, and the staff and janitors would have to put up big green garbage bags to catch the water. One teacher fell and broke her arm, and a child broke her leg. The restrooms in some buildings were in such deplorable condition that I actually became physically ill when I walked into them. But in spite of that, the teachers came to work every day, and those kids were in those buildings every day.

I asked for a meeting with Governor Clinton and took this opportunity to tell him how deplorable the situation was for the children. He went into his emergency fund and provided $460,000 for building repairs. In addition, I was able to get some loans from the state to buy new buses, and we were able to get new buses over the next three years, something we really, really needed badly.

Probably, the most memorable time of that experience was our planning a technology conference for these mostly poor students. This was an opportunity to expose them to careers most of them had never considered. There was a huge gathering of black and white people to attend this event, the largest in Marianna's history. We used that opportunity to speak to the community's leadership about the importance of communities working together. Those conferences continued for a number of years.

The first person to speak to the leadership was Governor Clinton. Black and white people stood on the streets of Marianna to see and hear him. Most rewarding was that the local leaders responded to his challenge to take responsibility for assuring that all children were well-educated. He walked through the high schools and interacted with the staff and the students, answering questions and asking the kids what they wanted to make of their lives. It was a wonderful experience for the eastern Arkansas Delta and the children of the Delta.

When Governor Clinton went to Washington, I was called by a wide array of media folk who wanted to hear what I thought about him as governor and his support of education. I had nothing but positive things to say, because I knew what he had done for the state and what he did for the children of eastern Arkansas.

I count his appointments of African Americans to key leadership positions as his most substantive accomplishment as president. People like Bob Nash, Wilbur Peer, Rodney Slater, Mike Espy, Jerry Malone, Alexis Herman. What will stay with me for the rest of my life is that for the first time ever, not only did I have access to people at the highest level of federal agencies, but I could call a cabinet secretary or a high-level White House appointee at their homes.

I could go to Washington, D.C., and meet with people who understood the South, who were friends of the South. Another reminder of the type of access we were provided is when the decision was made about enterprise communities and empowerment zones, and we had one zone and nine enterprise communities in our region.

One thing that has been so prevalent in Arkansas is the negative press—ongoing negative editorials and commentary. There are people who complain that Bill Clinton didn't do anything for Arkansas. I believe Arkansas didn't respond to the opportunities his administration availed them. Unfortunately, we missed out on some golden opportunities, because it seemed to me that we did not understand these processes.

I was in many, many meetings where people from the Clinton administration were making every effort to make people understand the process and how to take advantage of the process. There were people beating down doors to make sure people understood and had economic access.

I was disappointed that the Race Initiative didn't take off the way we hoped it would. I'm not sure what happened, but I worked very closely with Governor (William) Winter in Mississippi on that. I had also hoped to see more done in the areas of education and economic empowerment, policies and appropriations which would not have been "giving people the fish" but empowering people.

I think Governor Clinton as well as President Clinton has always wanted to do the best thing for those who have been left out, but those are the kinds of issues that not a lot of other people were interested in. I'm sure he encountered a great deal of opposition, and as a good politician, he tried to appease both sides.

The Clinton legacy? He is a man not only for this country, but who tried to make the world better. He tried to improve the quality of life the world over. The world yet views Bill Clinton as one of the greatest leaders in history. The news commentaries from other countries during the height of the Lewinsky case, and conversations I had as I traveled to the Philippines, East Africa, Germany, and France, bear this out. The world views Bill Clinton much the same as most African Americans do . . . they tend to look inside his heart and see how much he wants peace and equality for all.

Charity Smith, native of both Hope and Forrest City, Arkansas; assistant director, Arkansas Department of Education:

Bill Clinton was governor at the time I met him. Part of my childhood was spent in Hope, on Oak Street, not too far from the old Clinton house. I was born in the colored wing of the hospital there, but I didn't live in Hope very long and never went to school there. My father was a county agent, and my mother was a school-teacher. I went back and forth between Hope and Forrest City, growing up. But that genuine openness you find in Hope and the South is part of who Bill Clinton is . . . that down-home, Southern-fried-chicken, neighborly attitude.

The first time I met Governor Clinton was at my cousin Ralph Parker's funeral. Ralph was Mr. Clinton's chief of security, but died of cancer. Governor and Mrs. Clinton came to the funeral services, and the governor was one of the people who eulogized Ralph. He met privately with Ralph's family after the funeral and shared a lot of fond memories with us. We were so moved by that. We felt as if we knew him, from Ralph talking about him so much. They shared a wonderful relationship. What he wanted the family to know was how much Ralph had meant to him.

The next time I saw the governor, he was sitting in the gym at Southwest Junior High School. I was the principal at Southwest Junior High, and his daughter, Chelsea, played volleyball at Horace Mann. Her team happened to be playing against my school's team that day. My security officer had called me to tell me the governor was in my gym. I immediately got a little worried and asked why. The volleyball team was the furthest thing from my mind.

I rushed down to the gym, expecting to see the governor of the state of Arkansas in a dark suit, looking very serious. Instead, here was this tall man in jogging pants, a cap pulled down on his head. He looked like just a regular guy waiting to watch his kid play volleyball. If he had security, they were nowhere to be seen. There was no pomp and circumstance.

I asked him if there was anything we could do for him, and he said, "Oh, no, I'm just here to watch my daughter play, I'll be just fine." I was so pleased to see him just wanting to be a parent and to support his daughter. He sat in the bleachers, cheering for Horace Mann and his daughter, while I cheered for my school and our players. Chelsea, I remember, was a serious, focused player.

My school was one of the first in Little Rock to get a New Futures grant. Hillary wrote me a personal note, saying how proud she was about the work we'd done and to keep up the great work. The mission of the grant was to target low-performance students, work with them through the year, and, hopefully, increase their academic performance.

To prepare for implementation of the program, we visited some of the best schools in the country to find out what they were doing. When we came back, we were able to put into place some things that really worked. Southwest had been one of the lowest-performing schools in the district; with the New Futures grant, we improved to the point of becoming one of the highest performing schools.

Later, I recall the governor's office looking for a school site to announce a new scholarship program, the Academic Challenge Scholarship. Of course, every school wanted to have the governor announce new programs on their campus. Little Rock School District Superintendent Ruth Steele recommended Southwest Junior High.

I was so excited when they told me our school had been selected. This time, he did come with all the pomp and circumstance, all the fanfare, all the legislators who were part of that district. There were about 900 people in all on our school grounds that day.

I was asked to introduce the governor. It so happened that a flyer had been circulating on campus that morning about him possibly running for president. So in my introduction, I said, "I want to be the first to introduce him as the President of the United States." The kids just started screaming. He was very surprised and told me that was one of the best introductions he'd ever had.

It was so exciting when he actually ran for president. Because I was a principal, I didn't have time to do a lot of work in his campaign, but I was selected as one of the three personal pages for him and Vice President Gore at the economic summit held in Little Rock.

The Clinton era was a time of success in our country: the deficit virtually erased, no major wars, people loving and feeling good about their president for a change. For the first time, minorities had access to the White House and access to high-profile public meetings that they had never enjoyed before.

Not only was he a president, but he was a husband and a father. Chelsea was able to have a private life for herself. She was able to grow up as near a regular child as possible in that role. Everyone knew he respected Mrs. Clinton's opinions. She was truly what we biblically call a helpmate. I think they demonstrated that first ladies no longer had to be merely trophy wives, adornments, or window dressing. He introduced the country to a new way of leadership, new ideas that created a better country.

245

The Clinton legacy will be that he created a period of self-actualization for people of every race and for underrepresented groups: women, handicapped, the gays. It was a period of self-actualization that you could, without fear, state your beliefs and participate fully in the American dream, which we previously had not been able to do. The disparities in wages narrowed. The country prospered, and we all benefited.

He realized the American dream and proved that that being a great president doesn't depend as much on wealth or politics as it does on a sheer desire to achieve excellence . . . by simply wanting more than other people think is possible and expecting more than other people think is practical.

What some whites won't admit is that they benefited more from his administration than we did. What is true is that there are some in the white community who never experienced the American dream. There are little children here in Arkansas who never would have been full partners in their community, had this period not come about.

People will remember his fall but, more importantly, his restoration. Not only did that allow the presidency to be restored, but all those political figures who had fallen before. All those who had tried to shield themselves in perfection were able to say, "Here's my imperfection."

℺

Dr. Cora McHenry, Augusta, Arkansas; former president, Arkansas Education Association; president, Shorter College, North Little Rock, Arkansas:

Bill Clinton was selling sandwiches outside a convention center, campaigning for attorney general in 1976, when I met him. I introduced myself to him and volunteered to work with his campaign. I was impressed with his energy, with his freshness of thought as he walked around and talked to people.

The next time I met him, he was announcing that he was running for governor for the first time. He came over to the Arkansas Education Association, and the teacher leaders interviewed him. We had a chance to ask him about his ideas, his issues, and his platform.

• • •

Great leadership is when a person can visualize a positive solution to a critical challenge and is able to draw people in to help him or her solve that issue. There are a number of people who I define as great leaders, including Bill Clinton . . . the successes he had in the education arena that others said were impossible. That suggests to me that not only did he have the brainpower but the persuasive power and confidence of enough people to achieve objectives that benefited the state and individuals.

Mary Hatwood Futrell is another person I consider a great leader—her creativity and her innovation in dealing with difficult issues. When there was such an outcry about the national dropout rate, she asked the 2.2 million members of the AEA to donate $1 of their dues to a program called Operation Rescue, and in that one minute, she raised $2.2 million toward programs to keep kids in school. She came back the next year and asked for a $3 donation, and that was the birth of what is now the National Foundation of the Improvement of Education. Their resources now rival the Rockefeller Foundation.

John F. Kennedy is in that category because he was willing to swim against the tide and do what he believed was right, without regard to personal political consequences. There was a genuineness about him that common people recognized. We felt as if we knew him.

●　●　●

We had a few good governors before Bill Clinton came along, actually. Dale Bumpers did a good job, making sure blacks were hired in state government and making some critical appointments to boards and commissions. He established long-standing health initiatives, putting health centers around the Delta, which gave people—especially women—the opportunity to become independent and confident.

He was also very instrumental in moving the higher education institution from under federal court jurisdiction. He worked hard to get it into the state's jurisdiction. He took advice well from the education association when I was there, as well as from others who advised him. But in the end, it was his sheer will power to get it done. In fact, the records show there were more gains in teachers' salaries, dollarwise, during his administration than during any other administration.

It was during the Bumpers' administration that schools began giving free textbooks to all students. I always saw education as a civil right. Something as simple as free textbooks for all children came about under his administration. There were 13 of us (in my family) and I never had a whole set of textbooks, I had to borrow books from others.

Bill Clinton was something completely alien to Arkansas, refreshing. By far, the most substantial change during his governorship was the new education standards for accreditation for public education. Those standards have stood the test of time and have had a great impact on equalizing educational opportunities for all students throughout the state, and for raising the standards and achievement of all students.

It's hard not to put Hillary on the list of great leaders. I found her to be an extremely strong leader, and I just admire her so much. She and I had done a lot of work together with children and families before I met Bill Clinton.

Of course, every leader could have done something better or different. Perhaps he could have provided a stronger leadership in the area of economic development initiatives. He should have supported, more strongly, the repeal of sales tax. That is still a real issue for low-income people. I think he could have gotten that done.

The plight of the Delta is certainly something we'd hoped would improve but didn't get the kind of help it deserved under Bill Clinton's leadership.

You know, it's not so easy to pinpoint one or two specific things Bill Clinton did as president. What took place, though, was that for the first time in presidential history, blacks and minorities were able to demonstrate their talents on an amazing scale. He opened doors that had been closed to us throughout this country's history.

He set a tone of giving back, which I think inspired young people as well as minorities to return to their communities and help make them what they can be. His leadership, his smart choices of department heads, helped sustain economic growth in this country.

Internationally, President Clinton assured security for our country and peace to other parts of the world. He was considered a great negotiator as he dealt with other leaders to make the world a safer place for everyone. That will be a big part of his legacy.

Certainly, the legacy of empowering African Americans by bringing them into the mainstream of American culture and society will be long-lived. He didn't just help some blacks ascend to elitism but helped everyday people whose success could have an impact on their communities.

Even Bill Clinton isn't perfect. Brilliant, yes, but not perfect. Even though his health care plan didn't work in its entirety, there were elements of his national health initiative that benefited African American communities in a significant way.

He probably could have done even more with economic initiatives like the empowerment zones. I don't think he went as far as he could have with that concept, especially in the South and the Delta. Had he been there another term . . . I think more people and more communities would have benefited. It was a proven, successful concept. Who knows what would have happened, had he expanded it and left some kind of legislative mandate that it be continued?

The Clinton legacy? History will paint Bill Clinton as a man who put a human face and personality on the presidency of the United States. He was a president that the American people was proud of, had confidence in. He was also a compassionate president who was not afraid to try bold, new things. Personally, my life was changed after meeting and working with Bill and Hillary Clinton. He restored my confidence in the American system when he invited me to play a role in helping change what we viewed as wrong about our state.

Even though Bill Clinton and Arkansas teachers had their differences after teacher testing, I knew Bill Clinton had our children and our future at heart. I encouraged the AEA interview committee to understand that we were only hurting ourselves by not supporting the person who was obviously a great leader. When Bill Clinton was ready to run for president, he was clear that he needed the teachers' vote.

The AEA, at my encouragement, wrote letters to teachers and teacher organizations all over the country to let them know what kind of person Bill Clinton was. And although at the national level they still held teacher testing against him, they were able to look past that and support his presidency.

☉

Mrs. Liza Ashley, native of Pettus, Arkansas; former mansion cook for Arkansas governors from 1953-1989:

I began my career cooking for governors in 1953, when Governor Frances Cherry was in office. I worked for every governor after Cherry until I retired in 1989. Governor Clinton came to the mansion in 1979, and I retired 10 years later. It wasn't long after that he ran for president and went off to Washington, D.C. I still talk to all the governors I served who are still living and consider all of them my friends.

I was born in Pettus, Arkansas, in Lonoke County. I moved to Little Rock in 1942. I worked at the Pine Bluff Arsenal for a while, but they closed the arsenal down the day after Winthrop Rockefeller died.

In 1953, Mrs. Georgia Scrivner, who was Governor Cherry's cook, asked me if I was interested in working for the governor because she was leaving. She said if I was interested, she'd recommend me to Governor and Mrs. Cherry. I needed a job, so I told her to go ahead. They talked to me, and I went to work for them right away. After Governor Cherry came Governor Faubus. He was in the mansion for 12 years. Winthrop Rockefeller was there four years. I cooked for six governors over 36 years.

Though I met a lot of famous people working in the governor's mansion, for some reason I remember Gregory Peck the best. I think it's because I always liked his movies, and he was such a nice man in real life. I also remember meeting Colonel Sanders. He was visiting the governor's mansion once and asked me what kinds of food I liked to cook. I told him collard greens and cornbread . . . and he talked me into cooking some for him.

When my husband and I went out in the evenings, I would leave the food in the oven, so it would stay warm until the Clintons got home. Governor Rockefeller had left warmers there, and we used them so the families' foods wouldn't be cold when they came in.

My son was a little boy when I worked for some of the governors. He would sit there while I cooked and sometimes tell me he was hungry and ask why he couldn't eat. I would tell him we had to wait until the governor's family came home. He would ask, "Well, how come we got to wait for the white folks to eat?"

Some of Governor Clinton's favorite foods were corn pudding, greens, fried chicken, roast beef, and carrot cake. I always cooked carrot cake for Chelsea's birthdays, and she liked macaroni when she was little. Then, the only piece of the chicken she'd eat was the leg. She's a vegetarian now, though.

I can't remember Governor Clinton ever sitting down to eat a normal meal during the time he was governor. He was always on the go. He would walk through the kitchen, get him some kind of sandwich, and go on to his office to work. He loved roast beef sandwiches. I asked him once why he ate his food cold all the time.

I said cold food not good for your digestion. He said he started eating cold food when he was in college in London. I always told him he needed to eat more green stuff.

Now Mrs. Clinton ate real healthy, a lot of salads. She finally got him to eat some greens, too. I've heard the press say he would stop and eat hamburgers at McDonald's, I don't think that's really true. Knowing him, he was down there doing more talking to people than eating. He usually ate when he got back from jogging.

I never in a million years imagined walking into the White House. But when Bill Clinton was elected president, I made my first trip there for his inauguration. After that, I'd look forward to coming to the White House every year he was there.

☯

Ernie Green, Little Rock native; member, Little Rock Nine; Carter appointee; Clinton appointee:

I met Bill Clinton around 1977, just around the time I went to work in the Carter administration as an assistant secretary at Labor. Though I didn't meet him when he was teaching up at the University of Arkansas, my cousin, Bonita Terry, was a law student there at the time. She and a lot of other black law students talked endlessly about this white guy who had a great relationship with the black law students there.

In 1978, his first term as governor, his office helped coordinate a reception for me in Little Rock. I noticed then how at ease he was around black folk and how he knew all the people I knew in Little Rock. He had great personal relationships.

That was the same year he told me he planned to make appointments to boards and commissions where African Americans in Arkansas had never served. I specifically remember him mentioning the Highway Commission and the Game and Fish Commission. If you grew up in Arkansas in the '50s, to hear a white politician say they were going to appoint someone of color to the Highway Commission and Game and Fish Commission was just revolutionary, more difficult to conceive than my graduating from Central High School.

So early on, I realized Bill Clinton was a different kind of white Southern politician. I stayed in touch with him. In fact, he asked me to serve in his first cabinet. I thought about it, but there were

251

some restrictions, mainly pay. At that time in my life, I couldn't afford to move back to Arkansas and work in state government.

I was intrigued by this young white politician who felt very much at home with people I knew. And I liked the way he was running his government, and that whole accessibility . . . how he'd call people in the middle of the night to consult with them about some issue. All of that was just very refreshing.

●　●　●

Great leaders make others feel important, believing they have a stake. Great leaders don't restrict their audience to the elite, powerful, or rich.

●　●　●

In 1980, when Bill Clinton lost the race to Frank White, I got a call from Rodney (Slater) asking if I would be willing to come down and help out in the next campaign. I came up with all the excuses I could, but Rodney finally persuaded me to visit there during homecoming weekend at the University of Arkansas at Pine Bluff—always a big occasion in southeast Arkansas.

The amazing thing was that the number of blacks I talked to during that campaign genuinely felt Clinton was worth rehiring. All that business about blacks not expecting him to lose to White, just wanting to humble him a little bit . . . was not the attitude in the black community. People were sorely disappointed he didn't win and that we had to deal with a Republican governor for that term.

It was a real thrust on the part of the voters to make sure that that loss didn't repeat itself. I spent a couple of weeks working with Rodney, trying to make certain the turnout was significant, and the record shows that it was. So we all take a little credit for helping him get through Clinton II.

And from that point on, we really had what I consider a very good relationship. A number of times I would come down and call him and get invited over to the mansion. In 1987, the state made a big to-do about recognizing the Little Rock Nine. My understanding is that it was mainly Clinton-inspired. The reception at the mansion, the media exposure . . . all of that was something Clinton initiated and made happen.

So those of us who grew up in Arkansas were convinced that Clinton would outgrow Arkansas. No matter what he said, or other people said, Bill Clinton just had too broad a reach to remain governor of Arkansas. And while the rest of the country didn't know that, there were those of us who had been around him who just felt that at some point, he would break out and go for a bigger stage.

Had our two previous governors—Bumpers and Pryor—not been such outstanding senators, he certainly would have been considered for senator for the state of Arkansas. Really, there wasn't a lot left for him to do . . . he certainly wouldn't have been comfortable being a congressman.

The spring of 1991 was when he told me he was considering throwing his hat into the race. Now, this was when George Bush was at his height of popularity. I was thinking to myself, "Has Clinton gone off the deep end? Can he really pull this off?" I decided these two things: if he runs and loses, he was young enough that this run could just be his opportunity to put his marker down; and no matter what, he would be a political force for at least the rest of the century.

Secondly, I just enjoyed being around him, enjoyed his politics, and thought he had the right attitude to bring about change. Most importantly, his focus on race was the right way to approach it. No other white moderate Southern politicians were saying the same things Clinton was.

When he finally announced, Doug Wilder had also announced, and I had made a commitment to Wilder to stay with him for a moment. I did that until he bowed out around December. My first real involvement with the president was through the U.S. Conference of Mayors. He and Bruce Lindsey came there, right before the New Hampshire primary. Ray Marshall, Carter's Secretary of Labor, and I sat around talking with Bill Clinton. Before that night we'd both pledged to help him in any way we could.

That was around the time when the Jennifer Flowers story first started to break. There were no crowds around, no print, hardly anything. When it did break, I watched how he handled all that. I was convinced that if he could handle that the way he did, he could handle a lot . . . and he was going a lot further than anyone gave him credit for.

I came to Little Rock, took off weekends, did some speaking for him during the New York primary. Jerry Brown tried to beat up on him about membership at the Little Rock Country Club. I helped cut some ads saying, "This was the guy who invited me to an inaugural party at the Little Rock Country Club, and I'd never been there before, though my father was a waiter there." That was an emotional moment for me.

I watched Bill Clinton when Cuomo figured out he wouldn't be able to run and conceded that Bill Clinton was really the Democratic candidate. Clinton now had the Southern primary, he had an approach that would endear him to more and more people, and he had more and more black voters. He finally had the blacks from other parts of the country who kept asking me, "Now, is this guy for real? Do you Southern guys really feel this way about him?" And I kept telling them yes . . . and people started to buy it.

Then, I'll never forget the cover of *Jet* magazine. John Johnson did as much to help Bill Clinton become president of the United States as anyone I know, and it really shows the power of his publications. Ever since the 150th birthday celebration in Arkansas, when Johnson came and brought his wife and family and he did this whole spread, it was clear that John Johnson realized the importance of keeping this guy's political star up.

When history is finally written, I think Johnson publications made a huge impact on that election. I know it helped Bill Clinton get across the Illinois primary, and I think, in a way, that that cover story certified that this guy was not only comfortable with black people but would treat us as equals, and that was not something just for the campaigns, not just something to be used.

As we went into the final stretch, I think Bill Clinton's sincerity became clear to more and more voters. He would joke that he was one of the few white people who knew all the verses of (what's considered the black national anthem) "Lift Every Voice and Sing." Here was a person who took the time to know as much about what was going on in my community as his own.

As for his presidency, he did some really remarkable things: his trade initiatives and recognition of Africa; his firm stance on affirmative action; his creation of a robust economy that allowed millions of black folk to get into the workforce, buy homes, be stakeholders in the American dream. Most important was the way he worked the economy. Of course, critics argue that it occurred in spite of him, but it occurred during his watch, and he developed enough policies to continue it.

The real question about the Clinton legacy will be how well the American economy operated during his tenure. That will be clearly one of his major achievements. And his attitude about race defined George Bush's attitude. Bush announced that Rice and Powell would be in his cabinet before he got elected. All of this had to do with Clinton's attitude on race. Raising the importance of Africa, the trade bill, his relationship with Mandela, the trip to

Africa . . . all of these things are what Bill saw and felt needed developing.

Bill Clinton has been a tremendous asset for this country. He will make his Harlem move a plus for all the Harlems of this country, moving that area from being something marginal to being a part of New York. With all its history, the city never was able to see that. Bill Clinton moves there and in two weeks time, the rest of the country discovers Harlem.

If Bill Clinton does nothing else, I hope he'll work to focus the American attitude that all people have to be treated the same. This is the core of the problem of terrorism . . . there are a group of people out there who don't see America as ideal . . . as being in sync with one another. No country will ever have enough guns and tanks and planes to eliminate this. This is a battle for people's brains, not their brawn. As tragic as September 11 was, the only way you capture people's minds is to show this is a different place. Bill Clinton understands this better than any politician.

☉

Mrs. Josetta Wilkins, former state senator, Pine Bluff, Arkansas:

Our son, Hank, Jr., had returned home from the University of Michigan to go to the University of Arkansas' Law School. My husband, a state legislator, and I were in Fayetteville for Legislative Day. Back then, they always held Legislative Day on the same day as the Texas-Arkansas game in Fayetteville, so we took that opportunity to go there that weekend. Of course, my son wouldn't have been pleased to know that we were also there to check up on him.

We were roaming up and down the hallways of the law school looking for our son and didn't get a good reception from the people there. I think they were all getting ready for the game. My husband and I were getting pretty perturbed when this young man walked up and introduced himself as Bill Clinton. He asked if he could help us, and my husband said, "Yeah, my son is a student up here, and I wanted to find out how he's doing. It seems no one wants to pay any attention to us."

Bill Clinton started talking to us and steering us out on the patio. I thought he was just a very nice law student. He was so young, and I was thinking he's no more than a boy himself, and we're asking for a professor. But we soon discovered that he was a

255

professor, and he expressed genuine interest in our concern about finding our son.

He also told us he knew Hank, Jr., and assured us that Hank was doing wonderfully well. He was such a personable young man, and it was so unusual, in my experience, to have someone show that kind of interest. I guess I was surprised that he would actually put the Texas-Arkansas game aside to sit down and talk with us for as long as we wanted to talk. It made an indelible impression in my heart and in my mind.

When we left for home, my husband mentioned, "That young man is going to go far."

•   •   •

A great leader has to have strong character, and the human touch has to be there. Two great men, one a spiritual and civil rights leader, the other a political leader—Martin Luther King and Bill Clinton—marched toward the same thing, justice for all humanity, for all men and women.

•   •   •

When Bill Clinton decided to run against Hammerschmidt up in Fayetteville, I didn't really pay much attention to it, but I remember my husband saying young Bill Clinton would never win in northwest Arkansas. He was sorry he'd chosen to run up there, because he believed if he became known as a loser, he'd never make it.

But later on he came to Little Rock and ran for attorney general. Of course, we volunteered to help him win . . . based on that one experience in Fayetteville. Truthfully, we didn't know a lot about him other than that one experience, but we were sure he had the qualities that would be good for the people of Arkansas— and I mean all people.

From then on, we became big supporters of his. We decided that if he ran for dogcatcher we would be out there campaigning for him, because we believed there was such a dire need for people like him in public service, someone with genuine interest in people.

I'm convinced Bill Clinton will be recorded as the greatest president this country has ever known. They won't give it to him right away. There are those who would destroy him, even now. But one day someone will do an analysis that shows what he did to promote humankind, and to promote it in such a way that he gave opportunity where opportunity was not available before.

I think he would have done more if he had not been in a society that limited his abilities for more inclusion, but we have to face the realities of politics in this country. I think his hands were tied to a great degree, but he did all he could. He pushed the limits, raised the bar when it came to acknowledging diversity and getting behind his words, letting his actions support his words. And there were a lot of people angry with him about that.

His wife, in my estimation, is a super woman. You've heard the statement, "Behind every good man is a good woman." I think that Hillary was a living testament to that statement. She has gone through a lot, but at the same time, she stood by him. Most of us know that each president before Bill Clinton had their human weaknesses.

It may be years before the full realization of all he's done will come forward. If you think of throwing a stone in water and the rippling effect . . . many of our children and their children will be the real benefactors of his good works.

Since he left the White House, I have been invited to a number of events and parties with him. I have often thought, "Here's this brilliant man still in his prime. Most people didn't run for president until they were his age now. And he's served his terms, now what can he do?" He still has some people out there shooting darts and trying to destroy him, but he also still has people like us who are forever in his corner, supporting him. I think he could be one of the greatest peacekeepers for race relations, human relations.

His grandfather owned a store in an area where he was exposed to people of every walk of life. He was able to get a view of other human beings, people different from him. Let's face it, most presidents came from wealthy, prominent families and never interacted with a minority except for their house servants or laborers.

I would describe him as a young man with God-given abilities who used those abilities to go to school and to prepare himself. He achieved what a lot of us describe as luck, which is actually preparation and opportunity coming together. What happened was that he prepared himself, then took advantage of opportunities.

I was in Little Rock in June. I sat beside him, and the change I saw in him was that he had grown in wisdom. He's gained a lot of wisdom. Can you imagine being humbled when you've been president of the United States, and then talking about it with everyday people like myself? I saw the humility was greater and deeper, and wisdom greater and deeper. I saw him able to talk about the missteps, but he felt like he needed to say it, and I needed to hear it. The first experience that rests in my mind and will always be there was the time when he acknowledged my husband and me in Fayetteville when no one else would.

☉

Former Arkansas Senator Judy Smith, once voted one of the top 10 legislators by *The Arkansas Gazette*; director of Arkansas' Minority Health Initiative:

The very first time I met Bill Clinton was the summer of 1985. At the time, I was the executive director of a nonprofit called People of Concern in Camden. I met him at the first annual conference on the prevention of alcohol and drug abuse. I had taken three high school students to Little Rock for the conference, and I remember how excited they were to meet the governor.

He was very personable and knew a lot about my part of the state, Camden. He started talking about all these people I knew in Camden. After that year, I saw him at most of the conferences over the next few years. We were always happy to have the governor at the conference. It meant a lot, not just to the kids but to the parents who wanted to do something about alcohol and drug abuse in the state. At that time, there were at least 500 kids involved in that program.

• • •

A great leader is someone who is selfless and demonstrates a genuine care for others. My grandmother, Agnes Watson Bellard, was uneducated and didn't speak English until I was 15 years old. She spoke Creole but was the political matriarch of her community. Martin Luther King and Fannie Lou Hammer are on that list.

• • •

As for Arkansas governors, Bill Clinton would have to be at the top of the list of those who made a difference for the state. Governor (Mike) Huckabee is doing a better job than anyone expected. His challenges are that he's met with resistance from right-wing Republicans, and he has made genuine efforts to include African Americans. It doesn't matter what party you're in as long as the right people are benefiting. Blacks are in a better position than we've ever been before. The more we can't be taken for granted by either party, especially Democrats, the more inroads we can make.

Bill Clinton's education initiative had the potential for a major impact. I'm not so sure we took advantage of it. It was so critical for the time. I wish he had done more to assure that the 10 percent minority set-aside law had been implemented. That was critical for laying a foundation for our economic development. Though most people thought it was beneficial to blacks only, it would have helped the economy as a whole. New businesses—black or white—are good for the state. Unfortunately, a number of blacks with good ideas and willingness to work for their dreams ended up moving to other states where they could make them come true.

I think he did the right thing by signing the welfare reform bill. The law gave the states such an opportunity to invest in people who were poor, to provide educational opportunity, training, jobs with benefits. People were given an opportunity to become self-sufficient. When he signed the welfare reform bill and handed it over to the states with such broad flexibility, that was a great opportunity. Unfortunately, many states didn't know what to do with it . . . maybe it was too much flexibility. Nobody can tell you what happened to that money. It turned out to be more of an opportunity for providers, rather than people for whom the law was made.

There were some things President Clinton missed the mark on, including health care reform. What a sad moment when we saw that nothing could be done about health care insurance and the mounting costs of prescriptions. That one initiative could have been a great legacy for him. Of course, most African Americans were disappointed when he didn't stand behind Lani Guinier and Jocelyn Elders.

I've seen Bill Clinton grow during his eight years in office. I think he's learned from his mistakes. America never expected him to accomplish what he did. And if he hasn't accomplished all he wanted to, he still has time to do it. You don't have to have a title to make a difference. Bill and Hillary Clinton exemplify what parents should be and what a family should strive for . . . keeping your family together at all costs. They raised a child together and seemed to have done it very well.

Lottie Shackelford, Little Rock native; former mayor, Little Rock, Arkansas; global consultant, Washington, D.C.

Bill Clinton was running for U.S. Congress against Hammerschmidt in 1974 when I met him. I was part of a group in a campaign rally. I was just getting involved in Democratic politics and had been working with labor folk in the state. I started hearing about this person who was young and very dynamic and very progressive. Then I'd listen to him speaking, and he was constantly talking about moving Arkansas forward. He wasn't harping on what we didn't have but what we could have.

In 1976, he ran for attorney general, and I worked in his campaign. I also worked in his campaign when he ran for governor in 1978. It was after he lost in 1980 that I took a formal role, because it was very important to me that he was re-elected.

● ● ●

A great leader is a person with vision, ideas, and the ability to move the masses. He or she has the ability to garner enough confidence that others will buy into your vision. Martin Luther King, Jr., is someone who would definitely fall into this category.

Bill Clinton involved more blacks in his government than any other Arkansas governor. Winthrop Rockefeller, had the timing been different, probably would have come close. I also have to give Dale Bumpers and David Pryor their due . . . they were good for the state, progressive. And David Pryor actually was instrumental in helping me get started in state Democratic politics.

Governor Pryor called and asked me if I was interested in running for secretary of the state Democratic Party; there had been no African American serving in any position in the state before. I was successful in winning that seat with the help of a lot of people. Bernadine Wilson, a white woman, was slated to become secretary and could have gotten it, but she bowed out just a few days before the election. She came to me and said that what Governor Pryor was trying to do was more important to the state than her personal desires. And after that, I was elected without opposition.

But as far as someone reaching out to the masses, Clinton was the one who did that after Rockefeller. I will never forget hearing him say, very early in his political career, that there were very few things people couldn't do in America if they had the right training and ample opportunity. He didn't just say that, he practiced that.

What Clinton did could probably be compared to any state in the Union. Having a black head up a social service agency is outstanding, but appointing a black to head up financial services was completely unfathomable before Bill Clinton. There are very few states, even now, that can top that.

He pushed Arkansans to reach their potential . . . pushed Arkansas kicking and screaming. I don't know many folk who can extract every bit of effort from people like Bill Clinton. The key was you never thought you were outworking him.

Given different circumstances, he certainly would have pushed the whole issue of the Race Initiative to the forefront. As a country, we would have been further along. When you look at how September 11 brought out patriotism, Clinton had the ability to do the same thing with diversity . . . getting America to come to grips with the fact that the nation has to beat this cancer called racism, together.

Over and above the nation prospering, I still think his greatest legacy was making America reconcile with all of its people, having both women and minorities not be second-tier citizens. That, to me was historical . . . not having to be an afterthought. He also reinvigorated people's sense of why the government is important . . . the good it does. For 12 years, there was a real effort to diminish the importance of government. He made people feel proud of   government. Government is to work hand in hand with its people.

There was something powerful about having such a brilliant, intellectual president saying government is good, if we use it the way it was meant to be used. That's a great legacy. Bringing in high quality doers and thinkers to make government better, not get rid of it.

I am so hopeful that his library will have one component on race relations. I also hope he will help dispel the notion Americans feel about "to heck with the rest of the world." I'd like to see him continue to address the need for America to recognize that we're only super if we bring along others. He gave value to Third World countries and Africa, in particular. He was not an isolationist.

Rodney Slater, native of Marianna, Arkansas; former governor's aide; former U.S. Highway Administrator; former Secretary, U.S. Department of Transportation:

The first time I was formally introduced to Bill Clinton was by State Senator Henry Wilkins, who would later become my father-in-law. Governor Bill Clinton had called for a state constitutional convention in 1979, and I was a staff member.

I was, of course, in awe. He was very personable and engaging. I had all these deep questions about his politics I wanted to ask, but amazingly, he seemed as interested in asking me questions as I was in querying him. We talked briefly about mutual acquaintances at the University of Arkansas' Law School . . . Dick Atkinson, who was one of the professors at the law school; Hal Witty; Diane Blair and some others. His willingness to engage in a conversation with a young staffer was just amazing to me.

I had returned to Arkansas after undergraduate school, in 1978. I knew Arkansas had young leadership at the time: Bill Clinton was attorney general, Paul Revere was secretary of state, David Pryor was governor, Dale Bumpers was a senator, and Jim Guy Tucker was in the U.S. Congress at the time. All of this made it exciting to be returning home at that time after being away at college for four years.

I went to law school at the University of Arkansas, and during my first year there, all I heard was about this threesome they called the "Mod Squad." They were referring to Hillary Rodham, Bill Clinton, and a black law professor by the name of George Knox. All three of them, however, had moved on by the time I arrived at the law school. George had gone on to Miami, Bill had become attorney general, and Hillary Rodham had joined the Rose Law Firm.

I think they had left over a year earlier, but people were still talking about these young idealistic professors and how they could communicate with students unlike any law professors before. They didn't just talk about the outcome of a given case but the motivation and underlying principles and ideals of a given case . . . and how you can use a law degree in the public arena. That very much impressed me, because that's how I viewed the law . . . from a civil rights vantage point, and in terms of legal service and public policy.

The other thing that impressed me was that Bill Clinton had taken many of his former law students to the attorney general's office with him—not just one woman or one African American, but it was a very diverse office. I could see there was a new South being born then, shaped by the civil rights movement.

There were still a lot of people very tentative about breaking down walls and building bridges, but I found this person . . . Bill Clinton very proactive, very progressive . . . and in some respects, very aggressive about it. But that was the image from afar, and when that opportunity came at the constitutional convention to actually meet this unique leader up close, I was just so eager to ask him about all of this. But, really, I didn't get the opportunity because he was better at asking questions than I was. That genuine interest in people around him was just something brand new in a politician, for me.

So I think in a nutshell, it was my first experience of what I call the Bill Clinton touch . . . to look into a crowd, never see a stranger, to really focus on whomever he's talking to . . . especially when he's meeting someone who has thought a lot more about meeting him than he could ever have thought of meeting them.

I've seen that Clinton touch play out a million times with other people and have taken great joy in being a part of that when I served as a governor's aide, later on. What you figure out over time is, if you walk into a room at something like a convention, you've already spotted the people on the peripheral. You know the magic of that whole encounter, his ability to deal with those on the front row. But you learn that there are always those who are either sitting on the periphery or way back in the rear who had probably found it really difficult to get there but sacrificed because they wanted to see or hear him.

The magic of Bill Clinton is that he deals with those people as the valuable, special, dedicated individuals that they are. There were thousands of events like that, and Bob Nash, Carol Willis, and I worked diligently to make sure that that group of people— usually the less advantaged, poor, minorities—understood that he was as interested in meeting them as they were in meeting him. And to see them finally realize the truth in that, when he walked to where they were, made it all worth it. Sometimes they would be old women, old men, grandparents, young kids . . . and just the magic of that moment for him and for them. Frankly, that's what I remember most about the entire journey. I think that really speaks volumes about what he has meant, he literally empowers others.

● ● ●

Great leadership is dedicated to taking its followers to a new, different level of appreciation and achievement. Great leaders can always take more than just the people who are naturally in that arena, but can actually open that arena up and invite others in, not simply to participate in the victories but the effort as well. Great leaders go beyond their community of followers and loyalists; they bring everyone along. That's the kind of leadership President Clinton and Martin Luther King personify.

● ● ●

Interestingly, I lived in the small community of Marianna, the east Arkansas Delta. It was a very dynamic community in many respects and had strong educators like Mrs. Anna B. Strong, a contemporary of Mary McLeod Bethune. During my teen years, Governor Winthrop Rockefeller would host a function up at his farm on Petit Jean Mountain.

That was the first integrated event I had ever gone to. Mrs. Mamie Nelson, head of the Marianna NAACP, was responsible for me attending. I can still recall my amazement at seeing blacks and whites interacting at this function, and how unique that was for a teen-ager from the east Arkansas Delta. It just didn't happen . . . we didn't have integrated functions in town or in school.

As president, it came out more clear than all the years of his being governor, but Bill Clinton personifies a kind of boldness. It became most evident to me during his State of the Union address shortly after the Lewinsky scandal broke.

I remember saying to myself, "He's going to do this, but he's going to do this almost as if everything was in that moment." Watching him that night, it was as if the theme of that moment was, "I'm here to be dealt with, and I'm going to deal with you. And as I deal with you, I will have everyone watching. I will force you tonight to deal with me."

I remember thinking of that biblical verse: "Yea, though I walk through the valley of the shadow of death, I will fear no evil: for thou art with me." That was the most powerful thing, in a political sense, I've ever seen. And from that point on, given everything we had to deal with in those years, people would say, "Damn, I'm glad this guy is president."

The other very powerful moment in time was his walk down the hallway at the DNC Convention. It reminded me of a prize-fighter or a wrestler—it was the swagger. It's as if he was carrying all his enemies and all his friends, all those who sometimes tuned in, sometimes didn't, and everyone way back in the cheap seats, and the others who paid to get in the good seats but really preferred the cheap seats.

And all of us were tracing his steps with our own lives . . . those who walked into the factory each day, the cotton field, the pristine offices . . . all saying, "Eight long years, and he's still standing." It was *"High Noon"*. . . Gary Cooper. People were saying, in spite of everything that happened in those eight years, "I liked his performance." Many said it begrudgingly.

His leadership was seen in how he focused on education, on unifying the message and the issues. His opening the government to people who had never had access did more than just give individuals a chance, but something a lot larger than that. He was, forever, (Muhammad) Ali. Frankly, there was no way to really marshal his energies or his ability, so his foes came back with a force that would show the world that he was unworthy. But that's when his deep-rooted faith, spirituality set in, and they had no inkling of that.

When someone is spending $70 million to bring you down . . . with the authority of the United States, it must take a while to fully understand the gravity of it . . . you just take those punches, take those punches. I remember saying to someone, "Ali survived." Bill Clinton was more spiritually centered than ever, more powerful than ever before.

Most people didn't know the man as some of us knew him. My point was that we're going to beat this, and we're going to deal with this. We can all debate why we are where we are. The reality is that sometimes we wake up and we are there . . . so how do you deal with it? Do you blame yourself, blame someone else? The whole point is, you deal with it. To me, that was what coming down that corridor was all about.

Crack and powder cocaine was definitely an area that deserved more work by his administration. I know an attempt was made, and one of the things was that the judgment that was made included a limited amount of capital . . . but we certainly could have done more. Our failure on that one issue has such ramifications. What that has resulted in is thousands of our young men being incarcerated for crimes out of proportion with the injury caused. I believe the president acknowledges and recognizes that was a lost opportunity.

As governor, he took bold steps in the area of education and in opening up government to black Arkansans. More than giving an individual an opportunity, it allowed a state to see the full measure of its strength, what it can do when it taps the ability, soul, and spirit of all of its people.

Arkansas was able to elect a president of the United States. It was one thing for him to have the desire, but another for the Arkansas Travelers to leave the comfort of their homes to go out to places that were really tough, politically, and hold their own. I remember the slights and jokes about Arkansas . . . and the governor.

He suffered from the same thing that almost all Southerners have suffered from since the Civil War, the ability to declare themselves "fit" to represent the nation. Carter had that problem; Johnson had that problem. If you go back to the time when Clinton was elected . . . after Roosevelt's two terms, no Democrat served more than one term. Truman served one full term; Kennedy served part of one term; Johnson served one full term; Carter served one term. Then you have Bill Clinton, who changed the tide, after running against a president who had the highest approval rating of any president at that time.

He came from a small Southern state, and that was used as a statement against him. He overcame all of that. He went to New Hampshire, and it's raining and cold outside, and he is still on the streets waving at people, saying, "Remember me." And they tried to hit him with everything, questioning his audacity to be the "Comeback Kid."

The two most important contributions: focus on education, and broadening the circle. He gave Arkansas an opportunity to realize its real strength and allowed us to say to the nation, this is a good guy. A key part of that is the opportunity he afforded African Americans, unheard of opportunities. Generally, the weakness of a Southern politician is his relationship with African Americans. He was able to say that his first selection to cabinet was Mahlon Martin, for his finance department, then Dr. Elders and Bob Nash.

This is what Carol Willis and I were doing early on, reaching out to people where they were. We talked about the fact that he had blacks who managed big agencies and the state's money, billions of dollars. That went over really well.

Our black congressional leaders were not easily persuaded to back this Southern governor. People like Congressman (Charles) Rangel were at a different place. The only people with us early on were Bill Jefferson, Congressman Harold Ford, Congressman John Lewis, and Congressman Mike Espy. We had to go out and rally everyone else. They either had an allegiance to the Reverend Jesse

Jackson, or they had to get over this thing about Southerners. Finally, Los Angeles Mayor Willie Brown and Congressman Maxine Waters came aboard.

A large contingent of our supporters was African Americans that we'd invited back to Arkansas for the sesquicentennial celebration. We didn't know that would be a link back in the early '80s, but it did work. I think, tactically, what Bill Clinton did in 1982, he did in 1992.

Eastern Arkansas had always been one of the strongest support areas for him, but he sent a message to eastern Arkansas: he was not coming to any more segregated events. I admit I didn't understand it. But he was saying he didn't just want to get elected, he wanted to govern. And for him to govern, blacks and whites had to work together. Then, when I thought about it, I decided this is got to be a different kind of guy, and he's not just doing this for show. Even if we lose taking a stand like this . . . what he was saying was larger than that.

So the question became, where do we meet together? We can't go to a courthouse, a school, or a church. They ended up doing this great fish fry at the first integrated event at the Helena airport. This was the first time in history that black folks and whites did an event together, and there were hundreds of people there.

Eastern Arkansas has a rich history. There are two historic cemeteries in Helena—one black, one white. Six Confederate generals are buried in the white cemetery, including General Patrick Clymer, who recommended to Jefferson Davis to use black soldiers in the Confederate Army, and also suggested they be given their freedom in return.

Then in the black cemetery, Dr. William H. Gray, a hell of a guy who was the first black elected to the Arkansas General Assembly, is buried there. That was the only time both African Americans and whites played prominent roles in the administration, only time comparable to the Clinton era.

Bill Clinton did the same thing in Michigan and gave a speech to the Reagan Democrats, and went to Detroit and gave a speech to urban America. His message was, we cannot come back as a region, as a country, those who are running away from African Americans . . . the same thing as 1982. Tactically, those two events were most significant because they defined him as a politician. It's all about drawing that circle bigger. You're saying to yourself, I've been to segregated events, especially when it's your base.

The only time Governor Clinton and I had a serious, public disagreement was when he and Buddy Romer and Governor Mabus all ended up appointing themselves head of the Delta Commission. I didn't have an issue with that, but there were no African Americans appointed. I only said I was disappointed that he hadn't made any African American appointments. We talked about it later, and he said he had done so with the expectation that he would appoint African Americans.

What happened was, you're looking for every opportunity for an African American to be appointed, and you see that all the slots were filled up . . . then they appoint themselves. Bob was a designee, and Louisiana also had an African American.

The Reagan years were not bitter years for me, because it seemed as if every day there was something cutting edge and exciting and new . . . not that we didn't stay in touch with the news and see what was going on, but I was so excited about those years.

The Clinton legacy? His genuine belief in the worth of all people is the strength of our nation, and all the communities that make up our nation. You can exercise fiscal discipline, but still, through strategic investment and with the right focus, emphasize the right things. That is the hardest thing to do, and when a person does it, it should be acknowledged. The president did a very effective job. He instilled in the country his own belief that tomorrow could be better than today, that we can do even better.

Q

George Knox, Miami attorney; former law professor, University of Arkansas at Fayetteville; and a member of the Fayetteville "Mod Squad."

I was interviewed for a professor's job at the U of A at Fayetteville in 1975. Bill Clinton was a faculty member at that time . . . and the other faculty members were very anxious to meet him, as he and Hillary were probably the youngest faculty members.

I first met Hillary at a recruitment conference in Chicago, along with the dean and another staff member. I was one of the people Hillary and other professors interviewed. Subsequently, I was invited to the university campus to meet other faculty members and to look around the campus. That evening, they had a cocktail party, and that was where I met Bill. One of the professors' wives said, "You know, Bill's going to be president one day."

I went to work at the law school in 1975 and stayed there about 18 months as a junior faculty member. The law school faculty was in transition at the time. They were actively looking to get a younger, more diverse staff. Bill and Hillary and one or two other people came from Yale, all about the same time. Coming out of the revolutionary phase, the system was very, very interested in recruiting black faculty and recruiting and maintaining black students. All of this converged at the same time.

So I think Bill was regarded as the native son who had gone away and gotten his western European education, then came back home to begin his march toward the presidency. And this was all a part of the endowment and the legacy of William J. Fulbright: pick the best and brightest young men of the state of Arkansas, bring them back to govern the state, and position them for great things.

When I got to Arkansas, it was just after Bill had lost his congressional race, and the university was a place he could earn a living, do some good, and still have enough free time to campaign and work the state. There was a kinship between us by virtue of our relative ages, a kinship because we were perceived to be change agents. There was also a kinship because he had this charismatic ability to get everybody to buy into this notion that they should support him in his efforts.

And of course, Bill Clinton was a very decent, committed, compassionate, down-to-earth person. Both he and Hillary were traveling most of the time, so the only time we got together was between classes or at faculty meetings. But there was one very special occasion of gathering in northwest Arkansas that I found quite charming: hanging wallpaper. This activity involved traveling around from house to house and pitching in to help each other hang wallpaper. And of course, one of the homes I recall hanging wallpaper was at Bill and Hillary's home.

There had long been a feeling of alienation between black lawyers and the university. One of the things from that time I'm proudest of, was helping to heal that rift between the university and black lawyers. I brought Yale-educated civil rights lawyer John Walker up to the campus to help me do that

During just about every faculty meeting, the staff would discuss ways to help black students become more academically competitive without appearing patronizing. Bill Clinton's answer was that something had to be done, and now. My position was that something had to be done, but it couldn't be seen as condescending.

• • •

A great leader is someone who goes through the effort to embody what America should stand for in their everyday lives, in their official conduct and private lives as well. There are so few presidents who pass that litmus test. You can't define justice as treating blacks as three-fifths of a human being. When you empower people politically but don't allow them to participate economically, how are you ensuring them all the freedoms afforded the rest of the country? Every president to this day, save Bill Clinton, can be criticized for showing indifference, unwarranted patronization, or unwarranted paternalism.

Lyndon Johnson raised the consciousness about civil rights and opportunity. Kennedy charmed with his intellect, when it was Johnson who rolled up his sleeves and fought for civil rights. But then, we can't forget Ronald Reagan, who we have to thank for making us realize the critical need to continue affirmative action. Bill Clinton was more inclusive of blacks and other minorities than any other president.

The Clinton legacy? Bill Clinton was the first president in history to appreciate the value of the African American constituency and what they were worth as human beings. He lived the Constitution, things that other leaders simply gave lip service to: equal protection, equal opportunity, and fair play. He wanted blacks to contribute to the governing of America. I don't think anyone can ever accuse Bill Clinton of making a token appointment. He exposed talent and exposed substance.

His influence provided opportunities for African Americans to move into high-level organizations and allowed Fortune 500 companies and other major players to appreciate blacks as consumers and blacks as a market. His closely-watched friendship with Vernon Jordan is a good example. No president has allowed such open access to blacks. That led to a kind of black power. By putting blacks into positions, into cabinet positions that weren't all human services departments, some such as Frank Raines, whose position affected the economy.

After he figured out the conservatives had it in for him, I think Bill Clinton moved too far the other way. His leadership was diluted by political correctness, rather than being forthright and standing up for issues we all know he felt in his heart. Unfortunately, he didn't have enough people around him to tell him that. The first thing they told him was to remember re-election and, secondly, to preserve his legacy.

His future should include serving as an ambassador and continuing to teach Americans. His decision to place his office in Harlem is only appropriate: black Americans gave him unprecedented support throughout his political life. When he returned to Arkansas in 1974, Bill Clinton began a quest, but what is so rare is that he accomplished it . . . exactly what that professor's wife told me in 1975. Twenty years later, it was reality.

I don't think his eight years in D.C. changed his core; that part of him is fossilized. But there are now layers between his core and reality. When I think back, what I remember most fondly is our hanging wallpaper while he drank beer and sang limericks He never stopped working. He never took a break, never was deterred by those around him.

Conver

WILLIAM JEFFERSON CLINTON
FROM HOPE TO HARLEM

PART VII
A DAY IN THE DELTA

The issue of race is possibly the most difficult issue for this nation to come face to face with, to be completely honest about. It has been now, for centuries, this great nation's Achilles' heel. This doesn't mean we are not yet a great nation. But I ask you to dream how great a nation this could be, should we resolve this painful issue.

—Former President William J. Clinton
at the Shorestein Center

CHAPTER 20
CHANGE
— IN THE —
Delta

It was spring in West Memphis, Arkansas, and pleasantly cool. The small town was the lesser-known, less-sophisticated half of Arkansas' twin cities bordering Tennessee. The better-known twin, Memphis, sat less than a mile away, beyond an Arkansas mound. Memphis was the real city, with bright lights and world-renowned barbecue and a history of the blues. Most importantly, it was home to the Elvis mansion.

A buzz of small conversations wafted through the Holiday Inn conference room. The sparse group of men and women took peeks at their watches, growing a bit restless. "The governor supposed to be here about now," they mumbled softly to themselves or whoever might be listening. No response was needed.

Their conversations meandered from their children, to the weather, to their truck patches, and back to the governor's appearance here this morning. William Jefferson Clinton—"The Guv," in these parts—was already known for showing up just in the nick of time and sometimes a little past that.

In Arkansas' early spring seasons, the cotton seedlings are transforming themselves into promising young plants, turning the scorching brown rows a heartbreaking green. It's a time when Delta natives become so attuned to the mosquitoes' constant buzzing that they hardly hear them at all. The faraway sounds of giant John Deere tractors rolling through the endless fields, plowing and tilling the rich northeastern land, from dawn to dusk, appear to be nothing more than the hoot of midnight owls or the sound of roosters' early morning crows.

Northeast Arkansas, like most of the Delta, was Bill Clinton country. It was as if he had scribbled his name in the red dirt and dared another white Southern politician to try and step over it. The governor's fate, most believed, was a life of running. Hadn't it been said he'd come here knowing he wanted to run for something? By the spring of 1990, he was moving closer to that next, inevitable starting line, the one that would really count. Everything, even this small gathering of mostly black politicians and community leaders in this wannabe Memphis suburb, was part of that fate.

Governor Clinton walked into the room that morning looking as if he had all the time in the world and, at the same time, as if he had come to save the world. He had the unusual ability to evoke both ease and excitement. He strode with long, fast steps into the small crowd of loyalists, his entourage in tow. "Sorry I'm late," he mumbled with the smile that had already melted at least a million hearts over his 43 years.

He was a welcome sight at just about any gathering, big or small, black or white, backyard barbecue or sit-down dining, as long it was in Arkansas. He had shown up at the *Arkansas State Press'* annual political exchange for the last three years. Each time, his scheduler had offered a strong "maybe, we just can't be sure." But it was the only black-owned publication in Arkansas and a staunch Clinton backer to boot. Like his incorrigible charm, Bill Clinton was also born with his finger on the political pulse of Arkansas. He knew when a quick stop-by would make a difference and when it wouldn't.

While politics and local politicians' issues were the fare for the morning, Bill Clinton was—by a long stretch—the highlight of the morning's event. The people in this room have real concerns, of course: the loss of jobs in their communities, the growing price of groceries, the poor quality of their children's educations, and the list could go on. But more than anything, their early rise to get here this morning and their patient waiting were in anticipation of being in the presence of young Governor Clinton and his boyish grin and personal hellos. Nobody gave a heck about the weak apology.

A hush fell over the crowd just about 8:10 a.m., when the slightly rumpled governor strode into the oversized room, "sucking up the air . . . and pulling the attention from every other human being in the room." What must a child with that kind of crowd control have been like in his birthing room? He was now waving at old friends and nodding at unfamiliar ones as he walked toward the stage. This white man was used to being the token in a sea of black faces.

If it wasn't a political season, and if you didn't know Bill Clinton, you might think he was a country preacher toting a big Bible into the room. In fact, Bill Clinton carried a different kind of Bible this morning under his right arm and a Styrofoam cup, something to attend to his sleepiness, in his left hand. As he mumbled his good mornings to some in the group, calling most by their first names, they heard the gravel in his throat and knew that meant he'd awakened just minutes ago, just in time to get here before it was too late.

The familiar buzz quickly followed the hush, as "The Guv" strolled down the front of the room, eyeballing each little old woman and man sitting there. He stopped at the end, took a sip, and acknowledged the rest of the group with a smile and nod before stepping up on the stage that looked like so many thousands of others he'd stepped up on over the last 10 years.

The crowd, too, was pretty much indistinguishable from so many others he'd stood before in this part of the state. He eyed the seat awaiting him, offered one more smile and nod to the crowd, and disappeared behind the podium to settle in for the few moments he had before speaking to the group. He sipped from his cup and browsed through the heavy document he had brought. This was his first stop of the day, and he was mulling over what other gatherings awaited him on this Saturday in 1990.

The governor held the heavy document protectively, almost lovingly, against his chest. Later, he would describe it to this group as a blueprint for change in the Mississippi Delta. Though the study had been commissioned by the mostly white men who made up that estimable body called Congress, in Washington, D.C., it was the brainchild of progressive Southern leaders like Bill Clinton, Mississippi Governor Ray Mabus, Mississippi Congressman Mike Espy, former Mississippi Governor William Winters, and a collection of other stellar Southern politicians.

Bill Clinton had, in fact, played a significant role in developing this document, a State of the Mississippi Delta. He had implored Congress to help move the region into the 20th century as he described the atrocities of poverty, poor health care, and illiteracy. The white men and few women and minorities, dressed in their dark suits and ties, shook their heads in horror, muttering that the region sounded like a "damn Third World country, or something."

This powerful group of oversized egos rarely found much to agree on, but that day they were in agreement: the Southern Delta region was an embarrassment to the rest of America. And while most of them decided the region was virtually beyond repair, they voiced commitment to seriously study what could be done to turn the region around.

Bill Clinton had an enviable knack for rubbing America's nose in a reality it knew but refused to acknowledge, such as the fact that almost half of all the poor and minorities in the Delta region were either undereducated or illiterate; that children were having children there at an unimaginable rate; that almost half of all black adults in the Delta were unemployed, and jobs were getting scarcer every day; that the schools in the region only half-educated the children; and that poor and inadequate health care allowed for a proliferation of sickness and diseases throughout the Delta region.

Arkansas' youngest governor sat with the state's senior U.S. senator, Dale Bumpers, during this early Mississippi Delta Commission meeting. The men differed in age, demeanor, and political profile, yet had much in common. They both had large hearts and sharp political minds; they both had soft spots for the region's disenfranchised and saw the commission's efforts as a way to put federal dollars to good use and help themselves politically to boot.

The less-than-teeming group that gathered in West Memphis on that Saturday morning in May knew their governor would give them something in exchange for what he wanted from them. Today he would tell them that the Lower Mississippi Delta region was rife with tremendous human resources, productive land, water, timber, energy, and natural beauty. But he would also, because he was Bill Clinton, induce them to try harder to get water out of a turnip.

The young governor gave as complex an explanation of what the plan was about as he felt the audience could absorb this early in the morning. And an outside observer might have heard the "Wham!" as Bill Clinton laid down the race card as smoothly and bravely as any Southern politician could before this all-black audience. He stared straight into the eyes of the black men and women as he told them they had to take some blame for the region's economic and social stagnation just as white residents did; and no matter how much money Washington poured into the place, nothing could really change for the better until the region got a handle on its historical racial conflicts.

The gist of what Bill Clinton said that morning was nothing new to this group. In fact, he had said much of it many times before. Bill Clinton understood that most people, especially the disenfranchised, took you at your word when the promise of a brighter tomorrow was contrasted with the ugly reality of today, as long as your promises were wrapped in hope. The commission's plan for an improved Delta region was just such a gift of hope.

Bill Clinton's message of hope would go beyond this room and end up a conversation piece during Sunday dinners, or during a ride to the cotton fields, or while standing on the church grounds after service, or at coffee breaks at their 9 to 5s.

Later today, the people here would slowly nod their heads and agree that some responsibility for the mess that was the Delta region belonged to them. Certainly, they knew they weren't powerful enough to deserve much of the blame, but they'd take what was theirs. Bill Clinton's heart was in the right place, they would always decide, giving him credit for wanting to make things better.

It would be long after the hubbub of the commission's study had subsided that some would realize just how big this commission's job really was, and that the only part they could really play in assuring change in the region was giving Bill Clinton their vote whenever his name showed up on the ballot.

While there were no hallelujahs or amens voiced that Saturday morning in West Memphis, there was rousing applause, conciliatory smiles, and nods of approval. Once again, Bill Clinton had brought them hope for change. Bill Clinton always promised change, and that promise almost always guaranteed their vote on Election Day.

Though a light would turn on in many of their heads later on down the road, and they would realize a study is just a study, not a magical cure, they wouldn't hate the messenger of hope who made the study sound like so much more. Bill Clinton had allowed them to believe that Saturday morning; no other white politician even bothered. He had painted pictures prettier than they actually were; he'd also gotten what he'd come after: another round of adulation for thinking first about the people of Arkansas that few politicians ever thought of first.

Bill Clinton and his fellow commissioners had met in a number of small and medium-sized towns in Arkansas, Louisiana, Mississippi, Tennessee, and Missouri. They'd listened to hundreds of Delta residents: black, white, church leaders, restaurant owners, health care workers, cab drivers, and even local politicians.

The commissioners' aides would sit close by, listening, documenting the locals' harrowing stories and concerns about their home towns, their educational systems, their hospitals, their roadway systems. The concerns were endless, all perfectly credible reasons why the Delta was still mired in hopelessness, poverty, and racial conflicts. Bill Clinton never left one of these sessions without asking, "What do we need to do to make things better for you and your family here in the Delta?"

Arkansans would later believe that the Delta Initiative was a part of the governor's lifelong race for something more. The almost 200-page document was an agate marble that might just help propel him to that starting line. William Jefferson Clinton told Congress that "real change is hard, frustrating, complicated, and takes time." In essence, it needed someone like him—methodical, strategic, brilliant, and visionary—to see something so complex to fruition.

Few Arkansas Democrats, black or white, disagreed. They had believed for a long time that they had something special in Bill Clinton. For the many who believed special and good were synonymous in this case, their fear was that the governor's ascension to bigger and better things would come too soon, before he had completed the hard job of making substantive changes in his own back yard.

The Delta Commission's study has been characterized as Bill Clinton's legacy as governor of Arkansas. Synonymous, even, with him, the man and the politician said to overlap more often than not. While the young governor was honest and sincere in his efforts to bring change to the Delta region, they say, the brilliant politician in him knew that his political star lay not with its success, but with his valiant effort. His hand would be solidly imprinted on the political sidewalk.

CHAPTER 21
—— THE ——
Delta Blues

Judge Ollie Neal, tall and straight as the trees that cooled and shaded the Delta summers he'd known in Marianna, Arkansas, where he grew up, wears a perpetual smile. His humor is legendary, as is his sharp insight into Arkansas politics . . . particularly politics centered around the Delta. The black robe he wears these days shows how far he has come since his days of vocal and consistent activism against the status quo.

The revered former activist, who donned dashikis and sported an afro many years before the judge's chambers became his domain, concedes that Arkansas has seen some positive changes over the last 20 years. His Paul Robeson-like voice would sound just as natural reciting soliloquies from Shakespeare's *Othello* play or Martin Luther King's "I Have a Dream" speech as it does orating about the problems that seem to never die in the Arkansas Delta.

"Changes, yes, but nothing like it should'a been," he smiles, "nothing close to what most of us dreamed it would be." Neal admits he takes it personally, given his lifelong work in the area, that the Delta Commission didn't live up to its promises. "Their reach came far short of what black Arkansans expected . . . far short."

The hard part, he says, is when you see that Clinton *got* it. "There is no question that Bill Clinton understood the depth of the problems in the Delta," Neal says, describing the 12-year governor as maybe the most brilliant man he's ever met. "He empathized with their plight but failed to make the kind of impact . . . to go the full length of making the kind of difference we had all hoped for."

It there is disappointment, Neal says, it is because of Bill Clinton's effective leadership. "If he had concentrated more of his political capital in the Delta, I know he could have made long-term changes. He did some short-term things, and he made progress in highways and construction, and we were real happy to get the research center; but given his leadership, I believe he could have gotten away with more long-term changes in that area."

CHAPTER 22
An
Arkansas Star
is Born

Arkansans, for the most part, hung their stars on the young, brilliant governor for 11 years. They were proud to call Clinton their own. His outgoing personality and incredible intellect had helped put the state on the map. His vision had been the impetus for new industries to arrive from countries that otherwise would never have given Arkansas a second look. That same vision encouraged the creation of a Motion Picture Department that drew Hollywood to the small Southern state.

The Saturday morning meeting in the room half-filled with Arkansas' African American leaders, politicians, and community leaders, and his arrival bearing the gift of the Delta Initiative, tell the story of the Bill Clinton that most Arkansans know well. He was there when nobody thought he would be, and he always had a piece of hope to share. Never mind that the hope didn't always pan out in the end. He was the first to offer it—often the only one to offer it—and he truly did want it to happen.

Black Arkansans don't agree that Bill Clinton had a certain smile for them and another for the white folks. They didn't accept outsiders' claims that he never slapped a white man on the back or laugh as raucously when in their company. Most folks who knew him believe that Bill Clinton was Bill Clinton, no matter what side of the track he happened to be on.

Professor Theman Taylor teaches African American studies at the University of Central Arkanas, in Conway—a long way from Dallas, Texas, where he grew up.

The former radical continues to vent his conscience in newspaper editorials and essays. Taylor holds up a now-worn newspaper clipping of an editorial he wrote in 1990, encouraging Arkansans to push to get Hillary Rodham Clinton to the White House rather than Bill Clinton.

"Bill Clinton is about as smart a politician as you'll find. Smart enough to put some time in studying our culture and the way we think. And he knew what was acceptable in the different environments, that's a fact . . . but that's being smart, not necessarily disingenuous.

"I personally never got the feeling that he was putting one group down and building the other one up. It was just respecting the culture of the people he was around . . . and it paid off for him."

What some astute politicians point out is that Bill Clinton had grown up enjoying the company and culture of black friends and associates, but that had changed into something more when he decided he wanted to be a Southern politician. Now, he needed the very people he had always simply enjoyed being around.

As attorney general, then governor, Bill Clinton brought much of that kind of sensitivity and inclusiveness into his office. Arkansas' racially exclusive state government embarrassed him. He made it known that he would not stand for a lily-white attorney general's office, and, according to some, he took it upon himself to recruit the best and the brightest African American attorneys to his office.

Bill Clinton was the first attorney general in Arkansas' history to appoint African American assistant attorneys general. It helped that Clinton knew many of them, since the overwhelming majority of black attorneys practicing in Arkansas had attended the University of Arkansas during Clinton's tenure there.

☾

CHAPTER 23
FOOTSTEPS
IN *History*

When Bill Clinton became governor of Arkansas in 1979, he followed on the heels of two progressive leaders, David Pryor and Dale Bumpers. Dale Bumpers had replaced a far-left liberal and Yankee-turned-Southerner, Winthrop Paul Rockefeller, who many believe set the groundwork for Clinton's efforts to level the racial playing fields inside and outside state government.

Winthrop Rockefeller had beat out an Arkansas governor with a dubious history of railing against race mingling, the man who had stood in the doorway of Central High School to bar the entrance of nine black children during the infamous 1957 Integration Crisis at Central High. The notorius Governor Orval Faubus had followed in the wake of a one-time friend and colleague, Syd McMath. While Faubus was a conservative-turned-rabid rightist, McMath had been a progressive who went as far left as his south Arkansas roots would allow—this at a time when the words "white Southern liberal" were rarely uttered in the same breath.

McMath was a native of southwest Arkansas, growing up in Smackover, just a stone's throw from Clinton's birthplace of Hope, and moving at the age of 10 to Hot Springs, also the second home of the future president. The attorney-turned-prosecutor-turned-public servant has been credited by African Americans with exhibiting almost as much sensitivity to Arkansas' racial problems as Bill Clinton later would.

Given the times, he positioned himself as a moderate when it came to race relations, while Bill Clinton would dance on the edge of liberalism but call himself a staunch progressive. McMath's work for the underdog is said to have begun when he witnessed a black man being horsewhipped in the city of Hot Springs. His son-in-law, Richard Hatfield, says his sensitivity had much to do with his growing up dirt poor in southwest Arkansas and understanding how tough life was for the rural poor.

In 1957, McMath openly criticized his one-time protégé, Orval Faubus, for his stance on school desegregation. He had helped propel Faubus to prominence during his own governorship, placing him on the Highway Commission, then hiring him as his administrative assistant. Yet he lamented Faubus' role in keeping blacks out of Central High and called on the governor to "quit playing politics with the lives and educations of our boys and girls." McMath believed Faubus' political campaign had no place in the classrooms.

Sid McMath was governor from 1949 to 1953 and was eulogized in 2003 by Senator David Pryor as the man who "invented charisma long before the word appeared in politics." At the age of 36, he was the youngest governor elected since Reconstruction and the second youngest in Arkansas history. President Bill Clinton, at McMath's funeral, called him one of Arkansas' true heroes.

Ironically, the prosecutor-turned-reformist made his name sweeping out Hot Springs' corrupt political machine, headed by Mayor Leo McLaughlin. Political incumbents were charged with fraud, malfeasance, bribery, and even armed robbery, according to one report. Fraudulent poll taxes, he'd found, had helped perpetuate McLaughlin's machine. His role in cleaning up the city helped propel him to the nomination for the 1949 Democratic gubernatorial primary. He won that election and a subsequent one in 1950.

McMath was credited with keeping Arkansas behind Harry Truman when some other Southern states defected from the Democratic Party in favor of segregationist Dixiecrats. He is also credited with putting in place equal facilities and educational opportunities for blacks.

In 1952, there was a national discussion by the Democratic Party as to whether McMath should be offered up as the Southern prospect on the 1952 presidential ticket. He was outvoted, however, and Adlai E. Stevenson received the nomination. McMath left the governor's office in 1952 under a cloud of scandal after being accused of misappropriations of funds. Though no convictions ensued, and he claimed the charges were being brought by political opponents, he lost the next term to Francis Cherry.

Arkansas' racial history mirrors that of many Southern states. The leaders have historically dealt with much the same problems as "business as usual." Bill Clinton was the first governor beside Winthrop Rockefeller to have the guts to be open and vocal about his commitment to racial equality and diversity in state government.

It was due to Bill Clinton's leadership that, for the first time, the state's governmental departments were headed by a diverse cross section of the populace, including women and minorities. As governor, he appointed more African Americans to cabinet-level posts, boards, and commissions than all other Arkansas governors combined—22 percent in 1990. For most of his tenure, his cabinet was representative of the state's diversity.

Those who know him best are convinced that Bill Clinton is as close to color-blind as any white Southerner can get. His tenure as governor includes a record of challenging Arkansas' history, replacing antiquated practices with those that were equal and fair to Arkansas' population.

When he stepped into the governor's office in 1979, Clinton told aides he was appalled that so little change had been made over the years in the monochromatic boards and commissions that served an appreciatively growing minority constituency. That year, as Clinton had promised, dramatic changes began to take place in Arkansas' state government.

Some of the state's most visible commissions—the Public Service Commission, the State Highway Commission, and the Game and Fish Commission—were filled by African Americans during Clinton's second term.

Dr. Jocelyn Elders, a prominent physician and professor at the University of Arkansas' medical school, was tapped to head the state's health department. And just shortly before announcing his bid for the presidency in 1991, Governor Clinton appointed a former Little Rock city manager, Mahlon Martin, to head the state's Department of Finance and Administration. For the first time, black judges represented constituencies in predominantly black judicial districts. Within a span of four years, four black juvenile judges were appointed, as well as two black appeals court judges, two black Supreme Court judges, and a number of trial judges.

CHAPTER 24
—THE—
Education Governor

I f a legacy was what William Jefferson Clinton sought in return for his 11 years at the helm of the small state of Arkansas, his education record would give him just that. One of a handful of "new generation" Southern leaders, the young governor put education at the top of his political agenda early on. In 1983, the state Legislature approved the most comprehensive education program in the state's history, designed to lift its schools from the bottom of the national rankings.

Dr. Cora McHenry, who now heads up a local historically black college, is an eastern Arkansas Deltan who credits her parents for teaching their 13 children the importance of a solid education. She credits Bill Clinton for bringing that same kind of understanding of the power of education to the state of Arkansas.

The petite woman, who speaks with a soft and measured cadence, shakes her head and smiles. "I remember all those trenches I shared with Bill and Hillary Clinton during those early years." Bill Clinton's greatest talent, McHenry says, was his ability to do amazing things with little early support. "He was able to do so much in the area. His greatest accomplishment by far as governor of Arkansas was his pushing of the new education standards and accreditation for public education.

Bill Clinton, the "progressive pragmatist," persuaded Arkansans to accept their first sales tax increase in 26 years to help pay for a teacher salary increase, arguing that education was vital to the economic and social future of the state. Then, in one of the most controversial political moves of his career, he demanded that teachers be tested for competency, putting himself squarely in the national spotlight.

To drive his point home, the governor spouted the statistics: more than 100 high schools didn't offer chemistry, foreign languages, or advanced mathematics; more than 200 did not offer physics. Many students were never offered art or music. The state had been, for years, the most underfinanced school system in the nation, ranking last in per-pupil expenditures and teachers' salaries. A 1978 study concluded that students would be better off in any other state.

On January 21, 1991, Governor Clinton outlined a plan to raise $287.2 million over the next two fiscal years, all for education. On January 29, to many observers' amazement, the plan was made law. So began the education legacy of Governor Clinton and the saga of the state of Arkansas' controversial road to education reform.

No one was much surprised in 1986 when Clinton became the new chairman of the National Governors' Association. His visibility as a national leader helped his efforts to keep education on the national front burner, and he introduced issues such as at-risk youth and illiteracy to the education reform agenda.

During the years between 1983 and 1992, Bill Clinton fought for and passed major reform legislation when the odds were against him. The state's wealthy constituents and its business lobbyists fought successfully to prevent him from increasing personal and corporate income taxes in order to fund his reforms. Instead, he settled for raising the sales tax, which fell the hardest on the poor, but followed that up with the passage of a tax cut for the poor and elderly.

In February 1984, the Arkansas State Board of Education unanimously approved new education standards, culminating a yearlong effort by Governor Clinton, the Educational Standards Committee, and the Arkansas Legislature. The new law authorized new school reforms that would raise graduation requirements from 16 to 20 units and establish a minimum number of course units that high schools must provide. It would also set maximum class sizes and require minimum competency tests for students in the third, sixth, and eighth grades.

Arkansans were in awe of the cooperation the governor garnered from the Legislature as well as of his dogged determination to change Arkansas' educational horizons. It was an unusual partnership between a progressive thinker and traditionalist lawmakers. Education administrators celebrated the content of the reforms, realizing the boost this would be to educators, administrators, and teachers statewide.

Syd Johnson, president of the Arkansas Education Association, said of the state Legislature's passage of the education bill, "They've never moved anything that cost money through the Legislature that fast . . . even the old-timers said they'd never seen anything like it."

Were the stars aligned just right for the young governor, or was his passion for this issue so deep as to enhance his persuasive abilities as he stood before the staid lawmakers?

Few in the state would dispute that this governor had made education reform a personal mission or that the children of the state would be its beneficiaries. The young, progressive pragmatist was, in fact, part of an emerging group of Southern Democrats who sought to mesh their social ideals with a public policy that proved itself workable, affordable, and accountable.

Those who followed Clinton's bold engineering of education reform, in a state most considered backward, were not surprised when he was elected to chair the Education Commission of the States, an influential meeting ground for state education leaders. Yet in spite of his national and local recognition, many traditional educators believed the governor had bitten off more than he could chew and was in some ways going about things in the wrong way.

The American Federation of Teachers president, Al Shanker, was adamantly against the teacher testing part of Clinton's reform, predicting that it would result in severe teacher shortages and force states to grant teacher certifications to ill-trained substitutes, thereby exacerbating an already difficult situation.

John I. Goodlad, who conducted a seven-year study of high schools, argued that a pilot test of the teacher examination requirement was desperately called for. Goodland, the former dean of UCLA's Graduate School of Education, believed that Clinton should not be focusing on asking practicing teachers to take the test but on identifying prospective teachers. In fact, Clinton's plan called for all Arkansas teachers to take the competency tests in reading, writing, and mathematics. Those who failed would have to take further training; if they didn't pass the test within four years, they would lose their jobs.

Governor Clinton argued, "You can make all sorts of arguments about how we should have tried this on an experimental basis, but I tell you, if we had let four or five years pass without acting, we would have wound up with nothing, in my view. The time to act was then . . . it's not often that the nation's attention is focused on education. If we had waited, we would have had more business as usual."

The 1991 Education Reform bill would give teachers an average $4,000 pay raise in addition to the $1,000 raise they were already slated for, boosting their pay to 45th in the nation. This raise, however, came in exchange for the governor's controversial effort to increase the quality of teachers through tests—what many teachers and educators saw as a "weeding out" of instructors.

The radical new education bill also called for eighth graders to pass a test before going on to high school, required schools to shrink class sizes, and mandated that all districts offer college prerequisite courses in math and science.

No matter who came up against him, Clinton defended his reform efforts. He smoothed the ruffled edges of the state's teachers during his January 15 inaugural speech, saying, "We cannot ever hope to have the education system we want if we try to add new standards, new programs, and new opportunities on the backs of the school teachers. They have done all they can do, and they have produced for you more results with less money than any state in the United States of America."

Clinton said his education package represented the kind of real financial investment that the state needed to move out of poverty.

By the time Clinton would hang up his hat at the Arkansas State Capitol in 1992, Arkansas was 10th in the nation in the number of computers per pupil and 17th in teachers per pupil. The dropout rate had shrunk lower than the national average, enrollment in advanced math and science classes had tripled, and the proportion of high school graduates going on to college had risen from 38 percent to more than 51 percent, bettering the national average.

On another level, white flight, which had plagued the capital city of Little Rock, leveled off, as white families returned to public schools; they had been lured back by greater parental involvement and school restructuring, according to school administrators. The governor consistently put money where his mouth was when it came to education reform for the state, spearheading the state's provision of $1,000 college scholarships to more than 12,000 students who otherwise couldn't afford college. He divided the remaining funds from the package between preschool programs and college scholarships for high school seniors with a B or better average and funded pilot apprenticeship programs for students not going on to higher education.

Mathematics and science schools were established to train teachers, experiment with alternative curricula, and serve the state's brightest math and science students. Funds were also slated for the creation of rural magnet schools in the state's poverty-ridden Delta region.

One might say that young Governor Clinton admitted his mortality in 1991, when he told his state Legislature that, in many ways, Arkansas was no better off that day than it was when he'd taken office 10 years earlier. While he owned up to his own shortcomings, he placed much of that blame on the deeply ingrained poverty, illiteracy, and unemployment that still troubled the Delta region.

Bill Clinton warned the group of men and women lawmakers that the Delta region would continue to haunt the state until they faced up to its deep-seated and debilitating problems of class, culture, and race. The bright spot in the forecast, he pointed out, was the education reform bill, a ladder they had built together to help Arkansas' children climb up and out of the state's abyss of impoverishment and hopelessness.

In deference to his wife's unflinching work for education and children, he lauded the Home Instructional Programs for Preschool Youth (HIPPY), which had been introduced by Hillary Rodham Clinton in 1985 and which helped prepare children from poor homes for kindergarten. HIPPY had been modeled after an Israeli program that had been acclaimed for its success and which was the largest preschool program in the world.

Arkansas' program was now the second largest in the United States, even though it only reached 20 percent of Arkansan children needing it. The governor lamented that he hadn't been able to convince the legislature that preschool was just as important as elementary or high school.

In February 1992, the *Christian Science Monitor* featured the HIPPY program in its newspaper, highlighting the community of College Station, a suburb of Little Rock. The article noted that HIPPY students, who were predominantly low-income students, historically began school more academically prepared than other kindergarten students. The program had just doubled its participation to more than 4,500 families—more than all other states combined—thanks to funding from a state education bill pushed by Governor Clinton.

Conver

WILLIAM JEFFERSON CLINTON
FROM HOPE TO HARLEM

PART VIII

CONVERSATIONS WITH
BLACK AMERICA

Among the really profound and difficult problems of the world . . . they tend to fall into two categories. Some are like old wounds with scabs on them, and some are like abscessed teeth.

Old wounds with scabs eventually will heal if you just leave them alone. And if you fool with them too much, you might open the scab and make them worse. Abscessed teeth, however, will only get worse if you leave them alone, and if you wait and wait and wait, they'll just infect the whole rest of your mouth.

There are many everyday problems this country faces that, I believe, are becoming more like the scab. Even though we wish we could completely solve the many problems of our world, we know, in time, many of them will eventually heal themselves and hold no dire harm for this country, as a whole.

But this country's longtime struggle with the race issue is not just an old scab that will heal itself. It is a potentially poisonous abscess that will take strong medicine and real commitment from the "doctors," the "nurses," and, especially, the lay people of this country, to heal . . . for us to absolve ourselves of this dangerous toxin.

**—William Jefferson Clinton,
at the Shorenstein Center**

Tom Williamson, Washington, D.C., attorney; longtime Bill Clinton friend:

> Bill and I met in 1968, on a ship taking us from New York City to England. We were both Rhodes scholars, and it was tradition that Rhodes scholars sailed over together to get acquainted. Once we got there, we'd be scattered all over the campus; the structure was very decentralized.
>
> Bill came over and introduced himself as we were leaving, and we'd all said our goodbyes. "Hi, my name is Bill Clinton," you know, with this Southern drawl. I was still focused on my girlfriend rather than on him or the rest of the group. I'm sure he saw my lack of enthusiasm when he approached me. I was also wary that he had singled me out to get acquainted with me only because we were the outsiders: he was a Southerner and I was black. This was the late '60s, and I figured he wanted to make a point of being the impeccable defender of the South, so he was going to reach out to me.
>
> I began to think he could read my response, but still was absolutely not deterred. He seemed to have both the perception and conviction that "I know you may not think I'm that interesting to get to know, but I also know you're wrong, and I'm going to put some energy into showing you."
>
> We spent a lot of time together during the three-day trip and began to get to know each other pretty well. He was one of the more notable members of the Rhodes scholars group because he played the saxophone, even performed during one of the parties aboard the ship.
>
> There were about 160 students on the ship, and the usual sorts of things took place during our trip that you'd expect when girls and guys are stuck together like that for any length of time. Both Bill and I met and became friends with some very interesting young women. Ironically, the girl I met was named Hillary, and the person he ended up dating was named Martha. Martha was going to study in Paris, and Hillary was to study in Dublin.
>
> Our ship docked in Southampton three or four days after we left New York, and we took a bus to Oxford. Over the next few days, and later on, we both made frequent efforts to do things together. By the time we arrived in London, this Southern fellow had persuaded me it was worth my time for us to become friends. We both enjoyed discussing political issues. I enjoyed talking about issues, and Bill liked talking about the political process.

We hitchhiked from the campus into downtown London and always made a day trip out of it. We quickly learned that wearing our Oxford scarves just about guaranteed we'd be picked up. The scarves symbolized status there. We'd often hitchhike to one point, then take a ferry between England and Ireland, where we'd meet Hillary and Martha. Because hitchhiking was not rapid transit, Bill and I ended up spending a lot of time talking, reflecting, and sharing stories about our backgrounds.

● ● ●

As to his presidency, there were some things I wish he had done differently. When the debate was going on about affirmative action, I felt Bill stalled on how to "reform" affirmative action. His commitment didn't take place until much of the debate was mooted by the Adarand decision. I wish he had acted more decisively.

I was disappointed when he backed off support for Lani Guinier. It didn't harm blacks as much as it harmed his presidency. Once people know you can be pressured to abandon your friends, they'll exert that pressure on you time and time again.

The greatest disappointment was an issue that indirectly affected hundreds of thousands of Rwandans. It is inconceivable that the United States would have chosen not to send troops in. If 800,000 whites were going to be killed, I can't imagine the administration wouldn't have taken some strategic action. This was an opportunity for the U.S. president to make a very important statement—that black peoples' lives are just as important as the lives of any others, including Europeans and the Middle Easterners. But we did nothing as hundreds of thousands of blacks were being slaughtered.

● ● ●

Bill Clinton's legacy will be his overall commitment to appointing African Americans to a wide range of senior positions within federal government, not just traditional roles . . . which helped us as American citizens make a quantum step forward in this country.

As for his future, I'm a big admirer of Jimmy Carter. I think Carter figured out how to focus his life as a past president in a way that speaks to his values and his commitment to service to the needy of this country and the world.

Bill has, at his core, a very similar sort of compassion—using his knowledge, skills, and connections to make situations better for everyone. But he needs to focus on something that isn't a part of a conventional political debate, because some will wonder if he's trying to patch up his legacy or to continue to wield political power. Once you've been president, you can never have the luster of power that you had as a president.

Serving as president of the United States, you have to change to some extent. Bill has a remarkable ability, when he is with you, to regenerate the care which is at the core of the friendship. What changed was the nature of his accessibility.

When he was governor, we would hang out for the weekends. He'd be doing his political stuff, but we could also walk down the streets of Little Rock, and he'd tell me about all the different sites downtown. We'd go raid the icebox late at night like we were still in our college days.

Presidents of the United States lose that kind of accessibility to their friends. There is always that artificial shield between him and the rest of us, nothing like those days of hanging out or raiding the refrigerator in the governor's mansion. He still has the remarkable ability to, within a few moments, make you know that he is still in touch with that feeling you shared in the past. He had to deal with a lot of people . . . an enormous number of friends. Sometimes it's the friend's responsibility to decide whether to impose on his friendship.

Professor William Julius Wilson, director, Joblessness and Urban Poverty Research Program, John F. Kennedy School of Government, Harvard University:

I met Bill Clinton at the economic summit conference before he took the presidency. I think that was December of 1992. We were in a ballroom, and he came in. This was before the conference began, the night before the conference. He came into the ballroom and he just exuded a confidence and a sort of charismatic appeal. He looked like some type of king walking in . . . the way in which he lit up the room was just incredible.

I remember him walking over to where I was . . . apparently he had commented on my book, saying he had read about it somewhere, and I thanked him for the comment. He said it was a very good book and was pleased to have read it.

On the next day, at the conference, I gave a presentation, and he chaired the panel discussion. After my talk, he did a brief follow-up and told the group, "I don't know how many people have read Professor Wilson's book, but I highly recommend it . . . it's only 187 pages of text." Well, when I got home, one of the first things I did was pull the book off the shelf. The book was exactly 187 pages. I found that incredible.

• • •

A great leader has to have a vision of how the world works, a comprehensive vision that will integrate critical issues and policies, social issues and policy. That's very, very important to have, that comprehensive vision of the world. Secondly, he or she needs leadership skills to push that vision forward, to command the attention of the constituency—the people he's trying to reach.

Clinton was certainly one of the leaders who had that comprehensive vision . . . along with Martin Luther King, Jr., Bayard Rustin, Mahatma Gandhi, Winston Churchill, and Franklin Delano Roosevelt. I think Roosevelt and Clinton are the two presidents in recent years that had that kind of comprehensive vision. I would like to add Carter, but I really can't.

Franklin Roosevelt created programs that had long-term cumulative effects on the black population. The New Deal led to lots of programs that positively affected blacks, including protective union legislation, which enabled unions to compete for blacks and brought blacks into industrywide unions. Prior to that, blacks had been excluded. Add to that social security legislation, welfare legislation. The cumulative effects of these policies on the black population, over time, put Roosevelt at No. 1.

Lyndon Johnson's administration created civil rights legislation, the Great Society program. But again, I think Roosevelt's social programs had the longest-lasting impact. Given Johnson's civil rights legislation, it's a close call between the two.

• • •

Bill Clinton put in place race-neutral programs and positions that positively affected blacks, such as the Earned Income Tax Credits and raising minimum wage after years of not being increased under the Reagan and Bush administrations. Blacks disproportionately benefited from these types of initiatives.

He can be credited also with a continued commitment to affirmative action when it was under real attack by his opponents. His theme was "mend it, don't end it."

Clinton probably used the bully pulpit to talk about race more than any other president. He should receive some credit for reduction of racial tension during his tenure. Both his Memphis speech and his Austin speech were greatly covered by the media. Following the Austin speech, he created the Race Initiative . . . a very important symbolic message that said the president of the United States is concerned about race issues. He went against his political advisors with this, but he showed that he really did want to end racial disparities. Unfortunately, the sustainability of this effort was lost.

His appointments of a significant number of African Americans to major positions in government and to his cabinet—Elders, Herman, Brown, Slater, Pena, West, Cisneros—was an unprecedented number. On the basis of all that, I'd say he has been one of the great presidential leaders for African American causes.

Clinton had a comprehensive vision reflected in his economic and social policy outlines, except for welfare reform. We all knew there could be no meaningful welfare reform without health reform. My concern was that there wasn't sufficient communication with the public about this bill. He needed to talk about his opposition with groups who had a vested interest. He lost an opportunity by not anticipating organized opposition.

He would have had an incredible accomplishment if he had gotten a health reform bill. Instead, he signed a very, very weak welfare reform bill. Even with people saying it is effective, timing could not have been better. The economic boom aided that decision . . . that, and the minimum wage increase. He was very lucky, fortunate for the string of economic successes.

My worry . . . concern is, what will happen if we enter a real inflation? I wish we had gone before the American people and said this is a Republican bill that is based on the belief that people are on welfare because they choose to be. Right now, we're lucky that conditions are favorable. The long-term effects, I predict, will be negative.

The Clinton legacy? Bill Clinton, in a way, spoiled us. We got very accustomed to having a president who was very intelligent, with incredible energy, tireless, working at these problems. His legacy is not so much in terms of substantive actions or policies as it is a fact that he was a model for what a president of the United States can accomplish. There is no reason for us to elect a president who lacks intelligence, lacks vision, after a Clinton, who had extreme intelligence and broad vision. Unfortunately, he couldn't run for a third term.

The president changed. When he first entered the White House, he had really a progressive agenda. I was very concerned about poverty and welfare . . . social issues. If he had had a strong Congress to work with him, you would have seen him do some of the progressive things he promised during his campaign. I was always struck by his ability to pull together groups, to meet with progressive popular groups and make them see they were being manipulated. He had real progressive, comprehensive vision, and if he'd had a strong Democratic Congress behind him, he could have done some great things.

His wake-up call came in 1994. That forced him to shift away from the progressive agenda he had wanted to move forward. At that point, he was listening to his advisors telling him about political survival. For those of us who are progressives and liberals, that was a big disappointment. The years between 1994 and 1996 were definitely a "down" period in his presidency. He regained himself in 1996, when he was re-elected.

What does tomorrow hold for Bill Clinton? He has a very good understanding of domestic and foreign policy. I would like to see the Democratic Party use him more, rely on his judgment. I was very disappointed in the Democratic Party in how they responded to George Bush. They all seemed intimidated. Clinton should be encouraged to speak out more. They should put him out there, in front, to address the Bush administration.

Another thing that impressed me about Clinton was his respect for scholarship. He was widely read, knew the work of leading social scientists and relied on us. He used to have a number of meetings with experts on various issues. He was exposed to our work, and I think that was very unique for a president.

Wellington Webb, former mayor of Denver; former president, National Conference of Mayors:

I met Bill Clinton in 1992. Of course, I knew of him much earlier than that. I had sat in a number of meetings which probably contributed to his 1981 loss to the Republican governor in Arkansas. I was at the Department of Health, Education, and Welfare at the time. I vividly recall one meeting I participated in, when HEW Secretary Joe Califano and President Carter were discussing the whole issue of moving Cuban refugees to Arkansas.

There were a number of such meetings, and the general consensus there was that bringing Cuban refugees to Arkansas probably wasn't a good idea. No one was sure this young governor could effectively handle it if a problem arose. Well, I understood later that that was one of the issues the Republicans used against him.

During a trip I took with the president on Air Force One, I told him how I'd sat in on the meeting when it was decided to send Cuban refugees to Arkansas. He thought that was amazing that I had participated in the government adding a new population count to northwest Arkansas.

Before his election, I met a number of times with the governor and Mrs. Clinton during their visits to Denver. I had just been elected mayor in 1991when he started letting people know he was running. Several presidential candidates voiced an interest in meeting with me because of Denver's political electorate. Bill Clinton, though, was the only one who came to my office and met with me and my staff to share his vision, platform, and programs.

Those kinds of things, the small things that other candidates thought wouldn't be noticed, put him ahead of the crowd. He wasn't put out or concerned about having to come by my office. He certainly would have a larger audience than a small meeting with me and my colleagues. Other candidates felt they were above that. Shortly afterwards, I was convinced that Bill Clinton would be the next president.

The staff fell in love with him because he'd always remember their names. Once his campaign began in earnest, his numbers spiraled up, and his popularity grew in our state. He started out with 7 percent of the voters saying they'd vote for him, but he ended up winning the election with 57 percent of the vote.

● ● ●

I think great leadership can be defined as the ability to grasp the issues of the day, at home and internationally, take those complex issues and simplify them in a way the average American citizen can understand. A great leader understands that a leader is a creation of his followers, and thereby that leader must consistently seek ways to better serve those who honored him or her with leadership.

● ● ●

What he did for Democrats was prove that you can be liberal on social issues, fiscally responsible, and tough on crime. That's an important lesson for Democrats and Republicans . . . to know they can care about our fiduciary well-being, about safety and security and not abdicate those issues to Republicans, carte blanche. That gave Bill Clinton a lot of support from unaffiliated voters.

He learned from watching and studying previous administrations that had very popular presidents but drove the country in the ground, fiscally. He was able to, through his leadership, challenge Congress and pass proposals that eliminated the deficit. It was absolutely phenomenal how he crafted an economic strategy that assured good economic times for that many years.

His interest in world affairs outside the U.S., and his understanding of the importance of the continent of Africa was so important...and, then, to have a U.S. president land an aircraft in Nigeria and Ghana.

Because of his centrist policies, he was criticized by those on the left and by some within his own administration. Certainly, the conservatives believed he wasn't conservative enough. But he did not equivocate on the issues of women, and children, and of inclusion of minorities. His administration reflected the nation as a whole.

He would stand up shoulder to shoulder with those whom history has named our greatest presidents. Roosevelt has long been at the top of the list given his outstanding and, to a great extent, creative leadership during the Great Depression. He led us through not only the Depression but part of the Second World War.

We have to, of course, credit Truman for the Marshall Plan and desegregating the armed services, and Kennedy for bringing something that is very difficult to quantify. Much like Clinton, he made Americans proud to be Americans and inspired young people to get involved in public service. I even think Woodrow Wilson's League of Nations during World War 1 was very important to the country's stability.

But more than any other U.S. president, Bill Clinton came in with the expectation that he was there to serve all Americans. No special interest group or constituency was deserving of better treatment than any other group. He came in wanting to make the federal government, which is responsible for so very much in everyday people's lives, be representative of all those people it served . . . or was put there to serve.

What I always found interesting about Bill Clinton was his love of politics. Not just the campaigning and shaking hands part, but using politics to make the world better. He absolutely loved to discuss public policy, even though the average person's eyes glaze over after a few minutes of discussion. Most people who have not spent time with him in small settings would be amazed at how quiet and introspective he can be.

Finally, his power was in the fact that people from every spectrum of society identified with him . . . from the most economically or socially challenged to the wealthiest person in the nation. That was a big part of his success and his mystique.

There is still this archaic notion by many in power that if you don't come with that pedigree or the nobility of birth or wealth, there are limitations to where you can and should go. In case anyone missed it, Bill Clinton proved without a doubt that, in the end, none of that mattered. And because of his inclusive philosophy, people of color were able to prove that they were much more than the color of their skin or the part of town they grew up. What an amazing legacy!

☉

Bill Campbell, former mayor of Atlanta, Georgia

I met Bill Clinton when he was governor of Arkansas. He came to a National League of Cities conference in San Antonio and spoke to the black municipal elected officials. I saw his presentation as fairly remarkable, even then. That was well before 1990. I was struck by his ease with African Americans and the ease they felt with him. I have, on occasion, seen a kind of symbiotic relationship between Southern blacks and whites who grew up around each other. His, though, had something more to it.

I learned more about Bill Clinton through Rodney Slater, who convinced me that his governor was a man to watch, that he was going places. I began to follow him at that point and was convinced he had a real political future. It's really hard, now, for people to realize just how distant his chances were back then. Bush's approval ratings were so high.

It was fascinating to watch and participate in Bill Clinton's race to the presidency. Without a doubt, he won because of his very strong black support, the women's vote, and blue-collar whites. He had an "everyman" kind of appeal about him that he still has.

In my estimation, Lyndon B. Johnson was the most important president for black America . . . because of his voting rights amendment, his civil rights legislation, and a host of other initiatives for poor and working class people. Yet Bill Clinton, without any equivocation, has been the most important president for minorities . . . and for cities. He understood the role and the needs of cities for the economy of this country. No other president in history has engineered such changes in America's cities— revitalization of cities for the first time in 30 years; urban America saw the most astounding growth ever; crime significantly reduced; prosperity; more movement back to the cities; rebuilding. All the things cities have needed to grow and prosper for many, many years. He made cities an essential part of the domestic agenda, no longer as an afterthought but a vitally important link to the country's economy.

The Mayors Conference's unambivalent support of this president through his dark days symbolized their appreciation for his treatment of cities during his administration. But he brought forth some intangibles, too—empowerment of minorities and African Americans. The Carter administration wanted to and tried to do this, but the system fought him harshly.

Certainly, the rock solid support of the African American community surely was a big part of saving the Clinton presidency.

The only action I wish Bill Clinton would have taken during his presidency was the appointment of an African American Supreme Court judge. Having Clarence Thomas as the only African American Supreme Court judge is an abomination. Such an appointment would have outlived us all. So much in our society is impacted by the makeup of the Supreme Court: affirmative action, women's rights, and even who becomes our next president. Of course, he made some important judicial appointments, but a Supreme Court appointment would have meant a lot.

Bill Clinton should stay involved in issues of the day. Though, understandably, he is constrained by September 11, but hopefully, when this is behind us he will again speak out on the important issues.

Hank Aaron, baseball great, Atlanta, Georgia:

I met Bill Clinton in Atlanta a number of years ago, but it seems as if I've known him a lot longer. While I knew of him before our relationship or his presidency, we'd never had the opportunity to meet. We've kept in contact since he left office, and I'm scheduled to travel to Africa with him.

●　●　●

Of all the presidents in the 20th century, President Clinton and President Johnson contributed most to the African American community. Certainly President Carter's heart was in the right place, but he just wasn't able to do a lot. Bill Clinton's major contribution was proving to all the country . . . the world, that if the opportunity was ever given to minorities, we could perform in either public or private enterprise.

He was a very courageous leader, to put so many minorities in important positions. I think many people believe his openness and inclusiveness turned out to be a lightning rod for him . . . an ended up being the root of many of his problems while he was in office. The conservatives just couldn't understand him or why he was trying to change the status quo.

He was a fair president. Although he was a Democrat, he didn't pit himself against Republicans. He tried more than most presidents to work with his opponents.

I've been blessed to meet a number of presidents, including John Kennedy, Richard Nixon, and, of course, Georgia's own Jimmy Carter. I've been invited to the White House by Presidents Nixon, Carter, and, then, President Clinton. Though they all treated me cordially, I wouldn't call any of those relationships a friendship. Though I visited the Clinton White House many times during his eight years, it wasn't just going to the White House, but the fact that he made Billye and me feel it was our White House, too. He treated us like a warm host would treat a valued guest.

I never believed he said one thing and believed something completely different. Not like some other presidents have in the past who gave lip service to equal opportunity or made promises that they never followed through on. Bill Clinton shot the bow and arrow straight. That's what made him stand out so far above other presidents.

●　●　●

Bill Clinton's future? He should continue to voice his opinion about fairness for all people. I'm particularly concerned about our future, about our leadership.

Like a lot of people, the closer it came to the end of Bill Clinton's eight years, the more I dreaded seeing him leave the White House. January 20, 2001, was a very sad day for me . . . and a lot of people I know. I laugh now, because the way I felt reminds me of the time I promised my youngest son I'd take him to the circus. He would ask me every day how long was it before we went. The first day was three months, and when it was just a week away, I said, "You just have seven more days," and he started to cry, because he didn't understand that seven days was actually shorter than three months.

William Jefferson Clinton will go down in history as one of our greatest presidents, but more importantly, one of our most memorable world leaders.

☉

Eddie Williams, founding president, Joint Center for Economic Policies:

I first knew about Bill Clinton through the Children's Defense Fund chaired by Hillary Clinton. I recall looking up Governor Bill Clinton's policies and being impressed with some of the changes he was making in Arkansas. I didn't actually meet him until his campaign for presidency and spent a substantial amount of time with him after that. To my great honor, he invited me once, during his first term, to Camp David with him and Mrs. Clinton. The vice president and Mrs. Gore were also there.

The most memorable experience we shared, I think, was when we invited him to the Joint Center's annual fund-raising event. Given his hectic schedule, he was only able to attend the VIP reception. We had the whole floor blocked off, and people were everywhere, most of them trying to say hello to the president. There must have been over 800 people there. But through all of that mayhem, he and I were completely engrossed in a discussion on some of his policy issues.

Toward the end of that evening, as the crowd started thinning out and he had shaken at least half of those people's hands, he still seemed as fresh as he probably did starting out that evening, and asked me if there was another reception!

310

Great leadership is the ability to get people to trust you and follow you just with the sheer force of your passion, your chemistry, and charisma. It's the ability to arouse in people the need to follow. Timing and circumstance is important in great leadership, so our current president (George W. Bush) has been able to ride the crest of America's overarching need for great leadership. Clinton had it, and Johnson had it . . . in a different kind of way. Johnson had what I'd describe as a wicked charm. Kennedy and Roosevelt had it. It remains to be seen exactly where Clinton will fit in with the likes of Kennedy, Roosevelt, Eisenhower. But he definitely has the makings of a great president. He is a man with a phenomenal human touch.

• • •

President Clinton's greatest contribution was his demonstration, publicly and unabashedly, that he cared about all Americans' concerns, including minorities, who for so long had not had a seat at the table at the federal level. This also played out in the fact that most of the social policies he championed were either liberal or progressive. History will grade him as America's most popular president in our time. Who knows what would have happened if he had been able to serve out both terms without the infinite distractions. I hope he will continue to pursue the conversation on race. It would have been so important to move this country forward.

While Bill Clinton, I think, has been the best president ever for the minority communities, Lyndon Johnson gets high marks for putting civil rights on the front burner at a critical time in American history. Johnson took advantage of stepping into the presidency after Kennedy's death and his Southern heritage to push that law forward. No president except Clinton has addressed the race issue since. Both Johnson and Clinton used political capital to try to move this country beyond its terrible history with slavery and racism.

I do wish President Clinton would have had the opportunity to play out the Race Initiative, unfettered. It just didn't get off the ground, given other things that were going on. I worry more about those kinds of things than about policies. I also wish the president and vice president had gotten their act together before the 2000 election. We'd be living under a different political landscape today.

Dr. Dorothy Height, president emeritus/founder, National Council of Negro Women:

I got to know Bill Clinton over 25 years ago, when Hillary chaired the Children's Defense Fund and I was a board member. This was well before Bill Clinton was governor, but he would join her at some of the fund's conferences. Even then, he showed a genuine interest in important social issues, especially the needs of families and children.

. That sensitivity I noticed when I met him, he brought to the presidency—that interest in just everyday people. You know, many politicians like the people who will vote for them, but Bill Clinton was a person who liked people ... whether they voted or not. That was one of his endearing characteristics. He also had a wonderful ability to communicate with just about any crowd, often without actually saying a word.

Early on, I noticed that he took things seriously, yet most people I know describe him as easy to meet. He is so good at interacting with people at all different levels. He had that charisma, too, that was absolutely universal in its scope.

It's true that Bill Clinton and Hillary often brought to mind the partnership between Franklin and Eleanor Roosevelt during their tenure in the White House. Their programs were rooted in what was actually happening in the real world, and they had a keen awareness of what was happening . . . not just in the U.S. but throughout the world.

• • •

Great leadership? I think a great leader has to be a visionary rather than someone who is good at carrying on what already is. He needs to be telling us what ought to be. He or she also must be willing to risk favor and popularity to stand up for what they really do believe. When people asked Mahatma Gandhi about his role in India's revolution, he said, "The people want freedom, and therefore I follow them, because I am their leader." A leader has to see people as they are and issues as they are, and be concerned about what's happening. That was a great strength of President Clinton's. You see that in the social issues he focused on and attempted to change. The leader sets the climate . . . because when it's clear that the leader isn't concerned about something, that attitude trickles down.

• • •

Bill Clinton deserves a great deal of credit for going as far as humanly possible to assure civil rights for all Americans and for assuring equal opportunities for all Americans. He made that an important part of his administration. It was especially refreshing to have a president who used his bully pulpit to talk about race in America. That really helped to carry this to the next level. Yes, we have the law, but now we have to move people beyond just the written law.

When he was running for president in 1992, he visited our Black Family Reunion Celebration on the city mall. There were about 4,000 or 5,000 people there, including lots of children . . . and I would ask a lot of them who they would vote for president if they could vote, and every one of those children would say, "I'd vote for Bill Clinton."

The country moved ahead under President Clinton because he was concerned about working people, children, and human rights. We were making steady progress in improving conditions for workers, wages, hours, working conditions, and safety. His recognition and support for the family was so very important. It is shameful that the U.S. is the only Western country without a family policy. At least his family leave policy and some other initiatives he put in place for families brought us into the 20th century.

He was the first American president to really take the continent of Africa seriously . . . not only their problems but their contributions to the world. He won the hearts of many Third World populations when he saw value in Africa, in its people as well as its resources. Because he took such a critical step in opening up about race on a national and international stage, private and public organizations began to feel more comfortable addressing this issue. I just hope he will continue that discussion now that he doesn't have the same constraints and distractions.

There is one thing I thought about a lot during his presidency. I'd always counted Lyndon Johnson as the one president that made substantial contributions to the black community. In some ways, I find Bill Clinton and Lyndon Baines Johnson's passion for change similar. Johnson would let everyone know what he thought or felt, even though he knew he would pay a price.

Shortly after passage of the Civil Rights bill, I was invited to a meeting at the White House with a group of black leaders, and Jack Valenti, one of Johnson's special assistants, was there. Valenti told us that Lyndon Johnson had gone into the Oval Office after the announcement of passage of the bill, very depressed. Of course, we asked why. Valenti said, "Because he is a realist." He told Jack, "I have delivered the South to the Republicans."

That, to me, shows his determination to do what he feels is right, regardless of the consequences. Then, some years ago, after he'd left the presidency, the late Barbara Jordan hosted a reception for the Delta Sigma Theta sorority down in Texas. President Johnson invited the group of us to visit his ranch. Lady Bird wasn't there that evening. He showed us all around the house, even showed us how the closets had been built, and his and Lady Bird's bedroom. I still get tickled when I remember that, because I know Lady Bird would not have been happy to know he was exposing her home like that.

Of course, we had a wonderful time. And I asked him a question before I left that night: what was his greatest contribution to the American people? He told me, beyond anything else he'd done as president, the passage of the Voting Rights Act was his greatest contribution. He said he knew that giving blacks the right to vote was the only way they'd ever have any real influence on how the country operated.

I was there when Martin Luther King made his "We Shall Overcome" speech, and I was in Memphis when he was assassinated. I was always part of that civil rights leadership group that went to the White House and met with President Johnson. It was very clear to me that this was not just something he was doing easily . . . but it represented a major change.

When the question of the Fair Housing Act came up, the civil rights leaders were saying, "Let's go easy." It was Lyndon Johnson and Clarence Mitchell who fought for fair housing. Once he bought into doing what's right, you didn't have to push him on it.

When Johnson was vice president, he hosted a group of about 400 African American leaders at the White House to talk about civil rights. Back then, President Kennedy designated anything that had to do with civil rights or equal opportunity to Johnson. When we'd all sat down, one of the first remarks he made to this large group of black leaders was, "I know you all have questions about me, my background. I know that you wanted John F. Kennedy so bad that you took me along with him. But what you did not know is that Mary McLeod Bethune put my integration diapers on me during the NYA (National Youth Administration) days."

He told us how he had been a designated area person in the South, and when he'd been asked to go to Tallahassee to speak at a black school, he had called Mrs. Bethune and asked her what he should do. She told him: "Lyndon, you are representing the United States of America. You work for the federal government, you go wherever you are sent. It doesn't matter what color the people are . . . I'm asking you to go."

He said he got off the phone, got dressed, and flew to Tallahassee. That, he said, was his first lesson that the federal government is for all the people. I'll never forget that. It exemplified the kind of drive he had about doing what he believed was right. It reminds me of what Lillian Smith once wrote, that a reconstructed Southerner is often more vigilant about improving race relations than someone who grows up saying, "We never had a problem." The difference between Lyndon Johnson and Bill Clinton is that Bill Clinton never needed to be reconstructed.

Dr. David Levering Lewis, Pulitzer Prize-winning author; professor of African American Studies, Rutgers University:

Though I was actually born in Little Rock, Arkansas, I left there when I was 10 years old and never returned until recently, when I visited my old home on 1204 Ringo in downtown Little Rock. My father was a school administrator for many years at Little Rock's Dunbar High School-the same school that served as a voting poll and where Governor Clinton voted during election seasons.

So I'd never met President Clinton until I was invited to a Ghana state dinner at the White House in 2000. I was standing in one of those long receiving lines before the dinner when I met Mr. Clinton, and, frankly, there wasn't enough time for me to talk with him. But my wife, who is such an ardent Clinton fan, embarrassed me by throwing herself in the president's arms. I did have a nice exchange with Mrs. Clinton, and my impression of her was positive. Overall, I was pleasantly surprised by the cordiality of both Clintons.

● ● ●

A great leader is someone with the ability to articulate and, to some degree, implement an agenda, whether it's a political, social, or economic agenda. While all platforms, policies, decisions will be controversial, leaders are measured on the degree to which they mollify their opponents and end up with what they want.

A bonus, of course, in great leadership, is charisma. Not all great leaders enjoy charisma, but it is always a plus. I count people like Charles de Gaulle, Franklin Roosevelt, Nelson Mandela, and Mikhail Gorbachev as great leaders.

• • •

I think his signing the welfare reform bill was one of his greatest contributions to this country. Just this morning, the papers have the Republicans tinkering with it . . . in a Draconian way. Their bill is reminiscent of what we'd expect in the early 1800s. But Clinton made fundamental changes in welfare as we knew it.

His inclusion of all Americans in the operation of the federal government was groundbreaking. This is hard to quantify or measure, but he had a welcoming ethos to all Americans, which included African Americans. We saw this in his appointments to very important government positions. He exemplified what seemed to be a genuine affinity for the masses and the reciprocation from the masses. While most people took Toni Morrison's quote of him being the first black president out of context, I think we can understand the meaning behind it.

In my recent visit back to Arkansas, I was more convinced than ever there was never a real Whitewater story there. It was the Republicans' effort to balloon this story into huge proportions. It made me understand why the Clintons felt they were being unfairly persecuted.

His missed opportunities resulted from President Clinton's lack of discipline. Not only were African Americans hurt, but the American people, in general, were affected by his lack of discipline. It was costly and almost fatal to the presidency. The Contract with America victory can largely be accredited to this.

He wasted an enormous opportunity . . . particularly with health care reform, which was so badly needed. The consequences of these mistakes made the Republican agenda very appealing when Gingrich came on the scene. What President Clinton did, however, was co-opt the Republican agenda . . . moving beyond the center toward the right. So while the Democratic Party suffered, he gained. The consequence was that we now have a country where market solutions are seen to be the way to deal with our social problems . . . and we know that is not going to work for all communities.

The Lewinsky scandal—it's hard to put into words just how goofy that whole thing was. One might make a judgment: if you are going to sin, as previous presidents have certainly done, one might choose people who know how to keep their business to themselves. That was a juvenile mistake. Beyond that, the management of that scandal was a disaster.

Because of his charm, his brilliance, and the fact that he is probably the greatest politician we will ever see, Bill Clinton is often his own worst enemy. Lyndon Johnson and Bill Clinton, while very different individuals, were amazingly alike in their abilities to wield power.

☉

U.S. Congressman John Lewis, Georgia:

The first time I heard of Bill Clinton was in the early '70s. I was living in Georgia, working for the Southern Poverty Law organization, when someone told me about this young, emerging leader in Arkansas who served as attorney general, then later became governor.

I think I paid more attention to him at the 1988 Democratic Convention, when he was asked to introduce the presidential candidate and took up far more time than was allotted to him. After he became involved with the Democratic Leadership Council, I would run into him from time to time. But it was one of his aides, Rodney Slater, who actually introduced us in 1991 and asked me if I would support his presidency.

Rodney gets the credit for convincing me that Bill Clinton was "the man," when he told me all he had done in Arkansas to help change the layout of that state. In the summer of 1991, I hosted a breakfast for him in the Rayburn Building. Congressmen Mike Espy and Bill Jefferson were there. The three of us were trying to convince the Democratic Black Caucus to endorse Clinton. Most Northern members didn't know him and wasn't very interested. Only a few members of the Black Caucus came to the breakfast, but those of us there had a wonderful discussion. Several staff people came from different offices, and they all came back to me later to say how wonderful he was.

What was so striking about Bill Clinton was that here was a governor and a presidential candidate, and he actually made you feel as if he knew he needed you. He was warm, engaging, and comfortable with the African American audience. We literally began to feel he was one of us. The people there were amazed to see this white Southerner so comfortable around blacks. I think we

317

all decided that morning that he was a different kind of Southern politician. But I've always felt that white and black Southerners have a lot in common.

After that icebreaker, I found a way to endorse him in Georgia before the primary. Alvin Brown, one of his campaign aides, said, "Let's find a way to endorse him," and I did. It was at the Martin Luther King, Jr., Chapel at Morehouse. I publicly endorsed him and called him "the man who talks the talk but also walks the walk."

● ● ●

Great leadership is a headlight, not a taillight. Courage is so important in a great leader. Roosevelt, Kennedy, Johnson, Carter, and Truman all exemplify great leadership in their own ways. But I have to say, before Clinton came on the scene, Lyndon Baines Johnson, by far, had done more than any president for our community.

● ● ●

Much like John Kennedy, President Clinton's greatest contribution to America and our community was simply being there at that time in history. Just being there changed America's attitudes about themselves, thanks to his openness about race, about minorities. There was something very significant about his being there at the time he was.

African Americans have this antenna that other races don't have. We can sense when people are real, authentic. Our antennae told us that Bill Clinton was real, authentic. Black America identified with this man, no matter where they were in the stream of things.

Where President Kennedy created a similar sense of hope in Americans, his contributions weren't as real or substantive as Bill Clinton's. Who knows what he could have done, had he lived? While the Civil Rights Act of 1964 may have passed in memory of Kennedy, LBJ literally knocked heads to get it done. That was a revolutionary step for America, just as the 1965 Voting Rights Act.

I was there when President Johnson spoke to the Joint Session, and I continue to believe that address was the most significant speech by any president of the 20th century. He condemned the violence in Selma (Alabama) and repeated black America's mantra, "We Shall Overcome."

I was sitting next to Martin Luther King, Jr., during that speech, and there were tears streaming down his face. Lyndon Baines Johnson would have gone down in history as one of the greatest presidents ever, had it not been for the Vietnam War. All the things that mean so much to our communities-fair housing, Head Start, Medicare, higher education, the War on Poverty. He did a great deal for the Southern region.

I sometimes wonder if Bill Clinton is aware of just how loyal African Americans are to him, what he has meant to our community. During the whole impeachment efforts, black folk would say the most unbelievable things to me, like, "Please, take care of my president." There was this strong bond . . . I saw the same type of thing when I traveled with the president to Africa. It was almost a defense mechanism for black America, as if "their" president's critics were trying to run him out of office because of what he stood for. For the first time, maybe ever, black America felt they had a president who was on their side. You heard that here, and you heard it in Africa.

I always felt that maybe some American president . . . maybe this president would have apologized for slavery. It makes me so sad that the American government has never yet issued an apology for slavery.

Bill Clinton is the one president who could have done it. I think he could've said to this nation that it was a gross mistake, this nation made a serious blunder. He would have been criticized for it, but it would have been the right thing to do . . . it would have righted a long history of wrongs by this nation.

Bill Clinton's future? As a former president, I don't think he should just travel around the world. He has as much to offer here as abroad. We still need him, and he should continue to provide a sense of hope, faith. He should not give up . . . there are too many people feeling lost right now, feeling as if they have no place to turn, have lost "their" voice. Maybe he can help us find that voice.

When you think of Jimmy Carter, it wasn't so much what he did as president but what he has done as a former president. He's been out there doing good, fighting for free and open elections in Central Africa, Haiti, working for improved health care. He's taken a tremendous lead on housing issues—his Habitat for Humanity is a global effort. He's made a lot of difference in Third World countries. Bill Clinton could do as much good or more. We still need him.

Michael White, former mayor of Cleveland, Ohio:

I learned about Bill Clinton through the media, and then I began reading about him. I'm not sure whether it was his Southern boyishness, the fact that he was an outsider, or the fact that everyone was saying he couldn't win, that drew me to him. I actually met him in 1991 at a mayors' meeting. He made a presentation, and while the fundamentals of his presentation were good, I was still a doubting Thomas. I mean, I had been in politics since I was 13 years old.

As time went on, and as I got to know him better, I began to think, "This guy seems to be genuine." His roots had a lot to do with it . . . this fellow wasn't born with an oil well in his mouth, wasn't supposed to make the team. Every step he took . . . throughout his whole life, he had to kick the door down. That was one of the things I liked about him, because I came from that same mold.

● ● ●

A great leader is someone who will lay it on the line to improve the lot of those he is leading. That encapsulates a great leader and pretty much encapsulates Bill Clinton's leadership. Some others I consider worthy of that title are: Martin Luther King, Jr., former Cleveland Mayor Carl Stokes, President John F. Kennedy, and civil rights leader Medgar Evers.

● ● ●

In my lifetime, there have been very few common people or people with the common touch in the White House. Jimmy Carter had it, but he couldn't execute.

John F. Kennedy didn't have it, but he could empathize with the common man. Bill Clinton genuinely understood the common American . . . because he was a common American. He understood economic disenfranchisement, giving the poor a hand up, not a hand out. This guy lived it.

He not only had the common touch but was clearly the smartest president of my lifetime. Unfortunately, after he made the team, the team began plans immediately to cut him from the team. The moment his hand came down after his oath, there were forces in place whose total commitment was not just to defeat Bill Clinton but to destroy him—with special prosecutors, with seen and unseen investigations, with a Republican congressional onslaught that no Republican president has ever experienced. The American people can tell a fake a mile off. They also know that no man is perfect. Bill Clinton's greatest strength was that he could walk with kings and still maintain the common touch.

He was very serious about getting people to think about the racial problems, the economic problems in our society . . . and he began, through his political power, to effect some changes in the poverty rate, in the economic factors. None of this happened by coincidence. He set a different tone, and more than any president in history, he had a genuine comfort with minorities and, certainly, African Americans. Jimmy Carter had a certain comfort, nothing near Bill Clinton's. But they were alike in other ways, both smart, both from the South, and neither were blue bloods.

Bill Clinton assured African Americans, not in words but in deeds that this was our country, and he was our president, too. I think LBJ is the only other president who came close to that. Bill Clinton didn't have to say it. He didn't have to wear the dashikis to make us know . . . it was his manner, his comfort level, that I'm convinced was genuine.

He surpassed Lyndon Baines Johnson, whose civil rights bills brought an end to legal, overt racism; or Abraham Lincoln, who freed the slaves but had an ulterior motive. Bill Clinton was in many ways like Johnson, but his approach wasn't to attack overt racism because we were beyond that. It's like the recent issue about employers screening applicants based on ethnic names— Ebony vs. Jill. This is the kind of racism Clinton was fighting against.

John F. Kennedy was one of those great communicators, but his deliverability was questionable, in contrast to Johnson, who wasn't good at communicating his vision but was great on delivery. There are stories of how Johnson would call senators into his office and dress them down like children if they didn't vote the way he wanted.

Both Clinton and Johnson put the prestige of the presidency behind the issues they believed in. Unlike many presidents who husband presidential power, refusing to expend it, these two men spent their currency on the issues they felt were important. They were visionaries and were willing to expend the currency on delivery. I'm not sure people like Kennedy were willing to lay it all out there like that.

First of all, although he clearly made some mistakes, I like him. I have been in politics for 30 years and have been an elected official for 25 years. You happen up on very few people in today's environment that you can truly call a friend. I have always maintained a personal like for Bill Clinton and still consider him a friend, which means I'll always wish the best for him.

Notwithstanding that, his biggest misstep was his failure to tell the truth about the Lewinsky affair. That one misstep diminished the presidency. He should have told the truth. He reacted as most men would. What man willingly goes on television and admits to the world and to his wife that he's had an affair?

• • •

Yet, he wasn't most men. He was the president of the United States, and the presidency is more than a man: the presidency is a symbol. I've seen politicians do all kinds of things: steal, lie, cheat, use drugs, take money under the table . . . but yet, what he did to the presidency is like someone telling you that Santa Claus is a child abuser. Although we accept the fact that there are child abusers in the world, no one wants to believe that Santa Claus is a child abuser. For me, more than getting caught . . . the thing that bothered me most was that it was Bill Clinton, my president, getting caught.

While what he did with Monica Lewinsky is pardonable, it hurt his presidency and is the one thing that will probably stay with him for the rest of his life. It's that whole thing about America and its sexual repression . . . hypocrisy. George Bush can go all over the world embarrassing the United States, but when it's sexual, Americans seem to have more of a problem with it.

The Clinton legacy? Bill Clinton is one of the very few presidents who was actually in tune with the common American, including the poor and lower middle class, the farmers, and the factory workers. From what I witnessed, he was the same 24 hours a day. I recall critics commenting on his attending so many tragedies. Those critics failed to realize that his presence was not only a message to the victims' families but a message to America that "here is a president who cares and will be there for you." He gave Americans a sense of security.

His appeal internationally never diminished. Here's a leader of the free world who didn't treat the rest of the world like his colony. And by doing that, he raised the stature of America throughout the world. Bill Clinton made a huge contribution to our standing in the world during his eight years in office, and as yet he hasn't gotten the credit he deserves for his many international accomplishments. Ironically, there is more anti-America sentiment around the world than ever before. South Korea has "Americans not welcomed" signs in their stores.

◎

Carla Williams, former president, Jack and Jill International:

I met President Clinton during his presidency. I was invited by a friend to take a tour of the White House, and the highlight of that was a tour of the Oval Office. To all of our surprise, the president stopped in the Oval Office unexpectedly. He had just returned from visiting a senior citizens facility in the city and was on his way to play golf. He was dressed in his sports shirt and khakis and golf shoes.

I had heard about how charming and charismatic this president was but was not prepared to experience that charisma in person. He was gracious enough to greet us, chatted with us for a while, and even took photos with us. We couldn't believe this was the president of the United States being so gracious and warm and down to earth.

I compare Bill Clinton to another young, handsome president—John F. Kennedy, who had such a positive impact on our country in the early '60s. Just as Mr. Clinton is, Kennedy also believed in all Americans finding a way to give back. Sadly, he was right on the cusp of the civil rights changes when his time was cut short. I truly believe he could have done great things. Maybe Bill Clinton was somehow fated to live out his term.

Lyndon Baines Johnson implemented the civil rights laws that Kennedy left undone. Before him, Franklin Roosevelt was good for America and did many good things through his wife, much like President Clinton, who has such respect for Hillary's intellect. Kennedy and Roosevelt, however, would be second and third on my list after Clinton as far as great presidents.

● ● ●

Great leadership? A person who develops leadership in others, recognizing that no one man or woman can ever do it all. If you aren't developing people around you, you end up burning yourself out and get little done. Clinton was one leader who developed and empowered others. Great leaders understand the importance of diplomacy and develop an art of interacting with people from all

323

different persuasions, interests, and cultures. They must be great communicators.

• • •

Bill Clinton's warmth and personality was important, but his knowledge of the issues and willingness to learn what he didn't know were invaluable. I know blacks who had been interested for a long time in starting their own businesses who were able to do so during the Clinton administration, as small business loans became more accessible. He put initiatives in place that helped grow and develop minority businesses. He did an exemplary job in the most important areas—economic policy, jobs, health care. It is so unfortunate that the health care reform initiative didn't happen.

I certainly got mad at Bill Clinton more than once during his eight years. Personally, I am against people remaining on welfare forever. But the welfare reform act he passed doesn't address the problem. I saw far too many poor women with children forced out of the home to find jobs when they weren't adequately prepared for the workplace.

I don't know what could have been done differently, but I know I was personally dismayed with the outcome. I'm sure the president saw the bill as a way of rectifying the waste of human capability and federal money, but from my viewpoint, the law hasn't benefited the people it's supposed to have served.

I wish the Race Initiative hadn't come to a standstill in the middle of his terms. Who would think that in the 21st century we would still be talking about racial profiling? The Clinton presidency encouraged me. I'm more aware of what our possibilities are and less willing to accept anything less.

President Clinton's legacy will be the empowerment of all people, but most importantly, the disenfranchised. He made some of the smartest appointments of any president. Commerce Secretary Ron Brown opened the doors of commerce for people to have worldwide opportunities.

Very often, economic opportunities are what make all the difference in people's lives. Those opportunities allow us to make long-term decisions rather than live day to day. It gives us the flexibility to give back to our communities. We've never had a president give us these opportunities before. Bill Clinton is much too young and has too much energy to think about retiring.

Bob Johnson, founder, Black Entertainment Television:

I met Bill and Hillary Clinton in the early '80s up in Martha's Vineyard. Marian Wright Edelman had rented a summer home there and was hosting some type of retreat. She invited a number of people, including my wife Sheila and I. We also took our 3-year-old daughter. Andy Young was there, Bill Snyder of CNN, and James Hormel. Someone later told me that Uma Thurman's mother was there. It was a pretty eclectic group of people.

Bill and Hillary Clinton joined Marian in facilitating interactive discussions on public policy issues. They did some interesting role-playing kinds of things. I imagine it was something like the Renaissance Weekends that were held for years in Hilton Head. That was my first encounter with Bill Clinton, and I'm not sure whether that was during or after his first term as governor.

We talked quite a bit and had an interesting time. About a month later, I received a letter from him reiterating some of the issues we'd talked about and even adding others for me to think about. I was amazed and thought, "Who is this Bill Clinton?" After that, there were a number of years when we didn't communicate much. Then I hear he's running for president. While I was surprised, something told me I shouldn't have been.

Ron Brown was heading up the DNC at the time and working hard to pull more blacks into politics. He was the one who told me I should get involved with Bill Clinton's campaign. I decided I would and sponsored a few events for the DNC and made some contributions. Before I knew it, Bill Clinton had gotten the nomination. The rest is history.

I still hadn't run into him during his campaign, but I ran into Hillary at a party at Hugh McCall's home in New York. We talked and reminisced about that first retreat at Martha's Vineyard. Then, a little later on, I got a call from Bill Clinton asking me if I wanted to come down to the economic summit in Little Rock. I was surprised and happy to do so.

As I walked into the reception that first evening, in the midst of a crowd of people talking, Bill Clinton came over with a big grin on his face and said, "Hi Bob, I bet you don't remember where we met." From that point on, we sort've renewed our friendship and started interacting whenever we'd meet at various Democratic Party events. Whenever I did fund-raisers for certain people, the president was willing to show up as an added bonus. He invited me to the White House pretty frequently, too, especially if it was an issue where he really needed some feedback from a black person's perspective.

I never wanted anything from him, no ambassadorship or federal role. I had no particular agenda other than just to be a part of his support group. He did, however, appoint me to a number of boards during his tenure. One of the most substantive, I think, was the information superhighway initiative headed by Delano Lewis. I'm sure Del wanted someone on the board he knew and considered a friend. I was also invited to go up to Camp David a few times. Ours was more of a friendship than a political relationship.

● ● ●

A great leader? A great leader is someone who has a vision and can articulate that vision and motivate people to follow it.

● ● ●

What President Clinton did was to bring the African American community to a level of decision making on public policy issues that we had never been before. And he brought to center stage the dialogue on race in this country. That hadn't been done, ever, by a president. Beyond that, America hadn't really talked about race, the root of it, the far-reaching consequences of it, since the '60s.

His commitment to create a White House and cabinet and federal government that looked like America set the foundation for future presidents. Every president, henceforth, will have pressure to at least live up to his accomplishments in that area. While much of his legacy will be what he tried to do on the race issue, it has to be rekindled. Unfortunately, it was short circuited by his other problems . . . Monica Lewinsky, namely.

I think most African Americans see Lyndon Johnson as the predecessor to Bill Clinton. In many ways, his accomplishments were further reaching and substantive . . . when you think of the Voting Rights Acts, equal opportunity, Fair Housing Act, Head Start for our children. He was an insurmountable politician, a politician who learned the race issue while he was in office, then virtually forced the Democrats' hands on it. It's a toss-up between these two men when it comes to who is our civil rights president.

Bill Clinton is probably one of the smartest people you'll ever meet and has infinite charisma and personality. His strength will not be in the policies or programs he implemented. His strength was Bill Clinton. His ability to mobilize people, to get people to identify with things that he was concerned about, and his ability to get a dialogue between people going, to get people to work towards solving problems . . . any problems.

I don't think Bill Clinton ever met a problem that he didn't believe he could solve, if he could gather enough people in a room and get them to reason. His greatest strength was the ability to get people from across the spectrum in ideology, cultures, politics in a room together, and by the time they walked out, they had learned how much they had in common.

He can certainly take credit for economic growth between 1991 and now. He has this great track record on the economy. A lot of Americans, blacks and whites, benefited from the economy.

Thankfully, he saw the importance of keeping affirmative action around, even if he had to water it down with his "mend it, don't end it" tagline.

When you look back and ask what did Bill Clinton do, the most important answer is, he was there . . . thank God. He was leader of the free world, and everyday Americans felt they had access to him. Many minorities and blacks could literally pick up the phone and talk to him. There was this amazing attitude shift about how to deal with concerns that black people brought up . . . you knew you had a voice in the '90s . . . an in.

Missed opportunities? Under Bill Clinton, the House voted down affirmative action. During Bill Clinton's term, they never changed the law on the disparity between sentencing for crack and powder cocaine. As for welfare reform, the jury's out on welfare reform; all of a sudden when the time runs out and people are out of jobs, we can decide whether it was a good bill or a bad one. You look back at some things and say, wow, these things should never have happened under a guy who had so many good programs and policy issues. But policies and programs will not be his legacy.

The Clinton legacy? Bill Clinton should continue providing a voice to disenfranchised people around the globe because he can have an impact on the world. I told him we could build his library out of the best bricks and mortar, and it can be a $200 million edifice down here in Little Rock, but that wouldn't be his strength. He's not going to lift this building up and take it to India, or take it to Africa, take it to Newark. Bill Clinton has got to go to Africa, to India, and to Newark. Bill Clinton going to the people will be the key to his legacy, not this shining building on the river.

Bill Clinton is the one person who, when he calls people for a meeting, they know that no matter what, when they leave that meeting they will have been a part of a solution, a way to do something positive.

I never questioned whether Bill Clinton's relationship with the African American community was genuine . . . I certainly viewed it as genuine. He gave credibility to the African American community. One of his most significant actions during his presidency was his trip to Africa, and that was the first time I asked Bill Clinton for anything. I wanted to be a part of that, because I saw the historical significance of it. It was one of the hottest tickets going during that time. Everybody wanted to be a part of it. He did something so symbolically significant in those 10 days.

☙

Anthony Williams, mayor, District of Columbia:

My association with President Clinton began when I was a state official in his Connecticut campaign office. I was appointed as chief financial officer for the agricultural department in 1993 but still didn't really know the president at that time. When I first came to D.C., I had this expectation that most appointees quickly develop this really close relationship with the president. It didn't take me long to learn that's just not the way Washington politics operates.

I did become much more involved with the White House after I was appointed chief financial officer of Washington, D.C. I worked very closely with people like Treasury Secretary Bob Rubin, OMB director Frank Raines, and District Congresswoman Eleanor Holmes Norton. We got to know each other pretty well as we worked to put together a recovery package for the District.

I didn't personally get to know President Clinton until after my election as mayor of the District in 1999. After that, the doors of the White House were always open to me and my family. The president and first lady were extremely gracious to us, inviting us to most of the major state dinners and other White House events. It was a great honor to sit at the president and first lady's dinner table and spend the evening chatting with them about various issues.

President Clinton was very, very supportive of everything we were trying to do in the District. I talked with him on a fairly regular basis about issues surrounding the District. His support for the District was total and unequivocal. He and Bob Dole, in fact, hosted a bipartisan fund-raiser for me and raised almost $1 million. He's been very supportive of the city and to me.

Clinton's impact on the country and the African American community was phenomenal. It's not a myth, but reality. I don't know about this whole "first black president" thing, but I do think he's probably the first president who ever understood, as a white man, what it means . . . the whole idea of what we go through as citizens of this country, such as standing on a corner trying to get a cab and having cabs bypass you consistently. Or for hard working black families, not being able to get a loan for your house or your business, or the glass ceiling that stops so many of us from achieving our all because the corporate ladder just doesn't take us there. I think he understood the depth of that kind of prejudice and the unjustness of it.

President Clinton's most far-reaching initiative was his Africa initiative. He made us and America know that the continent of Africa was important. In the new emerging geopolitics, that was very important. He really was looking at much more than what the media or others give him credit for. He focused on long-term issues for which there were no short-term political benefits. Health care was certainly one of those issues that affect the working poor at a much greater rate . . . and so many African Americans are part of the working poor.

He showed leadership in finessing the very difficult problem of affirmative action, when so many powerful politicians and constituents were calling for an end to it. He did a great job of focusing on the long term, focusing on the cities like Atlanta, a beacon in the African American community. Economic empowerment for the people in these cities was something he wanted to see. He was a big proponent of the Emerging Markets Initiative.

Lyndon Johnson is the only other U.S. president comparable to Bill Clinton in both his impact on the black community and his political agility—his Voting Rights Act, his civil rights bill. When you drive the streets here, you might criticize urban renewal, but you have to credit Johnson for trying to make life better. Head Start, too, was one of his major initiatives and had a huge impact on black families, on our children's welfare.

The Clinton legacy? I think it will be his role in institutionalizing the Emerging Markets Initiative. His push to get jobs and investment opportunities into the cities will have long-term effect on America's cities, as the demographics of cities continue to change, and as the labor market continue to reach deeper and deeper into the inner city in a way it hasn't since the 1990s.

I don't think that's an aberration anymore. If the market performs reasonably well, it will be tapping into sectors of the economy that were marginalized and structurally excluded before. That is an important change. So now there is a real opportunity for investment in our cities.

One final and major accomplishment: he changed the conversation on race. Now President Bush can appoint blacks into high-level roles and it's not even discussed. That's a real accomplishment of Bill Clinton's. William Jefferson Clinton is a brilliant leader who, some say, should have focused better. That must have been very hard, though, when you have so many things coming at you from every direction.

❦

Marc Morial, former mayor of New Orleans; current president, National Urban League:

I received a call in 1991 from a young man who had served with me as a delegate to the Democratic Convention. I don't remember all the conversation, but the most important part was that Bill Clinton was throwing in his hat for the presidency. I had just been elected to the Louisiana Senate at that time.

I wasn't sure about how that would play out. I had been in Atlanta in 1988 when Bill Clinton made his infamous speech, and now major Democratic candidates were deciding they weren't going to run, because George Bush had just come off the Gulf War and was strong, and the perception was that he was unbeatable.

My image of Bill Clinton wasn't a bad image, but it was of a young guy who had been elected to the governorship of Arkansas and got defeated his second term. I'd followed his career, but, unfortunately, the only time I'd seen him make a public presentation was the speech he made to the Democratic Convention in Atlanta. I was also wary about a Southern Democrat positioning himself as a moderate-conservative Democrat. I had some real problems with that.

But what changed my mind about Bill Clinton was one visit he made to New Orleans in January 1992. Lindy Boggs hosted a fund-

330

raiser for him on this rainy, rainy night in the Quarters. He made a speech before 60 or 70 people, standing on the steps of her house. I was blown away, and that rainy night in the New Orleans Quarters was when I began changing my views about Bill Clinton.

Shortly after that, Congressman Bill Jefferson, John Lewis, and Mike Espy got together and decided they would endorse him early. Congressman Jefferson invited him back to New Orleans. He held a reception with New Orleans' black leadership in his home. Jefferson made a compelling case that we should get on with Clinton early to help shape his candidacy.

I worked very hard in the campaign in '92. In fact, as a young state senator, I was thrust into a role I didn't ask for. I served as a surrogate for the campaign in a series of debates with Republican state representative Quinton Gastugue, who had a reputation of being a very aggressive, forceful kind of debater. No one with any sense wanted to tangle with him.

But I was young and brash and said, I'll tangle with the guy, no problem. So we went into the television studio for a live debate on the morning show, and we mixed it up pretty good. The news director liked it so much he asked us back every week for four or five weeks straight. Even after the election was over, we continued this Crossfire type of dialogue.

Since Congressman Jefferson and Senator Breaux were in Washington, mostly, I was stuck in New Orleans carrying the load for the Clinton campaign. The mayor at that time wasn't really into the campaign, so by default, I was the Clinton spokesman in our area.

He had been president for a little while when I was elected mayor of New Orleans in 1994. I was really surprised when the president called and congratulated me on my victory, because even then I didn't really know him that well.

My first visit to the Oval Office was in 1995. I had been in office six or seven months, and Jay Bennett Johnston orchestrated the visit. I'd gone to see Johnston the day before to get his support for funding for New Orleans' water system. On this particular day, the Arkansas Razorbacks had won the national championship, and the president was talking stuff about Arkansas basketball. And I thought to myself, OK, he's talking basketball, and I'm here to ask for money. We got around to it, finally. I asked for $100 million over a 10-year period. Though New Orleans has had an historical problem with the water system, no city official had ever been aggressive in asking for federal assistance.

Leon Panetta was there in that meeting and was just kind'a shaking his head as if to say, "Mr. President, don't commit to this man . . . how in the world do you expect us to find this money?" The president, though, was in a great mood. He was saying, "Come on, Leon, we need to help New Orleans. The mayor's here with our friend, Bennett, and besides, I like New Orleans. We have to help New Orleans." I guess God and the Razorbacks were with us. We walked out with a commitment from the president, and it was a good feeling, a great moment for New Orleans.

One of the defining times in Clinton's relationship with the black community probably came in 1995 when the controversy over affirmative action really, really, really erupted. I remember because, prior to his "Mend it, don't end it" speech, I was on a panel in New Orleans with Jesse Jackson, Kweisi Mfume, Maxine Waters, and Al Sharpton. You don't have to wonder how that conversation was going.

There was a room full of folk talking affirmative action and being real strident about it. This was before the president took his position, because I think there was a fear at that time that he was going to retrench, because there was a lot of heat on him, a lot of pressure from moderates and conservatives. We had just lost control of the House, re-election was coming, and Gingrich was on a roll.

I was working on the conference of the Council of Mayors at the time and went to a meeting in San Antonio where Vice President Gore made a presentation. This was basically a private retreat with about 15 mayors. It was shortly after Gingrich had proposed this crazy, Draconian budget. Some of us thought the vice president was trying to soft-pedal Gingrich's budget, as if to say we couldn't stand up and get into a big fight, as if we should accommodate Gingrich.

I think Mayor Ed Rendell of Philadelphia and I both got our backs up on this and said, "Wait a minute now, the president got to veto this stuff . . . he's got to fight. We can't sit here and see all our programs go away and keep our mouths closed . . . we're not going to do it."

So that time was a defining moment in his presidency, because literally, the right wing had taken over Congress and had achieved a public opinion beachhead, going into early 1995. They had us over a barrel with affirmative action and their budget cuts. And I was like, "Oh, God, we got the presidency, but they took over Congress, and they're working to kick us out of the White House."

The president, much to our relief, came out with what was a sensible position on affirmative action, saying that he supported it in principle, but gave enough, rhetorically, to those concerned about affirmative action. He was able to, with that, to refine and strengthen his relationship with the African American community.

I remember that a large group of mayors went to the White House just after Labor Day in 1995 to discuss what Gingrich's budget would do to cities. Basically, we ended up saying, "Mr. President, if you want to veto these budgets, we'll stand behind you. If you need us to ask you to, or support you after you veto these budgets, we will. But we do not want to see you concede. Our cities just couldn't withstand cuts in programs like the Community Development Block Grants and education. We had fought hard to get the crime bill passed, and it had been a great success, but it was a great success before Republicans took control of the Congress."

That was a defining time for the president, when he decided to stand these guys down and vetoed the budget. Gingrich made the awful mistake of blocking a continuing resolution, which ended up having the effect of shutting down the government, and that was the beginning of the end for Gingrich. He'd lost his credibility.

A lot of credit goes to President Clinton for knowing who to place in certain positions to make him successful. His decision to choose someone like Bob Nash to manage and oversee his appointments allowed him to keep his promise to the American people. At long last, the federal government and his administration mirrored American demographics. His commitment to diversity made so much difference. Clinton brought his history with blacks to his campaign and then to the White House, something pretty much unheard of with presidents before.

• • •

What is great leadership? Drive, compassion for people not in a superficial way, vision and the ability to communicate it, and the ability to act on it. It all goes hand in hand: the vision, the articulation of it, and the implementation of it.

• • •

A major defining moment in the Clinton presidency was his appointments of African Americans to the judiciary and the U.S. attorney general's office, which creates a depth . . . a reservoir that will have a long-term impact. It will take away an excuse for people to say we don't have the experience.

When a Bob Nash goes to work as VP at a world-renowned development bank, or Alexis becomes a consultant to a Fortune 500 company, they come with cachet because of those experiences that had never been available in that fashion before. Bill Clinton empowered so many people. That's how the real world works for other Americans. Finally, it's working for us.

Many of the lost opportunities (during his administration) were due to his personal issues. President Clinton performed beyond most people's expectation and, in spite of his personal problems, we were his allies because we understand the senseless attacks, the elevation of personal problems to political landmines.

We were all privately pissed off in '96 with the welfare reform bill, even though we understood election politics. Cisneros met with us in Chicago before the Democratic election primary to talk about the welfare-to-work bill. Even with the compromises, we had grave reservations.

Bill Clinton grew in the presidency. I saw tremendous growth—personal, professional, and political. It would be amazing to see a side-by-side comparison of President Clinton from the time he was a candidate to the time he left office.

C. Payne Lucas, president emeritus and founder, AFRICARE:

It seems like I've known Bill Clinton forever . . . that's the feeling you get with Bill Clinton. You never meet him for the first time. That's because of his enormous personality and enormous capacity to create lasting relationships. And later, you think to yourself, "Hell, I just met the man."

It was fascinating to be sitting in a room with him when there were Republicans and critics there, also. The moment they got the opportunity to engage him in a conversation, they were totally disarmed. He had this rare magnetism, and his critics found themselves having to work at remaining critics. How do you criticize a person when you want to be his brother or sister, somebody you want to go shoot marbles with?

I've known other presidents. I knew George Bush, Sr.; Johnson; Nixon; Reagan; Kennedy; I knew Carter better than others. Once I was introduced to these presidents, the next time I saw them, I'd have to be reintroduced. Bill Clinton was completely different. And it was more than just his phenomenal memory. He connected with people.

334

* * *

This might even be seen as a problem for minorities, the disenfranchised . . . in the sense that the president could have, should have done more, but we didn't press him to do more. We loved the man. You don't knock on somebody you love. The black community could have probably gotten a lot more from Bill Clinton if we hadn't been so disarmed by the fact that he saw us as equal citizens. We probably should have asked for more jobs, insisted on more programs.

But how do you ask for more jobs when it seems like you're being a critic, and arming the other side with ammunition? While we have always respected the presidency, African Americans loved this president as much as we respected the presidency. It was an unbelievable eight years of pride and self-pride. We had a president who commanded such enormous knowledge of details . . . that cut across all these disciplines—economics, sociology, psychology.

There were some memorable times in the Clinton presidency. I'll never forget that walk he made down the streets of Washington, D.C., in 1992, up Georgia Avenue. I hadn't seen African Americans respond to a leader like that since Martin Luther King, Jr., walked the streets.

The Africa trip was more than any of us expected from him. The African continent liked Kennedy a lot, had his picture up in lots of places after he was assassinated. But take my word for it, Jack Kennedy was no Bill Clinton. While the Kennedys had marvelous oratory skills, nice presence, no African I know felt he was their brother. But they felt that way about Bill Clinton. If Bill Clinton could run for president in Africa, he would have won it.

What you saw in him, and what we hoped that America would evolve into, was an America that disregarded color. People he met went away feeling that, though he was a white American, there were no differences in the two of you. The trip to South Africa was a once-in-a-lifetime experience. Here were all these people in all their pain, no jobs, HIV, rampant crime in South Africa. America was in Africa, saluting Mandela. No one had anything ugly to say about America when Bill Clinton was there. They truly believed that with Clinton in Washington, he could fix anything, make the world better. They were ecstatic that they had the leader of the free world on their side, wanting to fix everything.

I don't feel Bill Clinton ever went into a meeting with black people and spent time thinking about what he should say, and how he should behave that would be acceptable to blacks. In some way, that's almost a major part of his legacy. But that's Bill Clinton. He has such a comfort level thinking and talking about race that he failed to take into consideration that many Americans may not think like he does. I'm not sure he ever knew why he didn't have super success with his Race Initiative. Maybe he really thought that most people just want to figure out a way to get along . . . and that they'll expend energy or capital doing it. So we get to the end of the thing, and we still have church bombings.

Sometimes, you can't do more because you're inclined to think people around you are like you. He may have assumed that people are better than they really are. But if he had made a decision to get beyond putting people in high places, but not in the bowels of the agencies, where we deal with welfare and social security . . . .

There were missed opportunities during the Clinton years. Africa was a lost opportunity . . . he made a giant step but stopped there. If he had put the same amount of energy into Africa that he put into the Middle East and the Balkans . . . applied it to the center of Africa, zeroed in on Congo, the center of Africa, where so much of her resources and so much stability is required in order to get peace in the continent . . . it would be a different Africa today.

While Clinton's involvement with Africa was greater than any president's before him, and he engendered more respect from African leaders than ever before, the fact of the matter is, he could have done much more in that continent. There were all these naysayers when it came to the discussion about us getting involved in Somalia. Unfortunately, he followed the advisors' advice on that. I think that was a major mistake for America.

He should have devoted more manpower and resources to battle AIDS. This is fast becoming a universal problem, and he could have made a world change. Bill Clinton was not only liked here and Africa, he was liked all over the world.

The welfare legislation was a disgrace to who Bill Clinton is. Passing that welfare legislation hurt poor and minority communities. While it always surprised us when some of Bill Clinton's decisions were painful to the community, we had to remember he was a brilliant politician, and survival is as natural as eating to a politician.

You have to wonder how in the hell a man as brilliant as Bill Clinton got himself involved in the Lewinsky scandal. I really do believe he wants to solve all the problems of the world. He didn't want any unsolved problems left over when his presidency was over. In a way, had there not been a constitutional amendment for third terms, and had there not been the Whitewater/Monica Lewinsky affair . . . Bill Clinton might have been president for life.

The Whitewater issue was one thing, but I think if Clinton had not had that Lewinsky thing hanging over him, he could've recruited anybody. He could've taken the country to another level of understanding. The White House could've really become the people's house. It was still a miracle what he was able to achieve under those times.

The Clinton legacy cannot be measured in a policy. Black America now believes that the presidency is ours, too. You can't find that in a piece of legislation, it's not written anywhere. Black America has now experienced being officially included in the American presidency.

Bill Clinton broke the mold: American presidents usually travel to Europe, China, and Russia. The trade bill was a Clinton product and could have worked wonders for Africa had it been implemented there.

While the Race Initiative will be part of his legacy, it is also unfinished business. Unfortunately, he thought he could get Americans to the same place he was. If I were rating presidential legacies, I would rate Clinton first, then Johnson, Truman, Roosevelt and Carter.

On Clinton's future? He could be invaluable to the problems of Africa. He commands so much respect. A Clinton/Mandela team is unbeatable, in the area of conflict resolution. We have to develop good leadership in Africa. Clinton could play a major role in that. He has the energy and the intellect.

Conver

WILLIAM JEFFERSON CLINTON
FROM HOPE TO HARLEM

PART IX

THE CLINTON PRESIDENCY:
BLACK AMERICA'S REPORT CARD

Bill Clinton did not and has never appealed only to black voters. He could never have served as Arkansas' governor for 11 years or made it to the White House, where he stayed for a second term, with just the votes of African Americans. While records show that the vast majority of African Americans did vote for Bill Clinton, most blacks also voted for Franklin Roosevelt, John F. Kennedy, Lyndon Johnson, and Jimmy Carter as well. Where was the outcry about blacks' blind loyalty to these candidates?

CHAPTER 25
THE CLINTON PRESIDENCY:
—A Report Card—

A merica is rife with black and white myths about William Jefferson Clinton. The myth that refuses to die, in Main Street America is that African Americans—regardless of geographical or cultural backgrounds, experiences, or personal likes and dislikes—are monolithic when it comes to the country's 42nd president.

Most white Americans, in fact, believe it is pure hogwash when dissidents argue that there are more than a handful of African Americans who see beyond Bill Clinton's charismatic smile and soulful saxophone blowing. That, in fact, there is a human being below the surface that either we identify with—given our own experiences, beliefs, and principles—or we do not.

Black America's mythology is centered around white America's distrust and disdain for this former president. Most African Americans believe white America's falling out of love with Bill Clinton has more to do with his affinity for blacks and minorities than any policy or initiative. Half in jest, they say white America's jaundiced eye turned red with rage when network news showed a laughing Bill Clinton chauffeuring the affable Vernon Jordan around in a golfing cart.

Though the myths serve to highlight America's great, ongoing racial divide, Clinton shrugs off both opinions as narrow assessments. In truth, there are more than a handful of African Americans who are neither Clinton loyalists nor Democratic liberals. The more conservative blacks, in fact, view the charismatic and shrewd politician as a white man who has black America's number. It doesn't hurt, they say, that he can preach with the best of them on Sunday mornings and blows a mean, if a bit rusty, saxophone on Saturday night.

Even his detractors admit that it is Bill Clinton's openness and his daring to go where no other white politician will that gain him entrée into the hearts of African Americans. The two-term president's charisma, complex ideologies, and political acumen make both whites and blacks ask, "Can this guy be for real?"

The former president says he has heard endless variations of those and other myths throughout his political career and has never allowed them to stop him from doing what he thought was right. "What I have decided is that . . . I tend to make some whites nervous, because I do feel so comfortable within the black community, and, of course, there are some blacks who just flat out refuse to believe that any white man could be so accepting of another culture." Clinton insists, however, that he couldn't fool the black community if he wanted to. "Black Americans," he says, "are like any other culture . . . people know in their hearts when you're selling them a bill of goods and when you're acting or speaking from your heart."

Bill Clinton has never in his 30 years of political involvement had only a black following. He was elected to serve as Arkansas' governor for five terms and was voted the most popular governor in the country by an all-white group of governors. He has been compared to John Kennedy throughout his presidential stint, in both his intellect and his charisma. And if he ends up in America's history books on the list of the top 10 most popular presidents, it won't be based solely on his relationship with black America.

Bill Clinton won his political races because both blacks and whites believed he offered something more than the other candidates; he could not have won any other way. His appeal, then and now, crosses all social, cultural, and ethnic lines, just as those who don't like him or his politics come in all persuasions. While records show Bill Clinton consistently enjoyed a 90-plus percentage of African Americans' votes, that number equals roughly 90 percent of less than 12 percent of the country.

The inordinate focus on black America's loyalty to Bill Clinton seems disingenuous. Blacks, since Reconstruction, have overwhelmingly voted Democratic, from the "Give 'em Hell, Harry" days to the Peanut President. Bill Clinton was just the latest in a string of Democrats who could boast overwhelming support from black voters. One might argue, however, that Bill Clinton was the first president to reciprocate black voters' loyalty.

One writer scathingly dubbed Bill Clinton the "O.J. President. Were black Americans, then, the ignorant and hapless jurors who "sprung" him for president? Bill Clinton, in fact, has African American detractors; they were around throughout his eight years as president.

A *Baltimore Sun* writer criticized the fact that blacks turned their heads as the pardons scandals broke in January 2001 and lamented that blacks had welcomed Bill Clinton into Harlem with open arms. He questioned the whereabouts of the Reverends Jackson and Sharpton when troubles abounded around Clinton. Vocal and credible opinions all, yet the vast majority of black Americans believe they, and America, were better off under Bill Clinton's leadership.

For additional assurance that not all blacks are sycophants of Bill Clinton, Adonis Hoffman, a Washington lawyer and political columnist for the *Washington Post*, wrote in 1996 that "Nowhere has Bill Clinton been more successful at projecting a more beneficent and larger-than-life persona than his relations with African Americans. Clinton's down-home familiarity with the cultural idioms and lexicons of black folks has engendered a genuine comfort level and earned him the trust of a supermajority of black voters."

Hoffman, however, points out that in the wake of several policy decisions, welfare reform in particular: "The president is facing a clash of icons. Clinton points to a record of achievement on issues of concerns to African Americans, and yet, during his presidency, he has overseen one of the most dramatic declines in black political empowerment in decades. Something is clearly wrong with this picture."

There are reasons, logical reasons, that African Americans overwhelmingly supported Bill Clinton through his roller-coaster ride in the White House, not the least being, as Toni Morrison said it best, their ability to identify with his roller-coaster ride. His nightmare on Pennsylvania Avenue was probably only a tad better than an African American's experience would be, given a chance at the White House.

Yet with all our affinity for this president, and all his comfort with us, there are black leaders who rate Bill Clinton's performance in the White House with mixed grades. In the end, they point out, all people are the same, and black Americans are just as concerned about the bottom line as other Americans—it's about whether there are more pluses than minuses for us and our families.

Conversations with African Americans throughout the country resulted in interesting and diverse thoughts and views on the 42nd president. There are some universal responses lauding his domestic policy initiatives that addressed the issues of economic and health inequities, racism, and gender and age discrimination. Welfare reform probably garnered the most vocal dissatisfaction, as most viewed his signing of the Republican-led bill as "selling out" politically.

In the end, as the following conversations will show, African Americans are neither monolithic nor blind to the former president's strengths and weaknesses. What almost all the interviewees agree on is that for the first time in presidential history, when the president spoke of America, they believed they heard their names.

CHAPTER 26
—THE CLINTON—
Race Initiative

B ill Clinton is the first to say he failed to take the Race Initiative where he had hoped he could during his presidency. The public dialogue on race was, in fact, much shorter on dialogue than he had hoped; yet most interviewed for this book gave the president high marks for his courage in broaching such a burdensome issue with America.

Johnathan Capehart wrote in the New York *Daily News* in 1997 of his memories of summers in the South, which included staring at pictures of Martin Luther King, Jr., Jesus Christ, and John F. Kennedy on the walls of black folks' homes. "Spiritually," he writes, "Christ has always been there for blacks. But Kennedy and King were seen as heroic mortals who died for true freedom for the descendants of slaves. For that, they won the hearts of generations of African Americans. Now comes a man who is carving out a frame where his likeness might one day be added . . . President Clinton and his crusade to improve race relations."

Hugh Price, former president of the National Urban League, admits that he was a vocal detractor of Bill Clinton during much of his presidency. Price said that the president's efforts to start a dialogue on race, while commendable, were "stillborn," never getting off the ground because Bill Clinton and his White House were distracted by the Lewinsky issue. The major problem with the effort, Price points out, and the reason he couldn't give it high marks, was that the president was seeking to strike up a conversation when white America didn't want to come to the table. "You can't have a one-sided race conversation in this country."

Lottie Shackelford, longtime Clinton supporter and former mayor of Little Rock, says there is no question that given more time and under different circumstances Bill Clinton would have pushed the race issue to the forefront—forcing Americans to recognize that racism does exist and how it's hurting this country. "The incredible thing is that he made it a White House initiative—he used his bully pulpit to lead and encourage others to buy into the racism issue, bringing Americans from all backgrounds together and talking about the root of all our problems."

Susan Taylor, former *Essence* magazine editor in chief, joined President Clinton, the Reverend Jesse Jackson, and other luminaries at the Rainbow/PUSH Coalition's Second Wall Street Economic Summit. It was there she made her eloquent and fiery speech in which she credited William Jefferson Clinton with bringing African Americans into a club that, heretofore, had allowed in only rich white males.

In her speech, Taylor said: "I feel so blessed to have this opportunity to express a little of what black women feel, and a bit of what we know. We feel amplified by your bold spirit that has in so many major ways moved our nation toward healing the old wounds that still divide us.

"Your bravery in bringing us into the club—that before you came was almost exclusively the reserve of rich white men—has rallied us in our weary days and put a creeping cynicism to flight."

"In an unprecedented way, your White House—your history-making cabinet and the thousands of people you've appointed to key positions in the executive branch of the federal government—helps us to imagine something this world has never seen: women and men of all colors, cultures and religions—rainbow people—using all the oars we have in the water to pull smartly in the same direction."

Baseball great **Hank Aaron,** who retired from baseball and began to build wealth in Atlanta, said: "Though I was invited to the White House many times during my baseball career, it was only during Bill Clinton's presidency that I truly felt welcomed in the White House. He made you know that that house was as much ours as it was any other Americans'.

"It wasn't just visiting black churches on the Sunday before Election Day or going to a black night club to drum up votes . . . this man lived this race thing every day. It was as if he woke up and went to bed conscious of it."

Some political pundits, noting George Bush's photo ops with Condoleezza Rice and Colin Powell before the 2000 election, believe that Bill Clinton's position on race helped define the Gore-Bush campaign and will continue to define the ethnic and racial makeup of presidential administrations to come.

Harvard Professor **William Julius Wilson** was tapped to participate in the historical economic summit held in Arkansas in 1992, soon after Bill Clinton's election to the presidency. Wilson says Clinton certainly deserves credit for using the bully pulpit to talk about race and for reducing racial tension during his tenure.

The speeches Clinton delivered in Austin, Texas, and Memphis, Tennessee, Wilson says, were early indications of his willingness to "get out there" on race. "It was a strong symbolic message that the president of the United States was concerned about the race issue . . . he went against some of his political advisors and showed real courage in his hopes of ending racial disparity."

Eddie Williams, president of the Joint Center for Economic Studies, says everyone has their own perception of the story when it comes to Bill Clinton's performance, but that from his standpoint, the president's greatest contribution to the black community was his ongoing demonstration—publicly and unashamedly—that he cared about our issues.

But I truly believe his efforts at forging a national dialogue on race will go down as a large part of his legacy. That is something that's important to us, and that the Center has been trying to get off the ground for some time here.

"I had hoped he would have had the opportunity to play out the Race Initiative unfettered by other distractions. Unfortunately, the initiative coincided with the peak of his problems, and without his direct personal involvement, I don't think it got off to a good start. It just seemed that some of the other people left to try to shape it weren't as committed, didn't have the same kind of leadership, or couldn't inspire the same kind of following that he had.

"That was so unfortunate because that whole effort is so vital to America. I worry about those kinds of things more than policy A, policy B, versus policy C . . . because if you get the race issue resolved, the policies will fall into place, because people will have respect for one another."

CHAPTER 27
AN ADMINISTRATION
— THAT LOOKED LIKE —
America

Never before in American history has so many African Americans populated the halls of federal government and the White House. Bill
Clinton's White House was the residence of over 60 black appointees,
ranging from the highest level of assistants to the president, down to staff
assistants.

At one point during his first term, there were five African Americans heading either agencies or departments in the administration, including the late
Ron Brown, Secretary of Commerce; Mike Espy, Secretary of Agriculture;
Hazel O'Leary, Secretary of Energy; Jesse Brown, Secretary of Veteran Affairs;
and Togo West, Jr., Secretary of the Army. And then there was Clinton's first
surgeon general, Jocelyn Elders, and Willie Brown, the White House drug
czar. Cabinet member photos, some point out, looked more like the United
Nations than ever before, even if half of the African American members
became targets of the Republican-led Congress during their tenure.

Bob Nash headed the White House Office of Personnel for six of the years
Bill Clinton was president. Nash, who half-jokingly called his job the most
difficult in the federal government, says that beyond any other achievements
Bill Clinton might have made during his presidency, the most remarkable was
in the area of appointments.

Nash points out that the inclusion of blacks in highly visible and non-
traditional positions did not begin with Bill Clinton's arrival in Washington,
D.C. Nash, who served in Arkansas as Governor Clinton's senior economic
advisor, says, "I could give you 10 names of African Americans who served Bill
Clinton with distinction, and in high positions, in Arkansas' state government.

"It became clear to me, early on, that we were facing a different kind of obstacle to diversity here from the kinds we found in Arkansas. It was a more subtle, sophisticated, 'inside the beltway' kind of exclusion that had been nurtured and survived presidency after presidency. There weren't too many people who didn't know him who believed him when Bill Clinton said he wanted an administration that looked like America. They found out he really meant it."

In fact, Nash says, Clinton's record as governor of Arkansas closely paralleled his presidential record of changing the status quo and the complexion of government. "What amazed me—educated me early on—was the insensitivity of many cabinet-level people seeking department heads or assistants. I would say, 'I have this minority candidate I'd like you to look at,' and the first thing out of their mouths would be, 'Well, we already have a black in the office,' or, 'We actually need someone who can do the job.' Not only was that insensitive, it was senseless. How many blacks would arrive at that level of consideration without having at least as much going for them as the average white candidate?"

Nash says that Bill Clinton's position was definitely not business as usual in the federal government; he was breaking new ground and upsetting lots of apple carts on the way. "There were departments, agencies that had terrible reputations when it came to diversity. There were large offices where every employee was a white man or woman. Under the Clinton directive of an administration that looked like America, we went in and changed a lot of that, and I have to admit it gave me some personal satisfaction to be a part of that kind of history."

The verdict on whether such changes are long-term or will continue at some level is still out. Nash says that after someone like Bill Clinton puts his prints on the way federal government does business, things can never completely revert back to the way they were. "His changes, as far as bringing in people of color, were such drastic changes that it would be really blatant for department heads to revert completely back to business as usual, no matter who is in the White House."

CHAPTER 28
CLINTON'S DOMESTIC
Policies

I t is the nation's domestic policy initiatives, most social scientists agree, that most affect Americans' day-to-day lives. And whether they are good or bad policies, they always affect African Americans disproportionately. While most mainstream polls give President Clinton a passing grade on his domestic affairs approach over his eight years in the White House, African Americans have surprisingly mixed reviews on his performance.

President Clinton received overwhelmingly high marks from the American community, based on his early passage of the economic stimulus bill and his ability to forge an economic team to assure continued growth in the American economy.

Hugh Price of the National Urban League says, "President Clinton's greatest contribution to this country and the African American community was his economic success . . . he stands head and shoulders over any other president in recent history in that area . . . the brilliant orchestration of the strengthening of our economy after the recession."

Price says that as a result of the economic upturn under Clinton and the decline in unemployment, the African American middle class grew, and lots of people who had been on the outside looking in were now part of the economic mainstream for the first time. "While Bill Clinton can't claim all the credit for that huge success, it was also through his fiscal policies, the federal government he had responsibility for, his economic team—Rubin, Raines. Without a doubt, his primary legacy is his economic legacy."

Price adds that the strong economy helped young people decide that having babies out of wedlock was nonsense. For the first time, he said, some youth saw a legitimate way to move into the mainstream.

"Most importantly," he says, "the economic growth pushed recovery deep into our communities . . . you see that in the revivals of the Harlems of the world. It placed retailers into our community; our communities became safer, too. This economic recovery was not a macro-recovery, it impacted our communities like it never has before . . . the idea that we could have economic recovery without inflation broke all the rules."

CHAPTER 29
THE OTHER SHOE THAT DROPPED:
Welfare Reform

In spite of Clinton's overwhelming popularity in the African American community, many of those loyalists broke ties with him after passage of his welfare reform bill. For some it was the one indicator that the president was not as empathetic to the plight of the poor and the underclass as he'd led black America to believe. Others thought it was a very bad judgment based on pure politics. For certain, it took its toll on his relationship with the African American community and brought loud criticism from all corners of the black leadership.

Professor William Julius Wilson, longtime admirer of Bill Clinton and an early advisor to the president on welfare reform, was also one of the early detractors of Clinton's ultimate position on welfare reform.

"I give the president credit for a number of things, including putting in place a number of race-neutral programs that had very positive effects on our communities, programs like the Earned Income Tax Credit; raising minimum wage after so many years of it not being increased under Reagan and Bush, which blacks disproportionately benefited from; and his commitment to affirmative action when it was under real attack from his opponents.

"I am, however, very critical of the president for what he didn't do—that is, take a courageous stand on the welfare reform issue," Wilson says. The professor, who has made a career studying, teaching, and writing about the health and welfare of African Americans, said he took offense at Clinton's center-to-right position on welfare reform, an issue so important to the well-being of the African American community.

"I was grossly disappointed in how the president and his administration handled welfare reform. He signed a very, very weak welfare reform bill whose success depended completely on a continuing economic boom. Even with some people declaring it as successful right now, time will tell. The timing for him, when he signed it, could not have been better . . . the economic boom was in full throttle.

"I worry about what happens to all these people if we enter a real depression. I frankly wish he had gone before the American people and said, 'This is a Republican bill that is based on the belief that people are on welfare because they are lazy and choose to be on welfare.' " Wilson says that now we're just lucky that economic conditions are still formidable, but he is still afraid that the long-term effect of the bill will be negative.

Wade Henderson, president of the Leadership Conference on Civil Rights, who has worked on immigration policies with both the ACLU and the NAACP, says he was an early admirer of Bill Clinton.

"There was a real sense of optimism with the new president and a hope that the advance characterizations in his presidency would hold true. He was surrounded by more progressive and diverse support than had been seen previously in most Democratic candidates, and his affinity for African Americans was well known.

"Clinton's ties with the civil rights establishment through the Little Rock Nine and a host of others were really quite positive," Henderson points out. He says he was quite enthusiastic about a Clinton presidency, believing it afforded tremendous hope, especially after the Reagan and Bush administrations which, except for programs like fair housing and the Americans With Disabilities Act, had really been years in the wilderness for African Americans.

"Ironically, the Reagan years were the most productive in terms of legislative accomplishments in the modern day civil rights period," said Henderson. It was a strange anomaly because the Democrats controlled Congress, and in spite of the White House being in Reagan's hands, we still made progress.

"My exposure to the White House during President Clinton's tenure was substantial . . . he opened his doors to a diverse group of people on a variety of issues. That engendered a feeling of being at home politically in the White House, reinforcing our appreciation of Bill Clinton."

However, Henderson says it was these kinds of unique overtures that made the president's missed opportunities most disappointing. "You expected more from him."

"I was woefully disappointed in some of the positions President Clinton took in respect to the welfare of the African American community, and his position with Lani Guinier was a major disappointment."

Henderson describes what he calls the "welfare reform debacle" as a result of the president and his administration's less-than-artful handling of a number of complex issues early in his administration.

"The problem with the welfare reform issue was that he had to ultimately ignore the policy recommendations of the people he knew, and instead took the politically expedient route, which appeased his political interest on the one hand but cost him his moral integrity on this critical domestic policy issue."

Henderson believes that the bill signed by the president had long-term and far-reaching importance for the minority community. "Welfare reform was so important, because it involved this question of rewriting the social contract in America. This was a big piece of rewriting the contemporary social contract. It wasn't just about more money . . . you were redefining the government's role."

Henderson, like other African Americans who have seen how disproportionately the ups and downs of the economic climate affect the minority community, believes a big allure of the welfare reform bill was the economic good fortune that occurred during Clinton's tenure. He laments, however, that "we are just one economic downturn from economic disaster."

Henderson said that while the president "shared our interests in many ways, his political interests overruled everything else." One example, he says, was the president's attitude about reducing penalties for crack cocaine.

Henderson took part in the early 1990s effort to overturn a decision that Congress had made at the height of the drug wars to establish a 100-to-1 disparity in sentencing guidelines for crack and powder cocaine offenders. He says it was clear that "crack sentences were largely associated with African Americans and, to a lesser extent, Latinos," while powder cocaine was more closely associated with whites.

When the federal sentencing recommendation came to Congress, he says, it was one of only a handful of times Congress had rejected sentencing commission recommendations. He echoes others who voiced disappointment in the administration's response to the Rwanda tragedy, but gives the former president points for his humanitarian efforts in Somalia and Haiti, and his historical effort to change political attitudes on Africa.

"I'm sure he'll look back on Rwanda and know that we turned our backs on a situation that he should have known would result in genocide, and yet this country failed to act."

To sum it up, Henderson describes Bill Clinton as a paradox, an enigma, a puzzle. He says there are many things for which we should have expected a more enlightened response from someone like him and a less enlightened response from someone else. "When I look back at his presidency, I do see missed opportunities."

Hugh Price of the National Urban League has a different take on the Clinton administration's welfare reform bill. With the realization that he has isolated himself from most African Americans on this issue, Price gives Clinton a passing grade on welfare reform.

He believes the policy was helpful in persuading teens that having kids out of wedlock was the major obstacle to economic parity. He says, however, it was only due to the historical economic upturn, however, that Bill Clinton could get away with such a policy.

"It was good as long as the economy was good, but it's certainly not for a soft economic market," says Price. "What we have now is a 'perfect economic storm.' "

AFTERWORD

AFTERWORD

— A Conversation With —
William Jefferson Clinton

No fact, no story, no opinion inside these pages came near to answering the question of how William Jefferson Clinton came to be such a socially conscious idealist, coming out of the narrow, constrained world of Hope, Arkansas, or the more worldly yet patently Southern Hot Springs.

Neither the most sardonic of critics nor the most sycophantic of loyalists can explain what makes Bill Clinton continue tilting at windmills even now, when there is no outward compulsion, no elections, no poll results egging him on. The reader then might conclude that this complex man's legacy is inextricably tied to his early passions: the need to transform the world into that colorless, classless nirvana he believes it should be; maybe an early need for recognition as the good son or later the good politician who is more than just another politician?

Was that seed—the root of all things Bill Clinton—sowed in Hot Springs, that city of miraculous spas and forgiven indiscretions . . . or back on Hervey Street when he was then too young to understand the things his heart took note of, in that place called Hope?

And, finally, what might have been left behind, or replaced, or stored away for safekeeping, making room for the more acceptable pragmatism and political wisdom in that long journey from Hope to Harlem?

The following is a conversation with America's 42nd president:

What defines a great leader . . . My definition of a great leader is a man or woman who understands the moment in which he or she serves: how it relates to the past, how it relates to the future. It's very difficult, because you can have a vision, but it can be totally out of whack with what's possible unless you understand how the present fits with the past, as well as the future you're try-ing to achieve. I was lucky that I had served 10 years as a governor (in a state) that had all the problems of America . . . and the prom-ise. So I had a chance to learn in a way that I couldn't have learned just from reading about where we were in that particular moment.

Vision, practical ability to develop a strategy and to implement it and to go about realizing that vision . . . it is important that a leader has a reasonably good mind. It is more important that a leader be curious than that he or she is brilliant. Good imagination and a generous heart, so you can always put yourself in the other person's shoes.

A great leader cannot be small-minded, can't be distracted by criticisms, attacks, or little things. If you give your mind over to them you are, in effect, stealing the time people have given to you to help them and giving it to pettier concerns. Every leader falls prey to this at times, but it should be something that lasts maybe a minute or two, not a week, a month, a year, or a term.

Leaders have to be strong and willing to fight for what they believe in. And they have to be constant. That was one of the things we had going for us in the Middle East conflict. Both leaders—Israelis and Palestinians—viewed me as constant. That's why I was viewed favorably by both Israelis and Palestinians. They both believed that I wanted the best for each of them; and I was constant in the pursuit of whatever that was.

Mahatma Gandhi would go high at the top of my list as a great leader because he understood the moment, had a vision, had a big and generous heart and a fine mind. He was tough as nails and gave up his small-mindedness. Then there are Prime Minister (Yitzhak) Rabin and South African President Mandela. Those are three great men who lived during my lifetime. All three had egos, but their purposes were designed to help other people live their dreams. Great men from the past would be Presidents Roosevelt and Lincoln.

But I'd also add Napoleon Bonaparte to that list, one of the greatest leaders to ever live, and an absolute genius. He actually did a lot of good, but in the end, leadership that is about conquest doesn't stand up too well in the light of history.

America's greatest presidents . . .   As for great U.S. presidents, I would cite George Washington, Abraham Lincoln, and Franklin Roosevelt, who all served as presidents at a time when we could have lost the country. I don't really think we could have lost World War II, but America could have been diminished forever if we hadn't responded both to the war and to the Great Depression the way we did. But each of these men was in a position to do something really great, and they did it.

Thomas Jefferson was a great president in his first term. He bought Louisiana and sent Lewis and Clark on their expedition. He built a political dynasty that lasted longer than anyone since. So while his second term was something of a disappointment to people, and he made policy mistakes, he was a great man and a visionary.

Then there is a close call between Presidents Theodore Roosevelt and Harry Truman. Teddy Roosevelt basically crystallized our emergence as an industrial nation as we became more urbanized and more of an immigrant nation, and he articulated the role of the national government in trying to build one nation. He humanized the worst excesses of the industrial revolution and became our first great environmental president. And while he could be a little bellicose, he could also work peace. He won a Nobel Peace Prize for settling that war between Russia and Japan.

Harry Truman was the completely accidental president. He basically finished Roosevelt's vision of creating a United Nations and the international institutions of cooperation, all the international financial institutions. He supported the Marshall Plan, rebuilding our friends and foes after the war, and established NATO and other institutions that allowed us to avoid the third world war . . . and to win the Cold War.

U.S. presidents' impact on black America . . .   As far as presidents who contributed most or had the greatest impact on the African American community . . . it would be either Abraham Lincoln or Lyndon Baines Johnson. Lincoln's primary purpose was to save the Union, but he always knew slavery was wrong, and the more he thought about it, the more determined he became to support emancipation, in spite of the fact that a significant percentage of those fighting on his side of the Civil War only wanted a union and were prepared to take the South back in with slavery still in existence. So I think the 13th, 14th, and 15th Amendments, which were the legacy of his life and his death, were very important.

When John F. Kennedy was killed, Lyndon Johnson got that enormous vote of confidence in 1964 with a big majority in Congress, enough to overcome the Southern Democrats' reluctance to buy into his program. With the new Democrats who came into Congress and the Republicans who were pro-civil rights, he was able to enact the civil rights laws, the voting rights laws, and the open housing laws.

Bill Clinton's contributions to black America . . . I think my contributions to the African American community would be the general sense of empowerment and recognition that African Americans had as citizens. I think during my administration, for the first time, they felt they were equal players in America. No administration—Democrat or Republican—will be able to ignore that and treat the black community simply as another vote.

I am proud that I kept my promise to create an administration that "looked like America." One of my regrets, however, is that I was not able to appoint one more Supreme Court justice, either an African American or Hispanic. I think an administration that looks like America in the future will have to have more Hispanics, more Chinese, Japanese, and other Asian Americans.

I do believe that America will come to view both the African American and Hispanic communities in less monolithic terms. We have people from Africa, the Caribbean, people from South America, even, that have African blood in them. So our generalizations will begin to give way to more sophisticated views of whether the administration is representative . . . and just how far the reach of Africa is into the heart of America.

I tried to go a step further during my presidency, to integrate the concerns of African Americans into all the policies of government—the economic policy, our social policy, and our foreign policies. They were all reflected to a degree, to an extent they never had before. Whether it was in health care, policies impacting the working poor, or the crime and hate bills, I knew that any problems in America were exacerbated in the minority communities.

Beyond that, I made it my business to keep raising the race issue every chance I got. Whether it was economic policy, home ownership policy, small business policies, or family leave and insurance policy . . . we basically set up a framework for considering the impact of various policies on our neglect, historical neglect of the African American community that had not been there before.

We did a lot of things to correct the historic record—the implementation of the Empowerment Zones, micro-credit banks, community lending banks, more esoteric efforts like apologizing for the Tuskegee experiments, going to Africa and saying how sorry I was about slavery and how wrong it was, the military recognition we gave to people who were wronged, going all the way back to the 19th century. My policies, while affecting the masses, had a disproportionately positive effect on African Americans because they needed more.

In the One America Initiative, we made specific efforts to highlight disparities in areas such as medical research, health care and treatment . . . we basically set up a framework. But on the other side of the equation, two of the missed opportunities could have meant a safer, healthier country—the inability to pass a health insurance law for all Americans and failure to pass a hate crime bill.

The one most controversial Clinton policy . . . Out of all my policies, the greatest criticism I received from the black community was over the welfare reform bill. And I think the evidence so far shows I was right. There has been a decline in inequality, a decline in poverty.

What remains to be seen is whether, when the Bush administration reauthorizes welfare reform, will the president and Congress take into account the changed economy and the fact that many states took the welfare money and didn't save it for a rainy day, and didn't spend it on welfare recipients . . . in which case, they should have to make some adjustments for that.

Words of wisdom for government leaders . . . What would my advice be to government leaders as it relates to continuing to try to resolve our historical racial problem? I would tell them three things: 1) make sure their governments are fully representative of the communities they serve; 2) set up a systematic approach to identifying continuing problems and resolutions to them; and 3) to continue to speak out about the importance of not just respecting diversity but celebrating it . . . but always in the context of building a better community

How Governor Bill Clinton impacted Arkansas and black Arkansans . . .

While serving as a governor of Arkansas helped prepare me for the role of president of the country, it also opened my eyes to the limitations that a leader, whether a governor or president, is faced with.

I was fortunate that I came into office after Winthrop Rockefeller, Dale Bumpers, and David Pryor. I was the fourth Arkansas governor in a row with basically progressive views, but I was the first person who had a number of relationships in the African American community. So I thought all I had to do was take what I knew and make sure the state did it. But like other governors of poor Southern states, there were huge challenges.

For example, in the three years I taught at the University of Arkansas' Law School, and afterward, I actually taught 75 percent of the African American lawyers in the state. There had been an extremely low percentage of blacks admitted to, or graduates of, the university law school before Hillary and I arrived there. We worked to change those statistics and began working with some of the students to make sure they didn't fail.

There was one student in his 30s who had gone to a black, segregated high school. He had a great mind but couldn't spell. I actually worked with him after seeing he was doing terrible on his exams. I brought him in and went over the material with him. We got him through it and he took the bar a few times, then finally passed. All the problems he had were due to things that weren't done during his developmental years, when he was very young. He was trying to make up for years and years of lost opportunities.

Fair and equal representation has always been a philosophy of mine. As attorney general, I had 20 lawyers on my staff and always had five (black) lawyers in that group. My top cabinet person at one point during my gubernatorial administration was black: Bob Nash headed up Housing and Finance, the largest bonding department in the country at the time. He handled all the New York bond daddies, along with Arkansas' political pressures brought on by that job.

My biggest challenge, apart from developing the economy and the educational system, was to overcome the still-present legacy of discrimination and segregation in the state, just making sure that people of my state were fundamentally fair-minded. So I felt that by just giving people a chance to serve and empowering them, we could go a long way toward inspiring other young African Americans, and help change the attitude of the state. To a large extent we succeeded in that.

There were specific things I had to do. I remember very well when three of my aides, all of whom happened to be African American—Rodney Slater, Bob Nash, and Carol Willis—warned me about the political consequences of my attending a segregated event in the east Arkansas Delta, in a county where I was told "that is the way they'd always done it." I needed that county real bad, but I told them I wouldn't come if they were having a segregated event. They complied, and after the event, they were all wondering why they'd ever had segregated events.

I also tried to make sure we didn't just do things in areas that were vote-rich. There were lots of little black towns that had no clean water, no sewer systems . . . just the basic indices of normal life. When I was a boy growing up in Hope and Hot Springs, the only streets those cities failed to ever pave were the streets in the black neighborhoods. That had a big impact on me. So we spent a lot of time and effort making sure that when we put out the water and sewer projects, these little towns, some of them no more than 150 to 200 people, got their fair share.

All these changes, these efforts were good for the white community as well. I remember during the terrible economy of the '80s, there were two towns, 18 miles apart, in southeast Arkansas. One was doing well and the other wasn't. And the one doing well had a totally integrated decision-making process. Blacks were heavily involved in the community; there was no white flight from the schools, no kids going to white academies. There were blacks as well as white administrators in the public school system. This was the early '80s, and the community was, by far, the most successful community in southeast Arkansas.

That was the city of Dumas, Arkansas, about 80 miles south of the state capital. I was absolutely convinced that the success of that small city was because a man named Merle Peterson and two or three other residents had enough sense to know that they had a massive human resource there, and if they spent all their time trying to recapture their past, all they were going to do would be to sink into it. And so . . . instead, they built a different future together.

And in the toughest of times, during the '80s, when we were all having a tough time down there, they were doing better than virtually anybody else, because they had the level of racial cooperation that enabled them to be creative in other ways and to be more sophisticated in other ways about how they courted business, kept business, and diversified their economy.

I think my most lasting contribution to the state of Arkansas was school reform . . . smaller classes in early grades, summer programs, guaranteed scholarships for students with B averages. Again, we changed the rules. Nobody can be governor again without having substantial involvement in the African American community.

William J. Clinton's Southern experience . . . I grew up in a segregated environment, the state as well as my high school that I graduated from in Hot Springs. But I had a few opportunities to interact with black people that a lot of people didn't have. Hope was a small town; and you couldn't avoid people even if you tried to.

My grandparents, though, as I've said so many times, were very liberal on civil rights issues, which was very unusual for middle class or lower middle class white people. My grandfather owned a general store in the black community, across from the cemetery. So I played with black children and knew black people as people in a way that most white people didn't.

When I moved to Hot Springs, which was more segregated, I was more sensitive by then. My father went into business with my uncle, who owned a car dealership. Lots of his workers were black, so I would go back in the back of the dealership and sit down and talk to them. One of them had a wife who worked for my mother for a while. You know, it just enabled me to have some human contact that I wouldn't have had. I don't think people realized just how segregated America was . . . even when I went to Georgetown, it was mostly segregated.

But personal contact makes a difference. Even when I became governor, the legendary cook at the mansion, Liza Ashley, this little, old black lady, used to say to me, "We never had a white governor who had black folks to dinner before . . . you sure that's not gone hurt you?" She was scared I was going to lose my election . . . and it turned out I did, but it didn't have anything to do with who I invited to dinner.

I was able largely to prove that doing the right thing is good politics, not bad politics. I always wanted to take the partisanship out of race. I could never understand why Republicans had to run away from that historic legacy. Well, I did understand it, too . . . they got a lot of votes for doing it.

I always felt, when I was in office, if I could prove that broad-based involvement was good politics, it would change forever. Look at the former President Bush and the current administration, which is the most diverse Republican administration you've ever had. They're doing it partly because they'd like to have a larger share of minority votes, partly because there's a larger pool of educated African Americans—and some of these, alas, will become conservative Republicans. But they're also doing it because there is no downside to it now. There isn't a downside. There's a culture war on other fronts, but at least we're moving past that one.

Black people are better judges of that than white people are. Lots of white Americans, especially a lot of my critics, felt threatened by my relationship with the black community. They didn't understand it. But the truth is, once you get past the politics of it, I think a lot of them wish they had the same sort of relationships I did. But what they don't understand is, it's not rocket science.

It is true that any group of people who have known long, long periods of segregation and discrimination have an extraordinary ability to judge the sincerity of people . . . it became necessary for survival, something almost handed down genetically through the generations. Civil rights was at the core of my being, it was what gave me the heart, the love for public life . . . the idea that you could do something to give everybody a fair chance.

Also, I couldn't imagine why white Americans thought they were so much better than everybody else that they wouldn't be interested in other people . . . different races and people with different backgrounds. I was just always interested, and I think African Americans knew that.

Yes, I enjoyed the political support, and as it turned out, because I embraced the African American community so strongly, and if they hadn't returned the embraces, I couldn't have been elected, because a lot of conservative whites didn't like me because of that. But there was nothing phony about it . . . when white people say that, they're basically saying, "Well, I always thought I was a little liberal, and I don't have all these kinds of feelings." For most of them, they haven't had the opportunities I have.

For some of them, they're still afraid, a little ill at ease, but that's natural. If you look at it, civilization has only been around about 6,000 years, and most of that time, people have stuck to their own kind and built group loyalty from within, in part by promoting opposition to those outside the group. Even in this enlightened age, we're still trying to unlearn habits we've learned over a millennium ago.

I've always felt at home in conversations, friendships, work, in casual encounters with African Americans . . . I don't know exactly why, but I just know I have. Maybe because I always identified with people who had been left out and left behind and had tough times. But I think mostly it was that I found it interesting. I couldn't imagine why anybody would shut themselves off from a major portion of the human race.

I think as more and more white people have more and more contacts and get over a lot of their subconscious stereotypes about what black people are like and what it means to be friends with them, I think those criticisms will fall away. But when people say that, I never really take it that seriously. I would take it seriously if a lot of black people believed I was insincere. I think it's almost a hopeful sign when a lot of white people start knocking on the door, wanting to be part of that, too. And it's not complicated . . . just show up.

If the good Lord came to me tonight when I walked out of this room and said, "Mr. President, now I'm not going to let you serve the end of your term, I'm taking you home tonight, and I'm no genie, I'm not going to give you three wishes, but I will give you one—what do you want?" I would wish for our country to be truly one America.

—President Clinton, speaking at an NAACP dinner

William Jefferson Clinton

TIMELINE

1946	Born William Jefferson Blythe III on August 19 in Hope, Arkansas
1951	Attends Miss Mary Perkins Kindergarten
1952	Attends St. John's Catholic Ramble Elementary
1953	Attends Brookwood Elementary
1953	Moves with his mother and stepfather to Hot Springs, Arkansas
1953	Attends Hot Springs Elementary School
1962	Changes his name to William "Bill" Jefferson Clinton
1964	Graduates with honors from Lakeside High School
1964-68	Attends Georgetown University
1969	Attends Oxford University in England as a Rhodes scholar
1970	Graduates from Georgetown University
1972	Directs McGovern for President campaign in Texas
1973	Graduates from Yale University Law School
1973-76	Teaches at University of Arkansas Law School
1974	Runs for U.S. Congress and loses
1975	Marries Hillary Rodham, fellow Yale graduate from Lake Forest, Illinois
1976	Manages Jimmy Carter's presidential campaign in Arkansas
1976	Elected State Attorney General of Arkansas
1978	Elected governor of Arkansas at age 32; youngest U.S. governor in 40 years

1980	Loses re-election campaign for governor
1980	Daughter Chelsea Clinton born to Hillary and Bill Clinton
1982	Re-elected governor of Arkansas (serves 1982-1992)
1991	Cited as country's Most Effective Governor
1991	Announces candidacy for U.S. president, October 3
1992	Accepts Democratic nomination at DNC Convention in New York, July 15
1992	Wins presidential election on November 3, first Democrat elected since Carter
1993	Inaugurated 42nd president of the United States on January 20, at age 46 (youngest U.S. president since John F. Kennedy, who was elected at age 43)
2001	Ends second term as president; moves to Chappaqua, N.Y., with wife, Senator Hillary Rodham Clinton
2002	Opens office in the middle of Harlem
2004	The William Jefferson Clinton Presidential Library and Museum officially opens in November in Little Rock, Arkansas

Since 2001, former President Clinton continues to work on social, economic and political issues that impact the well-being of human beings and the peace of the universe. He continues to speak out on issues of racial and ethnic reconciliation and promotion of economic empowerment for the poor and disenfranchised. Clinton joined former South African President Nelson Mandela in working to combat HIV/AIDs in Africa and Third World countries. He also joined former President George H.W. Bush to raise disaster relief funds after the tsunami and Hurricane Katrina disasters. In 2005, he founded the Clinton Global Initiative, which brings together world leaders to address world problems.

Clinton Administration Policies and Initiatives

1993 CLINTON ADMINISTRATION POLICIES ENACTED

Abolished Restrictions on Medical Research and the Right to Choose: Abolished gag rule prohibiting abortion counseling in clinics receiving federal funds to serve low-income patients. Revoked restrictions on a woman's legal right to privately funded abortion services in military hospitals; import on RU-486, the morning after pill; and restrictions on the award of international family planning grants—the "Mexico City Policy." Lifted the moratorium on federal funding for research involving fetal tissue, allowing progress on research into treatments for Parkinson's disease, Alzheimer's, diabetes, and leukemia.

First Step Toward Welfare Reform: Ordered the federal government to make it easier for states to receive waivers from government regulations in order to implement innovative welfare reform projects. The administration granted waivers to a record 43 states.

Family and Medical Leave Act: First piece of the legislation signed into law, enabled millions of workers to take up to 12 weeks unpaid leave to care for a new baby or ailing family member without jeopardizing their job.

"Reinventing Government" Initiative launched: Initiative imed at making government work better for less. Result: 377,000 fewer civilian employees, the lowest level since the Kennedy administration; federal spending reduced from 22.2 percent in 1992 to 18.5 percent in 2,000, the lowest percentage since 1966.

Childhood Immunization Initiative launched: In 1992, less than 60 percent of 2-year olds were fully immunized, the third lowest percentage in the Western Hemisphere. The number of children immunized during the Clinton administration reached an all-time high—90 percent of toddlers and the highest rate in history for America's preschool children for all racial and ethnic groups.

Motor Voter Registration signed: Law made it simpler and easier for millions of Americans to register to vote by allowing registration at drivers license venues. More than 28 million new voters registered with the new law—a higher percentage of registrants than with passage of the 26th Amendment, which lowered voting age to 18.

Clinton-Gore Deficit Reduction Plan enacted: Though it passed without a single Republican vote, it established fiscal discipline by cutting the deficit in half—the largest deficit reduction plan in history. Plan included investments in education, health care, science, and technology, and extended the life of the Medicare Trust Fund by three years. The Clinton-Gore Deficit Reduction Plan resulted in the largest budget surplus in American history.

Earned Income Tax Credit Expansion/Working Family Tax Cut: Passage of an expansion of the Earned Income Tax Credit gave tax cuts to 15 million of the hardest-pressed American workers. In 1999, EITC moved 4.1 million American workers above the poverty line.

Student Loan Reform: The Direct Student Loan Program cut red tape and administrative costs by eliminating subsidies and bureaucracy in the student loan program. $4 billion was saved due to the program.

Empowerment Zone/Enterprise Communities Program: The Empowerment Zone represents the federal government's most ambitious incentives program to promote private sector investment in distressed areas in America. The program includes nine Empowerment Zones and 95 Enterprise Communities with tax incentives and $100 million per EZ in discretionary investment dollars. Congress expanded the program in 1994, 1997, and again in 2000.

AmeriCorps Community Service Initiative enacted: Initiative allowed individuals to serve communities across the country while earning money for college or skills training programs. 150,000 volunteers participated during the Clinton administration—more than participated in Peace Corps during its first 20 years.

Brady Act: This legislation, which was debated seven years during previous administrations, was signed into law under President Clinton. The law required background checks before the purchase of a handgun and established a national instant check program. The law prohibited more than 600,000 felons, fugitives, and domestic abusers from purchasing guns. Gun-related crime went down 40 percent during the Clinton administration.

NAFTA Ratified: Bipartisan legislation implemented the North American Free Trade Agreement, creating the world's largest free trade zone. More than 400,000 new jobs were created, and exports to Canada and Mexico supported 600,000 more jobs than in 1993

1994 CLINTON ADMINISTRATION POLICIES ENACTED

Goals 2000 Education Standards enacted: Legislation provided assistance to states to implement high standard and challenging curricula to help all children succeed.

Head Start Reform and Creation of Early Head Start: The president advocated for legislation increasing Head Start participation and quality. This new bill established minimum performance standards, strong accountability, and created the Early Head

Start program for children aged 0 to 3. Funding for Head Start programs increased 90 percent. Approximately 93,000 children were affected by the initiative.

Crime Bill signed: The Clinton-Gore Crime Bill contained tougher penalties, including "three strikes and you're out" legislation, which helped states build more prisons and increased prevention and victim rights. The overall crime rate dropped for eight years in a row, the longest continuous drop on record. The crime rate was at a 26 percent low in 2001.

Assault Weapons Ban: Nineteen of the most dangerous assault weapons were banned to help decrease the crime rate.

100,000 Community Police Officers: Bill authorized local governments to fund the hiring of 100,000 community police officers.

Violence Against Women Act: Bill contained new penalties and resources to prosecute more domestic violence offenders and quadrupled funding for battered women's shelters. A nation-wide 24-hour Domestic Violence Hotline was established, the first federal effort to address domestic violence and violence against women. Resulted in a significant decrease in domestic violence cases since the law was established.

Community Development Financial Institutions (CDFI) Fund: Legislation creating the CDFI Fund to support both specialized financial institutions and traditional banks that serve lower-income communities. As of 2000, the CDFI Fund had certified over 400 community development banks, community development credit unions, housing and business loan funds, and venture capital firms as CDFIs. Over $427 million have been allocated to institutions providing capital and services to underserved markets.

Improving America's Schools Act: Reauthorization of the 1965 Elementary and Secondary Education Act, ending the era of lower expectations for disadvantaged children by insisting that all students be held to the same high academic standards. This act strengthened accountability for student performance and required states to turn around low-performing schools.

1995 CLINTON ADMINISTRATION POLICIES ENACTED

Loans Preventing Economic Collapse in Mexico issued: President Clinton issued $20 billion in emergency loans to Mexico to stabilize the country's financial markets after Congress refused to act. Monetary funds prevented the collapse of the peso, prevented economic crisis, and helped the country return to solid economic growth. Mexico repaid the loans with interest three years ahead of schedule, resulting in a U.S. taxpayers' net gain of $580 million from the loan.

Federal Child Support Enforcement Expanded: Executive order stepping up federal efforts to collect child support payments. Child support collections doubled from $8 billion in 1992 to $16 billion in 1999.

Comprehensive Plan to Reduce Youth Smoking: This proposal would require youth to prove their ages to buy cigarettes, banned vending machines in places where minors can go, ended the marketing of cigarettes and tobacco to minors, and required the tobacco industry to fund an education campaign to prevent kids from smoking.

Dayton Peace Accords: President Clinton led talks that resulted in the signing of a peace treaty by leaders of the rival factions in the Bosnian civil war.

1996 CLINTON ADMINISTRATION POLICIES ENACTED

National Campaign to Prevent Teen Pregnancy: In response to President Clinton's challenge for all Americans to participate in preventing teen pregnancy, the National Campaign to Prevent Teen Pregnancy was launched. Teen birth rates and teen pregnancy rates fell 18 percent, to the lowest level on record.

Telecommunications Reform signed: First major overhaul of the tele-communications laws in 60 years. Reforms of the 1934 Telecommunications Act opened up competition between local telephone companies, long-distance providers, and cable companies The law also required the use of new V-chip technology to enable families to exercise greater control over the television programming; the E-rate proposal provided for low-cost Internet connections for schools, libraries, rural health clinics, and hospitals.

Adoption of School Uniforms: President Clinton was convinced that school uniforms led to safer schools and more disciplined and orderly classrooms that freed teachers to focus on teaching and students to focus on learning; public schools were encouraged to voluntarily adopt school uniform policies.

Antiterrorism Law: President Clinton signed the Antiterrorism and Effective Death Penalty Act into law, which included measures to fight terrorism at home and abroad and to provide broad federal jurisdiction to prosecute terrorist acts, bar terrorists from entering the United States, and toughen penalties over a range of terrorist crimes and increase controls over biological and chemical weapons. This bill was first sent to Congress in February 1995, calling for additional antiterrorism measures and actions after the bombing of the federal building in Oklahoma City.

Megan's Law: Legislation was signed into law requiring states to notify communities when a dangerous sexual predator resides or moves into a community. This legislation built on the 1994 Crime Bill, the Jacob Wetterling Crimes Against Children and Sexually Violent Offender Registration Act requiring state sex off enders registration for child molesters and other sexually violent offenders.

Welfare Reform Bill: President Clinton took the first national steps to require welfare recipients to move to work. An executive memorandum issued by the president required participants in federal training programs for welfare recipients to agree to go to work within two years or face the prospect of losing their federal assistance.

Minimum Wage Increased: The president signed into law the first minimum wage increase in six years; the 90-cent per hour increase was the largest ever. Ten million workers were affected.

Kennedy-Kassebaum Health Insurance Reform (Health Insurance Portability and Accountability Act): This bipartisan insurance reform bill prevents individuals from being denied coverage because they have pre-existing medical conditions. It requires insurance companies to sell coverage to small employer groups and individuals who lose group coverage without regard to their health risk status. It also prohibits discrimination in enrollment and premiums against employees and their dependents based on health status. Finally, it requires insurers to renew policies they sell to groups and individuals. As many as 25 million people benefited from this act.

Requiring Mental Health Parity for Annual and Lifetime Insurance Limits: To help eliminate discrimination against individuals with mental illnesses, the president enacted legislation containing provisions prohibiting health plans from establishing separate lifetime and annual limits for mental health coverage.

Protection for Mothers and Newborns: Common sense legislation requiring health plans to allow new mothers to remain in the hospital for at least 48 hours following most normal deliveries and 96 hours after a Cesarean section.

Eliminating the Discriminatory Tax Treatment of the Self-Employed: HIPAA increased the tax deduction from 30 percent to 80 percent for the approximately 10 million self-employed Americans. Also signed into law were provisions to phase it into 100 percent in the Balanced Budget Act of 1997.

Fighting Fraud and Waste in Medicare: The Kennedy-Kassebaum legislation created a new stable source of funding to fight fraud and abuse, coordinated by the Departments of Health and Human Services, the Office of the Inspector General, and the Department of Justice. Nearly $1.6 billion in fraud and abuse savings were returned to the Medicare Trust Fund during the Clinton administration. A 410 percent increase in convictions for fraud abuse was reported, saving $50 billion in health care claims.

Health Care Reform: This bipartisan law was the end result of President Clinton's promise to end welfare as we know it. The law required welfare recipients to move within two years from welfare assistance to work, limited the time recipients stayed on welfare, and provided childcare and health care assistance to parents making the move from welfare to work. The landmark law also enacted tough new child support enforcement measures proposed by the president. The number of Americans on welfare fell by nearly 60 percent from 14.1 million to 5.8 million, the smallest welfare population in 32 years. Millions of parents joined the workforce during that time.

Designated Commission to Design Patients' Bill of Rights: President Clinton created the National Commission on Health Care Quality that included health care providers, insurers, and businesses, and charged it with studying the need for consumer protections and ways to guarantee the quality of care. Their recommendations formed the basis of the Patients Bill of Rights.

1997 CLINTON ADMINISTRATION POLICIES ENACTED

Launched Youth Anti-Drug Media Campaign: National Drug Control Strategy was unveiled, a long-term effort to reduce illicit drug use; it included $175 million national media campaign targeting drug use by youth, 500 additional border patrol agents, and $40 million for counter-drug programs in Peru, the primary source of cocaine.

Banned Federal Research on Human Cloning: The president issued a memorandum prohibiting the use of federal funds to clone human beings and urged the entire scientific and medical community to adopt a voluntary moratorium on the cloning of human beings.

Chemical Weapons Convention Ratified: The Senate ratified the Chemical Weapons Convention, which makes the production, acquisition, stockpiling, transfer, and use of chemical weapons illegal.

Welfare to Work Partnership Launched: A partnership between federal government and private businesses to hire welfare recipients. 20,000 businesses partnered with the government, and 1.1 million welfare recipients moved from welfare to employment. The federal government, under Vice President's Al Gore's leadership, hired more than 500,000 welfare recipients and fostered relationships between employers and community and faith-based organizations that help families move from welfare to work.

Individuals With Disabilities Education Act reauthorized: The expanded IDEA applies the same high academic standards for all children, ensuring that children with disabilities learn the same things with the same curricula and the same assessments as all other children. It also assures that more children with disabilities are placed in regular classrooms and take part in regular school functions.

Initiative for One America: In an effort to initiate a national dialogue aimed at narrowing America's racial divide, the president appointed a seven-member Advisory Board on Race. During the next 15 months, board members held meetings with thousands of black and white Americans and organizations throughout the country. The commission proposed several policies which helped guide the administration's efforts to close the racial gap still existent in America.

Many of the policies resulted in civil rights and education policies. A One America office was established in the White House and continued throughout the Clinton presidency to work with federal agencies to carry out the president's vision of One America.

Stronger Air Quality Regulations released: The president approved the strongest air quality standards in history to control pollution from smog and soot. The standards could prevent 15,000 premature deaths every year and will improve the lives of millions of Americans suffering from respiratory illness.

Balanced Budget Agreement reached: On August 5th, the president signed the Balanced Budget Act of 1997, which finished the job of eliminating the $290 billion deficit.

$500 per Child Tax Credit: As part of the balanced budget agreement, the president secured a $500 per child tax credit for approximately 27 million families with children under 17, including 13 million children from families with incomes below $30,000.

Children's Health Insurance Program created: At the urging of the Clinton-Gore White House, Congress invested $48 billion for the State Children's Health Insurance Program, the single largest investment in health care for children since the enactment of Medicaid in 1965. Up to 5 million previously uninsured children would now have coverage for prescription drugs, vision, hearing, and mental health services. All 50 states had implemented S-CHIP programs within three years, and 2 million children had been covered. States covering children up to 200 percent of poverty increased sevenfold.

Strengthening the Medicare Trust Fund: President Clinton, through the Balanced Budget Act, extended the life of Medicare, which had been projected to become insolvent in 1999, by an additional 10 years, resulting in the longest Medicare Trust Fund solvency in a quarter century (for a total of 26 years, and offering premiums nearly 20 percent lower than projected in 1993).

Modernizing the Medicare Benefit Package: Implemented a series of structural reforms modernizing the Medicare program and bringing it into line with the private sector and preparing it for the baby boom generation. Reforms included waiving cost-sharing for mammography services and providing annual screening mammograms for beneficiaries age 40 and older to help detect breast cancer; a diabetes self-management benefit; and Medicare coverage for colorectal screening and cervical cancer screening.

Hope Scholarships/Lifetime Learning Tax Credits: President Clinton proposed and passed the largest increase in college opportunity since the GI Bill. The Hope Scholarship provides a tax credit of up to $1,500 for tuition and fees for the first two years of college. The Lifetime Learning tax credit will provide a 20 percent tax credit on the first $10,000 of tuition and fees for students beyond the first two years or taking classes part-time.

Welfare-to-Work Grants: The Balanced Budget Act included $3 billion over two years for Welfare-to-Work grants to help states and local communities move long-term welfare recipients and certain noncustodial parent into lasting, unsubsidized jobs.

Landmark Education Investment: America Reads, Charter Schools, Education Technology: The president succeeded in doubling investments in education technology, increasing charter school funding, expanded Head Start to reach more than 800,000 children, and increased the maximum Pell Grant by 63 percent to the largest maximum award ever. The budget also provided $300 million for the President's America Reads Challenge—the most significant increase in education funding at the national level in 30 years.

More Empowerment Zones and More Rural Enterprise Communities: Following Congress's 1994 designation of Cleveland and Los Angeles as Empowerment Zones, President Clinton requested a Round 2 of 20 new Empowerment Zones and 20 new rural Enterprise Communities.

Requirement that Drug Companies Provide Adequate Testing for Children: President Clinton directed an important Food and Drug Administration regulation requiring manufacturers to do studies on pediatric populations for new prescription drugs and those currently on the market, to ensure that prescription drugs have been adequately tested for the unique needs of children.

American Reads Child Literacy Initiative launched: The America Read Challenge called for 1 million tutors—college, university students, senior citizens, and private sector employees—to help reach the national goal of every child reading by the end of third grade. Congress funded the initiative with $300 million in grants to help states improve children's reading skills. More than 2 million children were tutored by national service programs such as AmeriCorps, VISTA, and Foster Programs during the three years of operation.

Agreement to Provide Child-Safety Locks with Handguns: An agreement negotiated between President Clinton, eight of America's leading gun manufacturers, and the Shooting Sports Council was announced. The voluntary agreement marks progress in the ongoing effort to include child safety locks with all new handguns. The president previously issued an Executive Memorandum requiring federal law enforcement authorities to provide child-proof locks for their officers' firearms.

Adoption and Safe Families Act passed: To meet the president's challenge of doubling the number of adoptions by 2002, this act provides incentives to states to permanently place children in foster care. In 1999, 46,000 foster care children were adopted, more than a 64 percent increase since 1996 and the biggest increase in adoptions since the National Foster Care Program was created 20 years earlier.

Endorsed Recommendations of Quality Commission: In 1996, the president created a nonpartisan Commission on Quality and charged commissioners with developing a patient's bill of rights. In 1997, he accepted the commission's recommendation that all health plans should provide strong patient protections, access to emergency room services, and access to a fair, unbiased, and timely appeals process.

1998 CLINTON ADMINISTRATION POLICIES ENACTED

Child Care Initiative: An historic effort to address the struggles of working parents to find child care they can afford, trust, and rely on. The initiative helped families pay for child care by more than doubling funding for child care subsidies and for Head Start. Quality after-school programs were established and were estimated to serve 1.3 million children in 2001. The initiative also sought to improve the safety and quality of care and to promote early learning through the Early Learning Opportunities Act.

Child Support Incentives: The Clinton administration's ongoing efforts to promote responsible fatherhood included the Child Support Performance and Incentive Act of 1998, built on prior legislative and executive actions to improve child support collections by establishing performance-based rewards for states. Paternity establishment tripled and child support collections doubled during this time.

GEAR UP Initiative: At the urging of President Clinton, Congress unanimously voted to enact GEAR UP to provide intensive early intervention services to help prepare students at impoverished middle schools for college. Over 700,000 students were helped by this initiative. The initiative is part of the Higher Education Amendments of 1998, which reduced student loan interest rates, supported partnerships that would strengthen teacher preparation and quality, and created the first federal performance-based organization to administer student aid.

Class Size Reduction Initiative: Congress agreed to provide $1.2 billion for the first year of the president's new initiative to hire 100,000 new teachers to reduce class size in the early grades, decreasing the average national class size to 18. This is the first comprehensive effort to reduce class size across the nation.

21st Century Community Learning Centers: The Clinton administration launched a series of dramatic funding increases for before and after school programs, turning a small demonstration program into an $846 million program (up from $1 million in 1997) that would serve about 1.3 million children and become one of the most popular federal education programs in history.

Wye Middle East Peace Agreement signed: After nine days of negotiations at the Wye Conference Center, Israeli Prime Minister Benjamin Netanyahu and Palestinian Authority President Yasser Arafat signed an agreement that strengthens Israeli security, expands the area of Palestinian control in the West Bank, and enhances opportunities for the Israeli and Palestinian people.

Head Start Expansion and Reauthorization (Human Services Reauthorization Act): The reauthorization of Head Start paved the way for further quality improvements, doubled participation in the Early Head Start program, and moved toward the president's goal of providing quality Head Start opportunities for 1 million children. The Human Services Reauthorization Act of 1998 also created the Individual Development Account Demonstration Program, which encouraged low-income families to save for a first home, post-secondary education, or to start a new business.

1999 CLINTON ADMINISTRATION POLICIES ENACTED

Education Flexibility Act of 1999: Ed-Flex was designed to help districts and schools carry out educational reforms and raise achievement levels of all children by providing increased flexibility in the implementation of federal education programs. In exchange, states are required to demonstrate enhanced accountability for the performance of all students.

The Ed-Flex Partnership Act signed: This legislation expanded the Ed-Flex demonstration program to enable all states, the District of Columbia, Puerto Rico, and the territories to form Ed-Flex partnerships. States could also waive many of the federal education program requirements in exchange for accountability for results.

100,000 Officers Funded: The president's successful community policing initiative played a key role in America's longest continuous drop in crime on record. Under budget and ahead of schedule, the president's goal of funding 100,000 officers was reached in May 1999. Over congressional opposition, President Clinton secured the first installment of funding for his new 21st Century Policing Initiative in November 1999. This initiative would fund up to 50,000 additional community police by 2005.

Child Labor Convention Adopted by the International Labor Organization: At the urging of President Clinton, an historic international convention that would ban the worst forms of child labor was unanimously adopted by delegates at the international organization's annual conference. This marks the largest investment in ending abusive child labor globally.

Victory in Kosovo: President Clinton led the NATO Alliance in a 79-day air war that expelled Serb forces from Kosovo and restored self-government to the province, ending a decade of repression and reversing Slobodan Milosevic's brutal campaign of ethnic cleansing.

Financial Modernization Legislation enacted: President Clinton signed the Financial Modernization Act into law, revamping a banking system in place since the Great Depression. The new law increases innovation and competition in the financial services industry, gives consumers greater choice and lower prices, and mandates that banks satisfactorily serve the credit needs of their communities.

2000 CLINTON ADMINISTRATION POLICIES ENACTED

Africa Growth and Opportunity Act and the U.S.-Caribbean Basin Trade Partnership Act signed: This act expands two-way trade and creates incentives for the countries of sub-Saharan Africa and the Caribbean Basin to continue reforming their economies and participate more fully in the benefits of the global economy. This area forms the sixth largest export market for the United States.

Campaign Finance Disclosure Act: President Clinton signed the first new campaign finance reform legislation in 20 years, closing a loophole that allowed tax-exempt groups to use undisclosed donors to pay for political ad campaigns.

Providing Health Insurance to Women With Breast Cancer: The president enacted legislation to provide a new Medicaid option to provide needed insurance coverage to the thousands of uninsured women with breast and cervical cancer detected by federally supported screening programs.

Reauthorization of the Older Americans Act: This act ensures that millions of seniors have access to meals, nursing homes ombudsmen, legal assistance, elder abuse prevention, employment, and transportation services that are essential to their dignity and independence. This act also includes the National Caregiver Support Program, designed to provide respite care and other supportive services to help hundreds of thousands of families struggling to care for older loved ones who are ill or disabled.

$1.2 Billion Initiative for Emergency School Repairs: Passage of an historic initiative for emergency school renovation makes possible much-needed repairs, such as roofs, heating and cooling systems, and electrical wiring in public schools in impoverished or stressed districts. $75 million was earmarked for public schools with high concentrations of Native American students.

New Markets and Community Renewal Initiative: The historic New Markets initiative was the most significant effort ever to help hard-pressed communities lift themselves up through private investment and entrepreneurship. With the help of the New Markets tax credit, 40 strengthened empowerment zones and 40 renewal communities, this initiative was expected to spur billions of dollars in private investment and ensure that every American shares in the nation's economic prosperity.

Investments in Health Care: President Clinton's longstanding commitment to expand access to quality health care for all Americans is reflected in the fiscal year 2001 budget, which includes a multi-billion dollar effort to provide health care coverage to low-income children, seniors, people with disabilities, and those leaving welfare to work. It also expands preventive benefits like cancer and glaucoma screenings for Medicare beneficiaries.

Interviewees

ALL INTERVIEWS CONDUCTED BY THE AUTHOR, JANIS F. KEARNEY

HOPE INTERVIEWS

1. **W. LaDell Douglas,** pediatrician and chair, Southwest Regional Hospital; Hope, Arkansas; June 2002
2. **David Johnson,** former deputy mayor, former National Football League athlete; June 2002
3. **Tillmon Ross,** military veteran; Hope, Arkansas; June 2002
4. **Autrilla Watkins Scott;** Long Beach, California; June 2002
5. **Hazel Simpson,** beauty and barbershop owner; Hope, Arkansas; June 2002
6. **Mary "Nell" Turner,** former school teacher; Hope, Arkansas; June 2002
7. **Hosea Watkins,** former worker for Eldridge Cassidy and Clinton auto dealership; Hope, Arkansas; June 2002
8. **Floyd Young,** former teacher and mayor of Hope; Hope, Arkansas; June 2002

HOT SPRINGS INTERVIEWS

1. **Ruth Mae Atkins,** former Hot Springs spa aide; Hot Springs, Arkansas; June 2002
2. **The late Larry Bonner,** barbershop owner; Hot Springs, Arkansas; June 2002
3. **The late Early Marbry,** Clinton Buick dealership employee; Hot Springs, Arkansas; June 2002

4. **Petrilla Bonner Pollefeyt,** first black female country entertainer; June 2002

5. **Junious Stevenson,** former educator; Hot Springs, Arkansas; June 2002

ARKANSAS INTERVIEWS

1. **Annie Abrams,** veteran educator; Little Rock, Arkansas; March 2002

2. **Liza Ashley,** former cook to Governor Clinton; Little Rock, Arkansas; March 2002

3. **Judge Wiley Branton,** county judge, juvenile court; Little Rock, Arkansas; March 2002

4. **Rep. Irma Hunter Brown;** Little Rock, Arkansas; March 2002

5. **LeRoy Brownlee,** Arkansas commissioner for the Department of Corrections; Little Rock, Arkansas; March, 2002

6. **Arkie Byrd,** attorney, Mays & Crutcher law firm; Little Rock, Arkansas; March 2002

7. **Dale Charles,** former state NAACP president; Little Rock, Arkansas; March 2002

8. **Thedford Collins,** former aide to Senator Dale Bumpers; Washington, D.C.; January 2002

9. **Othello Cross,** Pine Bluff attorney and former Clinton law student; Pine Bluff, Arkansas; March 2002

10. **Dr. Beverly Divers-White,** Mid-South Foundation; Little Rock, Arkansas; March 2002

11. **Cleola Dozzell,** former Arkansas educator and Clinton appointee; March 2002

12. **Reggie Favors,** Blue Cross Blue Shield; Little Rock, Arkansas; March 2002

13. **LaVerne Feaster,** former president, Arkansas Future Homemakers of America; Little Rock, Arkansas; June 2002

14. **Patsy Gatlin,** former appointments assistant, Governor's Office; Little Rock, Arkansas; June 2002

15. **Judge Wendell Griffin;** Little Rock, Arkansas; March 2002

16. **The late Bill Hamilton,** former director, Arkansas Family Planning Services, and Mrs. Hamilton; Little Rock, Arkansas; June 2002

17. **The Reverend R.J. Hampton,** longtime Arkansas political activist, one-time gubernatorial candidate, and current presiding elder, east and northern Delta district; June 2002

18. **Former Judge Perlester Hollingsworth,** Arkansas native; Atlanta, Georgia; January 2002

19. **Judge Marion Humphrey;** Little Rock, Arkansas; March 2002

20. **Judge Henry Jones;** Little Rock, Arkansas; June 2002

21. **The late Ernest Joshua,** former CEO, JM Products; Little Rock, Arkansas; March 2002

22. **Jack Kearney,** attorney and former Clinton appointee; Little Rock, Arkansas; June 2002

23. **James Kearney,** retired Arkansas farmer and sharecropper; Gould, Arkansas; March 2002

24. **Jesse Kearney,** former Clinton law student and aide; Pine Bluff, Arkansas; March 2002

25. **John L. Kearney,** attorney and former Clinton law student; Pine Bluff, Arkansas; March 2002

26. **Julius D. Kearney,** attorney and former Clinton cabinet member; Little Rock, Arkansas; March 2002

27. **Loretta Lever,** former director, NAACP Fair Share Initiative; Little Rock, Arkansas; March 2002

28. **Former Judge Richard Mays,** attorney, Mays & Crutcher law firm; Chicago, Illinois; April 2003

29. **Cora McHenry,** president, Shorter College; Little Rock, Arkansas; June 2002

30. **Gene McKissac,** attorney; Pine Bluff, Arkansas; March 2002

31. **Katherine Mitchell,** Arkansas native and veteran educator; Little Rock, Arkansas; June 2002

32. **Bob J. Nash,** former Clinton advisor; Chicago, Illinois; April 2002

33. **Judge Ollie Neal;** Little Rock, Arkansas; March 2002

34. **Jan Pascal,** Hot Springs educator, friend and Clinton appointee; February 2002

35. **Judge Andree Roaf;** Little Rock, Arkansas; March 2002

36. **The Reverend William Robinson,** Hoover Methodist Church; Little Rock, Arkansas; March 2002

37. **The Reverend Larry Ross,** former senior official, Southwestern Bell; Little Rock, Arkansas; March 2002

38. **Lillian Ross,** former Arkansas educator and longtime Clinton political volunteer; Little Rock, Arkansas; March 2002

39. **Lottie Shackelford,** former mayor of Little Rock; Global USA; Little Rock, Arkansas; March 2002

40. **Rodney Slater,** former Transportation Secretary; Washington, D.C.; May 2002

41. **Charity Smith,** Arkansas education administrator, Forrest City native; Little Rock, Arkansas; June 2002

42. **Judy Smith,** former Arkansas senator, Little Rock, Arkansas; June 2002

43. **Tommy Sproles,** Hot Springs native and Clinton gubernatorial cabinet member; Little Rock, Arkansas; June 2002

44. **Senator Tracy Steele;** Little Rock, Arkansas; March 2002

45. **Charles Stewart,** vice president, Regions Bank; Little Rock, Arkansas; March 2002

46. **The Reverend Hezekiah Stewart;** Little Rock, Arkansas; March 2002

47. **Sherman Tate,** vice president, Alltell; Little Rock, Arkansas; March 2002

48. **Theman Taylor,** professor, University of Central Arkansas; Conway, Arkansas; June 2002

49. **Minnie Jean Brown Trickey,** member of the Little Rock Nine; Little Rock, Arkansas; November 2002

50. **Judge Joyce Warren;** Little Rock, Arkansas; March 2002

51. **Senator Josetta Wilkins;** Pine Bluff, Arkansas; March 2002

52. **Carol Willis,** senior advisor, Democratic National Committee;

Little Rock, Arkansas; March 2002

53. **Clevon Young,** director, Arkansas Human Development Corporation; Little Rock, Arkansas; June 2002

NATIONAL INTERVIEWS

1. **Hank Aaron,** baseball great; January 2002
2. **Bill Campbell,** former mayor of Atlanta, Georgia; Atlanta; January 2002
3. **Former President William J. Clinton;** Harlem office, New York City; February 2002
4. **Ernie Greene,** native Arkansan and managing director of Amex; Washington, D.C., January 2002
5. **Dorothy Height,** president emeritus, National Council of Negro Women; January 2002
6. **Wade Henderson,** director, Leadership Conference on Civil Rights; Washington, D.C.; January 2002
7. **Bob Johnson,** president and CEO, Black Entertainment Television; Washington, D.C.; January 2002
8. **George Knox,** Miami attorney and former University of Arkansas Law School colleague of the Clintons; March 2002
9. **Congressman John Lewis,** civil rights legend; Washington, D.C.; February 2002
10. **David Levering Lewis,** professor of African American studies, Rutledge University; May 2002
11. **C. Payne Lucas,** president, AFRICARE; Washington, D.C.; January 2002
12. **Glen Mahone;** Washington, D.C.; May 2002
13. **Marc Morial,** former mayor of New Orleans; Chicago, Illinois; January 2002
14. **Hugh Price,** former president, National Urban League; New York City; February 2002

15. **Ozell Sutton,** former regional director, Office on Civil Rights, Justice Department; Atlanta, Georgia; January 2002

16. **Michael White,** former mayor of Cleveland, Ohio; Cleveland; March 2002

17. **Mayor Wellington Webb,** Denver, Colorado; March 2002

18. **Mayor Anthony Williams,** District of Columbia; Washington, January 2002

19. **Carla Williams,** former president, Jack and Jill International; February, 2002

20. **Eddie Williams,** president, Joint Center for Economic Studies; Washington, D.C.; January 2002

21. **Tom Williams,** D.C. attorney, friend and Oxford Fellow; Washington, D.C.; January 2002

22. **Dr. William Julius Wilson,** professor of sociology, Harvard University; April 2002

Bibliography

Ashmore, Harry S. *Arkansas: A History.* New York: W.W. Norton, 1978.

Baker, T. Harri and Jane Browning, *An Arkansas History for Young People,* Second Edition. Fayetteville: University of Arkansas Press, 1991.

Bush, G.M. *Reflections on Babysitting a President.* Long Beach Press-Telegram, February 23, 1996.

Capehart, Jonathan. *Black & White: Three Views Bill Gaining Spot in Black History.* New York Daily News, June 24, 1997.

Center for Earth and Planetary Studies, National Air and Space Museum, *The Dust Bowl,* http://www.nasm.si.edu/research/ceps/drylands/dust.html.

Clinton, Bill. *A Deep Debt of Gratitude for a Valuable Lesson.* Crisis, October 1997.

Clinton for President Committee. *A Commitment to Opportunity for All.* Little Rock, Ark.: Clinton for President Committee, 1992.

Clinton for President Committee. *Governor Bill Clinton's Record in Arkansas.* Little Rock, Ark.: Clinton for President Committee, 1991.

Deane, Ernie. *Arkansas Place Names.* Branson, Mo: Ozarks Mountaineer, 1986.

Duffy, Joan I. *Clinton Signs Preschool Measure.* Commercial Appeal, February 21, 1991.

——. *Arkansas Students to Get Aid Notices this Weekend.* Commercial Appeal, July 13, 1991.

Education Week, *Arkansas Governor Defends Tests in Debate with A.F.T.'s Shanker,* April 10, 1985.

Education Week, *Education Package Barrels Through Arkansas*

389

Legislature, Hot Springs High School Torch Light, February 6, 1991.

Esanu, Benny Traian. *Living in the Great Depression.* Taken from a Study of the Great Depression by the students of the Lake Hamilton Jr. High Gifted and Talented Program, Lake Hamilton, AR. http://wolves.dsc.k12.ar.us/jrhigh/media/%20ACE/%20Forsaken.../Html's/main.htm

Franklin, John Hope. *Reconstruction: After the Civil War.* Chicago: The University of Chicago Press, 1961.

Garland County Historical Society, 25th Edition. Hot Springs, Ark.: PHOEBE/ The Uzuri Project, n.d.

Hoffman, Adonis. *Clinton's Black Problems: Image vs. Reality,* Washington Post, August 11, 1996.

Hope Hempstead County Chamber of Commerce, *History of the Hope Watermelon Festival,* http://www.hopemelonfest.com/festival.htm.

Hope Star. D-Books Publishing, 1998.

Hot Springs High School Torch Light, May 29, 1964.

Hot Springs Sentinel-Record, *Most Businesses, Professions Found Among City's 8,000 Negro Citizens,* February 18, 1962.

Howe, Edna Lee. *A City of Racial Harmony.* Hot Springs Sentinel-Record, February 22, 1959.

Lower Mississippi Delta Development Commission. *Body of the Nation: The Interim Report of the Lower Mississippi Delta Development Commission.* Memphis, Tenn.: The Lower Mississippi Delta Development Commission, 1989.

Minton, Mark, and Charlie Frago. *State Luminary McMath, 91, Dies: Ex-governor Left 'Deep Footprints.'* Arkansas Democrat-Gazette, October 6, 2003.

One America in the 21st Century—Forging a New Future: the President's Initiative on Race. The Advisory Board's Report to the President. [Washington, D.C.]: The Initiative, 1998.

Paulson, Alan C. *Roadside History of Arkansas.* Missoula, Mont.: Mountain Press Publishing, 1999.

Pendleton, Scott. *Clinton's Record: Strong on Education and Welfare Reform.* Christian Science Monitor, February 19, 1992.

——. *Governor gets High Marks for Public Education Reforms*. Christian Science Monitor, July 21, 1992.

Provost, Richard. *Governor Sees Plan as 'Bible': Pleads for Change*. Arkansas Democrat-Gazette, May 13, 1990.

Ranborn, Sheppard. *Arkansas Board Approves New Standards After Yearlong Effort*. Education Week, March 14, 1984.

Reed, Roy. *Faubus: The Life and Times of an American Prodigal*. Fayetteville, Ark.: University of Arkansas Press, 1997.

Sandomir, Richard. *Mainstream Press Gave Minor Play to Robinson Breakthrough*. New York Times, April 13, 1997. http://www.nytimes.com/.

Scully, Dr. Francis J. *Notes From Cutters Guide, 1888*. Hot Springs, Ark.: PHOEBE/The Uzuri Project, n.d.

Sawyer, Jon. *Poverty in the Delta: Report Urges Action*. St. Louis Post-Dispatch, May 16, 1990.

Taylor, Orville W. *Negro Slavery in Arkansas*. Fayetteville: University of Arkansas Press, 2000.

Taylor, Susan. *Comments to President Clinton*. Speech presented at the Second Annual Wall Street Conference, Rainbow/PUSH Coalition's Wall Street Project, New York, N.Y., January15, 1999.

United Press International (UPI), *Arkansas Overhauling its Education System*, New York Times, November 20, 1983.

Whayne, Jeannie, and Williard Gatewood. *The Arkansas Delta: Land of Paradox*. Fayetteville: University of Arkansas Press, 1993.

White House Communications Office. *The Clinton Presidency: Eight Years of Peace, Progress, and Prosperity*. Washington, D.C.: White House Communications Office, 2001.

Who's Who in Little Rock, Nineteen Hundred and Twenty-one. Little Rock, Ark.: Who's Who Publishers, 1921.

Williams, C. Fred, Charles Bolton, Carl H. Moneyhon, and Leroy T. Williams, eds. *A Documentary History of Arkansas*. Fayetteville: University of Arkansas Press, 1984.

Williams, Charlean Moss. *The Old Town Speaks: Reflections of Washington, Hempstead County, Arkansas*. Houston, Tex.: Anson Jones Press, 1951.

Index

Note: Entries in **boldface** represent interviewees.

Subject Index